# Indian Sociological Thought

# Indian Sociological Thought

Third Edition

**B.K. NAGLA**

**RAWAT PUBLICATIONS**

Jaipur • New Delhi • Bangalore • Guwahati • Kolkata

ISBN 978-81-316-1296-5 (hb)
ISBN 978-81-316-1297-2 (pbk)



First Edition, 2008
Second Edition, 2013
**Third Edition, 2024**

**Reprinted, 2025**



*Published by*
Prem Rawat for **Rawat Publications**
Satyam Apts., Sector 3, Jawahar Nagar, Jaipur 302 004 (India)
Phones: 0141 265 1748 / 265 7006
E-mail: info@rawatbooks.com
Website: www.rawatbooks.com

*New Delhi Office*
4858/24, Ansari Road, Daryaganj, New Delhi 110 002
Phone: 011-23263290

Also at *Bangalore*, *Guwahati* and *Kolkata*

Typeset by Rawat Computers, Jaipur
Printed and bound in India

*To my teacher*

Professor Yogendra Singh

# Contents

# Preface to the First Edition

There is an old Hindustani story of seven blind men. They had not seen an elephant. Nor did they have any idea about one. Once they were all taken to see the elephant; one of them touched the trunk of the elephant. He said that the elephant was like a serpent. Another one touched the tail of the elephant and gave his explanation: The elephant was like a long rope. One of them who put his hand on the body of the elephant, called it like a wall. Thus, all the seven blind men provided their respective ideas about the elephant in parts. Nobody could see and explain the whole elephant. Similarly, Indian society is analysed partially, that is, in parts. The Indian Constitution is very clear in its definition of society. It is also clear about the government policies to be adopted and practised from time to time. Indian society is industrial, capitalistic, technological, secular and plural. Above all, it is democratic and is embedded in scientific spirit. This is precisely a constitutional, formal and official statement about the meaning of Indian society.

But, there are also other historical and intellectual definitions or projections of Indian society. Gandhi and other national leaders all through the period of freedom struggle argued for a moral society. Gandhi stood for the values of truth, non-violence and manual labour. There is another view about Indian society. It looks at it in the form of national culture, which is manifested in 'Hindutva' ideology. It described modernity, socialism and other secular values. Cultural nationalism labels modernity as reactionary modernity. There is yet another projection of Indian society. It is Naxalism. It argues that revolution comes only through the bullet of barrel. In another words, Indian society needs to be defined in terms of violence. India did not have any experience of bloodshed.

As a matter of fact, the Indian society, like a huge body of elephant, is interpreted differently in different ideologies. The basic problem for social scientists is to find out the meaning, truth and reality of Indian society. August Comte was the first sociologist to take up the task of defining society. Since then, gallons of ink have been put on the paper to define and redefine the Indian society. Those who worked on this issue are mostly sociologists. In the present work we have presented the analyses of society in both scientific and humane perspectives. The volume elicits the views of some of the leading Indian sociologists and a few western sociologists who have done research in India and developed the perspectives on Indian society. The volume includes historical, Indological/textual, structural-functional, Marxist, cultural and civilizational perspectives besides development of sociology in India and a discourse analysis. In the next edition, we will include some other perspectives, mainly, social stratification (André Béteille, K.L. Sharma and Dipankar Gupta), family, marriage and kinship (K.M. Kapadia, Irawati Karve and Leela Dube), etc. We believe that both teachers and students would be able to understand the contributions of our sociologists.

We have gone through the original writings of the scholars mentioned in this volume to understand their perspective about the Indian society and also consulted reference and textbooks, the most important amongst them are: Yogesh Atal (2003), *Indian Sociology: From Where to Where*; D.N. Dhanagare (1993), *Themes and*

*Perspectives in Indian Sociology*; S.L. Doshi (2003), *Modernity, Postmodernity and Neo-Sociological Theories*; Ramkrishna Mukherjee (1979), *Sociology of Indian Sociology*; Surendra Sharma, (1985), *Sociology in India: A Perspective from Sociology of Knowledge;* and N.K. Singhi (ed.) (1993), *Theory and Ideology in Indian Sociology.* Besides these books, we have also consulted some papers – both published and unpublished.

The book is dedicated to my teacher – Professor Yogendra Singh, who taught me at M.Phil level (JNU, New Delhi) and inspired me not only during my doctoral research work but also throughout my academic life. I always found him up-to-date in readings and with refreshingly new ideas. He kindled my interest in sociology and made me understand that sociology should always include both theory and empirical research. I enjoyed his professional visibility with affection to make me fearless and created confidence in me whenever I consulted him.

In the preparation of this book, the inspiration has come from diverse sources, such as classroom teaching and several special lectures to different universities, participation in seminars and symposia, and interaction with scholars. Without naming each of them individually, I wish to acknowledge my grateful thanks to all of them.

The present work is thus, a kind of friendly venture. However, I am alone responsible for the shortcomings. My wife, Madhu, has assisted me enough. I highly feel obliged to her. My teachers and friends like Professors Yogendra Singh, K.L. Sharma, J.S. Gandhi, S.L. Doshi, Ravi Kapoor, I.P. Modi, Jayaram Panda, Satish Sharma and many others have provided me all insights in the presentation of sociological thinkers. I thank Bonny Doshi who devoted her time in the proper handling of the manuscript. Last but not least, my thanks to my son Gaurav and my daughter Radhika for their constant encouragement. Finally, I also wish to thank Shri Kailash Rawat and his son Pranit – the publishers – for publishing this volume in an attractive form. I look forward to receiving comments from teachers, students and readers to enable me to further improve this book.

# Preface to the Second Edition

*Indian Sociological Thought* is being published in its second edition. To me, it is deeply satisfying to find that this book is becoming more and more popular and useful among students and scholars as one of the few books which provides synthetic and different perspectives of Indian sociological thought, namely, indological, structural-functional, dialectical-historical, cultural, civilizational and subaltern, along with discourse analysis in the end.

In this new edition, I have added another perspective – social stratification – highlighting the contribution of André Béteille. Besides this, I have also included a new chapter on Irawati Karve in indological/textual perspective.

So far, to my knowledge, there is no single published work which gives a composite picture of the Indian sociological thought. Therefore, I feel a sense of fulfilment in bringing out this book which is recognized as a necessary reading, a reference book and a textbook for the university courses related to the perspectives on Indian society. The book is written in a particular framework highlighting the perspectives on Indian society contributed by different scholars.

I am grateful to Dr Yogendra Singh, Emeritus Professor at Jawaharlal Nehru University, New Delhi for his affectionate and valuable guidance. I am fully conscious of its many limitations. However, I consider that the book will stimulate interest in the understanding of perspectives on Indian society. I am also thankful to Rawat Publications for bringing out the book in the shortest possible time in a nice manner.

# Preface to the Third Edition

It gives me immense pleasure to come out with the third edition of the book. This has enabled me not only to correct mistakes but also to add material to improve the quality.

A new chapter on D.N. Dhanagare in the section on 'Marxist Perspective' and two new chapters 'Globalization: Indian Perspective' and 'Privatization of Education: Challenges Ahead' in the section on Contemporary Discourses would fulfill the demand of the readers at large. It is my endeavour to go by suggestions I receive from scholars and academicians alike.

I look forward again to receiving comments from teachers, students and readers to enable me further to improve this book. I am thankful to Rawat Publications for bringing out this third edition and continuously reprinting the book to cater the demand of scholars and readers.

# Introduction

India has a chequered history. It has grown from monarchy, feudalism and colonialism to democracy. It has a civilizational depth. All through its history the country has promoted certain values, traditions and ideologies. We believe that sociology, and for that matter, social sciences in India can be properly analysed with reference to its social background. Social thinkers in India are the products of prevailing reality and truth of particular point of time. India has witnessed the exploitation and authoritarianism of colonial rule. It is expected that our social thinkers will bear the stamp of colonialism and feudalism. Our objective in this work has been to evaluate the works of sociologists who have tried to understand or who have been products of the colonialism and feudalism.

Raymond Aron, in his two-volume classical and eventful work, *Main Currents in Sociological Thought* (1965) has taken a critical review of the pioneers of sociology. He concludes that social thinkers are those who dwell on the rising problems of their country and struggle to come with some solutions. If we follow Aron, we would argue that sociologists who are reckoned to the social thinkers in India would dispassionately diagnose the ills or disorders of Indian society and provide a solution.

What have been the problems of Indian society? First and foremost, our millions of people have suffered a lot under the yoke of colonial and feudal rule. During the colonial rule in India, the native people were reduced to an inhuman life. Under the leadership of Gandhi, the freedom movement mobilized the people to rise against the British power. And, all this revolution was charged by the values of non-violence, non-cooperation and *satyagraha.*

At the level of princely states, there was feudalism and in many parts of the country the *zamindari* system prevailed. At a broader plane, the whole country was bonded to exploitation and submission. The system of colonialism and feudalism had a long-standing imprint on the psychology of people. Sycophancy has now become an idiom of the mindset of the people. We believe that our sociologists and particularly social thinkers are the production of such a social background of the country. They should have a chilling urge to analyse our struggle for independence. They should have made critical case studies – *Chori-Chora, Jallianwala Bagh* and the martyrdom of our people. Feudalism was, it is said, much more ghostly.

In the freedom struggle, it must be observed throughout, there was no discrimination between the rich and the poor; between the high caste and the subaltern; between the urban and the rural countryside. The British took advantage of the social diversity of the country, and Gandhi brought this diversity to unity. In any account of Indian society, a specific impact of India's struggle for freedom must occupy a prime place. Our writers of Hindi and regional languages have shown enough awareness and imprints of the national uprising. Munshi Premchand's *Godan*, a classical novel, very tacitly narrates the linguistics done by the *zamindars* on Hori. The whole fiction literature of Sharat Chandra describes how the Bengali society was made a victim of colonialism. Amrita Pritam, the Punjabi writer, clearly shows the imprint of foreign rule in her novels and stories.

The struggle for independence has been an event which has moved the masses of people and the intellectuals alike. What has been its impact on Indian social thinkers? This is our first question.

What is the situation of contemporary Indian society? Perhaps V.S. Naipaul (1990), not a sociologist but a fiction writer, has provided the profile: "With industrialization and economic growth people have forgotten old reverences. Men honour money now. The great investment in development over three or four decades led only to this: to 'corruption', to the criminalization of politics, in seeking to rise, India had undone itself. No one could be sure of anything now; all was fluid. Policeman, thief, politician, the roles had become interchangeable".

It is not that masses of people are unaware of such a kind of disorder. There is a wide network of social workers and NGOs spread over to the length and breadth of the country. They have a deep understanding about the reality or truth of the country. There has been an awakening in the country.

To quote Naipaul again, he says that people all over India are so much agitated that they are likely to commit 'mutiny' any time. And not one or two mutinies but a million one. Perhaps, Naipaul has exaggerated his predictions. But the matter of fact is that such a situation of contemporary Indian society cannot fail to 'influence' the thought process of our sociologists.

Have the happenings of post-independent India really brought about any impact on our present-day sociologists, this is our second question. What we have been arguing is that the social thinkers must respond to the callings of the nation. If there are refugees in the country, if there is disharmony among the sections of people, if there is genocide in Gujarat, if the community development fails in the country, if the green revolution ends up with the enrichment of propertied classes, and if our education system renders millions to unemployment, what do the sociologists write? Do they have any solutions? logic would say, these writings are not worth the salt.

Let us now take a short recapitulation of the social thinkers we have included in this work. To begin with, we would say that

Indian social thinkers/sociologists have discussed the Indian society in all its aspects. But they have dealt with the parts of the society, viz., family, kinship, caste, village, religion, and not the whole of the society. While discussing the society, they have suggested measures for reforms of the parts – untouchability, widow remarriage, demerits of caste, village factions and dominant caste and others. And doing this they have remained unaffected by the current of freedom struggle or current problems.

Take for instance, N.K. Bose. He has studied tribals and their integration. For him, the method of tribal absorption seems to be quite suitable. He was very close to Gandhi but he did not take up the issue of the need for communal harmony. In fact, he was far away from the prevailing national mainstream.

Most of our social thinkers have preferred to take up the issue of caste. At the most, they are rich in depicting the caste ethnography. In fact, they have followed the officials-turned-anthropologists of British times, to depict caste which could be useful for the exploitation of the poorer masses of people for whom caste is not an institution but a way of social, ritual and sacramental life. It gives moral strength to bear the atrocities of the high castes, kings, *jagirdars* and *zamindars.* Such has been the contributions of caste sociologists.

McKim Marriott, M.N. Srinivas and S.C. Dube, the towering social thinkers, have made studies on caste along with the village studies. In fact, these social thinkers brought about a flood of village studies in our country. Admittedly, Dube opened up some new pathways in the much needed field of village development. He argued that people were prepared to accept development plan which suited them to their traditions. When Dube talks about the role of human factor in development, he actually stresses the importance of traditions in village life. As a matter of fact, tradition has been an obsession with Indian social thinkers. Even Yogendra Singh who sets out to study modernity, ends up with the conclusion that traditions die hard and are in turn become modern not in substance. Thus, the modernization of tradition is in reality a false modernization.

Srinivas makes an intelligent and excellent study of village Rampura. It is an anthropological study made with a prolonged stay in a village. He also studied the Coorgs of South India. His concepts of Sanskritization and Westernization have earned wide reputation. But, the usefulness of these concepts for a democratic-secular, capitalistic-socialistic Indian society is limited. What do we want to make out of Sanskritization from the lower sections of society? If the tribals become Hindus (and it is the mission of the Hindutva forces), how will they later get this identity? They do not get entry into the caste hierarchy. It appears that a section of our sociologists such as N.K. Bose, G.S. Ghurye and M.N. Srinivas has become protective of Hindu ideology. Their civilization is Hindu civilization, their history is *pedantic* history.

Marxism has been a powerful ideology among the world social thinkers. We may take up any social thinker of Europe, particularly France, Germany and Britain, we will find that at one time or the other in his/her life, he/she has been a Marxist. In India, Marxism is rare as religion matters to the people of the country. A.R. Desai is a rare Marxist. He belongs to Bombay University which is renowned for liberal sociology. Among all the sociologists of the development such as G.S. Ghurye, K.M. Kapadia, D. Narain, Bopadammi and Kulkarni, Desai was the lone Marxist. In his 'praxis' he was a field Marxian worker. He was adviser to a couple of trade unions. His house was always inundated by party workers. Doctrinaire Marxism was his credo. For him, state was a capitalistic organ. It exploited the people at large. He was so much buried in fundamental Marxism that he could not think about neo-Marxism which, then, had come to Europe and America.

Our objective in the present enquiry is to delineate the perspectives of different social thinkers on the reality of Indian society. Perspective means a particular standpoint in terms of ideology on the society. We found that a general perspective of Indian society is its evolutionary aspect. The 16th century in sociology has been a century of evolution. Indian thinkers were no exception. They looked Indian society from evolution point of view. Civilization, traditions, caste, tribe, village, polity and economy, that is, agriculture, industry and development, have been some of the major perspectives which help us to understand the Indian society. The nature of the society which is depicted in our Constitution and government policies of development plans, *Panchayati Raj*, decentralization, urbanization and capitalization along with democracy and secularism are some of the recent perspectives for understanding Indian society.

Indian society as the evolution theory has two major parts. Elite or the high castes, *ex-zamindars*, *ex-jagirdars*, landed peasants and the high-ups constitute the first part and second part includes the scheduled tribes, scheduled castes, the poor and the subalterns. In any analysis on the perspectives on Indian society, these parts cannot be overlooked or neglected.

Romila Thapar, as a traditional historian, has provided the ancient history of India. She talks about golden age of Indian history. She also informs us that India has always been a diversified country. Local battles were common narrative parts of this history. Alliances in these battles were brought by marriages. Ancient India was ruled by caste associations. In other words, the king or *zamindar* wielded his power through the caste association.

Ranajit Guha was the first subaltern historian who rejected the traditional history. He talked about the people's history in which he called subaltern history the history of the downtrodden people. Both Guha and David Hardiman have brought into light the subaltern people. One very powerful perspective on Indian society is that of subalternism. Hardiman who has worked on the Bhils of Panchmahals (Gujarat) brings out very substantive data. He says that even if there was famine in this area the Bhils never made an attack on the sores of food grains belonging to the *Sahukars*. He further says that the Bhils who feed the *Baniya* are tragically exploited by the latter.

It is difficult indeed to comment on all the thinkers included in this work at this place. We only want to stress that Indian society is very complex and a huge phenomenon. No single perspective can do justice to provide a holistic view of this society. It has a civilizational depth. It is pluralistic and at the same time secular-democratic. With this understanding of the society we have employed several perspectives. And, these perspectives have been drawn from a large number of thinkers belonging to a variety of social sciences. We further have a strong conviction that social thinkers are the products of their time, age and era. With this conviction we have analysed them in this book. We believe that we are not wrong to bring out the perspectives which would help us to understand our society.

# 1

# Development of Sociology in India

This textbook, in fact, constructs the structural frame for understanding how sociology advanced in India. In this introduction, author's efforts are to construct profile of historical and contemporary development of sociology in India based on scholars' ideas and contributions. The present chapter is an attempt to assess the development of sociology in India. It describes the historical background of the growth of sociology. It also tries to identify the emerging trends in the development of various specialities and sub-specialities within the discipline and how they found together their way into teaching programmes. Thus, the chapter deals with the major trends in the discipline of sociology and the gaps, which need special attention and the new direction for strengthening teaching and research. In this context, the chapter discusses the development of sociology in India with focus on:

(1) Sociology in Pre-Independence India
(2) Sociology in Post-Independence India
    (a) Developments in the Seventies

- (b) Perspectives in the Eighties
- (c) Imperatives in the Nineties

(3) Sociological Research in India

## Context

The origin of sociology and social anthropology in India can be traced to the days when the British officials realized the need to understand the native society and its culture in the interest of smooth administration. However, it was only during the twenties of the last century that steps were taken to introduce sociology and social anthropology as academic disciplines in Indian universities. The popularity that these subjects enjoy today and their professionalization is, however, a post-independence phenomenon. Attempts have been made by scholars from time to time to outline the historical developments, to highlight the salient trends and to identify the crucial problems of these subjects.[1]

## Development of Sociology and Social Anthropology in India

Sociology and social/cultural anthropology are cognate disciplines and are in fact indissoluble. However, the two disciplines have existed and functioned in a compartmentalized manner in the European continent as well as in the United States. This separation bears the indelible impress of western colonialism and Eurocentrism. However, Indian sociologists and anthropologists have made an attempt to integrate sociology and anthropology in research, teaching and recruitment. They have made a prominent contribution to the development of indigenous studies of Indian society and have set an enviable example before the Asian and African scholars. Another significant contribution of Indian sociology and social/cultural anthropology lies in their endeavour to synthesize the text and the context. This synthesis between the text and the context has provided valuable insights into the dialectic of continuity and change to contemporary Indian society (Momin, 1997).

It is difficult to understand the origin and development of sociology in India without reference to its colonial history. By the second half of the 19th century, the colonial state in India was about to undergo several major transformations. Land, and the revenue and authority that accrued from the relationship between it and the state, had been fundamental to the formation of the early colonial state, eclipsing the formation of Company rule in that combination of formal and private trade that itself marked the formidable state-like functions of the country. The important event that took place was the revolt of 1857, which showed that the British did not have any idea about folkways and customs of the large masses of people. If they had knowledge about Indian society, the rebellion of 1857 would not have taken place. This meant that a new science had to come to understand the roots of Indian society. The aftermath of 1857 gave rise to ethnographic studies. It was with the rise of ethnography, anthropology and sociology which began to provide empirical data of the colonial rule.

Herbert Risley was the pioneer of ethnographic studies in India. He entered the Indian Civil Services in 1857 with a posting in Bengal. It was in his book *Caste and Tribes of Bengal* (1891) that Risley discussed Brahminical sociology, talked about ethnography of the castes along with others that the importance of caste was brought to colonial rulers. Nicholas Dirks (*In Post Colonial Passages*, Sourabh Dube, Oxford, 2004) observes:

> Risley's final ethnographic contribution to colonial knowledge thus ritualed the divineness of caste, as well as its fundamental compatibility with politics only in the two registers of ancient Indian monarchy or modern Britain's 'benevolent despotism'.

Thus, the ethnographic studies came into prominence under the influence of Risley. He argued that to rule India caste should be discouraged. This whole period of 19th century gave rise to ethnographic studies, i.e., studies of caste, religion, rituals, customs, which provided a foundation to colonial rule for establishing dominance over India. It is in this context that the development of sociology in India has to be analysed.

Sociology and social anthropology developed in India in the colonial interests and intellectual curiosity of the western scholars on the one hand, and the reactions of the Indian scholars on the other. British administrators had to acquire the knowledge of customs, manners and institutions of their subjects. Christian missionaries were interested in understanding local languages, folklore and culture to carry out their activities. These overlapping interests led to a series of tribal, caste, village and religious community studies and ethnological and linguistic surveys. Another source of interest in Indian studies was more intellectual. While some western scholars were attracted by the Sanskrit language, Vedic and Aryan civilization, others were attracted by the nature of its ancient political economy, law and religion. Beginning from William Jones, Max Muller and others, there was a growth of Indological studies. Karl Marx and Frederic Engels were attracted by the nature of oriental disposition in India to build their theory of evolution of capitalism. Similarly, Henry Maine was interested in the Hindu legal system and village communities to formulate the theory of status to contract. Again, Max Weber got interested in Hinduism and other oriental religions in the context of developing the theory, namely, the spirit of capitalism and the principle of rationality developed only in the West. Thus, Indian society and culture became the testing ground of various theories, and a field to study such problems as growth of town, poverty, religion, land tenure, village social organization and other native social institutions. All these diverse interests – academic, missionary, administrative and political – are reflected in teaching of sociology.

According to Srinivas and Panini (1973: 181), the growth of the two disciplines in India falls into three phases: the first, covering the period between 1773–1900 AD, when their foundations were laid; the second, 1901–1950 AD, when they become professionalized; and finally, the post-independence years, when a complex of forces, including the undertaking of planned development by the government, the increased exposure of Indian scholars to the work of their foreign colleagues, and the availability of funds, resulted in considerable research activity. Here, three major phases in the introspection in sociology, which have been discussed by Rege (1997) in her thematic paper on 'Sociology in Post-Independent India' may also be mentioned. Phase one is characterized by the interrogations of the colonial impact on the discipline and nationalist responses to the same, phase second is marked by explorations into the initiative nature of the theoretical paradigms of the discipline and debates on strategies of indigenization. This phase also saw critical reflections on the deductive positivistic base of sociology and the need for Marxist paradigms and the more recent phase of post-structuralism, feminist and post-modern explorations of the discipline and the field. Lakshmanna also (1974: 1) tries to trace the development of sociology in three distinctive phases. The first phase corresponds to the period 1917–1946, while the second and the third to 1947–1966 and 1967 onwards respectively.

### *Sociology in the Pre-Independence Period*

As is clear by now that sociology had its formal beginning in 1917 at Calcutta University owing to the active interest and efforts of B.N. Seal. Later on, the subject was handled by Radhakamal Mukerjee and B.N. Sarkar. However, sociology could not make any headway in its birthplace at Calcutta. On the other hand, anthropology flourished in Calcutta with the establishment of a department and later on the Anthropological Survey of India (ASI). Thus, sociology drew a blank in the eastern parts of the country. But, the story had been different in Bombay. Bombay University started teaching of sociology by a grant of Government of India in 1914. The Department of Sociology was established in 1919 with Patrick Geddes at the helm of affair. He was joined by G.S. Ghurye and N.A. Toothi. This was indeed a concrete step in the growth of sociology in India. Another centre of influence in sociological theory and research was at Lucknow that it introduced sociology in the Department of Economics and Sociology in 1921 with Radhakamal Mukerjee as its head. Later, he was ably assisted by D.P. Mukerji and D.N. Majumdar. In South India, sociology made its appearance at Mysore University by the efforts of B.N. Seal and A.F. Wadia in 1928. In the same year sociology was introduced in Osmania University at the undergraduate level. Jafar Hasan joined the department after he completed his training in Germany. Another university that started teaching of sociology and social anthropology before 1947 was Poona in the late 1930s with Irawati Karve as the head. Between 1917 and 1946, the development of the discipline was uneven and in any case not very encouraging. During this period, Bombay alone was the main centre of activity in sociology. Bombay attempted a synthesis between the Indological and ethnological trends and thus initiated a distinctive line of departments. During this period, Bombay produced many scholars who richly contributed to the promotion of sociological studies and research in the country. K.M. Kapadia, Irawati Karve, S.V. Karandikar, M.N. Srinivas, A.R. Desai, I.P. Desai, M.S. Gore and Y.B. Damle are some of the outstanding scholars who shaped the destiny of the discipline. The products of this university slowly diffused during this period in the hinterland universities and helped in the establishment of the departments of sociology.

Certain trends of development of sociology may be identified in the pre-independence period. Sociology was taught along with economics, both in Bombay and Lucknow. However, in Calcutta, it was taught along with anthropology, and in Mysore it was part of social philosophy. Teachers had freedom to design the course according to their interests. No rigid distinction was made between sociology on the one hand and social psychology, social philosophy, social anthropology, social work, and other social sciences such as economics and history, on the other. The courses included such topics as social biology, social probiems (such as crime, prostitution and beggary), social psychology, civilization and pre-history. They covered tribal, rural and urban situations. At the general theoretical level, one could discern the influence of the British social anthropological traditions with emphasis on diffusionism and functionalism. In the case of teaching of Indian social institutions the orientation showed more Indological emphasis on the one hand and a concern for the social pathological problems and ethnological description on the other. Strong scientific empirical traditions had not emerged before independence. Sociology was considered a mixed bag without a proper identity of its own (Rao, 1982).

### *Sociology in the Post-Independence Period*

The next phase, as mentioned by Lakshmanna (1974: 45), in the growth of the subject, corresponds to the period between the attainment of independence and the acceptance of the regional language as the medium of instruction in most states of the country. Towards the end of this period, we also witnessed the interest on the part of the Central Government to promote social science research through a formal organization established for the purpose. This phase alone experienced tremendous amount of interaction within the profession as two parallel organizations started functioning for the promotion of the profession. In Bombay, Indian Sociological Society was established and *Sociological Bulletin* was issued as the official organ of the society. This helped to a large extent in creating a forum for publication of sociological literature. Lucknow school, on the other hand, started the All India Annual Sociological Conference for professional interaction. Lakshmanna (1974: 5) identifies that the research efforts mainly progress on three lines. First, there was large-scale doctoral research in the university. Second, the growing needs of the planners and administrators on the one hand and the realization of increasing importance of sociological thinking and research in the planning process on the other, opened up opportunities for research projects. Third, during this period, the growing importance of social science research also resulted in the establishment of research institutes. The development of research activity also meant the enlargement of the employment opportunities at all levels.

Correspondingly, there was also an increase in the number of universities and college departments. This period also noticed considerable vertical and horizontal mobility in the profession. Teaching of sociology got well established in the fifties. This period reflected three things as marked by Rao (1982). First, sociology achieved greater academic status. Not only many more universities and colleges began to teach at the postgraduate and graduate levels but the discipline itself became more focused in theoretical orientation and highly diversified in its specialization. Secondly, sociology established its identity as discipline by separating itself from psychology, anthropology, social philosophy and social work. Although, in some universities, still social pathology and social psychology are taught as a part of sociology courses. In many others, a highly diversified curriculum structure in proper sociology exists including such specialization as rural and urban sociology, sociology of kinship, sociology of religion, sociology of stratification, sociology of education, political sociology, medical sociology, social demography and sociology of economic development. Thirdly, diversification followed the lines of extension of sociological approach to different areas of social life. It was related to the growing needs of development in independent India. Colonial legacy became a thing of the past and democratic processes were introduced at all levels. Sociologists soon become sensitive to problems of development in the contexts of tribal, rural and urban situations. Problems of rural development, industrialization, expansion of education, control of population, new political processes and institutions, social and political movements attracted their areas of social life. They started conducting empirical research with a view to understand the structure, dynamics and problems of development. All these concerns had a feedback on the teaching of sociology at various levels.

Another important change in the teaching of sociology, which came after independence, has been in regard to the external intellectual influences. Before independence the teaching of sociology and social anthropology was mainly, if not wholly, influenced by the then current theoretical concerns in Great Britain. We have already mentioned the influence of diffusionism and functionalism (of Malinowski). The syllabi also reflected traditions of ethnology, evolutionism and Indology. After independence, however, American sociological traditions had a major impact on the teaching of sociology in India. This is evident from such topics in the syllabi as structural-functional theory (Parsons and Merton) and research methodology. Besides the American, the French, German and Marxian intellectual influences also had an impact. In the midst of such diverse intellectual stimuli, Indian sociologists began to criticize, modify and develop diverse sociological approaches in the study of Indian society and culture, and these are reflected in the course of study of different universities (Rao, 1982).

### *Developments in the Seventies*

There have been a few reviews of developments in sociology and social anthropology since earlier times till 1970s and onwards (see, for example, the collection of essays in Unnithan, Singh et al., 1965; ICSSR, 1971, 1974, 1985; Rao, 1974; Mukherjee, 1977; Mukherjee, 1979; Singh, 1986; UGC, 1978, 1979, 1982; Lele, 1981; Oommen and Mukherjee, 1986; Dhanagare, 1993; Singhi, 1996). Of these, Ram Krishan Mukherjee's review has been more exhaustive and substantial for the discipline as a whole. The ICSSR trend reports covered in detail the developments in each of specializations. Rao (1982: 16–23) reviewed the developments in the seventies under three heads: (i) areas of the interests and specialization which got crystallized; (ii) areas of interest which have developed but not got crystallized; and (iii) emergence of new approaches in the established areas.

The seventies of the last century saw a further continued diversification of interests and specialization in substantive areas of research and teaching in the sixties. While, earlier, village community studies dominated researches, but the interests in the areas of agrarian relations, land reforms, peasants, agricultural labourers, and scheduled castes and tribes began to attract greater attention of sociologists and social anthropologists in the seventies. The problems of rural society were formulated in the Marxian framework of analysis emphasizing conflicts and contradictions. The other areas of interests that were crystallized in the seventies were industrial sociology, urban sociology and social stratification. Secondly, there were six areas of interest that started getting some attention in the seventies but have not really got off the mark. These were: sociology of profession, sociology of organization, medical sociology, social demography and studies on women, Muslims and Hindu-Muslim relations. Thirdly, it is significant to note that the seventies saw new approaches and foci in the large areas of research and teaching such as caste, kinship, religion, politics and tribal studies.

### *Perspectives in the Eighties*

Many of the areas of specialization mentioned in the foregoing account, no doubt, gained strength in the eighties of the last century. Some areas of enquiry, such as social demography and medical sociology, were crystallized. A few other areas of investigation opened up and more research in the established areas was undertaken on new lines. Some of the new areas have been introduced. These were: sociology of deviance, sociology of knowledge, sociology of science and technology, and historical sociology. Rao (1982) anticipated these areas for research in the eighties. There was an indication that interest in sociology of science and technology might get more widespread (Uberoi, 1978; Vishwanathan, 1977). The growing interest in historical sociology was reflected in Fox (1977). Damle (1982: 57–58) anticipated the task of sociology for the eighties in India, which was to analyse (1) the transformation of Indian society, (2) the limits of such transformation, and (3) the impact of these limits to such transformation, which was reflected either in the frustrations of the efforts to surmount the obstacles. In this context, new ideologies and protest movements acquired a special significance. In many of the newly developing branches of sociology, scholars have made notable but isolated contributions. There has been thinking that research should be promoted in the nineties in the areas of sociology of planning and development, sociology of professions, sociology of organizations, social dimensions of poverty, law and social change, sociology of national integration etc.

### *Imperatives in the Nineties*

The country during the nineties of the last century was passing through radical political, economical and socio-cultural changes as a result of which the scope and focus of Indian sociology has expanded. Under the influence of such developments, the Indian government that adored the policy of mixed economy ever since independence and cherished the ideals of welfarism proceeded to allow the market-oriented policy to prevail. To achieve this goal, the government adopted a new policy of economic reforms in the year 1991 with a view to globalize its economy (Singh, 1997). Globalization is a move prompted by the leaders of the developed world. Liberalization policy, including the freedom accorded to the foreign companies and capital to enter into Indian market, are the two major steps of the government in this direction. The impact of globalization on Indian cultural heritage and general life situation of the people of the country has generated new areas that deserve the attention of Indian sociologists who do seem to be attentive to such relevant areas as civic society (Gupta, 1997), crisis and resilience in the process of social change (Singh, 1993) and secularism and national integration (Joshi, 1997)[2] but specific social implication of the new economic policy is yet to be analysed. A few courses have been introduced recently on global themes in some of the universities. They are as follows: ecology and society, issues of human rights, sociology of management, human resource development, media and society, action sociology etc. There is also need to start some more new courses like sociology of public order; peace, security and development; security management and information technology etc. These courses are not only important for teaching but also for research in the construction of society and useful for the modern occupation and profession.

## Teaching of Sociology in India

The origin of sociology in India as a distinct discipline can be traced back to the period around 1920s. Teaching of sociology started in Bombay University as early as 1914 but the birth of current academic sociology took place only with the establishment of departments of sociology in Bombay and Lucknow. As for teaching and research, nothing such happened except nominal teaching of the discipline wherever it was introduced for almost a quarter of a century. What Parvathamma states about Mysore University remains true for the entire country and for the discipline of sociology as a whole. "The undergraduate syllabi in sociology as framed by Wadia continued almost for a quarter of a century. Only in the late 1950's, it was changed" (Parvathamma, 1978). Though one finds a nominal beginning, nothing of any consequence happened in the realm of sociology. It remained more or less static during the 1920–47 period. This was the last phase of the colonial rule in India when the national leaders were preoccupied with the liberation movement. Pre-independence scholars have contributed to the foundation of sociology by providing a tradition in which sociology in India could grow and evolve (Unnithan et al., 1967). Their contributions, however, began to make an impact only after independence, though the number of universities increased from 11 in 1920 to 16 in 1945. However, the number of sociology departments remained just two and of these, only one was concerned for independent degree in sociology (Unnithan, 1982).

The percentage of universities, having sociology department, had been falling during 1920–50. It began to show a trend towards regular increase after 1950. By 1960, 23.8 per cent of universities in India had sociology departments. By 1965, this number rose to 29.6 per cent. Now, there are 95 universities including institutions that are deemed to be universities. Fifty-one of them or about 54 per cent accommodate departments of sociology. In spite of their relatively greater growth in sociology departments, it is interesting that 44 (46.3%) out of 95 universities do not have any sociology teaching at all. Of the 51 universities that teach sociology, only 32 have separate departments, whereas 14 conduct undergraduate and postgraduate programmes including PhD. There are 16 universities where sociology is combined with other social science departments but an independent degree is awarded; in three departments no degree is awarded though the subject is taught (Unnithan, 1982: 64). Besides these, according to the Universities Handbook of India, 1973, the 16 Agricultural Universities, the five All India Institutes of Technology, the three Institutes of Technology, the three Institutes of Management, the Indian Statistical Institute, Kolkata, the Tata Institute of Social Sciences, Mumbai, and the Gujarat Vidyapith, Ahmedabad also offered sociology as a subject of study and/or research.

Sociology is very popular subject in the universities and colleges of India today. Currently, out of 133 traditional universities, about 85 have departments of sociology apart from other departments of social sciences related to sociology like population studies and women studies. A majority of students opt for sociology as one of their subjects at graduation level. It is considered as an easy subject to get through in examination. It is usually preferred by girls particularly those who are not much career conscious. Similarly, at the postgraduate level too, sociology receives a large number of students.

The rank of sociology comes fifth in terms of the number of the universities offering social sciences and allied subjects. This shows that from the quantitative point of view, the position of sociology as an academic discipline is not very low in spite of the fact that it entered the university curriculum only very recently. It is also seen that at the postgraduate level, sociology has established itself as a subject of major importance, attracting the largest number of students next only to economics, history and political science. Postgraduate enrolment in the year 1969–70 was alone 4,918 – taking sociology (4,442) and anthropology (476) together which contributed 11.57 per cent of the total enrolment (42,479) for postgraduate education in social sciences. However, the percentage was a little higher for PhD (16.34%). Of the 2,153 students enrolled for PhD in social sciences, 352 were in the field of sociology alone. According to the UGC report, out of total 2,582 faculty members of the postgraduate departments in social sciences in the universities and colleges, 243 were sociologists and 119 anthropologists. Until 1971, the country has produced a total of 485 PhD scholars in the fields of sociology, social anthropology, criminology and social work. Since 1968, the average rate of PhDs in sociology was 46 per year. This is an impressive figure, indeed, compared to the figures for previous periods. Thus, 34 PhDs were submitted during the decade 1931–40 and 79 in the subsequent two decades of 1941–60. There were more than a hundred PhDs from the universities of Uttar Pradesh and of Maharashtra upto 1970 whereas the position in other states was as follows: Bihar (43), Delhi (42), Madhya Pradesh (23), Gujarat (15), West Bengal (14), Rajasthan (12), Punjab (9), Karnataka (7) and others (13) (Atal, 1976: 118–19).

The courses and the syllabi in sociology of the various universities reveal yet another dimension of development of the discipline in India. Sociology is being taught at all levels in the universities – from graduation to MPhil/MLitt level. Some courses give special emphasis to research methodology. As regards the subject matter taught at the graduate and postgraduate levels, there seems to be some rough similarity between universities in the course. Principles of Sociology, Indian Social Institutions and Social Change are offered at both the BA and MA levels in most universities while Research Methods, Rural and Urban Sociology, Social Anthropology and Social Psychology are among the other subjects included in the core courses at MA level. The rest of the subjects cover a wide range of special areas in the discipline, namely, political sociology, educational sociology, industrial sociology, sociology of kinship, religion, marriage and family, and so on. It seems that from the national point of view, there is a wider choice of optional subjects for the students of sociology than is available to students of other disciplines. An analysis of the courses reveals several deficiencies. At present, there is a lack of integration of syllabi at all levels that could ensure a standard of uniform minimal knowledge in sociology along with possibilities for specialization and advance training in sociology. Hardly any effort is noticed to introduce new courses on the basis of rationale societal considerations. Largely, the old courses continue. The gravity of problem is accentuated by the contents of the courses and the textbooks prescribed. The contents of the courses are often irrelevant to the students of sociology in India as instruction is based mostly on books written by foreign scholars for students elsewhere. All these points reflect to the overall underdeveloped nature of sociology in India (Unnithan, 1982: 68).

Overall, the quantitative expansion of sociology is increasing but the quality aspect of the development of sociology as an academic discipline in colleges and universities is appalling. Except a few prestigious universities, the status of sociology in most of the universities in the country is really degraded. Hence, the quality research and teaching in sociology has considerably slumped. Singh (1997) writes: "Professional anxiety, achievement, motivation, entrepreneurial aspiration and changing mode of consumption have immensely affected the standard of sociology." Therefore, the teachers and other scholars of sociology will have to take care and pains for its revival. Importantly, and specifically, we need to be academically and politically active to influence the development of a 'new' sociological curriculum.

## Sociological Research in India

Since independence, with the rapid development of the teaching of sociology in Indian universities and colleges, there has been a concomitant increase in the number of research studies on different aspects of sociology, resulting in doctoral dissertations and in the publication of many volumes and articles in various professional journals. Several previous surveys of the development of sociology in India present the process in different phases and trends, notably those by Becker and Barnes (1961), Saran (1958), Bottomore (1962), Clinard and Elder (1965), Vidhyarthi (1972), and the Indian Council of Social Sciences Research (ICSSR) (1972). Despite these attempts, little attention has so far been paid in the direction of proper research taking steps of methods of data collection, techniques, degree of quantity and quality, arial unit of study, and theoretical orientations in specific substantive areas of sociology.

Usually, it is seen that while at the university department level, there are facilities of doing research which do not exist at the college level. Even at the department level there is no system of sabbatical leave where the teacher can take time off for the research. Fieldwork is an essential aspect of research in sociology and unless a teacher has a year or nine months off, he cannot conduct research. The ICSSR and the UGC have suitable schemes for providing these facilities. There is thus now no dearth of money to conduct research. The problem is to control spurious research. The ICSSR, which is the main agency for promoting research in sociology and social anthropology, has laid down priorities in keeping with social goals. It is necessary to initiate research to teach new courses as research and teaching are intimately related in the development of the discipline.

Research in sociology got a considerable boost in the country since independence. Several studies conducted by sociologists were financed, sponsored and supported by several agencies. There was another welcome trend in the introduction of the courses on methods of social research as part of the MA syllabus. In fact, this was also emphasized by the UGC Review Committee on Sociology (1960). Significant sophistication in research methodology is an urgent desideratum for present assessment of the rapidly changing and complex social organization to which we belong. In the field of doctoral research, the progress in sociology has been remarkable. In spite of the fact that almost till the middle of the fifties, a much less number of recognized supervisors were available for the guidance of the doctoral research students in the departments of the universities. Besides these limitations, sociology and other allied fields granted as many as 438 doctoral degrees up to 1970 and economics and political science exceeded these figures.

The personnel position in sociology is still on the lower side. There are only 243 sociology teachers as compared to larger number in economics and political science, psychology and geography. This has to be further viewed in the light of the numbers of the university and college departments. In terms of the number of departments at the university level, sociology (51) is behind only from economics (72), political science (59) and commerce (56). The position at the college level is roughly the same. When we try to match the spread of the discipline and its manpower requirements, it becomes clear that there had been some defect in the recruitment pattern as revealed by the existence of a large number of unfilled professorial posts in several universities. Senior members of the profession should take note of this unsatisfactory situation. In spite of the limitation of personnel, a very large number of research projects (50), constituting the highest share (25.5%) of the ICSSR grants, were undertaken by the scholars belonging to the sociology discipline. A total of 19 theses were published in sociology. The position is still brighter if we add in it social anthropology. In fact, the acceptance of the largest number of projects (above 20%) in sociology was a matter of satisfaction because the formulation of the problems were realistic and sound (Lakshmanna, 1974: 10–11).

There has been a realization that diverse research methods were complimentary rather than conflicting. The early seventies saw a bitter debate between the surveyors and participant observers. But, both realized that the two could be complementary. There has been more researches using statistical surveys methods. There were a number of training courses in quantitative methods including computer programming. Besides quantitative techniques, other techniques such as historical analysis, case studies and participant observation are also increasingly used by sociologists and social anthropologists depending on the nature of the problem of investigation and its aim.

## Sociological Research in India: The State of Crisis

The recent years have seen the publications in *EPW* of a number of articles discussing and for the most part deploring the current state of research and teaching in sociology (see Das, 1993; Deshpande, 1994; and the latest of these, by Rege, 1994; Béteille, 1996). Speaking especially of the situation in western India, they support the view that sociology in India has become a rather lacklustre discipline, its leading concepts presented through outdated mass-market American texts, and notably devoid of engagement with the social world outside the classroom. The 1990s have seen engaged debate on the crisis in the discipline. This debate saw a series of responses from the scholars in the field assessing the 'tiredness of the discipline' (Deshpande, 1995), the possibilities of 'a community of discourse' (Giri, 1993), the dangers of 'uncritical metropolitanism' (Murthy, 1993) and the relevance of gender and feminist pedagogues as strategies to confront the crisis (Rege, 1994; Uberoi, 1994). The discussion has been made on the construction of sociological discipline (Thappan, 1991; Hegde, 1992) and teaching of sociology in Indian universities(Uberoi, 1989–90; Deb 1997). In the recent years, a new dimension has been reflected in the debate taking the issue of gender studies (Dube, 1986, 1996, 1997; Desai, 1997; Bhagwat and Rege, 1991; Patel 1994; Uberoi, 1994) and women's movement (Niranjana, 1992; John, 1996).[3]

Veena Das (1993) tries to locate the crisis in sociological research in India in three institutional structures – the universities, the UGC and the professional bodies such as the Indian Sociological Society. At the level of the universities, the proliferation of the subject has simply not been matched by the will to ensure competence in teaching and research. In several universities, textbooks such as that of MacIver and Page, written almost 50 years ago, continue to be taught. Second, where teaching and research are conducted in regional languages, students do not acquire proficiency even in reading in the English language. This is in fact that rhetorical statements about national self-respect notwithstanding, neither the translations of competent sociological works in the regional languages nor original contributions add up to a sufficient body of literature that may be available in these languages. Thus, a student fails to acquire competence in his subject on the basis of this literature. Third, the policies for recruitment and promotion of teachers increasingly sacrifice academic competence for political expediency. Fourth, the examination of PhD dissertations is managed within small coterie of scholars.

If the universities are to take a share of the blame for the falling standards for research, the UGC cannot escape its major responsibility either. The decision-making bodies in the UGC seem to have completely misguided notions about the state of social science research in the country. Finally, the professional bodies have done little to salvage the situations. The interests of the profession lie not only in producing greater number of jobs for sociologists but in ensuring that ethical practices in the discipline are maintained.

## Possible Sociological Discourses

We need to concentrate on some of the essentials of sociological discourses to develop sociology in India. They are:

(1) The development of sociology in India may be viewed in terms of the historicity of social conditions that have shaped the sociological perspectives from time to time. The theoretical and cognitive systems of sociology are socially conditioned (Singh, 1986). It is to be hoped that thinking in this direction will result in the concentration of contested themes and in the recovery of key Indian socio-cultural realities and textual traditions, traditions that have remained or continue to remain as an excluded part of hegemonic sociology or its margin (Nadarajah, 1996). Perhaps, this is the right time to resume the 'Indian sociology' by recognizing context and culture of the society and to overcome from the identification of sociology as solely a western.

(2) The production of sociological knowledge can be qualitatively changed with a sociological curriculum helping the multi-faceted contestation of western sociological knowledge. There is a need to consider not only the content of social science education in our universities but also the methodology used in the production of such knowledge (Nadarajah, 1996).

(3) Institutionalization of research requires a proper fit between the growing needs of theory and the increasing demands of society. Generally, public funds are made available by the government, UGC, ICSSR and other agencies in terms of the criteria set out for priorities. The question of priorities has to be answered in the context of the relevance of research.

(4) While paying attention to research priorities, the needs of individual scholars pursuing a promising but out-of-the- way enquiry should not be neglected. Research efforts involving interdisciplinary approach or bold methodological innovation should, on principle, be encouraged. The ICSSR standing committee has also recommended these suggestions in the eighties.

To conclude, the history of the development of sociology has not been much encouraging. At its beginning anthropology and ethnology helped the colonial rule to establish its foundation. In other words, the discipline of sociology was partly responsible for the survival of colonialism and feudalism in princely states. The feudal mentality of Indian people is thus due to sociology, anthropology and ethnology. It must be said that this discipline has not been worth its salt in India.

If we make a survey of the sociological literature which has cropped up during the last about 100 years does not take into account any massive event which took place in India. India's freedom struggle was a long struggle and it sought the participation of the masses. All the people participated in the movement notwithstanding the plural character of the Indian society. It was a great event in the history of India. The sociologists did nothing to analyse the freedom struggle. It is difficult to find any book on sociology written by our so-called sociologists. When the masses were busy fighting for their freedom, our sociologists such as N.K. Bose and G.S. Ghurye were writing on caste and ethnicity. Such a record of sociology can easily be called ungrateful to the nation. How can we be proud of such sociologists?

Another memorable event in India's history has been the mass exodus of people from Pakistan after the division of country between India and Pakistan. Burning trains from Pakistan were coming to India and the blood-stained trains were leaving India for Pakistan. Lakhs of refugees crossed the borders. It never happened earlier but the sociologists who claimed to be the analysts of Indian society did not mention anything about this tragic event.

Besides, an event, which is a remarkable in the building of our nation-state, is the era of building modern India. Nehru and his generation of national leaders started Five-Year Plans for the development of industry and village agriculture. The sociologists again turned their eyes to this era of development. It is discouraging to learn that the sociologists observed silence on this process of development. However, the sociologists made some village studies. Actually, there was a flood of such studies. These studies made some contributions. But, these contributions have false theoretical claims. Dominant caste, sanskritization, westernization, parochialization and universalization are some of the contributions which have not proved to be of any help for the development of villages. They have proved to be utopian for the nation.

There are several problems for the country. The problems are multi-ethnic, multi-caste, multi-religion, multi-region and multi-linguistic. Economic problems coupled with unemployment are disasters. It is expected of sociology to analyse the social ills and bring out some solutions. In the present work, we are discussing social thinkers of contemporary India. They are also responsible to relax-in comfortable armchairs and enjoy the academic status.

## Notes

1. See, for example, Baljit Singh (1955), Saran (1959), Dube (1962), Ghurye (1968), Majumdar (1968), Mukherjee (1973), Srinivas and Panini (1973), and Atal (1976). A decade ago, even an All India Seminar on "Sociology for

India: Teaching and Research" was held at Mount Abu which was organized by the Department of Sociology, University of Rajasthan with the patronage of the University Grants Commission (Unnithan et al., 1967). Moreover, some professionals in the field have attempted subjective appraisals of the academic standing of these subjects and certain other issues [see, for example Béteille (1973), Damle (1974), Lakshmanna (1974), Yogendra Singh (1967), Madan (1974), Ramasubban (1975), and Surendra Sharma (1985)].

2. The references of D. Gupta (1997) and P.C. Joshi (1997) have been quoted from S. Singh (1997).
3. The references of Béteille (1996), Thappan (1991), Hegde (1992), Deb (1997), Leela Dube (1996, 1997), Desai (1997), Bhagwat and Rege (1991), Patel (1994), Niranjana (1992) have been quoted from Rege (1997).

## Select Bibliography

Atal, Yogesh (1976), "Sociology in the Indian Campus", in Giri Raj Gupta (ed.), *Main Currents in Indian Sociology* (Vol. 1), New Delhi: Vikas, pp.117–31.

Becker and Barnes (1961), *Social Thought from Lore to Science* (Vol. III), New York: Dover Publications Inc.

Béteille, André (1973), "The Teaching of Sociology in India", *Sociological Bulletin,* 22 (2): 216–33.

Bottomore, T.B. (1962), "Sociology in India", *The British Journal of Sociology,* 13 (2): 98–106.

Clinard, M.B. and Elder, J.W. (1965), "Sociology in India: A Study in the Sociology of Knowledge", *American Sociological Review,* 30(4): 581–57.

Damle, Y.B. (1974), "Sociology in India: Its Teaching and Status", *International Social Science Journal,* 26 (2): 343–48.

—— (1982), "Theoretical Orientation and Methodological Perspectives for Sociology in India in the 1980's", in P.K.B. Nayar (ed.), *Sociology in India: Retrospect and Prospect,* Delhi: B.R. Publishing Corporation.

Das, Veena (1993), "Sociological Research in India: The State of Crisis", *Economic and Political Weekly,* XXVIII (23), June: 1159–61.

Deshpande, Satish (1994), "Crisis in Sociology: A Tired Discipline?" *Economic and Political Weekly,* XXIX (10), March 5: 575–76.

Dhanagare, D. (1993), "Sociology: Teaching and Research in Universities in Maharashtra and Goa" (A Regional Profile Status Report submitted to UGC).

Dube, Leela (1986) "Introduction" in Leela Dube, Eleanor Lea Cock and Shirley Ardener (eds), *Essays on Women in Society and Development*, Delhi: Oxford University Press.

Dube, S.C. (1962), "Social Anthropology in India", in T.N. Madan and Gopal Saran (eds), *Indian Anthropology: Essays in Memory of D.N. Majumdar*, Bombay: Asia Publishing House, pp. 237–53.

Fox, Richard G. (1977), *Realm and Region in Traditional India*, Durham: North Carolina: Duke University Press.

Ghurye, G.S. (1968), "The Teaching of Sociology, Social Psychology and Social Anthropology", in *The Teaching of Social Sciences in India*, Delhi: Universal, pp. 152–64. Seminar organised by UNESCO in 1954.

Giri, A. (1993), "Creating Community of Discourse in Sociology in India", *Economic and Political Weekly*, XXVIII (29–30), July 17–24: 1538–39.

ICSSR (1971). *Report on Social Sciences in India: Retrospective and Perspective* (Volume 1 and 2), Indian Council of Social Science Research, New Delhi.

— (1974), *Occasional Monograph on Research Methodology in the Social Science.* Training in Research Methodology in Social Sciences in India, No. 1, Indian Council of Social Science Research, New Delhi.

— (1985), *Survey of Research in Sociology and Social Anthropology (1969–1979)*, New Delhi: Satvahan Publications.

John, Mary E. (1996), *Discrepant and Dislocations: Feminism: Theory and Post-Colonial Histories*, Delhi: Oxford University Press.

Lakshmanna, C. (1974), "Teaching and Research in Sociology in India", *Sociological Bulletin*, 23(1): 1–13.

Lele, Jayant (1981). "Indian Sociology and Sociology in India: Some Reflections on their Beginning", *Sociological Bulletin*, 30(1): 39–53.

Madan, T.N. (1974), "The Teaching of Sociology in India: Some Comments", *Sociological Bulletin*, 23 (1): 113–18.

Majumdar, D.N. (1968), "Special Report on the Teaching of Social Anthropology" in *The Teaching of Social Sciences in India, Delhi*, Delhi: Universal. Seminar organized by UNESCO in 1954.

Momin, A.R. (1997), "Sociology in Post-Independent India: A Self-Assessment". Paper presented in *All India Sociological Conference held* on 22–24 December at Osmania University, Hyderabad.

Mukherjee, P.N. (1977), "Social Movement and Social Change: Towards a Conceptual Clarification and Theoretical Framework", *Sociological Bulletin* 26(1): 38–59.

Mukherjee, R.K. (1973), "Indian Sociology: Historical Development and Present Problems", *Sociological Bulletin*, 22(1): 29–58.

Mukherjee, Ramkrishna (1979), *Sociology of Indian Sociology*, Bombay: Allied Publications.

Murty, G.B.U. (1993), "Crisis in Sociological Research", *Economic and Political Weekly*, XXVIII (45), November 6: 2484.

Nadarajah, M. (1996). "Notes on the Teaching of Sociology", *Sociological Bulletin*, 45(2), September: 233–253.

Nandy, S.K. (1971), "Aspects of Development of Sociology in India: A Study in the Sociology of Sociology", in Edward A. Tiryakian (ed.), *The Phenomenon of Sociology*, New York: Appleton Century Crafts, pp. 121–45.

Oommen, T.K. and P.N. Mukherjee (eds) (1986), *Indian Sociology: Reflections and Introspection.*

Parvathamma, C. (1978), "The Remembered Village: A Brahminical Odyssey", *Contribution to Indian Sociology.* (N.S.), 12 (1): 91–106.

Ramasubban, Radhika (1975)."The Teaching of Sociology", *Journal of Higher Education,* 1 (1): 77–86.

Rao, M.S.A. (ed.) (1974), *Urban Sociology in India*, New Delhi: Orient Longman.

— (1982), "Sociology in the 1980: Retrospect and Prospect", in P.K.B. Nayar (ed.) (1982), op.cit.

Rege, Sharmila (1994), "If this is, Tuesday ... it must be Social Roles': Sociology and the Challenge of Gender *Studies*", *Economic and Political Weekly*, XXIX (19), May 7: 1155–56.

— (1997), "Sociology in Post-Independent India". Paper presented in *All India Sociological Conference* held on 22–24 December at Osmania University, Hyderabad.

Saran, A.K. (1958), "India" in J.S. Roucek (ed.), *Contemporary Sociology*, New York: Philosophical Library.

— (1959), "India" in Joseph S. Roucek (ed.), *Contemporary Sociology*, London: Peter Owen, pp.1013–34.

Sharma, Surendra (1985), *Sociology in India: A Perspective from Sociology of Knowledge*, Jaipur: Rawat Publications.

Singh, Baljit (1955), "The Development of Sociology in India" in Baljit Singh (ed.), *The Frontiers of Social Sciences,* London: Macmillan, pp. 463–69.

Singh, R. (1980), "Culture of Inequality", *Seminar*, No.225, November.

Singh, S. (1997), "Sociology in Post-Independent India: A Self- Assessment". Paper presented in *All India Sociological Conference* held on 22–24 December at Osmania University, Hyderabad.

Singh, Yogendra (1967), "The Scope and Method of Sociology in India" in T.K.N. Unnithan and Indra Deva (eds), *Sociology for India,* New Delhi: Prentice Hall.

— (1986), *Indian Sociology*, New Delhi: Vistaar Publications.

— (1993), *Social Change in India: Crisis and Resilience,* New Delhi: Har Anand Publications.

Singhi, N.K. (1996), *Theory and Method in Indian Sociology*, Jaipur: Rawat Publications.

Srinivas, M.N. and M.N. Panini (1973), "The Development of Sociology and Social Anthropology in India", *Sociological Bulletin*, 22(2): 179–215.

UGC (1978), Report on the Status of Teaching of Sociology and Social Anthropology, Part I: *Summary and Recommendations*, New Delhi: University Grants Commissions.

— (1979), Report on the Status of Teaching of Sociology and Social Anthropology, Part II: *Regional Reports*, New Delhi: University Grants Commission.

— (1982), *Status Report on the Teaching of Sociology and Social Anthropology,* New Delhi: University Grants Commission.

Uberoi, J.P.S. (1974), "New Outlines of Structural Sociology 1945–1970", *Contribution to Indian Sociology*, (N.S.) 8.

— (1978), *Science and Culture*, Delhi: Oxford University Press.

Uberoi, Patricia (1989 and 1990), "Some Reflections on Teaching the Sociology of Gender", *Samya Shakti*, III and IV: 279–89.

— (1994), "Sociology, Gender, Family Studies: Regressive Incorporation", *Economic and Political Weekly,* XXIX (27), July 2: 1686–87.

Unnithan, T.K.N. (1982), "A New Sociology for India: Review of Sociology in the 1970's and Perspectives in the 1980's", in P.K.B. Nayar (ed.) op. cit.

Unnithan, T.K.N. et al., (1967), *Sociology for India*, New Delhi: Prentice-Hall of India.

Unnithan, T.K.N., Indra Deva and Yogendra Singh (eds) (1965), *Towards a Sociology of Culture in India,* New Delhi: Prentice Hall of India.

Vidhyarthi, L.P. (1972). "Tribal Ethnography in India", *A Survey of Researches in Social Anthropology and Sociology,* New Delhi: ICSSR.

Vishwanathan, S. (1977), "From Laboratory to Industry: A Case Study of Transfer of Technology", *Contributions*, (N.S.), Vol. II, No. I.

# I

# Historical Perspective

It is not unusual to find inquiries of different sorts in the social sciences. These could be classified in two categories, viz., the nomothetic and the ideographic. According to this classification, the ideographic sciences are those which study unique and unrepeatable events, while the nomothetic sciences attempt to make generalizations. We can thus call sociology as a nomothetic science and history as an ideographic science.

Historians try to enhance our accurate knowledge of unique phenomena of the past, whereas sociologists try to seek information about certain uniformities in social behaviour under specific conditions. This, in principle, is the difference between the two modes of inquiry. However, the data of history are also widely used now by sociologists. This is indicative of the assimilative quality of sociological work. But, increasingly now, historians have also started using data generated by sociologists for their own writings.

Historians, philosophers, social psychiatrists, literary men as well as social scientists, use the historical approach as an aid in visualizing society as a dynamic organism, and its structures and functions as steadily growing and undergoing change and transformation. Since all groups, social institutions and personalities undergo changes to a lesser or greater degree, social scientists concern themselves with the process of social change.

Historical method has also been employed by Marx in conjunction with dialectical materialism in understanding the human societies. He took this philosophical device and applied it to the materialistic view of society. Accordingly, he believed that the materialistic structure of societies accounts for their changing evolution and development. Applying this to history, Marx delineated the societal dialectic sequence as follows: primitive communism – slavery – feudalism – capitalism – socialism. In this manner, dialectic materialism becomes a sociological tool in the historical analysis of societal development.

Still another form of historical approach is characteristic of the work of Max Weber, and of a number of later sociologists influenced by him. Criticizing the Marxist formulations of his time, Weber argued that "the so-called materialist conception of history, as a formula for the causal explanation of historical reality, has to be rejected". His own historical approach is exemplified especially in his studies of the origins of capitalism, the development of modern bureaucracy, and the economic influence of the world religions.

The main methodological features of these studies are that particular historical changes of social structures and types of society are investigated and are compared in certain respects with changes in other societies. In this manner, both causal explanations and historical interpretations find a place in the social explanation. It is also implicit in Weber's work that the general sociological propositions refer only to trends, while their application to particular societies and situations involves historical study in detail. A very convincing illustration of this approach of Weber is to be found in his treatment of the growth of capitalism in Europe. As he brings out in his book *Protestant Ethic and the Spirit of Capitalism*, "Capitalism grew in Europe through the influence of ideas located in Calvinist ethics which governed the lives of the Protestants in general and Calvinist in particular".

## Sources of Historical Data

In her book *Scientific Social Surveys and Research*, P.V. Young (1973) describes sources of historical data.

The social scientists generally confine themselves to three major sources of historical information: (1) documents and various historical sources to which historian himself/herself has access; (2) materials of cultural history and of analytical history; and (3) personal sources of authentic observers and witnesses. When, how and under what circumstances these sources are to be used depends upon the discretion of the student, his interests, the scope of his study, and the availability of the sources.

Historical data have some limitations too, which arise mainly because historians cannot describe all the happenings in time and space available at the time of writing history. Personal biases and private interpretations often enter unconsciously, even when honest attempts are made to select pertinent facts. This can be illustrated by reference to the current controversy that is raging on the writing of medieval Indian history. Here, we are concerned with the Indian historians, mainly D.D. Kosambi and Romila Thapar, whose writings reflect the historical development of Indian society.

# 2

# D.D. Kosambi

Damodar Dharmanand Kosambi (1907–1966) is best known as a mathematician, but he is endowed with a truly Renaissance versatility. His formula for chromosome distance occupies a central place in classical genetics. His work on coins makes the numismatics of hoards into an exact science. An unrivalled collection of microliths, the discovery of a Brahmi inscription at Karle, and of a remarkable number of megaliths with rock engraving form substantial contributions to archaeology. His editions of the poetry of Bhrtrihari and of the oldest known Sanskrit anthology are landmarks in Indian text-criticism.

## Methodology and Techniques

A fundamentally new approach to the study of Indian history, scientific methodology, modern technique of interpretation, selection and analysis of basic problems make the presentation vivid and absorbing. Kosambi's work is most refreshing in its range of new material, original discoveries of megaliths, microliths, rustic superstition, and peasant customs. He explains how to gain an insight into the past by examination of the monuments, customs and records. For this, makes an impressive use of scientific methods in many fields like archaeology, ethnography and philology.

### Works of Kosambi

1. *An Introduction to the Study of Indian History* (1956, 1975)
2. *Myth and Realty: Studies in the Formation of Indian Culture* (1962)
3. *The Culture and Civilization of Ancient India in Historical Outline* (1965, 1970)
4. *Indian Numismatics* (1981)

Kosambi's first book, *An Introduction to the Study of Indian History,* published in 1956, was a shift from what he professionally stood for. He had little use for a chronological narrative in history since he argued that chronology for the early period was too obscure to be meaningful. For him, history was the presentation order of successive developments in the means and relations of production. Because of the reliable historical records he argued that Indian history would have to use the comparative method. This meant a familiarity with a wide range of historical works. Kosambi's own familiarity with classical European history is evident in his writings; it also meant the use of various disciplines and interdisciplinary techniques to enable historian to understand the pattern of social transformations.

The knowledge of Sanskrit led Kosambi to a series of etymological analyses which he used to a great effect in reconstructing the social background, particularly of the Vedic period. Thus, he argued that the names of many of the established Brahmanas in Vedic literature and the Puranic tradition clearly pointed to their being of non-Aryan origin. From the study of *gotra* he went on to the logical point that the language of the Vedic texts could not have been pure Aryan and must have had an admixture of non-Aryan elements, reflecting the inclusion of non-Aryans as Brahmanas. This theory is now more acceptable to those who have worked on Indo-Aryan linguistics, on the basis of the linguistic analyses of the texts and language which clearly indicates non-Aryan structures both in syntax and vocabulary.

It was the recognition of cultural survival, which led Kosambi to weave so much material from ethnology and anthropology into his historical narrative. He mentioned that the presence of a tribe, which had once given rise to *jati*, and of another which became a quasi-guild. He noticed trees and sacred groves, stones making a sacrificial ritual, caves and rock shelters, which may have been occupied successively by prehistoric men, by Buddhist monks and later by practitioners of Hindu cult. Such places have a remarkable continuity as sacred centres and often provided a greater historical continuity both in object and ritual than many written texts. It is important to clarify that Kosambi was not arguing that religion played a more significant part in Indian culture than has been the case in other cultures, as has been the stand of those who maintain the greater spirituality of the Indian past; but rather, Kosambi's position is that there was a greater survival of the archaic in religious ritual than in other areas of Indian life which speaks of a certain conservatism but at the same time makes it worth investigating historically.

## Mode of Production

Kosambi (1975: 13) places emphasis on the mode of production. According to him, "the more important question is not who was king, but whether the people used a plough, light or heavy, at the time. The type of kinship, as a function of the property relations and surplus produced, depends upon the method of agriculture, not conversely." He further says: "Dynastic changes of importance, vast religious upheavals, are generally indicative of powerful changes in the productive basis, hence must be studied as such, not dismissed as senseless flickers on the surface of unchanging substratum." Thus, Kosambi accepts the basic tenets of the materialist interpretation of history. But he adds: "When one applies [historical materialism] to the Indian problem, it must be kept in mind that [it] speaks of all mankind, [whereas] we deal with a fraction." In certain regional contexts, variations cannot be ruled out. "For short periods in restricted localities, a dead end, a retrogression, or evolution by atrophy, are possible." Along with the mode of production, we have to reckon with the people mode of reflection as well. "Ideas (including superstition) become a force, once they have gripped the masses; they supply the form in which men become conscious of their conflicts and fight them out. No historian may dismiss or ignore such ideas nor can he be regarded as having fulfilled his task unless he shows why, how and when the grip was secured."

## Agriculture Pattern

At a wider anthropological level one of the clues to understand the Indian past was the basic factor of the transition from tribe to caste, from small, localized groups to a generalized society. This transition was largely the result of the introduction of plough agriculture in various regions, which changed the system of production, broke the structure of tribes and clans and made caste the alternative form of social organization. This process Kosambi traced in part from the evolution of clan totems into clan names and then into caste names. The agency through which plough agriculture was introduced would therefore become the major factor of control in caste society. This society he saw as the Brahminical settlements in various parts of the country. These led to the assimilation of local cults into the Brahminical tradition as is evident from the various *Puranas* and *Mahatmyas.* But equally important is his contribution to the sanskritization of local folk cults with the incorporation of Brahmin priests and rituals, the association of epic heroes and heroines, and by the inclusion of such cults in Sanskrit mythology.

## Marriage and Family

Kosambi attempts an anthropological functional analysis in which he argues that it reflects the institution of sacred marriage in prehistoric societies as well as the ritual sacrifice of the hero by the mother goddess. One of the frequent strands in his explanation of myth was related to his belief that societies were matriarchal in origin and many gradually changed to patriliny and that myths, therefore, reflect the transition from the one to the other. Bride-price is also for him a survival of matriliny. The insistence on a transition from matriarchy to patriliny in every case is not now acceptable since many societies are known to have been patrilineal from the beginning.

## Socio-economic Formations

Kosambi also refers to the agrarian technology in the Indus Valley. He assumed that it was a culture without the plough, that the river bank was cultivated with a harrow and that the seasonal flood water was utilized for irrigation with dams and embankments helping in retaining this water and the river silt for a longer period. The decline of the Indus civilization is attributed to the Aryans who destroyed the agricultural system by breaking the embankments, which, he maintains, is symbolically referred to in the Rigvedic descriptions of Indra destroying *Vrta*, and releasing the waters. Plough was brought by the Aryans (i.e., the speakers of Indo-Aryan) who thereby changed agricultural technology. Recent evidence on the Indus civilization makes it clear that plough agriculture was practised even as early as the Harappan period and that it was known to the non-Aryan since the more commonly used word for the plough in Vedic literature is of non-Aryan etymology.

Plough agriculture and iron technology, when introduced into the Ganges valley, led ultimately to the growth of urban centres as well as the recognizable forms of caste. Recent views would include as causal factors in this development the role of changes in crop patterns with a dependence on rice agriculture, the diversity of irrigation systems, the use of labour in the new technologies and the range of control over these factors by different social groups.

An evident departure from the orthodox Marxist pattern of historical periodization is Kosambi's refusal to apply either the Asiatic mode of production or the slave mode of production to early Indian history without modification of a major kind. For Marx, the Indian past conformed, by and large, to what he called the 'Asiatic mode of production' characterized by a static society, absence of private property in land, self-sufficient villages, lack of a commercial economy and state control over the irrigation system. Although he and Engles recognized derivations from this pattern, they saw this as a contrast to what was prevalent in Europe and argued that historical stagnancy in India was broken by the arrival of colonialism. Elsewhere, he has argued for the existence of the tenant and of the landowning peasant. He did concede that from the end of the Gupta period there was a relative increase in self-sufficiency. He also argued that the lack of a sense of history and the power of myth further reduced individuality. A static mode of production could not have co-existed with a form of feudalism since the latter breeds its own contradictions. Perhaps if he had been questioned on this ambiguity he may have modified his position to argue that the degree of self-sufficiency increased, but not to the extent of the static mode of production becoming the dominant future.

The feudal mode of production Kosambi accepts as relevant to pre-modern Indian history, although even here he makes his own distinction between what he calls, 'feudalism from above' and 'feudalism from below'. Feudalism from above was his characterization of the changes which came about in the late first millennium AD subsequent to the Gupta period. Incidentally, he has little time for the Gupta period and is justifiably contemptuous of the nationalist historians who described it as the golden age of Hindu revivalism. The changes noticeable in the post-Gupta period were mainly those of an increase in the granting of land with a greater frequency of transition from tribe to caste through the introduction of plough agriculture, a decline in trade and commodity production which adversely affected the growth of urban centres, the decentralization of the army and a concentration of wealth at local courts. With this was associated the spread of Bhakti cults whose emphasis on loyalty and devotion he saw as a characteristic feature of feudal society. In a discussion on private property in land, central to the concept of Asiatic mode of production, he argues that it should be viewed in the Indian context which implies that:

- actual cultivators were ex-tribals who still regarded land as territory deriving from kinship rights;

- the holding of a field was proof of membership of community rather than ownership of land; and
- in non-commodity producing village or one located near wasteland, land would have no sale value.

The only conditions were the regular payment of taxes to either the grantee or the king. But no generalization can cover the entire sub-continent since the changes varied from region to region. In his discussion on feudalism from below Kosambi draws his evidence mainly from Kashmir and Rajasthan and depicts a more clearly recognizable form of feudalism but with specific Indian features. This phase is characterized by political decentralization, accompanied by a low level of technology with production for the household and the village and not for market, and the holding of land by lords on a service tenure who also have judicial or quasi-judicial functions in relation to the dependent population. The backwardness of technology allowed an easy conquest of northern India by those with a more advanced military technology. Changes in the ruling class did not substantially affect the nature of feudalism in India and it continued until the coming of colonialism.

## Political System

The Mauryan monarchy, which controlled the Indian sub-continent, was a feasible political system according to Kosambi because of the expansion of the village economy through Sudra agriculturalists being settled on state lands and by the deportation of prisoners-of-war who were used for the same purpose. He argues against the use of slavery in production in early India. The decline of the Mauryan empire is attributed to economic crisis, the details of which are debatable. Double economic pattern indicated an economic crisis. Inability of the Mauryan polity to survive must be attributed to causes, which in part were certainly economic, cannot be doubted. Mercantile patronage extended to Buddhists and Jains and other sects which rooted them in a society more firmly than did the help they received from royal patronage. The punch-marked coins are an indication of developed commodity production, which provided a high status to artisans and traders as members of urban society and their link with religious preachers propagating a universal ethic would not be surprising. In the post-Mauryan period the role of guilds and artisans as donors to the Buddhist Sangha in the light of expansion and diffusion of trade is also visualized. The emergence of occupational *jatis* in urban areas can frequently be associated with this development.

### Myth and Reality

The essays, in Kosambi's book on *Myth and Reality*, are based upon profound study of library sources and carefully planned field work – a unique combination not to be found elsewhere. Fresh data and logical interpretation cast fresh and novel light on the origins and development of Indian culture. Kosambi has raised and solved questions of vital importance to all those interested in the study of Indology. The date of Karle caves; the background of Kalidas' plays; the significance of the great Pandharpur pilgrimage; the economic, cultural and historical basis of the Goan struggle for reunion with India – these are a few of the many fascinating problems analysed by the Kosambi.

### The Culture and Civilization in Ancient India

*The Culture and Civilization of Ancient India in Historical Outline* is a strikingly original work of Kosambi. This is the first real cultural history of India. The main features of the Indian character traced back into remote antiquity as the natural growth of a historical process. Kosambi tries to explore the answers of the following questions:

1. Did the change from food gathering and the pastoral life to agriculture make new religions necessary?
2. Why did the Indus cities vanish with hardly a trace and leave no memory?
3. Who were the Aryans – if any?
4. Did the caste system ever serve any useful social purpose?

5. How does it happen that the slavery of the type seen in ancient Greece and Rome never appeared in India?
6. Why should Buddhism, Jainism, and so many other sects of the same type come into being at one time and in the same region?
7. How could Buddhism spread over so large a part of Asia while dying out completely in the land of its origin?
8. What caused the rise and what led to collapse of the Magadhan empire?
9. Was the Gupta empire fundamentally different from its great predecessor, or just one more 'oriental despotism'?

These are some of the many questions dealt with fresh insight in this work. The book is divided into seven chapters as under:

1. The Historical Perspective
2. Primitive Life and Prehistory
3. The First Cities
4. The Aryans
5. From Tribe to Society
6. State and Religion in Greater Magadha
7. Towards Feudalism

### Caste in the Ancient India

In his book entitled, *The Culture and Civilization of Ancient India,* Kosambi felt that there is a need to study rural and tribal society in India. He says that the main feature of Indian society, seen as its strongest in the rural part, is *caste*. This means the division of society into many groups which live side by side, but often do not seem to live together. Members of different castes cannot intermarry by religion, though the law now permits complete freedom in this respect. This great advance is due to the bourgeois mode, because of which caste has begun to disappear in the cities, except for political and economic cliques.

Most peasants will not take cooked food or water from the hands of persons of lower castes. That is, caste has a rough hierarchy. In practice, the number of such caste groups goes into the thousands. In theory, there are only four castes: *Brahmin* or priest caste; *Ksatriya* – warrior; *Vaishya* – trader; and *Sudra*, the lowest caste, which corresponds in general to the working class. This theoretical system is roughly that of classes, whereas the observed castes and sub-castes derive clearly from tribal groups of different ethnic origin.

The relative status of the small local castes depends always upon the extent of, and the caste's economic position in the common market. A *Joulaha* of Bihar suddenly transported to some village of Agris in Maharashtra would have no definite status automatically assigned to him. But, in Bihar, his preliminary status is decided by that of his caste within the range of villages with whom he is in normal contact. This goes roughly by the relative economic power of the various castes. The same caste may have different positions in the hierarchy in two different regions. If this differentiation persists for some time, the separate branches may often regard themselves as different castes, no longer intermarrying. The lower one goes in the economic scale, the lower the caste in the social scale on the whole.

At the lowest end, we still have purely tribal groups, many of whom are in a food-gathering stage. The surrounding general society is now food-producing. So food-gathering for these very low castes generally turns into begging and stealing. Such groups were accurately labelled as the 'criminal tribes' by the British in India, because they refused as a rule to acknowledge law and order outside the tribe.

This stratification of Indian society reflects and explains a great deal of Indian history, if studied in the field without prejudice. It can easily be shown that many castes owe their lower social and economic status to their present or former refusal to take food production and plough agriculture. The lowest castes often preserve tribal rites, and myths. A little higher up we see these religious observances and legends in transition, often by assimilation to other parallel traditions.

## The Villages

Not only caste but the emphasis upon village life is also given by Kosambi in his writings. India is still a country of peasants.

Agrarian development is extensive, though still with primitive technique. Most of the land is over-grazed and over-farmed after two thousand years of cultivation. The yield per acre is abysmally low because the methods are primitive and holdings too small to be economic. The main feature of the land is the lack of transport. This means that a significant part of the production is local and locally consumed. It is precisely this backward, inefficient and local nature of production that has allowed so many older tribal groups to survive, albeit upon the verge of extinction. The whole rural economy is dominated by the seasonal rains, i.e., the monsoon.

The succession of seasons is all important, while there is little cumulative change to be noted in the village from year to year. This gives the general feeling of 'the Timeless East' to foreign observers. The bullock-cart and village huts seen in *Bharhut* sculptures of about 150 BC or the plough and ploughman in *Kushana* reliefs of AD 200 would cause no comment if they appeared suddenly in some modern Indian village. This makes it easy to forget that the very formation of a village economy with the plough used on fixed plots of land implies a tremendous advance in the means of production. The relation of production had to become correspondingly more involved than at the food-gathering stage. The modern Indian village gives an unspeakable impression of the grimmest poverty and helplessness. There is rarely a shop except in villages that serve many others as a market centre; no public building apart perhaps from a small temple which may be an outdoor shrine open to the elements. Consumer goods are purchased from the rare itinerant vendors or at the weekly market day at a few key villages. Sale of village produce is mostly in the hands of middlemen who are at the same time moneylenders.

Their grip on the rural economy and the resulting indebtedness of the peasantry is a problem. Once the monsoon is over, most villages experience a progressive scarcity of water; good drinking water is scarce at all seasons. Hunger and disease are the massive concomitants of village India. The lack of medical attention and hygiene brings out most sharply the traditional apathy of the village – always a basic factor in the political economy of the country. And secure foundation for despotism. The surplus taken away from people who live in misery and degradation nevertheless provided, and still provides the material foundation for Indian culture and civilization.

The uniform appearance of passive village distress hides a considerable differentiation. The bulk of the produces are peasants with small holdings. A few are self-sufficient. Some may rise to be powerful in the sense of a *Kulak* class, which is, in fact, being strengthened by current land legislation. Mostly, the richer holdings are possessed by people who are not peasants and do not labour on the land. The great landlords are generally absentees; their titles to land derive as a rule from the feudal period. Many of them shook off feudal obligations to become bourgeois landholders with the advent of the British. However, the British registered all land titles and fixed taxes in cash. This means that no village can today be self-contained. Even, the most secluded must sell something, not only to buy the little cloth and household goods required but to pay some tax or rent.

Even otherwise, the village could not be completely self-sufficient. In most of India, clothing is not a physical necessity, though it has become a social need. Salt, however, has always been indispensable; metals in some quantity had to be available before regular agriculture could be practised. These two necessities are not produced in most villages, but have to be acquired from outside. In spite of its timeless appearance, the village, too, is tied to commodity production, now in the framework of a bourgeois economy. Nevertheless, it does not remain true that the Indian village is nearly self-contained (Kosambi, 1970: 13–25).

Some production requires specialized technical knowledge. Though the Indian village uses very little metal, the villager does not need pots, usually of earthenware. This means that a potter must be available. Similarly, a blacksmith to repair tools and forge ploughshares, a carpenter for building houses and making simple ploughs, etc. The priest must serve whatever ritual needs the village feels. He is generally a Brahmin, though that is not obligatory for certain lower cults. Certain occupations such as that of barber, or skinner of dead beasts, are low; yet the barber's tasks and leather goods are essential. This necessitates the presence in the village of a barber and leather worker; of different castes naturally. Normally, each such profession forms a caste – the Indian substitute for the medieval guild.

## Kosambi's Framework Summarized

### *Background*

1. Educated and training in ancient history
2. Interests in ancient Indian history

### *Aims*

Analyse culture and civilization of ancient India

### *Assumption*

1. History is to be viewed for the presentation in chronological order of successive developments in the means and relations of production.

### *Methodology*

1. Archaeology
2. Ethnography
3. Philology

### *Typology*

1. Monuments
2. Customs
3. Records

### *Issues*

Different aspects of Indian society, namely,

1. Study of Indian history
2. Indian culture and civilization
3. Myth and realty
4. Indian numismatics

## Select Bibliography


Kosambi, D.D. (1953), "Brahman Clans", *Journal of the American Oriental Society*, 73: 202–208.

— (1956), *An Introduction to the Study of Indian History*, (1975) revised second edition, Bombay: Popular Prakashan.

— (1962). *Myth and Realty*, Bombay: Popular Prakashan.

— (1965), *The Culture and Civilization of Ancient India in Historical Outline*, London: Routledge and Kegan Paul, and (in 1970) Delhi: Vikas Publishing House.

— (1981), *Indian Numismatics*, Delhi: Orient Longman.

Thapar, Romila (2000), *History and Beyond*, Oxford: Oxford University Press.

# 3

# Romila Thapar

Romila Thapar was born in India in 1931 of a well-known Punjabi family and spent her childhood in various parts of the country, as her father was then in the army. She took her first degree in India from the Punjab University and her doctorate at London University in 1958. She has taught Ancient Indian History at London University, Delhi University and Jawaharlal Nehru University. She was also an honorary fellow of Lady Margaret Hall at Oxford, and has been a Professor-at-large at Cornell University in the United States. She is currently Emeritus Professor of History at Jawaharlal Nehru University, New Delhi.

## Ideology and Interpretation

Thapar has an interest in the social and cultural history of ancient India. The increasing interest in the historiography of the early period is an indicator of the awareness of the role of ideology in historical interpretation. She has also used comparative method to study similar societies with the evidence both literary and archaeological sources. Other sources include linguistic, ethnographic and other fields of Indology.

## Works of Romila Thapar

Thapar has travelled extensively in Europe and Asia. In 1957, she took a study tour of Buddhist cave-sites in China, including that of Tun-Huang in the Gobi desert. When in London, she used to broadcast frequently from the BBC. Among her other publications are:

1. *A Study of the Emperor Asoka*
2. *Asoka and the Decline of the Mauryas* (1961, 1973)
3. *From Lineage to State* (1984)
4. *Indian Tales*
5. *The Past and Prejudice*
6. *Exile and the Kingdom: Some Thoughts on the Ramayana* (1978)
7. *Ancient Indian Social History: Some Interpretations* (1978)
8. *The History of India* (1990)
9. *Interpreting Early India* (1993)
10. *History and Beyond* (2000)

In the following pages, we would discuss the writings of Romila Thapar related to the historical development of Indian society.

## History of India

There are two volumes of *A History of India*. While the first one contains a classic introduction to the history of India written by Romila Thapar, in the second volume, Percival Spear handles the Mughal and British periods.

The first volume begins with the culture of the Indo-Aryan civilization. There is already a useful study of Indian pre-history and proto-history in the Pelican series. Without repeating the same material, the first volume covers the history of the sub-continent until the arrival of Europeans in the sixteenth century. The choice of the date 1526 is terminal only. Thapar traces, in this volume, the evolution of India before contact with modern Europe was established in the sixteenth century. Her account of development of

India's social and economic structure is arranged within a framework of the principal political and dynastic events. This absorbing narrative covers some 2,500 eventful years of history, from the establishment of Aryan culture in about 1000 BC to the coming of the Mughals in AD 1526 in northern India and the first arrival of European trading companies. In particular, Thapar deals interestingly with the many manifestations of Indian culture, as seen in religion, art, literature, ideas and institutions.

## Division of History

Emphasis on dynasties led to the division of Indian history into three major periods: (i) ancient, (ii) medieval, and (iii) modern. The ancient period frequently begins with the coming of the Aryan culture (and in later publications with the Indus Valley Civilization) and concludes with the Turkish raid in Northern India in AD 1000, which in turn inaugurates the medieval period, lasting until the coming of the British in the mid-eighteenth century. The division was buttressed by the inappropriate equation of ancient and medieval with Muslim, since most of the dynasties of the first period were Hindu in origin and those of the second Muslim. Religion was by no means the pre-eminent motivating factor of change in Indian history, as these titles would imply.

There are five important aspects of Indian society:

1. Religion.
2. Culture: The study of cultural institutions did not receive much emphasis partly due to the belief that they did not undergo much change: an idea which also fostered the theory that Indian culture has been a static, unchanging culture for many centuries. This of course is an exaggeration. It is true that at certain levels there is in India a continuous cultural tradition extending over three thousand years, but this continuity should not be confused with stagnation. The chanting of the *gayatri mantra* (a hymn from the Rigveda dedicated to the solar god Savitri and regarded as the most holy verse in Hindu scripture) verse by a Hindu has a history of three millennia, but the context in which it is chanted today can hardly be said to have remained unchanged.

3. Caste: Caste system, as described in the Sanskrit sources and *Dharmashastras* (law books written by Brahmin priests), appears to have been a rigid stratification of society, apparently imposed from an early period and thereafter preserved almost intact for many centuries and also prevalent today with some variation in the process.
4. Agrarian system.
5. Polity.

### Geographical Structure

There are two parts of the geographical structure of the sub-continent: (i) the vast northern Indo-Gangetic plain lent itself more easily to the emergence of large unitary kingdoms; and (ii) the southern half of the sub-continent, the peninsula, was cut up into smaller regions by mountains, plateaux, and river valley. The northern kingdoms based their strength primarily on acquiring large areas of territory, and their revenue came mainly from the land. The structure of the southern kingdoms had also to take into account the more than marginal effects of sea power and the economics of maritime activities, which produced a more complicated pattern than that of the north.

### Population in the Past

An estimate suggested for the sub-continent at the end of the fourth century BC is 181 million (Datta, 1962) whereas another estimate for the early seventeenth century is 100 million (Moreland, 1962: 21). The first census of the British Indian Administration covering the entire sub-continent carried out in 1881 put the population at a little over 253 million.

### Ethnic Composition

The ethnic composition of the people inhabiting the various cultures of India was not identical. Ethnological studies have revealed six main races in the Indian sub-continent. The earliest was apparently the Negrito and this was followed by the Proto-Austroloid, the Alpine, the Mongoloid, the Mediterranean, and later those associated with the Aryan culture. There is evidence of the Proto-Austroloid, Mediterranean, Alpine and Mongoloid in the skeletal remains at Harappan sites. Presumably, by this time, the first five of the races mentioned above were well settled in India. The Proto-Australoids were the basic element in the Indian population and their speech was of the Austric linguistic group, a specimen of which survives in the Munda speech of certain primitive tribes. The Mediterranean race is generally associated with the Dravidian culture. The concentration of the Mongoloid people was in the north-eastern and northern fringes of the sub-continent, and their speech conforms to the Sino-Tibetan group. The last to come were the people commonly referred to as the Aryans. Aryan is in fact a linguistic term indicating a speech group of Indo-European origin, and is not an ethnic term. Their ethnic identity is not known on the basis of the Indian evidence (Thapar, 1990: 26–27).

The Golden Age in India had existed prior to the coming of the British and that the ancient past of India was a glorious period of this period of history. This view was natural and inevitable adjunct to the national aspiration of the Indian people in the early twentieth century.

## History and Beyond

(i) Historiography links many facets, concerned as it is with interpretations of the past. In recent years, historical interpretation has drawn on other disciplines and this is evident in *Interpreting Early India*. The subject is history, but the discussions in this work move beyond history to provide a glimpse of explorations of new historical territories relating to early India.

(ii) Time, as is argued in *Time as a Metaphor of History*, is an essential component of a historical perspective. Societies have varying forms of time, depending on functions and perceptions. Conventional attempts to assign these particular forms of time – either cyclical or linear – have now been questioned. The most meaningful understanding of time and history is to view time at the intersection of the cyclic and the linear within the same society.

(iii) Culture suggests alternative ways of assessing the early Indian tradition. Using more recent concepts of culture and tradition, it distances itself from the static notion of fixed traditions and exclusive high cultures.

(iv) *From Lineage to State* discusses the history of India from about 1000 to 400 BC Moving away from conventional treatment of this period, it attempts to locate the processes of state formation and social configuration. The evidence, both literary and archaeological, is linked, using a comparative framework, with studies of similar societies from other sources in order to suggest a multifaceted reconstruction of this history.

### Lineage

Among the early sub-periods, Vedic society has been described as tribal. The term 'tribal' refers to a community of people claiming descent from a common ancestor. In its application, however, it has been used to cover a variety of social and economic forms, not to mention claims to biological and racial identities; and this tends to confuse the original meaning. Lineages emphasize succession and descent with the implication that these are decisive in determining social status and control over economic resources. It also helps to differentiate between chiefships where lineage dominates and kingship, which as a different category, evokes a larger number of impersonal sanctions. The concept of *vamsa* (succession) carries a meaning similar to lineage and is central to Vedic society with its emphasis on succession even as a simulated lineage. Lineage also becomes important in the structure of each *varna* defined by permitted rules of marriage and kinship and by ranking in an order of status, the control over resources being implicit. In this sense, the emergence of the four *varnas* is closely related to the notions of a lineage-based society.

### Economy

In a stratified society the reinforcing of status is necessary. But, where there is no recognized private property in land and no effective state, such reinforcing has to be done by sanctions, which often take a ritual or religious form. In the absence of taxation as a system of control in the Vedic period, sacrificial ritual functioned as the occasion for renewing the status of *yajamana*, initially a *rajanya* or a *ksatriya*. Apart from its religious and social roles sacrificial ritual also had an economic function. It was the occasion when wealth, which had been channelled to the *yajamana*, was distributed by him in the form of gifts to the Brahmin priests which strengthened their social rank and ensured them wealth. The ritual served to restrict the distribution of wealth to the Brahmins and the Ksatriyas but at the same time prevented a substantial accumulation of wealth by either, for whatever came in the form of gifts and presentations from the lesser clans, the vis, to the ruling clans, the Ksatriyas, was largely consumed in the ritual and the remainder gifted to the Brahmins. Generosity being important to the office of the chief, wealth was not hoarded. The display, consumption and distribution of wealth at the major rituals, such as the *reajsauya* and the *asvamedha*, was in turn a stimulus to production, for the ritual was also seen as a communication with and sanction from the supernatural. Embedded in the sacrificial ritual therefore were important facets of the economy. This may be a partial explanation of why a major change to the state system and a peasant economy occurred initially in the mid-first millennium BC not in the western Ganga valley but in the adjoining area of the middle Ganga valley. This change was occasioned not only by an increase in economic production and a greater social disparity but also by the fact that the gift economy associated with the lineage-based society became more marginal in the latter region and in some areas was altogether absent.

For the early period of Indian history the term 'peasant' has been used to translate both the *Rigvedic vis* as well as the *Gahapati* of Pali sources. The Vedic *vis* was primarily a member of a clan although this did not preclude him from being a cultivator as well. The transferring of surpluses, in this case the voluntary gifts of the *vis* to the Ksatriyas, points to a stratified rather than an egalitarian society and the simile of the Ksatriya eating the *vis* like the deer eating the grain would indicate greater pressures for larger presentations. But, the transfer was not through an enforced system of taxation. In the absence of private ownership of land, the relationship of the *vis* to the Ksatriya would have been less contrapuntal with little need of an enforced collection of the surplus. The tax collections were voluntary and random although the randomness gradually changed. However, the three major prerequisites governing a system of taxation – a contracted amount, collected at stipulated periods by persons designated as tax collectors – are absent in the Vedic texts. The recognition of these prerequisites in the post-Vedic period and the collection of taxes from cultivators by the state would seem decisive in registering the change from cultivators to peasants in which the existence of an economy based on peasant agriculture becomes clear.

The introduction of taxation presupposes the impersonal authority of the state and some degree of alienation of the cultivators from the authority to whom the surplus is given, unlike the lineage-based society where prestations are more personalized. Taxation the quantity of prestations and became the more substantial part of what was taken from the peasant, but prestations were not terminated. The sanction of the religious ritual becomes more marginal and that of the state more central, the change occurring gradually over time. The formation of the state is, therefore, tried into this change. For the cultivator land becomes property or a legal entity and the pressures on the cultivation have to do not only with the subsistence but also with a provision for ensuring a surplus. This highlights the difference between appropriation in the earlier system and exploitation in the latter.

The gradual mutation which took place becomes evident from the frequent references in the Pali sources to the *gahapati*. The existence of the *gahapati* focuses more sharply on the presence of what might be called a peasant economy. *Gahapati* is a head of the household. *Gahapati* with reference to agrarian society, therefore, is perhaps better translated as the landowner of some substance who would generally pay taxes to the state except when the land which he owned was a religious benefice. Private landownership and the payment of taxes demarcates this period as one in which a peasant-based economy is evident. Traces of the lineage-based society continued in the making of status by *varna* and performance. Now economy has disturbed all this.

There is an evidence of luxury goods exchanged by ruling class groups as a part of gift-exchange. Marriage alliances between Ksatriya families involved an exchange of gifts. Less spectacular but more essential was another form of exchange, that of raw materials and commodities brought by itinerant groups such as smiths and pastoralists. Diverse forms of exchange suggest the co-existence of various economic levels within lager trading systems and sharpen the social contours of the groups involved.

In the post-Gupta period, due to requirement of land and labour, state systems became more heavily dependent on a peasant economy and has to absorb these societies and convert them into peasant economies in order to extract the benefits. Where trade declined or where new states were established, the need to develop the agrarian economy became urgent. The granting of land appears to have been the mechanisms adopted for changing the agrarian situation.

## Religious Ideology

A new religious ideology gained popularity focusing on the image and the temple and asserting an assimilative quality involving the cuts and rituals of *Puranic* Hinduism and the genesis of the Bhakti tradition. Ideological assimilation is called for when there is a need to knot together socially diverse groups. It is also crucial when there is an increase in the distancing between such groups as well as the power of some over others and the economic disparity between them. The significance of these new cults and sects may lie in part to focus on loyalty to a deity which has a parallel to the loyalty of peasants and others to an overlord. The egalitarian emphasis of the devotees in the eyes of the deity has rightly been viewed as the assertion of those lower down the social scale in favour of a more egalitarian society. But, its significance grows when the social background to this belief is one of the increasing disparity. Movements of dissent which had religious forms were often gradually accommodated and their radical content slowly diluted. The move away from community participation in a ritual to a personalized and private worship encourages the notion of individual freedom, even if it only at the ideological level. Central to any concern with ideology in the ancient past is the critique of religious thought (as distinct from religious practice for organization). Upanisadic thought is said to be a secret doctrine known only to a few *kastriyas* who teach it to select, trusted Brahmins. Even the most learned were said to be going to Ksatriyas for instruction. The doctrine involves the idea of soul, the *atman,* and its ultimate merging with the Brahmin as well as metempsychosis or the transmigration of the soul: in fact a fundamental doctrine of this age which was to have far-reaching consequences on Indian society. That it should have been secret and originally associated with the Ksatraiyas raises many questions. It is true that the *brahmins* and *ksatriyas* were both members of the 'leisured classes' in Vedic society and could therefore indulge in idealistic philosophy and discourses on the niceties of life after death. But this is only a partial answer and much more remains to be explained. The adoption of meditation and theories of transmigration had the advantage of releasing the Ksatriyas from the pressures of a preastation economy and permitting them to accumulate wealth, power and leisure. These are not the only kinds of connections relevant to a history of the period. Upper and lower groups or even classes, treated as monolithic, belie social reality. The tensions within these should also be noticed where the evidence suggests this. The competition for status between *brahmins* and *ksatriyas* and the separation of their functions, as well as their mutual dependence is symbolized in the sacrificial ritual which becomes a key articulation of the relationship. The new belief was the reversal of the sacrificial ritual in that it required neither priests nor deities but only self-discipline and meditation. At another level, the transmigrating of the soul through the natural elements and plants to its ultimate rebirth, carries an echo of shamanism which may remained popular outside priestly ritual.

## Polity

The political institutions of India visualized largely as the rule of Maharaja and Sultans. The rulers were dynastic. Therefore, the early histories were "administrator's histories", concerned mainly with the rise and fall of dynasties and empires. The protagonists of Indian history were the kings and the narration of events revolved round them. The autocratic king, oppressive and unconcerned with the welfare of his subjects, was the standard image of the Indian ruler, but for exceptions such as Ashoka, Chandragupta II and Akbar. As for actual governing, the underlying assumption was that British administration was in fact superior to any other known to the history of the sub-continent.

## Orientalists

The historians of India have in the past been regarded primarily as orientalists. They focussed on language. The nineteenth century concept of oriental studies has changed in the present century, both in Europe and in India.

The concentration on dynastic histories in the early studies was also due to the assumption that in 'oriental' societies the power of the ruler was supreme even in the day-to-day functioning of the government. Yet authority for routine functions was rarely concentrated at the centre in the Indian political systems. The unique feature of Indian society – the caste system – integrated as it was to both politics and professional activity, localized many of the functions which would normally be associated with a truly 'oriental despotism'. The understanding of the functioning of power in India lies in the analysis of the caste and sub-caste relationships and of institutions such as the guilds and village councils, and not merely in the survey of dynastic power.

The emergence of a state marks a qualitative change in the history of a society since it arises out and initiates a series of interrelated changes at many levels. The transition from an absence of states to state systems in the mid-first millennium BC (the earliest historical period for which there is sufficient literary evidence), has generally been treated as a sudden change. *Rigvedic* society has been described as a tribal society and that of the later Vedic period as one of the state-based kingdoms – the transition having occurred during the period from the late second to the early first millennium BC. This has sometimes been assumed on the basis of the conquest theory (Oppenheimer, 1914) of the rise of the sate, which argues that after the supposed conquest of the area by the Aryans, when they gained control over the indigenous society, the state almost automatically came into existence. Where the theory of internal stratification (Lowie, 1920) and diversification has been applied in preference to the conquest theory, it has been argued that class stratification is reflected in the caste structure, with the Ksatriyas forming the ruling class and the *vis* constituting the peasantry. In this situation, the increasing power of the former led to the emergence of states. Stratification has been viewed as a precondition to the emergence of the state since stratified groups become involved in internal conflicts, require contracts for agreements or result in the evolution of a powerful elite. The prerequisites for stratification are however under debate (Service, 1978).

Population growth and social circumscription are described as primary factors towards state formation where surplus can only be produced under coercion and population growth creates the need to produce and control surplus (Flannery, 1972).

Increasing social and cultural heterogeneity can also lead to social stratification and a tendency towards centralized political control. In the process of stratification and the building up of a hierarchy, marriage alliances are of some importance. Endogamous marriages strengthened a small group with potential and actual power, whereas exogamous marriages were more suitable for the assimilation of new groups. Differentiation in status is then wrapped up in legitimation which often derives sanction from religious beliefs and rituals in early societies. Legitimation increases the distance between those of high status and commoners. Sacral kingship is an aspect of this distance and is in turn tied to beliefs concerning the welfare and prosperity of a society being symbolized in that of the individual regarded as the chief.

State is differentiated from government and also, in turn, from society. The functions of the state are performed through the government in which the process of policy making is crucial and is the concern of political elites (Lloyd, 1965). Policy is usually in support of those interests which stem from privileged groups who have access to rights over land and over ideology in the form of religion, shared interests leading to the formation of an interest group. The privileged group, in addition to controlling resources, is often one, which is either the favour of the king or else a following of kinsmen, clients or professionals, makes the group important. The tension between the privileged and the underprivileged can either lead to the overthrow of the former by the latter where the existing political structure would have to be overthrown or more often, to attempts by the latter to enter the ranks of the former. This would result in the new group being accommodated as part of the elite directly or through some fictionalized relationship.

## Conclusion

The Vedic period saw a change from the lineage system (most closely represented by the data of *Rigveda*) to a combined lineagc and house-holding. Economy (as suggested by the later Vedic texts); that in the post-Vedic period the sharper stratification of the chiefdoms of the middle Ganga valley was in part of a continuation of the lineage system but in effect also germinal to the tendencies encouraging state formation and, therefore, these *gana-sanghas* were both a contrast to, as well as in some ways the pointers to the kingdoms of Kosala and Magadha which saw the emergence of a peasant economy and subsequently commerce.

Tribal society in the Indian context is ambiguous and includes a range of cultures from stone-age hunters and gatherers to peasant cultivators. In the Indian situation lineage society gave shape and form to caste structure. Lineage elements, such as kinship and marriage rules, are important to caste. When differing forms of stratification begin to emerge, an attempt is made through the *varna* framework to draw them, together into a holistic theory of social functioning. In the later stage the occupational groups employed in production, the *sudras*, are added on as a fourth category but denied a lineage form, so that their exclusion is made explicit. At the same time, their origin as a group is determined by occupation and locality and this makes a major difference in the *varna* system itself. When lineage-based societies gave way to state formation, the socio-economic changes reflected in the transition are also reflected in the structure of caste with the emergence of what is seemingly a duality between ritual status and actual status. The continuance of *varna* is in a sense the continuance of an aspect of lineage society and of ritual status. The latter becomes the survival of the lineage system and is most clearly articulated on ritual occasions. Economic status arises from new changes and has to be adjusted to ritual status. The latter is strengthened in those situations where the two statuses coincide.

On the whole, we have indicated the institutions and events which have contributed to the evolution of Indian culture. In the course of tracing the evolution of certain aspects of Indian life – the economic structure, changing social relationships, the historical contexts of religious movements, the emergence and growth of languages, to mention a few – certain patterns have emerged. Dynastic chronology has been treated largely as a framework in time.

In the preceding pages it has not been our objective to describe the history of ancient India. Nor are we capable of doing it. What has been our view is that Thapar was a social thinker fully embedded in history. Besides being a historian she was a cultural analyst. In all her works, she has tried to understand the evolution of Indian social institutions. She tries to establish the institutions of lineage and state. This makes her a social thinker with a historical bias.

If we try to understand our history, we will find that many of our battles were due to clash in lineage and state. During most of the occasions, alliance was sought through marriage. It is interesting to know that the present state, which is industrial, democratic and secular, was developed from lineage. At another place, Irawati Karve, the eminent anthropologist, established that caste in India is an extension of kin. Quite like Karve, Thapar has tried to formulate that the state has its origin in lineage kinship. In other words, both Karve and Thapar deny the divine right theory of kinship.

## Thapar's Framework Summarized

### *Background*

1. Educated and trained in ancient history

2. Academic career at Chandigarh, London, New Delhi, Oxford, Cornell
3. Interests in Indian history

### *Aims*

Analyse social and cultural history

### *Assumption*

1. History is to be viewed at the intersection of the cyclic and the linear change within the same society.

### *Methodology*

1. Historiography
2. Ethnography
3. Indology

### *Typology*

1. Textual categories
2. Indology
3. Language

### *Issues*

Different aspects of Indian society:

1. Indian culture
2. Social structure
3. Social system
4. Religious movements
5. Lineage
6. Orientalism

## Select Bibliography

Datta, J.M. (1962). 'Population of India about 320 B.C.', *Man in India*, Vol. 42, No. 4, October-December.

Flannery, K.V. (1972), 'The Cultural Evolution of Civilization', in *Annual Review of Ecology and Systematics*, 3.

Lloyd, P. (1965), 'The Political Structure of African Kingdom: An Exploratory Model' in *Political Systems and the Distribution of Power*, ASA Monographs 2, London.

Lowie, R.H. (1920), *Primitive Society*, New York.

Moreland, W.H. (1962), *India at the Death of Akbar*, Delhi.

Oppenheimer, F. (1914), *The State*, New York.

Service, E.R. (1978), 'Classical and Modern Theories of the Origin of Government', in R. Cohen and E. Service (eds), *Origin of the State*, Philadelphia.

Thapar, Romila (1961). *Ashoka and the Decline of Mauryas*, Oxford: Oxford University Press (Reprint 1973), Delhi: Oxford University Press.

— (1978), *Ancient Indian Social History: Some Interpretations*, New Delhi: Orient Longman

— (1978), *Exile and the Kingdom: Some Thoughts on the Ramayana*, Bangalore: Mythic Society.

— (1984), *From Lineage to State*, Delhi: Oxford University Press.

— (1988), *The Mauryas Revisited*, Calcutta: K.P. Bagchi.

— (1990), *The History of India*, Volume I, New Delhi: Penguin Books India (Pvt.) Ltd.

— (1993), *Interpreting Early India*, Delhi: Oxford University Press.

— (2000), *History and Beyond*, Oxford: Oxford University Press.

# II

# Indological/Textual Perspective

Indology, more specifically, the branch dealing with interpretation of ancient texts, and linguistic studies of problems of ancient Indian culture would be more fruitful if supplemented by archaeological, sociological, anthropological, numismatic and ethnographic evidence and vice versa. Available data in each of these fields are to be augmented by a great deal of honest and competent field work. None of the various techniques can, by itself, lead to any valid conclusion about ancient India; combined empirical operations are indispensable (Siddiqi, 1978).

The Indological approach rested on the assumption that historically, Indian society and culture are unique and that this 'contextually' specificity of Indian social realities could be grasped better through the 'texts'. It may also be viewed that Indological approach refers to the historical and comparative method based on Indian texts in the study of Indian society. Therefore, Indologists use ancient history, epics, religious manuscripts and texts etc. in the study of Indian social institutions.

The texts basically included the classical ancient literature of ancient Indian society such as Vedas, Puranas, Manu Smriti, Ramayana, Mahabharata and others. Indologists analyse social phenomena by interpreting the classical texts. Apart from Sanskrit scholars and Indologists, many sociologists have also used extensively traditional texts to study Indian society. Therefore, it is called as "textual view" or "textual perspective" of social phenomena as it depends upon texts.

Thus, textual variety of ethnosociology* that emerged in the late 1970s marks a noticeable shift from the European (a la Dumont) to the American tradition of social anthropology. The studies conducted during this period cover a wide range of subjects, such as social structure and relationships, cultural values, kinship, ideology, cultural transactions and symbolism of life and the world etc. The studies based on texts have been conducted by many scholars, such as, Bernett (1976), David (1973), Fruzzetti and Oslor (1976), Inden and Nicholas (1972), Khare (1975, 1976), Murray (1971, 1973), Marriott (1979), Pocock (1985), Eck (1985), Gill (1985), Das and Nandi (1985) etc. Most of these studies are based on textual materials either drawn from epics, legends, myths, or from the folk traditions and other symbolic forms of culture. Most of them have been published in *Contribution to Indian Sociology* (New Series), edited by T.N. Madan, replacing Dumont and Pocock. A good number of studies following this method have been done by foreign-based scholars (Singh, 1986: 39).

Bernard S. Cohn has analysed orientalists' perspective to explain the textual view. The orientalists took a textual view of India offering a picture of its society as being *static, timeless* and *spaceless.* "In this view of the Indian society, there was no regional variation and no questioning of the relationship between perspective, normative statements derived from the texts and the actual behaviour of groups. Indian society was seen as a set of rules,

---

* Ethnosociology seeks to explore the meanings and symbols, codes and substance that inhere in texts and languages of a people's own culture (Y. Singh, 1986: 37).

which every Hindu followed" (Cohn and Singer, 1968: 8). Bernard S. Cohn further writes: "The orientalists tended to be better educated and from the upper classes of Great Britain; same as Sir William Jones were trained as scholars before their arrival in idea and they wanted to treat Sanskrit and Persian learning with the same methods and respect as one would treat European learning..." (Cohn, 1998: 10–11).

When field studies in many areas of their interest in India became difficult, textual analysis, either of classics or ethics or field notes from an earlier data, represented a fruitful basis for continued analysis of Indian structure and tradition in the 1970s and 1980s (Singh, 1986: 41).

An Indological and culturological approach has also been the hallmark of several sociologists. They have hammered against the acceptance of theoretical and methodological orientations of the western countries. These scholars emphasized the role of traditions, groups rather than individual as the basis of social relations and religion, ethics and philosophy as the basis of social organization. For example, R.N. Saxena (1965: 1–13) agrees with this Indological or scriptural basis of studying Indian society. He stressed on the role of the concepts of Dharma, Artha, Kamma and Moksha. Dumont and Pocock (1957: 9–22) emphasize the utility of Indological formulations. They observe: "In principle, a sociology of India lies at the point of confluence of sociology and Indology". Indology is representative of people's behaviour or that guides people's behaviour in a significant way.

The use of the Indological approach during the early formative years of Indian sociology and social anthropology is seen in the works of S.V. Ketkar, B.N. Seal and B.K. Sarkar. G.S. Ghurye, Louis Dumont, K.M. Kapadia, P.H. Prabhu and Irawati Karve have tried to explore Hindu social institutions and practices, either with reference to religious texts or through the analysis of contemporary practices. Initially, Sir William Jones established the Asiatic Society of Bengal in 1787 and also introduced the study of Sanskrit and Indology.

The knowledge of Sanskrit also helps to understand the great culture and philosophical tradition of India. The Indological writings dealing with the Indian philosophy, art, and culture are reflected in the works of Indian scholars like A.K. Coomarswamy, Radhakamal Mukerjee, D.P. Mukerji, G.S. Ghurye, Louis Dumont and others. In this context, we are discussing here Radhakamal Mukerjee, G.S. Ghurye and Louis Dumont who used Indological approach in their research. They have tremendously enriched the field of Indian sociology.

# 4

# Radhakamal Mukerjee

Radhakamal Mukerjee (1889–1968) along with D.P. Mukerji – his colleague in Lucknow University – and G.S. Ghurye of Bombay University, are considered a great pioneer in sociology in India. Lucknow University was a major centre of sociology and social anthropology. Under the scholarship of the triumvirate – Radhakamal Mukerjee, D.P. Mukerji and D.N. Majumdar – Lucknow soon emerged as a leading centre for social science studies and it remained so until the mid-1960s. Our discussion here is mainly on Radhakamal Mukerjee.

## Life Sketch

Radhakamal Mukerjee was born on 7th December in 1889 in a large Bengali Brahmin family at Berhampur (Murshidabad), a small country-town in Western Bengal. He spent the first sixteen years of his life in this town. His father was a lawyer and the leader of the bar. He was an accomplished scholar with a great interest in history.

Mukerjee had his early education in Berhampur. He went to the Krishinath College of Berhampur. He got an academic scholarship in the leading educational institution in India – the Presidency College, Calcutta. He took his honours course in English and History in this college. Here, he came in contact with scholars such as H.M. Percival, M. Ghosh, brother of Aurobindo Ghosh, and the linguist Harinath De.

A brilliant student of Presidency College, Mukerjee read meticulously the works of Comte, Herbert Spencer, Lester Ward, Bagehot, Hobbhouse and Giddings. But, his interest in understanding the social life ameliorating the conditions of the poorer segments of the society was the result of his contact with the masses during the Swadeshi days of 1905–6. His patriotism found expression in his educational work among the slum dwellers in Calcutta. "Only educational and social work among the masses could be silently ... pursued without being nipped in the bud by political oppression".

During this period of his life, Mukerjee launched himself into the area of adult education which remained his interest till the end. He started an Adult Evening School in 1906 in the slums of Mechaubazar in Calcutta. He also wrote simple texts for adult education.

The Renaissance, particularly the intellectual and political ferment, specially caused by the partition of Bengal by Lord Curzon, kindled in Radhakamal the flame of patriotism and the eagerness to do something for the suffering masses. His interest in economics and sociology in preference to history was a sequel to this.

In 1910, Mukerjee joined his alma mater in Berhampur as a teacher in economics. He stayed there for five years. It was the busiest period of his life. During this period, he wrote his early works in economic, such as the *Foundations of Indian Economics*. At this time, he also became the editor of the renowned Bengali monthly, *Upasana*.

During 1915, when there were persecutions by the British government, Mukerjee was once arrested for a day and all his adult schools were liquidated. The charges against him were that he was a 'terrorist' or had sympathy with terrorism under the disguise of adult education. He was released very soon by the efforts of his lawyer brother. He was offered a position in Lahore College in Punjab. He went there thus, nipping in bud any interest in politics.

He went back to the University of Calcutta where Asutosh Mookerji had established the Post Graduate Council of Arts and Science in 1917. He stayed there for five years and taught economics, sociology and political philosophy. He was awarded the Premchand Raychand Scholarship in 1915 and PhD degree in 1920 (Calcutta University) on his study of "Socio-Economic Change in the Indian Rural Community". In 1921, he joined the University of Lucknow as Professor and Head of the Department of Economics and Sociology on the very day when the university started functioning. He introduced an integrated approach in economics, sociology and anthropology in both research and teaching in Lucknow University. He taught economics and sociology in Lucknow University for nearly thirty years upto 1952. He was Economic Advisor of the Gwalior State Government from 1945 to 1947 and Vice-Chancellor of the Lucknow University from 1955 to 1957. In 1958, he became Director of the J.K. Institute of Sociology and Human Relation of the Lucknow University. Thus, he stayed at Lucknow until his death, with interludes at the universities of Patna, Calcutta and Delhi, from 1925 to 1940.

Mukerjee also visited the universities of Cambridge, Oxford, Cologne, Vienna, Harvard, Columbia, Chicago, Michigan and Wisconsin for delivering lectures in economics and sociology in 1937, 1946 and 1948. He was nominated Chairman, Economics and Statistics Commission of the FAO at Copenhagen in 1946, a member of the Indian delegation to consider proposals for World Food Council, Washington in 1947, and as a member of the Technical Committee of the ILO for recommending names of countries for seats on its governing body. He served as a member of various committees appointed by the Government of Uttar Pradesh and the Union Government.

## Theoretical Formulation

According to Ramkrishna Mukherjee (1979), since human institutions form an indivisible unity of the individual, society and values, any consideration of social facts without their value component is unreal; instead, there should be a fusion of 'empirical' and 'normative' sociology, therefore, development of man is possible through commonality and cooperation in a free society, and not through contradiction and conflict.

Radhakamal Mukerjee's vision of sociology, though rooted in the Indian tradition, was still universalistic. He saw the possibility of developing a general theory of sociology based on a social action theory. In the Indian case this theory would be derived from Indian philosophy and tradition.

## Methodology

Beginning with the structural-functional approach to ascertain the interdependence between the economic sphere and the entire socio-historical-cultural order of Indian society, the 'transdisciplinary' approach was to be used for a comprehensive appraisal of social reality in the Indian world context. Mukerjee also suggested for the use of comparative methods in the study of social sciences in India. He said: "We must aim at the scientific study of the race and culture origins."

Inspired by Seal to investigate reality in the specific context of India, by Geddes to unfold in its empirical details, and in the light of his basic training in economics, Mukerjee began his research career with field investigations and bibliographical research in economic sociology and human ecology. He sustained his interest in empirical field investigations and throughout his life encouraged his students in this respect.

However, in course of time, Mukerjee empiricism became multidimensional, centred around the conceptualization of human institutions as forming an invisible unity made up of the individual, society and values.

Having received initial training in economics, Radhakamal began with a series of micro-level analyses of problems in economic sociology, such as rural economy and land problems (1926, 1927), population problems (1938), and the problems of the Indian working class (1945). In the late 1920s, when the great depression had set in, he initiated a number of micro-level inquiries into the deteriorating agrarian solutions and the conditions of the peasantry in Oudh (1929). This study should have been a pace-setter in agrarian studies in India, but, except for Ramkrishna Mukherjee, who conducted a series of studies on agrarian structure in Bengal in the 1940s, this aspect of Indian rural society remained neglected till the 1960s.

After receiving training in social anthropology in England, Radhakamal naturally took a more active interest in micro-level empirical field investigations. These included studies on 'inter-caste tensions' and 'urbanization', particularly cities in transition (1991, 1952, 1963, 1964) and the like.

What is interesting is that his involvement in micro-empirical sociology co-existed with his prediction towards a metaphysical and multidimensional philosophical view of human societies and social institutions. He thought that sociology and social anthropology were logged down by lower order empirical realities and were forgetting the higher order ones whose laws and processes governed them. He advocated and practised philosophical anthropology. In an almost meta-theoretical perspective, he tended to view individual, society and values as an apparent trinity, but quintessentially an indivisible unity (1931, 1949, 1950, 1956 and 1965). In this sense, Radhakamal was a pioneer of a transdisciplinary approach in Indian social science.

## Writings

Mukerjee wrote around 53 books on several issues. The basic nature of his writings is the integration of the social sciences. He has been a path-finder in many fields. Many of his students and associates reflect this approach in their writings. His contribution lay in the important areas of (1) developing interdisciplinary, rather, transdisciplinary approach in studying society, (2) social ecology and regional sociology, and (3) sociology of values or social structure of values. Commenting on his contribution to knowledge about social life of men and women, the celebrated philosopher, Sarvapalli Radhakrishanan correctly observed: "What interests me is (Mukerjee's) attempt to base his thinking on Indian mysticism, his perception that human life is whole and cannot be studied in fragments. Sociology or the science of man cannot ignore the question of values. Social sciences give us knowledge and if this knowledge is to be employed for the betterment or good of man, we must develop a sense of values. Mukerjee's great ambition is to work for a better social order."

A predilection towards metaphysics and the 'idealism' however was noticed in Mukerjee's earlier writings such as:

1. The Three Ways: The Way of Transcendalist-Religion as a Social Norm (1929)
2. Sociology and Mysticism (1931)
3. The Theory and Art of Mysticism (1937)

Mukerjee's other important writings are as follows:

1. The Foundations of Indian Economics (1916)
2. The Rural Economy of India (1926)
3. Regional Sociology (1926)
4. The Land Problems of India (1927)
5. Introduction of Social Psychology (1928)
6. Field and Farmers of Oudh (1929)
7. Regional Balance of Man (1938)
8. Man and his Habitation (1940)
9. The Institutional Theory of Economics (1940)
10. Indian Working Class (1945)
11. The Social Structure of Values (1949)
12. The Dynamics of Morals: A Socio-Psychological Theory of Ethics (1950)
13. Inter-caste Tensions (Co-author) (1951)
14. Races, Lands and Food (1946)
15. The Social Function of Art (1948)
16. The Social Structure of Values (1949)
17. A General Theory of Society (1956)
18. The Philosophy of Social Science (1960)
19. Social Profiles of a Metropolis (1963)
20. The Dimensions of Human Values (1964)
21. The Destiny of Civilization (1964)
22. Flowering of Indian Art (1964)
23. District Town in Transition: Social and Economic Survey of Gorakhpur (with B. Singh) (1964)

24. The Oneness of Mankind (1965)
25. The Way of Humanism: East and West (1968)
26. Social Sciences and Planning in India (1970).

We would like to discuss here the following major issues, which we find worthwhile in the writings of Mukerjee:

1. Indian culture and civilization
2. Theory of society
3. Concept of universal civilization
4. Economic transactions and social behaviour
5. Personality, society and values
6. The community of communities
7. Urban social problems
8. Social ecology

## Indian Culture and Civilization

Mukerjee (1964) writes extensively on Indian art and architecture, history and culture. He believes that Asiatic art aimed at collective developments. According to him, harmony is the basic value of life. He found this harmony amply illustrated in the Indian scheme of life of previous ages. Indian culture has viewed man as a responsible member of a community. Man is not isolated individual. In this context, Mukerjee writes: "Art in Asia became the torch bearer of social and spiritual upheavals for millions.... Oriental art is most intensively charged with community feeling and is thus chiefly responsible for the historical continuity of Oriental cultures." In contrast, such artistic endeavour in the West had been dominated either by individualism or feeling that art was an end in itself. This was just not conducive to either social solidarity or spiritual development.

Indian art is embedded in social or ethical sphere. Mukerjee writes: "The myriad temples, *stupas* and *viharas* of India bear witness to the link between art and ethics, religious and social values. Art in India is an enduring component of people's interaction with each other which shows in concrete forms the active relationship between people's aspirations and their artistic creativity."

Indian art is constantly associated with religion. Mukerjee is impressed by the largely non-aggressive nature of Indian religions like Hinduism, Buddhism or Jainism. The spirit of tolerance of diversities is reflected also in *Dharamashastras.* These codes are flexible enough to accommodate ethnic diversities of communities. Emphasis on the ultimate truth, rather than on a particular set of beliefs or rituals, has been a constant feature of Indian religions. It is through the peaceful agency of religion that the Indian culture and civilization spread beyond the natural geographic limits of India to Ceylon (Sri Lanka) and countries in the southeast. Therefore, Indian influences spread to many countries not through war or conquest but through friendship and goodwill.

## Theory of Society

Radhakamal Mukerjee emphasized interdisciplinary or transdisciplinary approach towards the understanding of human life. He sought to develop a general theory of society. To achieve this, first, he proposed to break the barriers between physical or natural sciences and sciences relating to man's social and psychological aspects. Secondly, the compartmentalization of social sciences like economics, sociology and psychology should also be avoided. There should be constant interaction among various social sciences. Mutual exchange of ideas between physical and natural sciences is necessary to adequately appreciate the multiple dimensions of human personality and its interaction with the natural environment and social environment.

## Concept of Universal Civilization

Mukerjee's general theory of society seeks to explain the values of a universal civilization. He used the term 'civilization' in an inclusive sense; culture is part of it. He proposes that human civilization should be studied at three interrelated levels. These are:

1. Biological evolution
2. Universalization
3. Spiritual dimension

### *Biological Evolution*

The biological evolution of human being has facilitated the rise and development of civilization. They have the capacity to change the environment as an active agent. The animals can only adapt to an environment, but human beings can mould it in different ways. The human beings, as biological species, are capable of overcoming competition and conflict and attain cooperation (symbiosis).

### *Universalization*

In social psychology, people are often depicted within the framework of race, ethnicity or nationhood. Human beings are seen as prisoners of little selves or egos, whose attitudes are parochial or ethnocentric. On the contrary, human beings have potentiality to overcome the narrow feelings and attain *universalization*, that is, to identify oneself with the larger collectivity such as one's nation or even as a member of the universe itself. In the process, common values help to subordinate the particularistic values to universal values. To Mukerjee, *ethical relativism*, which means that values vary from society to society, is not helpful in the present times. There is a need for ethical universalism, which affirms the unity of the mankind. In the new perspective, men and women become free moral agents who are capable of recognizing the common strands binding the humanity. They are no longer dictated by divisiveness or relativity.

### *Spiritual Dimension*

Mukerjee views that the civilization has a spiritual dimension. Human beings are gradually scaling transcendental heights. It means that they are moving up to the ladder of spirituality by overcoming the constraints of biogenic and existential levels, i.e., the physical and material limitations. In this endeavour, art, myth and religion provide the 'impulsion' or the force to move upward. As the social sciences have hitherto ignored these cultural elements, they are capable of providing a spiritual perspective. To Mukerjee, humankind's search for unity, wholeness and transcendence highlights the spirituality of civilization. In this respect, he commended the Indian and Chinese civilizations, which had endured as stable entities since 6th century BC. Their strength is derived from their universal myths and values which foster spiritual quest.

## Economic Transactions and Social Behaviour

Too much of specialization in a particular discipline may give only a one-sided or partial view of man's existence and behaviour. In his *Institutional Theory of Economics*, Mukerjee has shown that Indian western economics and that mostly neglected the traditional caste network in indigenous business, handicrafts and banking. It viewed economic development mainly as an extension of monetary economics or market phenomenon. The western model in economics focused on the market and industrial centres.

In a country like India, where a large number of economic transactions take place within the framework of caste or tribe, the market model has only a limited relevance. Economic exchange in the Indian setting has been influenced by traditional networks. The guilds and castes of India have been operating in a non-competitive system. The rules of economic exchange were largely derived from the norms of social or collective living. Interdependence or non-competition between groups has been emphasized in the norms of Indian tradition. They have not stressed promotion of self-interest but highlighted fulfilment of the well-being of the community as the proper goal of human life.

The economic values in India should be understood with reference to social norms. Sheer biological or physical drives do not generate economic transactions. Religious or ethical constraints have always given a direction to economic activities. Values enter into the daily life of people and compel them to act in collectively sanctioned ways. For example, a hungry upper caste Hindu would not eat beef; likewise, an orthodox Muslim or Jew would not eat pork, however, urgent may be the need for food. Therefore, it is wrong to always treat economic behaviour as separate from social life or collectivity.

## Personality, Society and Values

In his book *Personality*, Radhakamal views personality of individual as an agent, who takes decisions and makes choices, and seeks value-fulfilment. Man makes choices and acts in terms of values relating to (i) self, (ii) the other, and (iii) cosmos.

Individual man is, of course, subjected to two kinds of influences. On the one hand, there are the influences of nature, environment and biological drives and needs. Add to them are man's psychological impulses. On the other hand, there is the pressure of society or collectivity. Human personality is greatly influenced by these two influences. But, it is not determined by them. Human personality has the quality of transcending both kinds of pressures. It can even transcend itself. Indeed, personality is defined by Mukerjee as "the sum total of the individual's characteristic mode of adjustment at different dimensions: (i) biological, (ii) social, and (iii) ideal, cosmic or transcendent". The human personality transacts with the environment as a biological and social creature. But, it is something more than that. It is "the psycho-social whole responsive to the cosmic whole". According to Mukerjee, "personality essentially is transcendence". Personality of a man or woman has a social dimension. But, he/she may want isolation from his/her fellow beings in order to establish a communion between himself/ herself and the cosmos. He/she may require freedom from social pressures to realize the freedom of his/her inner self. The function of the society and its value system lies in facilitating the development of personality which would be a free agent.

Society is, according to Radhakamal, "the sum of structures and functions through which man orients himself to the three dimensions or levels of his environment: (a) ecologic, (b) psycho-social, and (c) moral". Thus, society "fulfils the basic requirements of sustenance status and value-fulfilment".

### *Values*

Values are "socially approved desires or goals that are internalized through the process of conditioning and socialization. They generate subjective preferences, standards and aspirations." Values help man in orienting his desires and goals in a set pattern. Thus, man resolves the inner tensions or conflicts of imperious biological drives. Besides this, he succeeds in achieving harmonious social roles and orderly relations with his fellow men with the help of appropriate values.

The concept of value cuts across desires, goals, ideals and norms. Desires in social action are goals. The ideal is constructed in a hypothetical social situation characterized by the conflict of goals. Norms are arbiters of opposing or contradicting ideals. They connote a beyond-human, teleological order of the universe. Social relationships are defined by Mukerjee as attitudes and behaviours of men towards one another as presented by their common goals and values. Groups are, according to Mukerjee, orderly social relationships and behaviours of associated persons that emerge out of the integration and fulfilment of their common goals and values. Institutions are more enduring than groups. Institutions are defined as more organized formal and enduring social relationships that fulfil certain common and stable goals and values of persons.

Position refers to the individual's capacity and achievement in the specific status within the institutional set-up. The institutional network of a society provides the matrix where multiple roles become complementary and facilitate the fulfilment and integration of the goals and values of society and personality.

The basic problem for modern societies is to create and nurture values which will lead to full development and expression of human individuality on the one hand and the generality of harmony order and solidarity on the other.

The social sciences as developed in the West propounded metaphysical individualism:

- First, it makes the mistake of isolating man and his atomic desires and preferences from his total group and institutional situation.
- Secondly, the atomism and rationalism of the social sciences have ignored the vast sector of human values that are sharable rather than competitive, integral rather than partial, and that

mark both maturation of personality and improvement of social culture.

- Thirdly, the notion of rational and atomized individual creates the artificial division between empirical sociology and ethics or metaphysics. Empirical sociological studies social structure and function through the method of natural science and ethics studies values. The dichotomy of the two in western social sciences gives the wrong impression that values cannot be studied objectively.

According to Mukerjee, the distinction between values and measurable facts is false. Values and valuations can be verified and validated in the social process. It is borne by three postulates:

- First, values play an important part in the integration and fulfilment of man's basic impulses and desires in a stable and consistent manner. It means that the selfish desires and interests are modified by collective living, where people give and take from each other.
- Secondly, values are generic in scope and are made up of both individual and social responses and attitudes. Values become shared by all through their symbolization. Symbols are condensed or epitomized expressions of commonly shared values. The national flag, for example, is a common symbol that constitutes a nation.
- Thirdly, despite the diversity and divergence of values of different peoples, and cultures, some universal vales are discernible.

A gradation of values is found on four levels of social integration:

(1) In the crowd there is a spontaneous, although brutal, expression of value – e.g., moral indignation, etc., directed against individuals and institutions.

(2) In the economic interest group, certain elemental values may be expressed, such as reciprocity, integrity, consideration, fairness level; they are susceptible to impersonal conflict and retaliation.

(3) In 'society' or 'community', equity and justice find expression.
(4) In 'general', the chief values are 'spontaneous love', and social co-cooperativeness. These values are necessary for the reconstruction of the world. In short, Mukerjee deals with values in several contexts.

Values are always accompanied by disvalues. Disvalues arise both due to individual's lags and social shortcomings. The disvalues are expressed not only in individual deviance but also in institutional deviance (criminal gangs, etc.). Mukerjee emphasizes treatment of disvalues. He would reintegrate deviant individuals and groups by working on the total social situation and on the social adaptability of persons and groups.

In two of his works, *The Dynamics of Morals* and *The Dimensions of Human Values*, Mukerjee discusses ethics from a global perspective. He refers to man's need to transcend selfishness and attain a universal brotherhood. The movement towards moral transcendence becomes almost an inevitable development. This is especially true in a world, which is ridden with violence and discord.

## The Community of Communities

In *The Dimensions of Human Evolution: A Bio-Philosophical Interpretation*, Mukerjee explored the creative, integrating and harmonizing principles of life, mind and society in evolution at successive dimensions, while in both *The Philosophy of Personality* and *The Dimensions of Values: A Unified Theory*, he has stressed the interpersonal nature of human existence and transcendence, and the unity, mutual involvement and fusion of all values and possibilities.

The book on *The Community of Communities* endeavours to use and develop the same contemporary seminal idea of the open human person-in-communication for the understanding and interpretation of human communion and community. Human person, values and community are all unities and transcendences.

Normally, man never expands his cosmos and its resources for the deepening, enrichment and expansion of life, values and community in a continuously creative, transcending process of evolution. The philosophy of community envisions it as the pattern of "one cosmos, one community". This widens the prospects of human evolution for both individuals and species within an overall unity of world science, communication and civilization. In this context, the philosophy of community means a profound study of the unforeseeable role of man in and with community and cosmos, of the values and potentialities of *Homo universalis*.

The meaning of community in evolution varies at the level of following dimensions:

1. Biological
2. Psychological
3. Moral
4. Philosophical
5. Metaphysical

At the biological dimension the true community comprises the entire species of *Homo sapiens* which guides and directs the psychozoic phase of evolution through human values and culture. At the psychological dimension the true community rests on man's self-extension and transcendence or transformation of *Homo sapiens* into *Homo universalis*, who consecrates himself to the infinite values and possibilities of both himself and the community for self-fulfilment and self-expression. At the moral dimension the true community grounds itself in man's vital communion with his fellow men, belonging to all races and continents. At the philosophical dimension the true community embodies faith in the vital principles of inner harmony and organic unity of mankind and cosmos and of the order, wholeness and togetherness of existence. Finally, at the metaphysical dimension, the true community realizes the truth of identity between the self and the Universal Other or the Community of Communities of which human love is capable, and embodies this truth in every goal and striving of human life in all interpersonal relations and values.

Contemporary man's history should strengthen his evolutionary trend by enlarging his communication and communion and extending and deepening his cosmos, making it more relevant to his meanings, values and possibilities.

## Urban Social Problems

Mukerjee envisages an ameliorative approach to the problems of working class. The industrialization in India, which has been taking place during the last several decades, succeeded in bringing together people from diverse regions and languages. But, the living conditions of workers in the urban centres, such as Mumbai, Kanpur, Kolkata and Chennai, were adversely affected by slum life. In the early days of industrialization, urban slums gave rise to vices such as prostitution, gambling and crime. It was, therefore, necessary to bring about drastic changes in the lives of workers to improve their economic and moral conditions.

Today, many private industries and public sector units have been providing facilities for social welfare to their workers. Besides, the central and state governments have promulgated legislative acts, which are binding on the employers. However, unorganized workers (i.e., who are unemployed, or temporarily employed) continue to live in slums. The rampant problems in the Indian slums at present are consumption of illicit liquor and drugs, crimes, and worsening housing conditions and civic facilities. Therefore, Mukerjee's analysis of the working class is relevant even for the present industrial organization in India.

## Social Ecology

Harmonious development of man requires that he should live with other members of the community and also with nature or environment or ecology. Radhakamal Mukerjee's contribution to the studies of what is called 'social ecology' is unparalleled. Social ecology, as a discipline, requires the cooperation of a member of sciences including social sciences. The geological, geographical and biological factors work together to produce an ecological zone. Ecological conditions also conditioned by social, economic and political factors. Indeed, human or social ecology is the study of all aspects of reciprocal relations between man and his environment.

In his book, *Regional Sociology* (1926), Mukerjee explains the scope of human ecology "as a synoptic study of the balance of plant, animal and human communities, which are systems of correlated working parts in the organization of the region". American pioneers in ecological studies did not give adequate attention to the factor of culture in their conception of ecological relations. They viewed such relations as similar to those which take place among plants and animals. Mukerjee argued that ecological relations among human beings are largely similar with those among lower organisms. But, in case of human beings, cultural norms have a very important role. Human ecology highlights this fact. In the formation of an ecologic unit like 'region' social habits, values and traditions become very important. Individuals having the same or similar values possess solidarity. The ecological standpoint in which man's constant strivings, aspirations and ideals mingle silently with the ecological forces and processes. Social ecology stresses the ever complex give-and-take relationship between man and the region.

There is a definite link between ecology and society. The development of ecological zones is the outcome of a dynamic process that is the challenge of the environment and the response of the people who establish a settlement. Ecological balance is not achieved by a mechanical carving out of a territory and setting people therein. Such an attempt weakens or destroys the social fabric. For example, in building industrial plants or constructing irrigation plants or constricting irrigation dams in India, very often, people of the concerned locations are moved to new settlements. It seriously affects community's life of the people. As a people lives in an area, it develops a symbiotic relationship with the ecology or environment of the area. In the new situation it may fail to develop that kind of relationship with the surrounding.

Mukerjee's ideas about social ecology advocated regional development. He stood for a balance between economic growth and ecological fitness. Traditional crafts and skills like weaving or engraving should be revamped for attaining economic growth of a region without any great damage to its ecology. Deforestation has created havoc. Long back Mukerjee cautioned his countrymen against it. He strongly advocated for conservation of forests and protection of ecological balance.

Mindless urbanization was also lamented by Mukerjee. From the ecological point of view he upheld the idea and process of urbanization. Urban development at the expense of the countryside should be kept in check. Agriculture should be diversified and industries should be decentralized.

Mukerjee notices with concern that (i) overgrazing, (ii) improvident destruction of trees and scrubs, and (iii) faulty method of cultivation bring about a serious imbalance in the biophysical constitution of the entire region. It seriously impairs nature's cycle. Removal of vegetation brings about a chain of unfavourable reactions such as (1) denudation of the top soil, (2) fall in the underground water level, (3) diminution of rainfall, (4) increase of aridity, and (5) acceleration of 'river', sheet or gully and wind erosion. These have led to serious and continuous agricultural deterioration.

Industrial civilization, because of its mindless exploitation of natural resources, finds its "security threatened due to the exhaustion of coal and petroleum" and the diminishing supply of minerals and vitamins, which cannot be synthetically manufactured. The importance of ecological values can hardly be overemphasized even in the industrial society. Of course, there is no need for loss of nerves. Man's success in his adaptation to the geographical environment rests on certain ideal values, which have their roots in ecological values. But it is necessary that these values should "have reached the level of standards of moral behaviour".

## Conclusion

It may be viewed from the above analysis that Radhakamal Mukerjee advocated a methodology reflecting the organic interdependence between the economic sphere and the entire socio-historical cultural order [see, e.g., *A General Theory of Society* (1956); *The Philosophy of Social Sciences* (1968)]. He proposed, therefore, a transdisciplinary approach to social research at a time when some social scientists in India were considering the need for interdisciplinary research.

Mukerjee has pioneered three approaches to social science for which he would always be remembered:

1. Conceiving economics as a specialization, and not as a discipline, in the realm of social science.
2. Introducing the 'institutional approach' to planning which should not be regarded as the exclusive prerogative of the economists but should be treated under the rubric of social science.
3. Raising the sight of appraisal of social reality from the *unidisciplinary* or *interdisciplinary* outlook of the social scientists to a *transdisciplinary* perspective, bearing in mind the common acceptance of the term 'social sciences' comprising various 'disciplines' like economics, political science, psychology, and sociology and so on.

Mukerjee started his career as an economist who, in those days, defined the framework of reference to the 'discipline' as the relation between man and his exploitation of the natural resources in successively compounded forms. At that time, the Marxists had raised the issue, but they were not seriously considered by the establishment of economics. Mukerjee was not a Marxist, but he clearly conceived economics as dealing with the relationship *among humans* with respect to the exploitation of natural resources and the consequent production and appropriation of material goods and services.

In his voluminous writing in this context, Mukerjee examined the nexus of human relationships in the totality of life and living. But that was transcending the boundary of economics as a discipline, which he regarded as a specialization within the unitary discipline of social science. This viewpoint was not acceptable to the contemporaneous mandarins in the 'economic' science; nor was Mukerjee acceptable to the contemporaneous mandarins of sociology or any other social science 'discipline'. Therefore, Mukerjee became a *bratya*, a marginal man in the realm of social science.

However, Mukerjee's empirical studies on various aspects of life conditions (e.g., land problem, working class, town and village life, ecology, food planning, etc.) were more and more appreciated on their own merit; that is, irrespective of the theoretical underpinning to these efforts and achievements of Radhakamal. But his advocacy of 'institutional planning' was not so readily accepted. As we live in a lunar world, where light is reflected from the sun rising in the West, the social scientists became vocal about institutional planning after Gunnar Myrdal posed it (1971) in terms of transplantation of the 'modernizing ideals' from the First (and the Second) to the Third World.

In his last years, Mukerjee postulated the need for a fusion of 'empirical' and 'normative' sociology in order that social engineering will have its disposal reliable knowledge concerning human behaviour, goals and values as well as means and techniques of analysis and feasible devices for social control [see, e.g., *A Philosophical View of Civilization* (1963); *The Oneness of Mankind* (1965)]. Although, his last writings were somewhat speculative in nature, however, he is distinguished among the pioneers of Indian sociology as one who clearly specified his factual foundations, arguments and proposals regarding what Indian sociology was in his time and how it should develop.

Mukerjee did not give adequate importance to the part played by conflicts in actual social life. He upheld the cause of harmony between man and man, one nation and another, between different regions, between human groupings and biological environment. His stress on the importance of values of understanding and toleration, moral responsibility of the individual to the community and human responsibility for protecting ecology would be considered very important by the students of sociology, even today.

That intellectual freedom is a precondition for an advancement of science and of the frontiers of knowledge was the basic faith of the founding fathers of Indian sociology and social anthropology. This explains why, despite their own preferences for certain perspectives and methodologies, their students could contribute appreciably to the development of alternative conceptual framework for studying Indian society – its structure and change in the post-1950 period.

## Radhakamal Mukerjee's Framework Summarized

### *Background*

1. Educated and trained in economics at Calcutta.
2. Academic career at Calcutta and Lucknow.
3. His interest in understanding the social life ameliorating the conditions of the poorer segments of the society.

### *Aim*

To work for a better social order.

### *Assumption*

Development of man is possible through commonality and cooperation in a free society, and not through contradiction and conflict.

### *Methodology*

1. Structural-functional approach
2. Comparative method
3. Transdisciplinary approach

### *Typology*

1. Field investigations
2. Bibliographical research

### *Issues*

Different aspects of Indian society, namely,

- Indian culture and civilization
- Theory of society
- Economic transactions and social behaviour
- Personality, society and values
- The community of communities
- Social ecology
- Urban social problems

## Select Bibliography

Bhattacharya, S.K. et al., (2003), *Understanding Society*, New Delhi: NCERT Publications.

IGNOU (2004), *Early Sociology: Sociological Thought*: ESO: 13.

Madan, G.R. (1972), *Western Sociologists on Indian Society*, Mumbai: Allied Publishers.

Mukerjee, Radhakamal (1957), *The Oneness of Mankind*, London: MacMillan.

— (1958), 'A Philosophy of Social Sciences'. Presidential Address to the Third All India Sociological Conference 1958. Also in R. N. Saxena (ed), *Sociology, Social Research and Social Problems in India*, Bombay: Asia Publishing House.

— (1966), *The Community of Communities*, Bombay: P.C. Manaktala and Sons Private Ltd.

Mukherjee, Ramkrishna (1965), *The Sociologists and Social Change in India Today*, Delhi: Prentice Hall of India.

— (1989), 'Radhakamal Mukerjee: A Note', *Sociological Bulletin*, Vol.38, No.2, September, pp. 261–266.

— (1979), *Sociology of Indian Sociology*, New Delhi: Allied Publishers.

Nagla, Madhu (2005), 'Approaches to Indian Sociology', unpublished paper.

Oommen, T.K. and P.N. Mukerjee (1986), *Indian Sociology: Reflections and Introspections*, Mumbai: Popular Prakashan.

Saxena, R.N. (1968), 'Obituary: Radhakamal Mukerjee', *Sociological Bulletin*, Vol. XVII, No. 2, September.

Singh, Yogendra (1986), *Indian Sociology: Social Conditioning and Emergent Concerns*, New Delhi: Vistaar.

# 5

# G.S. Ghurye

Govind Sadashiv Ghurye (1893–1984) is a towering figure in intellectual and academic circles for his unique contribution in the field of Indian sociology. He has often been acclaimed as the 'father of Indian sociology', 'the doyen of Indian sociologists' or 'the symbol of sociological creativeness'. Ghurye had been engaged in building up, almost single handedly, the entire first generation of Indian sociologists in post-independence period.

M.N. Srinivas has rightly said, "nothing disguises the fact that Ghurye was giant". Efforts of individuals, who have variously been regarded as the 'founding fathers', 'pioneers' 'first-generation sociologists' etc., constituted the most important factor in the growth of Indian sociology. These pioneers provided direction to shape the future of sociology in India. And, of all these, none did as much for sociology in India as Ghurye.

Two aspects of Ghurye's work are worth inquiring into:

— first, his role in promoting and directing the course of research in diverse fields of Indian society (as a teacher, as an institution builder and as a scholar); and

— second, his own substantive writings, his theoretical postulates, his vision of the role of sociology, etc.

Ghurye excelled in both of them. We would like to discourse upon these things in this chapter.

## Background

Ghurye was born on 12th December, 1893 in a Saraswat Brahmin family in Malavan, Maharashtra, the West Coast of India. He died on 28th December, 1983 at the age of 91 in Bombay. Sociology was not a school or college subject when Ghurye was a student. From the very early years, Ghurye showed a flair for Sanskrit. After passing the matriculation examination, Ghurye got himself admitted to the Elphinstone College, Bombay with Honours. He had a brilliant academic career throughout. He stood first class second at the BA examination and was awarded the Bahu Dazi prize – the blue ribbon of Sanskrit competence in the university. He stood first class first at the MA examination in English and Sanskrit in 1918 and was awarded the Chancellor's Gold Medal. None before that time had obtained a first class at the MA with Sanskrit. With this type of background in Sanskrit, Ghurye finally came to sociology, which profoundly influenced later Ghurye's own writings and the course of research made in the field of sociology under his leadership.

While teaching at the Elphinstone College, Ghurye submitted an essay to Patrick Geddes on "Bombay As An Urban Centre". It won him a foreign scholarship. The scholarship was instituted by the University of Bombay to train promising young men in sociology. Ghurye went to London School of Economics where he briefly worked with L.T. Hobhouse. He later moved to Cambridge where he worked with W.H.R. Rivers. Rivers died in 1922 before Ghurye completed his doctoral work. In 1923, he completed his PhD under A.C. Hadden on *Caste and Race in India*. His work was published by Routledge and Kegan Paul in 1932 in C.K. Ogden's *History of Civilization Series.* It immediately established Ghurye's reputation.

Sociology in Bombay developed under the leadership of G.S. Ghurye. Patrick Geddes was invited by the University of Bombay to start a Department of Sociology in 1919. Ghurye succeeded Geddes as head and as a Reader, took charge of the Department of Sociology at Bombay University in 1924. He was appointed as Professor in 1934 and retired in 1959. When he retired in 1959, the University of Bombay made him an Emeritus Professor. Ghurye was the first Emeritus Professor in Bombay University. He did not cease to be academically active after retirement from service. His last research student submitted thesis in 1971. During these about fifty years' span, he supervised as many as eighty theses. Of these, forty have been published as books.

As a *teacher*, Ghurye was very serious and meticulous in preparing his lectures notes. Many of his students have testified that his lectures were heavily documented. As a *research guide*, he was more impressive and more successful. He created a 'sociological awareness'. The 'second generation' of Indian sociologists was largely his creation. They include M.N. Srinivas, K.M. Kapadia, I. Karve, K.T. Merchant, I.P. Desai, A.R. Desai, Y.B. Damle, D. Narain, M.S.A. Rao, K.N. Venkatarayappa, A. Bopegamage, M.G. Kulkarni, K.C. Panchnadikar, M.L. Sharma, D.B. Unwalla and many others.

As an *institution-builder*, deservedly, the most profound impact on Indian sociology was made by Ghurye. Ghurye was the principal architect of the Department of Sociology of Bombay University and produced a batch of renowned scholars including M.N. Srinivas, who is now internationally known. His students headed (and many of them are still heading) the departments of sociology in many universities in India. Ghurye was the prime mover in the formation of Indian Sociological Society in 1952 and was also instrumental in the publication of its mouthpiece, *Sociological Bulletin*, as its official bi-annual journal. However, the first sociological journal in India, *The Indian Journal of Sociology*, was started in January 1920 under the editorship of Alban G. Widgery of Baroda College in Baroda.

Ghurye was elected the president of the anthropological section of the Indian Science Congress in 1934. In the same year, he was also elected as the nominee to the Royal Asiatic Society and continued to hold this position till 1948. During his lifetime, he won several top honours accorded to any intellectual in India.

As a *scholar*, in fact, throughout his life, Ghurye has been active from the academic standpoint. His 16 books, out of a total of 31 books, published during his lifetime. His output is indeed prodigious by any standard. Several of them are noteworthy as pioneering contributions to the sociology field. Even so, Ghurye is most likely to be remembered by *Caste and Race in India* (titled *Caste and Class in India* in subsequent editions). His persistent research endeavour, wide ranging interest and upholding of the base of academic tradition made him the centre of sociological creativity and research for several generations of Indian sociologists. Ghurye's broad area of interest was general process of evolution of culture in different civilizations in general, and in Indian (Hindu) civilization in particular. The origin and subsequent proliferation of the different varieties of Indo-European civilization constitute the range of Ghurye's study.

Indian society, through its long historical process of growth, presents a picture of a vast mosaic of culture held together by religion, values and norms of Hinduism. As a sociologist, Ghurye feels the imperative of exploring this unifying and synthesizing process. In spite of many diversions, exploration and analysis of the process of cultural unity in India through ages constitutes the major thrust of Ghurye's writing. He moves to establish his thesis with perfect case, back and forth, from the Vedic to the present-day India.

## Theoretical Approach and Methodological Application of Ghurye

Ghurye's rigour and discipline are now legendary in Indian sociological circles. In the application of theories to empirical exercises or in the use of methodologies for data collection that legendary rigour is not somehow reflected. To put it differently, Ghurye was not dogmatic in the use of theory and methodology. He seems to have believed in practising and encouraging disciplined ecclecticism in theory and methodology. Despite his training at Cambridge under W.H.R. Rivers and his broad acceptance of the structural-functional approach, Ghurye did not strictly conform to the functionalist tradition when interpreting the complex facets of Indian society and culture, which he chose to investigate.

The pioneers were 'armchair' or 'lecture-ism' sociologists. Even Ghurye had conducted village, town and community studies. It was said that "Ghurye insisted on fieldwork, though he himself was an armchair scholar" (Srinivas and Panini, 1973: 188). This was not intended as a pejorative comment (Srinivas, 1973), but it reflected the tremendous premium placed on single-handed 'anthropological fieldwork'. Therefore, it may be said that although trained in the craft of Indology, Ghurye was not averse to the fieldwork traditions of social and cultural anthropology. His field survey of *Sex Habits of Middle Class People in Bombay,* conducted in the 1930s and published in 1938 and the monograph on the *Mahadev Kolis* (1963) demonstrated Ghurye was far from promoting an armchair textual scholarship. He was an empirical field worker also. Later generations of Indian sociologists and social anthropologists used Ghurye's inexhaustible themes for their researches.

It would be appropriate to characterize Ghurye as a practitioner of 'theoretical pluralism'. Basically interested in inductive empirical exercises and depicting Indian social reality using any source material – primarily Indological – his theoretical position bordered on laissez-faire. Similarly, when Ghurye conducted survey-type research involving primary data collection, he did not conform to accepted methodological canons. He often ventured into generalization on the basis of scanty and unrepresentative evidence, e.g., *Social Tensions in India* (Ghurye, 1968). It is also likely that Ghurye's flexible approach to theory and methodology in sociology and social anthropology was born of his faith in intellectual freedom, which is reflected in the diverse theoretical and methodological approaches that his research students pursued in their works. Ghurye also used historical and comparative methods in his studies which have also been followed by his students.

Ghurye was initially influenced by the reality of diffusionist approach of British social anthropology but subsequently he switched on to the studies of Indian society from indological and anthropological perspectives. He emphasized on Indological approach in the study of social and cultural life in India and the elsewhere. This helps in the understanding of society through literature. Ghurye utilized literature in sociological studies with his profound knowledge of Sanskrit literature, extensively quoted from the *Vedas, Shastras*, epics, and poetry of *Kalidasa* or *Bhavabhuti* to shed light on the social and cultural life in India. He made use of the literature in vernacular, e.g., Marathi, and cited from the literature of modern writers like Bankimchandra Chatterjee as well.

## Works of Ghurye

Ghurye's writings have enormous diversity of themes and perspectives. The range is very wide, indeed. As the two principal branches of the Indo-European people subsequently prospered in India (the Indo-Aryan) and Europe (the Anglo-Saxon), for example, he has shown wide similarities between these two peoples as regards the two principal institutions, viz., the family and the caste. Not only this, a host of other things also came with Ghurye's range of interests. Rajput architecture and funerary monuments, sadhus in India and sex in America, Shakespeare and Kalidas, castes, tribes and races, metropolitan civilization – everything was grist to his sociological mill. His writings have been gathered from all sources – literary, historical, archaeological, sculptural, painting and iconography. This gives an extra dimension to his research.

Upto 1980, he authored thirty-one books; only five of them were written before 1950 and thirteen upto 1959 when he retired from the university service. The important works of Ghurye are as follows:

1. *Caste and Race in India* (1932, 1969)
2. *Culture and Society* (1947)
3. *Indian Sadhus* (1953)
4. *Bharatnatyam and Its Costume* (1958)
5. *Family and Kin in Indo-European Culture* (1955, 1961)
6. *Cities and Civilization* (1962)
7. *Gods and Men* (1962)
8. *Anatomy of a Rural-Urban Community* (1962)

9. *Scheduled Tribes* (first published as *The Aborigines So-called and their Future*) (1943, 1959, 1963)
10. *Religious Consciousness* (1965)
11. *Indian Costume* (1966)
12. *Social Tensions in India* (1968)
13. *I and Other Explorations* (1973)
14. *Whither India* (1974)
15. *Indian Acculturation* (1977)
16. *Vedic India* (1979)
17. *Bringing Cauldron of North East India* (1980)

The whole range of Ghurye's works can be classified into a number of broad themes. The classification has not always been a neat one, sometimes a little bit of discretion had to be used but this enabled us to arrange more systematically his ideas. Pramanick (1994) has divided Ghurye's writings into six broad areas. These are:

1. Caste
2. Tribes
3. Kinship, family and marriage
4. Culture, civilization and the historical role of cities
5. Religion
6. Sociology of conflict and integration

Besides these, there are a number of important writings of Ghurye, which could not be fitted into the above scheme. We would briefly discuss here the important works of Ghurye.

### Caste and Kinship

We first take up Ghurye's *Caste and Race in India* (1932), which cognitively combined historical, anthropological and sociological perspectives to understand caste and kinship system in India. He tried to analyse caste system through textual evidences using ancient texts on the one hand and also from both structural and cultural perspectives on the other hand.

Ghurye studied caste system from a historical, comparative and integrative perspective. Later on he did comparative study of kinship in Indo-European cultures. In his study of caste and kinship, Ghurye emphasizes two important points:

1. The kin and caste networks in India had parallels in some other societies also.
2. The kinship and caste in India served in the past as integrative frameworks.

The evolution of society was based on the integration of diverse, racial or ethnic groups through these networks.

Ghurye highlights six structural features of caste system as follows:

1. Segmental division
2. Hierarchy
3. Pollution and purity
4. Civil and religious disabilities and privileges of different sections
5. Lack of choice of occupation
6. Restrictions on marriage

Besides the above characteristics, Ghurye laid particular stress on endogamy as the most important feature of the caste system. Any effective unit of the caste hierarchy is marked by endogamy. Every caste had in the past segmented into smaller sub-divisions or sub-castes. Each of these sub-castes practised endogamy. For example, Vaishya (Baniya or Mahajan) castes are divided into various sub-castes such as Agrawal, Maheshwari etc.

Caste is also linked with kinship through caste endogamy and also clan (*gotra)* exogamy. *Gotra* has been treated as thoroughly exogamous unit by the Brahmins and later by the non-Brahmins. The basic notion here is that all the members of a *gotra* are related to one another, through blood, i.e., they have *rishi* (sage) as their common ancestor. Therefore, marriage between two persons of the same *gotra* will lead to incestuous relationship. It will lead the lineage of the *gotra* to near extinction.

The relationship between caste and kinship is very close because (i) exogamy in our society is largely based on kinship, either real or imaginary, and (ii) the effective unit of caste, sub-caste is largely constituted of kinsmen. To Ghurye, there are three types of marriage restrictions in our society, which shape the relationship between caste and kinship. These are endogamy, exogamy and hypergamy. Exogamy can be divided into two parts: (i) *spinda* or prohibited degrees of kin, and (ii) *sept* or *gotra* exogamy.

The *gotra* and *charna* were kin categories of Indo-European cultures which systematized the rank and status of the people. These categories were derived from *rishis* (saints) of the past. These *rishis* were the real or eponymous founder of the *gotra* and *charna*. In India, descent has not always been traced to the blood tie. The lineages were often based on spiritual descent from sages of the past. Outside the kinship, one might notice the *guru-shishya* (teacher-student) relationship, which is also based on spiritual descent. A disciple is proud to trace his descent from a master.

Likewise, caste and sub-caste integrated people into a ranked order based on norms of purity-pollution. The rules of endogamy and commensality marked off castes from each other. This was integrative instrument, which organized them into a totality or collectivity. The Hindu religion provided the conceptual and ritualistic guidelines for this integration. The Brahmins of India played a key role in legitimizing the caste ranks and orders through their interpretation of *Dharamashastras*, which were the compendia of sacred codes.

## Tribe

Ghurye's works on the tribes were general as well as specific. He wrote a general book on *Scheduled Tribes* in which he dealt with the historical, administrative and social dimensions of Indian tribes. He also wrote on specific tribes such as the Kolis in Maharashtra. Ghurye presented his thesis on tribes at a time when a majority of the established anthropologists and administrators were of the opinion that the separate identity of the tribes is to be maintained at any cost.

Ghurye, on the other hand, believes that most of the tribes have been Hinduized after a long period of contact with Hindus. He holds that it is futile to search for the separate identity of the tribes. They are nothing but the 'backward caste Hindus'. Their backwardness was due to their imperfect integration into Hindu society. The Santhals, Bhils, Gonds, etc., who live in South-Central India are its examples (Ghurye, 1963).

There has been fierce debate between G.S. Ghurye and Verrier Elwin. Elwin in his book *Loss of Nerve* said that tribals should be allowed to live in isolation, whereas Ghurye argued that tribals should be assimilated into Hindu castes.

Thus, Ghurye holds the view that a grand historical process of merger between two communities has almost been completed. Consequently, tribes, now, may be regarded as 'backward Hindus'. The incorporation of Hindu values and norms into tribal life was a positive step in the process of development. The tribes in India had slowly absorbed certain Hindu values and style of life through contact with the Hindu social groups. Today, it is being considered a part of Hindu society. Under Hindu influence, the tribes gave up liquor drinking, received education and improved their agriculture. In this context, Hindu voluntary organizations, such as Ramakrishna Mission and Arya Samaj, played a constructive role for the development of the tribes. In his later works of north-eastern tribes, Ghurye documented secessionist trends. He felt that unless these were held in check, the political unity of the country would be damaged.

Ghurye presents a huge data on the thoughts, practices and habits of the tribes inhabiting the Central Indian region. He quotes extensively from various writings and reports to show that Katauris, Bhuiyas, Oraons, Khonds, Gonds, Korkus etc. have substantially adopted Hinduism as their religion. Ghurye suggests that the economic motivation behind the adoption of Hinduism is very strong among the tribes. They can come out of their tribal crafts and adopt a specialized type of occupation, which is in demand in society.

## Rural-Urbanization

Ghurye remained occupied all through his life with the idea of *rururbanization* securing the advantages of urban life simultaneously with nature's greenery. Therefore, he discusses the process of rural-urbanization in India. He views that the urbanization in

India was not a simple function of industrial growth. In India, the process of urbanization, at least till recent years, started from within the rural area itself. He traced Sanskrit texts and documents to illustrate the growth of urban centres from the need for market felt in a rural hinterland. Development of agriculture needed more and more markets to exchange the surplus in foodgrains. Consequently, in many rural regions, one part of a big village started functioning into a market. This led to a township, which in turn developed administrative, judicial and other institutions. In the past, urban centres were based on feudal patronage, which had demands for silk cloths, jewellery, metal artifacts, weapons etc. This led to the growth of urban centres such as Banaras, Kaṇchipurum, Jaipur, Moradabad etc.

In brief, it may be said that Ghurye's approach to 'rural-urbanization' reflects the indigenous source of urbanism. During colonial times, the growth of metropolitan centres altered the Indian life. The towns and cities were no longer the outlets for agricultural produce and handicrafts but they became the major manufacturing centres. These centres used rural areas for producing raw materials and turned into a market for selling industrial products. Thus, the metropolitan economy emerged to dominate the village economy. Therefore, the urbanization started making inroads into the rural hinterland in contrast to previous pattern. A large city or metropolis also functioned as the centre of culture of the territory encompassing it.

For Ghurye, the large city with its big complexes of higher education, research, judiciary, health services, print and entertainment media is a cradle innovation that ultimately serves cultural growth. The functions of the city are to perform a culturally integrative role, to act as a point of focus and the centre of radiation of the major tenets of the age. Not any city, but large city or metropolis having an organic link with the life of the people of its region can do this work well.

According to Ghurye, an urban planner must tackle the problems of (1) sufficient supply of drinking water, (2) human congestion, (3) traffic congestion, (4) regulation of public vehicles, (5) insufficiency of railway transport in cities like Mumbai,

(6) erosion of trees, (7) sound pollution, (8) indiscriminate tree felling, and (9) plight of the pedestrians.

## Culture and Civilization

There are two conflicting views about the growth and accumulation pattern of culture. One theory maintains that in any community culture grows quite independently of similar events happening elsewhere or predominantly with reference to local needs and local situation. The other group believes that culture grows by *diffusion*. A single invention or discovery is made at one place and ultimately this cultural trait diffuses throughout the world. Sir G.E. Smith was the most ardent advocate of the diffusion theory.

In one of his papers, "The Disposal of Human Placenta", published in 1937, Ghurye examines the practices of human beings with regard to the disposal of discard of human body like first out hair, nail pairing, first fallen teeth and the after birth. The purpose of this paper is, as he says, to compare the methods of disposal of the human placenta in the different regions of the world to see if they shed any light on the problem of diffusion of culture. Culture diffusion is essentially an anthropological theory, which is concerned with the nature of culture contact operating principally among the preliminary people. According to Ghurye, culture constitutes the central or core element for understanding society and its evolution. In fact, culture is a totality involving the entire heritage of mankind. Ghurye's abiding interest was to analyse the course of cultural evolution and the nature of heritage which mankind has denied from the past.

Culture relates to the realm of values. It is a matter of individual attainment of excellence and creativity. Ghurye had a strong faith in the power of man to preserve the best of his old culture, while creating from his own spirit of new culture. He was more concerned with the process of evolution of Hindu civilization, which has been termed as a 'complex civilization'. And, Ghurye thought that for analysing the dynamics of culture in such a long historical civilization. In this context, the process of *acculturation* is more relevant than the process of diffusion. He thinks that the challenging task of a sociologist is to analyse this complex acculturation process in India. According to him, India has been the home of many ethnic stocks and cultures from pre-historic times. In his analysis of caste, Ghurye refers to how caste system was developed by the Brahmins and how it spread to other sections of the population. The operation of the process of Hinduization also provides the general backdrop of his analysis of the trial phenomenon.

Ghurye was promoted by the belief that there is a "common heritage of modern civilization" and that civilization is a "collective endeavour of humanity". He holds that behind the rise and fall of civilization, there has occurred a steady growth of culture. Cutting across the vicissitudes of civilization growth, there are certain values, which have been established as final. These values have been termed by Ghurye as the 'foundations of culture'. He delineates five such values or foundations of culture. These are:

1. Religious consciousness
2. Conscience
3. Justice
4. Free pursuit of knowledge and free expression
5. Toleration

According to Ghurye, "civilization is the sum total of social heritage projected on the social plane". It is also an attribute of the society. Different societies can be differentiated with reference to their civilizational attainment. Ghurye makes four general conclusions with regard to the nature of civilization:

— Firstly, as yet, there has been no society, which has been either completely civilized or very highly civilized.
— Secondly, Ghurye believes in the law of continuous progress.
— Thirdly, gradation of civilization is also correlated with the distribution of values. In a high civilization, the humanitarian and cultural values will be accepted by a wide cross-section of population.
— Fourthly, every civilization, high or low, possesses some distinctive qualities.

## Sociology of Religion

Religion is fundamental to man. Man becomes conscious of some power beyond his comprehension almost at the dawn of civilization. This field has drawn the attention of sociologists like Weber (*The Protestant Ethic and Spirit of Capitalism*, 1930) and Durkheim (*The Elementary Forms of Religious Life*, 1915). Ghurye thinks that religion is at the centre of the total cultural heritage of man. He gives the five foundations of culture as mentioned earlier in the description of culture and civilization, out of which 'religious consciousness' is most important. It moulds and directs the behaviour of man in society.

Ghurye made original contribution to the study of Indian religious beliefs and practices. He wrote six books to bring out the role of religion in society. These are: *Indian Sadhus* (1953), *Gods and Men* (1962), *Religious Consciousness* (1965), *Indian Accumulation* (1977), *Vedic India* (1979), and *The Legacy of Ramayana* (1979). All these works reflect Ghurye's interest related to the sociology of religion. For example, in *Gods and Men*, Ghurye discusses the nature of the Hindu ideas of Godhead and the relations, if any, between the climate of an age and the type of Godhead favoured. In *Religious Consciousness*, Ghurye analyses the three oldest human civilizations, viz., the Mesopotamian, the Egyptian and the Hindu, in their various aspects of mythological beliefs, speculation, cosmology, life after death, view of Godhead, temple architecture, etc. And, in the *Indian Sadhus*, Ghurye considers the genesis, development and organization of asceticism in Hindu religion and the role ascetics have played in the maintenance of Hindu society.

## Indian Sadhus

*Indian Sadhus* (1953 and 1964) is an excellent sociography of the various sects and religious centres established by the great Vedantic philosopher Sankaracharya and other notable religious figures. In this work, Ghurye highlights the paradoxical nature of renunciation in India. A *sadhu* or *sannyasin* is supposed to be detached from all castes, norms and social conventions, etc. He is outside the pale of society. Yet strikingly enough, since the time of Sankaracharya, the Hindu society has more or less been guided by the *sadhus*. These *sadhus* were not the lonely hermits. Most of them belonged to monastic orders, which have distinctive traditions. The monastic organization in India was a product of Hinduism and Buddhism. The rise of Buddhism and Jainism marked the decline of individual ascetics like Viswamitra. Indian *sadhus* have acted as the arbiters of religious disputes, patronized learning of scriptures and the sacred lore and even defended religion against external attacks.

## National Unity and Integration

Ghurye had interest in contemporary Indian situations. As a sociologist, he had been extremely concerned with the concept of integration, the process of national unity in India, and the contemporary challenges to the situation. This concern became apparent even at the time he wrote *Caste and Race in India* in 1932 and *The Aborigines-so-called-and their Future* in 1943. However, this concern with the present 'disturbing trends' in Indian society has come back in a big way in the later writings of Ghurye (Pramanick, 1994). There are three books of Ghurye, known as his 'triology' in this field, which are relevant in this connection. These are *Social Tensions in India* (1968), *Whither India* (1974) and *India Recreates Democracy* (1978). In these books he has developed a theoretical framework to explain unity at the social or cultural level.

Ghurye holds that though groups play an integrational role in society, this is true only up to a certain extent. In modern society, there are five sources of danger for national unity coming as they do form a sense of excessive attachment with groups:

(1) The Scheduled Castes
(2) The Scheduled Tribes
(3) The Backward Classes
(4) The Muslims as religious minority groups
(5) The linguistic minorities

As we know, the main focus of Ghurye's writings is on culture. He thinks that it is largely as a result of Brahminical endeavour that cultural unity in India has been built up. All the major institutions of Hindu society originated among the Brahmins and gradually they were accepted by other sections of the community. Though Ghurye calls it process of *acculturation*, it was basically a one-way flow, in which the Brahminical ideas and institutions infiltrated among the non-Brahmins. It is the background of such an approach that Ghurye analyses the problems and prospects of Indian unity in contemporary India.

Ghurye's concept of cultural unity is new one and is not secular in orientation. He is concerned with India of 'Hindu culture' and uses the terms 'Indian culture' and 'Hindu culture' synonymously. He is concerned with India, he says provided an excellent normative base for maintaining social and political unity in the country. Hinduism had brought within its fold widely different groups in India. The various sects of Hinduism constitute vast mosaic holding together millions of people in different parts of India. First, he analysed the normative structure of Hinduism, and the teaching of sacred religious texts such as the Vedas, the Upanishads, the Brahmins etc., to show how they provide the common cultural foundation. Second, the role of such great Hindu thinkers as Panini, Patanjali, Tulsidas etc. has also been discussed by Ghurye.

He blames the political leaders for this, because they followed a course of action, which was more or less exactly the one which should have been avoided but the foundation for this national cultural unity had been built and maintained by the Hindus for one hundred years. According to Ghurye, society is not just an aggregation of isolated individuals but that group life, which provides the bridge between the individual and society. An individual acquires social attributes and is socializes through groups. This is the integrative function of groups in society. When groups perform the function efficiently, integration is achieved. Tensions in the process of this integration in India arise today because the various groups of people have failed to transient their narrow group loyalties. Religious and linguistic minorities are the most potential source of danger to the unity in modern India. Religion and linguistic groups are the prime areas which came disintegration to India's cohesion.

Ghurye gives great importance to the role of language in the process of nation-building in India. Even, in case of tribes, tribal life and culture can be improved only when the pick up developed language of a neighbouring community. Ghurye holds the view that the regional language has a symbolic integrational value of the region. The regional languages ensure the unity of territory at the local level and all efforts should be made to improve.

## Discourse

During his creative period of writing, Indian sociology was engaged in the debate on tradition and modernity. Ghurye neither entered into this controversy, nor he took up the issue of the role of tradition in Indian society. He further stressed that Indian traditions are actually Hindu traditions. One must know the Hindu traditions to understand Indian society. In fact, Ghurye created a special kind of *Hindu sociology*. The traditions of India are only Hindu traditions. He did not define traditions. He also did not discuss the impact of modernity. His main concern was the core of Hindu society. In this sense, the traditions of Indian society have its roots in scriptures, which is a very narrow vision about Indian society.

It has been argued that the most of Ghurye's works are based on textual and scriptural data. The choice of scripture and the way of writing may have bias towards one section of society to another. Ghurye further fails to recognize that qualitative change has occurred in modern India. Past is important for present. The question is that how much of the past is useful. Some argue that Ghurye did not have this realization as his knowledge of the India's past, instead of helping him, stood in his way of analysis. However, Ghurye was not only concerned with the past evolution of Indian society but also with its present tensions and problems. The task of sociologists, according to him, is to explore the social history of past. He says, one cannot understand the present without the reference of the past. Ghurye introduced a down-to-earth empiricism in Indian sociology and social anthropology. He was an ethnographer, who studied tribes and castes of India, using historical and Indological data. His knowledge of Sanskrit enabled him to study the religious scriptures in the context of Indian society.

## Conclusion

The sweep of Ghurye's works and the wide range of his intellectual interests have had a profound influence on the development of the twin disciplines (sociology and social anthropology) in India. Like a discreet butterfly, Ghurye moved from one theme to another with equal interest, erudition and ability. He showed India to an inexhaustible mind where sociologists and social anthropologists could conduct endless explorations. He indicated innumerable but unexplored dimensions of Indian society, culture and social institutions, which would occupy social analysis for decades if they had both the desire and the ability to know.

Ghurye's basic discipline may be regarded as social anthropology, since his PhD was under W.H.R. Rivers at Cambridge (UK). The range of Ghurye's scholarly interests and research is astounding. Exploration of diverse aspects of Indian culture and society through the use of Indological sources permeated Ghurye's otherwise shifting intellectual concerns and empirical research pursuits. His erudition and versatility, therefore, are substantiated by the wide range of his research from Sanskrit text, through interpretation of Indian culture and society

This rare spirit of inquiry and commitment to advancing the frontiers of knowledge was one of Ghurye's precious gifts to Indian sociology and social anthropology. His diversified interests are also reflected in the great variety of works of his research students produced on themes ranging from family, kinship structures, marriage, religious sects, ethnic groups, castes and aboriginals, their customs and institutions, to social differentiation and stratification, caste and class, education and society, the Indian nationalist movement, social structure and social change in specific villages or religions of India, and also urbanization, industrialization and related social problems in India.

The range of Ghurye's interests is encyclopaedic. His abiding interest is in the course of world civilization in general and in Hindu civilization in particular. He has analysed various aspects like the origin and evolution of caste, the evolution of Indo-Aryan family structures and its connections with the Indo-European family structure, and specific institutions like *gotra* etc. Analysis of the diverse aspects of the evolution of Indian social history and culture thus constitutes the major preoccupation of Ghurye.

## Ghurye's Framework Summarized

### *Background*

1. Educated and trained in Sanskrit and sociology
2. Academic career at Bombay
3. Interests in Indian civilization and culture, national movement

### *Aims*

Ethnographic study of castes and tribes, rural-urbanization, religious phenomena, social tensions and Indian art.

### *Assumption*

Analysis of evolution and growth of social institutions in India

### *Methodology*

1. Indological and textual
2. Inductive-empirical method
3. Historical-comparative method

### *Theoretical perspective*

1. Functional approach

### *Typology*

1. Classical textual categories
2. Literary data

### *Issues*

Different aspects of Indian society such as:

1. Indian culture and civilization
2. Race
3. Religion

4. Caste and kinship system
5. Tribal studies
6. Rural-urbanization
7. Indian sadhus
8. Social tensions
9. Indian costume
10. Sociology of conflict and integration

## Select Bibliography


Bhattacharya, Gayatri (1977), "Menstruation and Alleged Pollution of Women: Ghurye's Ideas on Women's Dignity", *Journal of Indian Anthropological Society*, 32:55–64.

Bhattacharya, S.K. et al. (2003), *Understanding Society*, New Delhi: NCERT.

Breekenridge, A. and Peter van der Veer (1994), *Orientalism and the Postcolonial Predicament*, Delhi: Oxford University Press.

Momin, A.R. (ed.) (1996), *The Legacy of G.S. Ghurye: A Centennial Festschrift*, Bombay: Popular Prakashan.

Nagla, Madhu (2005), "Approaches to the study of Indian society", unpublished paper written for the NCERT book on *Teacher Handbook in Sociology*.

Oommen, T.K. and Mukherji, P.N. (1986), *Indian Sociology: Reflections and Introspections*, Mumbai: Popular Prakashan.

Pillai, S. Devadas (1997), *Indian Sociology Through Ghurye: A Dictionary*, Mumbai: Popular Prakashan.

Pramanick, S.K. (1994), *Sociology of G.S. Ghurye*, Jaipur: Rawat Publications.

Shah, A.M. (1974), "Historical Sociology" in *A Survey of Research in Sociology and Social Anthropology*, Vol. 1, Delhi: ICSSR.

Siddiqi, Majid H. (1978), *Agrarian Unrest in Northern India – The United Province, 1918–22*, New Delhi: Vikas Publishers.

Singh, Yogendra (1986), *Indian Sociology*, New Delhi: Vistaar Publications.

Srinivas, M.N. (1979), *Interview with G.S. Ghurye*, January.

— (2002), "Itineraries of an Indian Social Anthropologist" in *Collected Essays*, New Delhi: Oxford University Press.

Upadhya, Carol (2002), "The Hindu Nationalist Sociology of G.S. Ghurye", *Sociological Bulletin*, Vol. 51, No. 1: 28–57, March.

Venugopal, C.N. (1980), *G.S. Ghurye and Radhakamal Mukerjee: A Comparative Sociological Appraisal of Their Selected Contributions*, unpublished Ph.D dissertation of Jawahar Lal Nehru University, New Delhi.

— (1986), "G.S. Ghurye's Ideology of Normative Hinduism: An Appraisal", *Contributions to Indian Sociology*, Vol. 20, No. 2: 305–14.

— (1992), *Ghurye's Ideology of Normative Hinduism: An Appraisal*, New Delhi: Gyan Publishing House.

— (1998), *Religion and Indian Society: A Sociological Perspective*, New Delhi: Gyan Publishing House.

Verma, B.N. (1964), "The Caste System in India", in B.N. Verma (ed.), *Contemporary India*, Bombay: Popular Prakashan.

# 6

# Louis Dumont

Louis Dumont (1911–1998), an eminent sociologist and Indologist, was a towering figure in the fields of sociology and anthropology in the world. His focus of debate has been India and the West: his exemplary studies are best on methodologies that he constructed for the study of particular societies and for inter-civilizational comparison, and these are of universal combined. The present chapter, which deals with the main contributions of Dumont, focuses on the following:

1. Methodological perspective
2. Homo Hierarchicus: The Caste System and Its Implications
3. Concept of pure and impure
4. Theory of *varnas*
5. Religion, Politics and History in India
6. Homo aequalis
7. Criticism of Dumont

## Background

Louis Dumont, the French sociologist, is regarded as an Indologist. Grandson of a painter and son of an engineer, Dumont combined his way of looking at the world with the qualities of both vocations, namely, creative imagination and an abiding interest in the concrete. Dumont began his academic career in the mid-1930s under the guidance of Marcel Mauss, leading sociologist and Sanskritist. World War II interrupted his studies, but not entirely. He was taken as prisoner of war and was detained in a factory on the outskirts of Hamburgh. There, he studied German.

In 1945, at the end of the war, he came back to home. He returned to the Museeces Arts et. tradition populaires (ATP), where he worked earlier in a non-academic position. Here, he remained engaged in a research project on French furniture and undertook the study of a folk festival, the Tarascon, about which he later wrote a monograph, *La Tarasque* (1951). Dumont used ethnographic details in this study and applied holistic approach. He also learnt Sanskrit. He had a chance of meeting with Professor Schubring, a specialist on Jain studies. Around this time, he also carried forward his interest in India, generated by Mauss' teaching, and took lessons in Hindi and Tamil at the Ecole des Langues Orientals and studied ethnography of south India. Among his patrons were the comparativist Georges Dumezil and the Indologist Louis Renou.

Dumont spent the years 1949 and 1950 in Tamil Nadu studying the Pramalai Kallar who stands somewhere in the middle in the regional caste system. It is interesting to note that he chose to focus on south India because he believed that it was the encounter of the Aryan-speaking people from the north with the southern Dravidians that had been responsible for the genesis of post-Vedic Hinduism and the socio-cultural configuration of classical India.

The 1950 viewpoint of course for the usefulness of village as a unit of study persisted and, as late as in 1974, Dumont was looked down and criticized for "underrating the significance of the village as a principle of social organization by asserting factors of social organization in India, so is village" (Das, 1974). However, this kind of 'village' partnership was itself combined with taking note of alternatives in order to understand religion, politics and history in India (ibid.: 1974: 119–24).

From 1951 onward, Dumont had lectured and written about caste. The presence of castes everywhere, he had said in 1955, was a token of the cultural unity and distinctiveness of India. The fruit of this pedagogic-cum-research endeavour was his magnum opus, *Homo Hierarchicus* (in French, 1966; in English, 1970), which is the most widely discussed work on the subject, translated into many languages but not yet into any Indian language. However, its English translation offered an excellent opportunity for further discussion of Dumont's approach and its substantial analytical and interpretative results.

Dumont returned home from India in 1951 and came back at the ATP centre. A year later, in 1952, he succeeded M.N. Srinivas as Lecturer in Indian Sociology at Oxford University. There, he developed a close relationship with Evans-Pritchard. The years at Oxford were of critical importance in the formulation of Dumont's methodology for the study of Indian civilization.

In 1955, Dumont returned to Paris to take up a research professorship at the Ecole Pratique des Hautes Etudes (rechristened as Ecole des Hautes Etudes en Sciences Sociales in 1975). In his inaugural lecture, he declared that the sociology of India must lie at the 'confluence of sociology and Indology'. The method was dialectical in the sense that although Indology may provide points of departure, the principles derived from it were to be confronted by what the people actually did (their observable behaviour). An English version of this programmatic text was published jointly with David Pocock in 1957 in the first issue of *Contribution to Indian Sociology*, of which they were the founding editors. In this journal, Dumont published a number of studies on the themes like village community, caste, marriage, kinship, renunciation and nationalism.

Dumont spent fifteen months in 1957–58 in a village of Gorakhpur district in eastern Uttar Pradesh. Although, the duration of fieldwork was not much shorter than that in Tamil Nadu, north India did not attract him as the south had. The fieldwork, however, contributed to his interest in inter-regional comparison and he published searching analyses of marriage and kinship terminology. His main areas of interest in sociology are Hinduism, caste, kinship in ancient India, and social-political movements in modern India.

## Methodology

As a study of the caste system in India, Dumont's *Homo Hierarchicus* offers several new perspectives of social structure. The notions of ideology and tradition are intrinsic parts of his paradigm. He has brought the method of structuralism to bear upon his study of the caste system. The chief elements of his methodology are:

1. ideology and structure
2. dialectic transformational relationship and comparison
3. Indological and structuralist approach
4. cognitive historical approach

Dumont seeks the ideology of caste in Indology, and in the assumption of the unity of Indian civilization. Defining ideology, he writes: "it designates a more or less unified set of ideas and values". Indian civilization, to him, is a specific ideology whose components are in a binary opposition to that of West: modern against traditional, holism against individualism, hierarchy against equality, purity against pollution, status against power etc.... This opposition (dialectic) is basis for comparison at the level of global ideology within the specific ideology of the caste system. The opposite is between the principles of purity and pollution.

Apart from ideology and structure, the notion of hierarchy has a pivotal place in Dumont's study of caste system. Hierarchy implies opposition between pure and impure, which also determines its dialectics. Hierarchy also suggests the relationship of 'encompassing' and being 'encompassed'. In the caste system, the principle of purity encompasses the impure. Thus, Dumont's approach to the study of caste system in India provoked very substantial debate.

Based on intensive fieldwork and methodical study of literary sources, two important monographs, *one sous-caste de l'inde du sud: Organization sociale et religion des Pramalai Kallar* and *Hierarchy and Marriage Alliance in South India* were published in 1957. The first is one of the richest ethnographic accounts of India ever published, while the latter one was written in English and dedicated to Claude Levi-Strauss.

Dumont's *Homo Hierarchicus* (1970), to some extent, revived the interest in caste studies in the 1970s. He focused on the need to understand the ideology of caste as reflected in the classical texts. Dumont advocated the use of an Indological and structuralist approach to the study of caste system and village social structure in India. Thus, Dumont (1970: 1–30) views 'Indian sociology' as that specialized branch, which stands at the confluence of Indology and sociology and which he advocates as the right type of 'mix' prerequisite to the understanding of Indian society.

The French sociological tradition leads Dumont to stress the role of ideology in moulding human behaviour and, therefore, to bring together sociology and Indology. When a sociologist is engaged in the analysis of the evolution and growth of social institutions in India, he has to draw heavily Indological materials considering this close relation between sociology and Indology. Dumont and Pocock observed: "In our opinion, the first condition for a sound development of sociology in India is found in the establishment of the proper relation between it and classical Indology."

Analysis of social change from a cognitive historical viewpoint has been postulated by Dumont. He conceives of Indian society not in terms of systems of relationship but as systems of ideational or value patterns or cognitive structures. The focus in social change study, according to Dumont, should be on "the reaction of Indian minds to the revelation of Western culture", and on how under the impact of the cognitive elements of western culture such as individualism, freedom, democracy etc., the cognitive system of Indian tradition is reacting with rejection or acceptance. The contrast in the Indian and western cognitive systems lies in the holistic character of the former and the individualistic attribute of the latter; this contrast also poses the nature of tension between tradition versus modernity in India (Singh, 1973: 20–22).

## Writings of Dumont

As stated at the outset, Dumont's main areas of interest are social anthropology and Indology. He has written on wide range of subjects such as Hinduism, caste, kinship, and social and political movements in India. His major works are as follows:

1. *La Tarasque* (1951)
2. *One sous-caste de Inde du sud: Organization sociale et religion des pramalai Kallar* (1957)
3. Hierarchy and Marriage Alliance in South India (1957)
4. Homo Hierarchicus: The Caste System and Its Implications (1966, 1970)
5. Religion, Politics and History in India: Collected Papers in Indian Sociology (1970)
6. Homo aequalis (1977)

Our main focus here is to discuss the important work of Dumont, viz., *Homo Hierarchicus*, which highlights the caste and *varna* systems in India.

### *Homo Hierarchicus*

The *Homo Hierarchicus: The Caste System and Its Implications* (1966) is an unusual work of Dumont in its conception, design and execution. This is a complete, theoretical work that helps us to access the vast body of available ethnographic data on caste. This work is different from others as it begins with a cardinal explanatory principle – hierarchy – and wholly sets out to build a model.

Hierarchy is said to distinguish Indian society from 'modern' societies whose fundamental social principle is equality. The major theme of this review can be anticipated thus: any hierarchy, like any equalitarian system, is opposed by those who see its effect upon themselves as disadvantageous, no matter how loudly or piously it is advocated by those who benefit from it. Those low in a hierarchical system universally see it as disadvantageous to themselves and object either to the system or to the manner in which it is applied to themselves. Any social hierarchy, then, is perpetrated and perpetuated by elites and is struggled against as circumstances permit, by those they oppress. This is true in India and anywhere else. There are four specific facets of Dumont's argument, which Berreman (2001) takes in a specific way:

(1) *The assumption that there is a clear and consistent, universal and fundamental disparity between what the author terms 'traditional' or 'simpler' societies (e.g., Indian), and 'modern' ones (e.g., French, British).* Dumont finds 'traditional' societies to be characterized by conception of the collective nature of man, by the primacy of social rather than individual goals, and thus by 'hierarchy' (by which he means ritual hierarchy, based on the purity/pollution opposition). 'Modern' societies are characterized contrastively by individualism and hence by egalitarianism (the antithesis of hierarchy).
(2) *The notion that power and economic and political factors are distinct from and epiphenomenal to caste and that ritual hierarchy is the central fact of caste, independent of power.* Berreman asserts that the power status opposition is a false dichotomy in the context of caste. The two are inseparable.
(3) *The notion that caste occurs only in India and is not subject to cross-cultural comparison.* The theoretically weakest part of the book is where Dumont discuses and dismisses the notion of cross-cultural comparisons of caste organization.
(4) *The limited biased, albeit scholarly, sources of evidence upon which the arguments are based.* Dumont relies heavily on some classical Sanskrit texts while ignoring others.

We will now give a chapter-wise synopsis of the contents of the book to show how Dumont constructs his arguments as described by Madan (2001).

The introductory chapter explains the concept of hierarchy, which is contrasted with opposite values of egalitarianism and individualism. "The caste teaches us a fundamental social principle, hierarchy". Hierarchy is an indispensable element of social life.

After reading this chapter, we can fully understand the concept of equality with the opposite notion of 'hierarchy' and not inequality.

Chapters 1, 2 and 3 deal with the concepts employed in the work and the ideology of caste. Dumont introduced the notions of 'system' and 'structure'.

The *caste system* is above all a system of *ideas* and *values*, a formal comprehensible, *rational system*, a system in the intellectual sense of the term ... (Dumont: 35).

Chapter 3 deals with *hierarchy* and the theory of *varna*. It is a most crucial discussion and focuses on the differentiation (disjunction) of status and power and the subordination of the king to the priest in Hindu society. Hierarchy is said to involve gradation, but is asserted to be distinct from both power and authority. It is "religious ranking and classifies things and beings" according to their 'dignity' (ibid.: 65). It is an all-embracing, comprehensive concept. Hierarchy and the scheme of *varnas* are found to be in consonance with each other, as are *varna* and *jati*. In fact, hierarchy encompasses both the *varna* divisions and the caste system. What remains problematic, however, is the connection of hierarchy with power, for hierarchy cannot give a place to power as such, without contradicting its own principle. Therefore, it must give a place to power without saying so, and it is obliged to close its eyes to this point on pain of destroying itself (ibid.: 77).

At this point, Dumont undertakes a somewhat detailed examination of ethnographical evidence to examine the interaction between purity and power in 'actual situations'.

Having introduced the ideology, Dumont proceeds to consider aspects of behaviour within and between castes in terms of it. Chapter 4 shows the traditional division of labour (the *jajmani* system) is based on religious values rather than on economic logic. It does not, however, account for all economic transactions, and Dumont admits this. Chapter 5 considers the regulation of marriage (endogamy, isogamy, hypergamy) in terms of the key concept of hierarchy. Chapter 6 carries the argument further to cover rules connecting contact, untouchability, food and vegetarianism. The opposition between the pure and impure emerges clearly and convincingly in these three chapters.

Chapter 7 deals in power and territory and chapter 8 with justice and authority. It is here that the confrontation of ideology with observed social reality is most prominent. We are now brought face to face with territory, power, village dominance, and ownership of wealth, and their mutual relationship. These are said to be questions of fact and not at all of theory. Dominant castes, factions, and economics also are discussed in this very framework.

Chapter 9 deals in renunciation and sects – the opposites of the notions of 'collective man' and caste. An examination of these is a methodological necessity (device) for Dumont, for he seeks understanding of India (and of western society) through a dialectical process, through the juxtaposition of logically opposite cultural types.

Chapter 10 takes the problem of comparison: are there castes among non-Hindus and outside India (ibid.: 201)? Enlarging the scope of comparison, Dumont suggests that caste should be deemed to be present only where the disjunction between status and power is present and where castes exhaust the entire society (ibid.: 214–15).

In Chapter 11 (the last) comparison is continued, but in temporal, rather than spatial, terms. In other words, Dumont takes up the problem of change: "What is the caste system becoming nowadays" (ibid.: 217)? "One thing is certain: the society as an overall framework has not changed, there has been change *in* the society and *not* of the society" (ibid.: 218). And, again, in Dumont's view, the only significant change that does seem to have taken place is the traditional interdependence of castes has been replaced by a "universe of impenetrable blocks, self-sufficient, essentially identical and in competition with one another" (ibid.: 222). Dumont calls this 'the substantialization of caste'. An inventory of sources of change in the caste system lists judicial and political changes, socio-religious reform, Westernization, growth of modern professions, urbanization, spatial mobility, and growth of market economy. But, despite all these factors making for change, the most ubiquitous and general form that change has taken in contemporary times is one of a 'mixture', or 'combination', of traditional and modern features (ibid.: 228–31).

Dumont concludes by asserting that hierarchy is 'a universal necessity' and that, if it is not formally recognized in a society, it may assert itself in a pathological form (e.g., racism). It is, therefore, of greatest importance for the western man to endeavour to study and understand a social system in which hierarchy is recognized, and, in fact, accorded the status of a first principle. That is why, the book is offered to the French public.

The appendix contains Dumont's well-known essay, "Caste, Racism, 'Stratification' ", first published in 1960. It contains all the principle ideas elaborated in *Homo Hierarchicus* and should help the reader to recapitulate the argument.

The following discussion of Dumont is an extract from his book *Homo Hierarchicus: The Caste System and Its Implications.* Dumont, an Indologist, feels that the study of the caste system is useful for the knowledge of India, and it is an important task of general sociology. His study of caste is based on the classical literature, historical examples etc. He expressed his views on caste system, *varnas*, purity and impurity, hierarchy, power and territory, caste council, etc.

## Caste System

Louis Dumont was primarily concerned with the ideology of the caste system. His understanding of caste lays emphasis on attributes of caste, that is why, he is put in the category of those following the attributional approach to the caste system. For him, caste is a set of relationships of economic, political and kinship systems, sustained by certain 'values', which are mostly religious in nature. Dumont says that caste is not a form of stratification but a special form of inequality, whose essence has to be deciphered by the sociologists. Here, Dumont identifies 'hierarchy' as the essential value underlying the caste system, supported by Hinduism.

Dumont starts with Bougle's definition of caste and says that it divides the whole Indian society into a larger number of hereditary groups, distinguished from one another and connected together by three characteristics:

(a) Separation on the basis of rules of the caste in matters of marriage and contact, whether direct or indirect (food);

(b) Interdependent of work or division of labour, each group having, in theory or by tradition, a profession from which their members can depart only within certain limits; and
(c) Finally, gradation of status or hierarchy, which ranks the groups as relatively superior or inferior to one another.

Dumont views that this definition indicates the main apparent characteristics of the caste system. He describes mainly three things:

1. India is composed of many small territories and castes;
2. Every caste is limited to particular and definite geographic area; and
3. Marrying outside one's own caste is not possible in the caste system.

In fact, Dumont highlights the 'state of mind', which is expressed by the emergence in various situations of castes. He calls caste system as a system of 'ideas and values', which is a 'formal comprehensible rational system'. His analysis is based on a single principle, i.e., the opposition of pure and impure. This opposition underlies 'hierarchy', which means superiority of the pure and inferiority of impure. This principle also underlies 'separation', which means pure and the impure must be kept separate.

Dumont felt that the study of the caste system is useful for the knowledge of India, and it is an important task of general sociology. He focused on the need to understand the ideology of caste as reflected in the classical texts, historical examples etc. He advocated the use of an Indological and structuralist approach to the study of caste system and village social structure in India. He viewed that 'Indian sociology' is that specialized branch which stands at the confluence of Indology and sociology and which he advocates as the right type of 'mix' prerequisite to the understanding of Indian sociology. From this perspective, Dumont himself, in his *Homo Hierarchicus*, has built up a model of Indian civilization, which is based on a non-competitive ritual hierarchical system. Dumont's analysis of caste system is based on the classical literature, historical examples etc.

### *Concept of Pure and Impure*

While considering the concept of pure and impure, Dumont had two questions in mind: Why is this distinction applied to hereditary groups? And, if it accounts for the contrast between Brahmins and untouchables, can it account equally for the division of society into a large number of groups, themselves sometime extremely sub-divided? He did not answer these questions directly. But, the opposite has always been two extreme categories, i.e., Brahmins and untouchables. The Brahmins, assigned with the priestly functions, occupied the top rank in the social hierarchy and were considered 'pure' as compared to other castes, whereas the untouchables, being 'impure', and segregated outside the village, were not allowed to draw water from the same wells from which the Brahmins did so. Besides this, they did not have any access to Hindu temples, and suffered from various other disabilities. Dumont said that this situation was somewhat changed since the Gandhian agitation and when India attained independence. Untouchability was considered illegal. Gandhi renamed untouchables as 'Harijans' or 'Sons of Hari', that is, creatures of God (Vishnu).

Untouchables are specialized in 'impure' tasks, which lead to the attribution of a massive and permanent impurity to some categories of people. Dumont highlights temporary and permanent impurity. In larger areas of the world, death, birth and other such seclusion of the affected persons, for instance, the newly delivered mother was actually excluded from the church for forty days at the end of which she would present herself carrying a lighted candle and would be met at the church porch by the priest. In India, persons affected by this kind of event are treated as impure for a prescribed period, and Indians themselves identify this impurity with that of the untouchables. In his work, *The History of Dharmshastra*, P.V. Kane writes that a man's nearest relatives and his best friends become untouchable for him for a certain time as a result of these events. According to Harita, there are three kinds of purity: (a) bearing of the family (Kula), (b) objects of everyday use (Artha), and (c) the body (Sarira). For the body, the main thing is the morning attention to personal hygiene, culminating in the daily bath. Even, the objects are considered as pure and impure: silk is purer than cotton, gold than silver, than bronze, than copper. These objects are not simply polluted by the contact but by the use to which they are put and used by the person. Now-a-days, a new garment or vessel can be received from anybody. It is believed that a person's own bed, garments, wife, child and water pot are pure for his own self and family and for others they are impure.

### *Theory of Varnas*

Dumont feels one cannot speak of the castes without mentioning the *varnas*, to which Hindus frequently attribute the castes themselves. India has the traditional hierarchy of *varnas*, 'colours' or estates whereby four categories are distinguished: the highest is that of the *Brahmins* or priest, below them are the *Ksatriyas* or warriors, then the *Vaishyas*, in modern usage merchants, and finally the *Shudras*, the servants or have-nots. There is one more category, the untouchables, who are outside the classification system. Dumont maintains that many of the Indologists confuse the *varna* with caste, mainly because the classical literature is concerned almost entirely with the *varnas*. Caste and *varnas* are to be understood with relationship of hierarchy and power.

By his interpretation, caste was different from other forms of social stratification through the 'disjunction' of ritual status and secular (political and economic) power within the same social system. The subordination of the political and economic criteria of social stratification to that of ritual status in Dumont's model, however, plays down the significance of social change in colonial and contemporary times. Did not caste lose its political significance as late in the 18th and 19th centuries? As for what has happening in the 20th century, although Dumont explicitly recognized the emergence of inter-caste competitiveness in place of a structure of independence as a departure from tradition. He regarded this as behavioural change, rather than a radical transformation of the system as a whole, at the level of values or principles. Madan (1999) presumed that Dumont's analysis is an exercise in deductive logic.

In the last, Dumont discusses the significant changes in the castes. He views that traditional interdependence of castes has been replaced by "a universe of impenetrable blocks, self-sufficient, essential, identical and in competition in one another'. Dumont calls this the 'substantialization of castes'. An inventory of sources of change in the caste system lists judicial and political changes, social-religious reforms, westernization, and growth of modern professions, urbanization, spatial mobility and the growth of market economy. But, despite all these factors making for change, the most ubiquitous and the general form the change has taken in contemporary times is one of a 'mixture', or 'combination', of traditional and modern features (Dumont, 1966: 228–31).

### *Religion, Politics and History in India*

All the essays in this collection, except one (No. 7), have been published in the different issues of *Contribution to Indian Sociology*. According to Dumont, it is intended as a complement to *Homo Hierarchicus* and, together with it, makes available in almost everything that he has written on India (excluding special studies of kinship). Besides the introduction and conclusion, the book has six chapters, two each on the three broad topics set out in the title of the book, viz., religion, politics and history.

As in other works of Dumont, the aim here is also to explain the underlying unity of Hindu thought and practice in terms of a few structural principles. His attempt is to unite a single framework to all Hindu norms and ideas in all their diversity. This concern for unity, which runs through the entire length of the book, thus, brings into focus Dumont's basic approach to the study of Indian society. In Dumont's own words: "Here then is the complete precipitate, on the general level, of an approach intended as structural which was carried out from 1952 to 1966 from earlier monographic starting point to *Homo Hierarchicus*" (p. vi). The main points made in the book in which Dumont's position can be briefly summed up are as follows (Das, 1974: 119):

1. India is one;
2. this unity is found above all in ideas and values;

3. caste is the fundamental institution of Hinduism;
4. the opposition of the pure and impure is central to the caste system;
5. hierarchy and separation are two basic aspects of opposition between purity and impurity, and hence of the caste system;
6. the caste ideology is an all-embracing ideology and power is subordinate to status;
7. hierarchy distinguishes Indian society from 'modern' societies whose fundamental social principle is equality;
8. there cannot be any revolutionary sociology; and
9. the change in contemporary India is 'organizational', rather than 'structural'.

### *Homo aequalis*

To what extent Dumont is successful in his latter enterprise – i.e., in the effort to understand *Homo aequalis* in terms of the opposite of the *Homo Hierarchicus* – remains to be seen. Therefore, after the publication of *Homo Hierarchicus*, it was (in his own words) *Homo aequalis* – Europe and the West generally – that beckoned to him. It was India that helped him problematise the West. The individualism of the West and its sub-theme of egalitarianism are best understood, Dumont maintained, in the light of holism and hierarchy. Not only was the 'individualist configuration' of the West to be compared with the Indian configuration (not at too low a level of ethnographic description but in terms of the underlying principles), particular expression of individualism within the western setting were also to be compared tom deepen understanding. The intellectual tools shaped in the Indian forge were now to be applied to the understanding of another civilization.

The results of the studies of the ideological propositions of western civilization or, more precisely, of ideology of individualism, were published in the form of book followed by a number of essays that were later collected in two volumes. The following three works came out in English and French versions.

*From Mandeville to Marx: The Genesis and Triumph of Economic Ideology* (1977) – the French title was *Homo aequalis* – argued that, speaking the language of relations (which a structuralist must), the transition from tradition to modernity in Europe occurred when, among other change, the primacy of the relationship of person to one another (holism) was displaced by the primacy of the relationship of persons to things, conceived as property (individualism). This development ultimately freed economics from the constrains of both morality and politics. The second book, *Essays in Individualism* (1986) contained the examination of the modern ideology. Individualism was presented as the global ideology of modern society. The third and the most recent book in the series, *German Ideology: From France to Germany and Back* (1994) develops this theme. The focus is on the German variant. He explains that the beginning of the divergence are traceable to the distinctiveness of the German version of the enlightenment compared to the western (French), for it was religious rather than secularist. The situation is complex, and the German-French contrast has the ontological and epistemological significance; indeed, its ethical dimension may not be denied.

## Criticism of Dumont

Dumont wrote many articles and books on sociology in India. He has joint venture with Pocock in *Contributions to Indian Sociology*. He is criticized on various grounds:

1. Gupta (2001) demonstrates that Dumont's understanding of hierarchy is critically faulted in his application of the term to the caste system.
2. Dumont's work is based on traditional Indian texts. Consequently, the features of the caste system, as projected by Dumont, seem to be unchanging. In reality, the caste system has changed in various ways during a period of time. Dumont also seems to characterize Indian society as almost stagnant, since he emphasizes the integrative function of caste system. Yogendra Singh agrees with Bailey, who considers Dumont's

approach to sociology rules out a study of a host of crucial social facts of Indian life, such as, formal organizations, the industrial system, labour and agrarian social movements etc. It also rules out many key variables from being introduced into a 'Sociology of Development'. Dumont is more concerned with system integration and system maintenance than with change or conflict. Yogendra Singh views that Dumont postulates some 'functionally equivalent' concepts but his paradigm remains hidden from public view. He also points out that Dumont's emphasis on Indology has inadvertently led to a displacement of focus, as if there is no scope for comparison or abstract generalizations in his sociology.

3. The purity and impurity opposition highlighted by Dumont is also not universal. In certain tribal societies 'status' is not anchored in purity but in 'sacredness'.
4. Dumont's view of caste, as rationally ordered system of values (ideology), has also been questioned. Dumont seems to have ignored the number of protest movements, which emerged in Indian history questioning the ideology of the caste division itself, through his emphasis on values. He could not see the relationship between castes as conflict ridden. For him, the relations between *varnas*, especially the Brahmin and Ksatriya, is almost complementary.
5. McKim Marriott criticizes *Homo Hierarchicus* as containing a speculative sketch of a pair of models, strongly shaped and documented mainly with textual ideology of social science and philosophical allusions.
6. Berreman (2001) adds that 'hierarchy' is simply a lure: the superior castes conception of social system. Further, on the issue of Dumont's separation between power and status, Berreman argues that power and status could be two sides of the same coin as well.

Despite these criticisms, Dumont holds an important position in Indian sociology. Amidst the debates about appraising Indian social reality on the basis of caste, Dumont's *Homo Hierarchicus* represented an outstanding contribution, whether or not one agrees with his viewpoint.

## Conclusion

In this chapter, we have discussed broadly Dumont's contribution to the study of caste system in India. To Dumont, hierarchy is the essential value undertaking the caste system. His approach to caste is basically Indological and structuralist. To him, the hierarchy of caste is religious in nature and is marked by the disjunction between status and power. Dumont's understanding has been traced mainly from ancient texts. Therefore, we consider him in the category of cognitive-historical and Indological.

## Dumont's Framework Summarized

### *Background*

1. French sociologist and Indologist.
2. Studied German and also learnt Sanskrit.

### *Aims*

1. Primarily concerned with the ideology of the caste system.
2. Focus on India and the West

### *Assumptions*

1. Hierarchy is the essential value underlying the caste system. Hierarchy of caste is religious in nature and is marked by the disjunction between status and power.
2. Unity in the Indian civilization

### *Methodology*

1. Indological and structural
2. Cognitive and historical approach
3. Dialectic transformational relationship
4. Ethnographical evidence

### *Theoretical Perspectives*

1. Structuralism
2. Attributional approach of caste

### *Typology*

1. Indology: Sources of material: Ancient texts
2. Ideology and tradition
3. Holism against individualism, hierarchy against equality

### *Issues*

Different aspects of Indian society, namely

1. 'System' of caste
2. Concept of pure and impure
3. The theory of *varnas*

## Select Bibliography


Berreman, Gerald D. (2001), 'The Brahmanical View of Caste' in Gupta, Dipankar (ed.), *Social Stratification*, Delhi: Oxford University Press.

Das, V. (1974), 'Review of Louis Dumont's Religion, Politics and History of India: Collected papers in Indian Sociology', *Sociological Bulletin*, 23(1): 119–24.

Dumont, Louis (1966), *Homo Hierarchicus: The Caste System and Its Implications*, Delhi: Vikas Publications.

— (1970), *Religion, Politics and History in India: Collected Papers in Indian Sociology*, Paris: Mouton.

— (1977), *From Mandeville to Marx: The Genesis and Triumph of Economic Ideology*, Chicago: University of Chicago Press. French version: *Homo aequalis I: Genese et epanouissement de l'ideologie economique*, Paris: Gallimard, Bibliotheque des Sciences Humaines, 1977.

— (1986), *Essays on Individualism: Modern Ideology in Anthropological Perspective*, Chicago: The University of Chicago Press.

— (1994), *German Ideology: From France to Germany and Back*, Chicago: The University of Chicago Press.

Harper, E.B. (1970), *Contributions to Indian Sociology*, New Delhi: Vikas Publishing.

Gupta, Dipankar (2001), *Social Stratification*, Delhi: Oxford University Press.

Kaur, Navneet (2002), 'Louis Dumont's Approach to Caste System', in *Systems of Stratification*, Chandigarh, Panjab University.

Madan, T.N. (1999), 'Louis Dumont', *Contributions to Indian Sociology*, (n.s.) 33, 3.

— (2001), 'Dumont on the Nature of Caste in India', in Gupta, Dipankar (ed.), *Social Stratification*, Delhi: Oxford University Press.

Nagla, Madhu (2005), 'Approaches to the Study of Indian Society', unpublished paper written for the NCERT book on *Teacher Handbook in Sociology*.

Singh, Yogendra (1973), *Modernization of Indian Tradition*, Delhi: Thompson Press.

— (1986). *Indian Sociology*, New Delhi: Vistaar Publications.

# 7

# Irawati Karve

Irawati Karve was an Indian educationist, anthropologist, sociologist and a writer from Maharashtra, India. She was born to G.H. Karmarkar, an engineer in Myingyan, Burma, on December 15, 1905 and died on August 11, 1970. She was named Irawati after the great and sacred Burmese river, Irrawaddy. She grew up in Pune. She was the daughter-in-law of Maharshi Dhondo Keshav Karve. Her husband Dinkar was an educator and the Principal of Fergusson College. Anand, son of Dinkar and Irawati, runs an NGO in Pune called 'Arti'. Their youngest daughter, Gauri Deshpande, was a well-known Marathi writer of short stories and poems. Their eldest daughter, Jai Nimbkar, who lives in Phaltan, is also a writer of novels and short stories. Jai's daughter, Nandini Nimbkar, is a distinguished alumna of University of Florida, USA. Priyadarshini Karve, Anand's daughter, has been working on developing biomass energy technologies and their dissemination in rural areas since 1991.

## Education and Career

Irawati did her schooling from Huzurpaga, Pune and completed her matriculation in 1922. She received a Bachelor of Arts (Honours) degree in Philosophy in 1926 from Fergusson College, majoring in Sociology. In the same year, she married Dr Dinkar Dhondo Karve, the son of Maharshi Karve. Under the guidance of a senior social scientist, Dr G.S. Ghurye, she researched and submitted two essays, 'Folklore of Parshuram' and 'Chitpavan Brahman'. Before proceeding to Germany for advanced studies, she received her Master's in Arts in Sociology from Mumbai University in 1928. She did doctoral work in anthropology from the University of Berlin, Germany in 1928–30 under the guidance of Eugene Fischer on the Normal Asymmetry of the Human Skull and Bones. For her researches in anthropology, Berlin University conferred on her the D.Phil. degree in 1930.

Karve served as the head of the Department of Sociology and Anthropology at Deccan College Post-Graduate and Research Institute, Pune (University of Pune) for forty years till her retirement. She presided over the Anthropology Division of the National Science Congress held in New Delhi in 1947. She was also head of the Sociology Department at Pune University for a while. Later, she remained the Vice Chancellor of SNDT College for some time. She was invited by the School of Oriental and African Studies of the University of London in England in 1951–52 where she prepared her first draft of the book on *Kinship Organization in India*. She was also invited by the Humanities Division of the Rockefeller Foundation of the United States. Chadbourne Gilpatric enabled her to undertake the trip to the US and she travelled from New York to San Francisco meeting colleagues and talking anthropology with them.

Irawati was an independent thinker and she followed her beliefs strongly. By nature, she was a researcher who preferred to work independently. She developed her personality through different media like being an assiduous professor, a researcher, an author and an orator. She was an intelligent woman who spread her knowledge. Her enthusiasm for study, research and travel was of unmatched kind. She has the reputation of being the first woman two-wheeler driver of Pune in 1952. Her ideas of women's liberation were very modernistic. Addressing the women fighting for women's liberation, she said, "Ladies, while fighting with men for rights, why fight for only equal rights? Always fight for more rights". After the Second World War, the fields of Cultural Anthropology and Social Anthropology were developed as independent sciences. By studying and doing in-depth research of these subjects, she successfully analysed culture and history; she was an unparalleled researcher in the world (MNS, 2009). The researcher in her is still alive today through the work of her son – Dr Anand Karve.

## Methodological Perspective

Irawati Karve was India's first woman anthropologist at a time when anthropology and sociology were still developing as university disciplines. She was also the founder of Anthropology Department at Poona (now Pune) University, an indologist who mined Sanskrit texts for sociological features, an anthropologist, serologist, and palaeontologist, a collector of folk songs, a translator of feminist poems, and a Marathi writer and essayist of no mean repute whose book *Yuganta* transformed our understanding of the *Mahabharata*. The indological tradition that Karve subscribed to was of very different from Dumont's in that there was no attempt at building or eliciting an underlying model of social relations. Instead, she was an indologist in the classical Orientalist sense of looking to ancient Sanskrit texts for insights into contemporary practice (Cohn, 1990: 143). Ghurye's influence is apparent in much of Karve's work. They shared common belief in the importance of family, kinship, caste and religion as the basis of Indian society, and also a broad equation of Indian society with Hindu society (Sundar, 2007).

## Works/Writings

Karve wrote in both Marathi and English on topics pertaining to sociology and anthropology as well as on non-scientific topics. The following are some of her books:

1. *Kinship Organization in India* (1953)

2. *The Bhils of West Khandesh* (1958)
3. *Hindu Society: An Interpretation* (1961; 1968)
4. *Group Relations in Village Community* (1963)
5. *The Social Dynamics of a Growing Town and Its Surrounding Area* (1965)
6. *Maharashtra: Land and People* (1968)
7. *Yuganta : The End of an Epoch* (1968)
8. *Paripurti* (in Marathi) (1949)
9. *Bhovara* (in Marathi)
10. *Amachi Samskruti* (in Marathi)
11. *Samskruti* (in Marathi)
12. *Gangajal* (in Marathi) (1972)

Irawati is known in Maharashtra for her work in Marathi literature. But, at the international level, she is known for her study of various social institutions in India, and through her book on *Kinship Organization in India* (1953). She created a mark for herself in all the branches of sociology, like social, cultural, human body, anthropology, language, etc., as a scholar and a writer. She was not just an armchair researcher, but she also traversed all over India and walked the Pandhari Wari (an annual walking pilgrimage of several days and kilometres) for several years and observed many fairs and pilgrimages from up close.

She draws a parallel between society and a quilt: just as a complete quilt is formed by pieces of different colours and sizes, so is the society formed by different people who come together, form relationships with each other, mix with each other and break up, and yet, the thread that ties them to society still remains. She has written considerably, both light prose as well as research-oriented and thought-provoking essays. She has also written amply on topics like kind heartedness of women, tremulous complaisance, and contemplation, with equal aplomb; *Paripurti*, *Bhovara*, *Amachi Samskruti*, *Samskruti* and *Gangajal* are some such examples. She was called the forerunner of light prose. Her prose blossomed through her flexible, natural style of language.

Irawati studied the humanity of the Mahabharata's great figures, with all their virtues and their equally numerous faults. Sought out by an inquirer like her, whose view of life is secular, scientific and anthropological in the widest sense, it is also appreciative of literary values, social problems of the past and present alike, and human needs and responses in the present and past. She wrote both in English as well as in Marathi. Her book *Yuganta*, based on the main characters of the Mahabharata, won the Sahitya (Literary) Academy Award in 1968. She has presented these characters from a unique unparalleled perspective. Written originally in Marathi, it was later translated by her into English too. We see Irawati at a completely new level as a woman, a researcher and an author in this book.

*Marathi Lokanchi Sanskruti* (The Culture of Marathi People), *Dharma* (Religion), *Hindunchi Samajrachna* (The Social Organization of Hindus), *Maharashtra: Ek Abhyas* (Maharashtra: A Study), *Hindu Society: An Interpretation* (1961) (it is a study of the Hindu society based on data which Karve had collected on her field trips and her perusal of texts in Hindi, Marathi, Sanskrit, Pali and Prakrit. In this book she discusses the pre-Aryan existence of caste system in Hinduism and traces its development to its present form), *Kinship Organization in India* (1953) (it is a study of various social institutions in India), *Maharashtra: Land and People* (1968) (it describes various social institutions and rituals in Maharashtra), and *Bhils of West Khandesh* (1955), are some of her important contributions. In addition to these, Karve's work on caste is collected in *Hindu Society: An Interpretation* (1961; 1968), though this book too was preceded by several articles on caste in different volumes of *Economic Weekly* (1958–59). These are: what is caste?: (i) caste as extended kin, (ii) caste and occupation, (iii) caste as a status group, and (iv) caste society and Vedantic thought.

Karve had recognized the importance of English as the language of knowledge. She knew by heart several Sanskrit compositions of Ramayana and Mahabharata, poems and fine quotations of famous poets. Besides the articles in books, she has also contributed several research papers in technical journals.

After a brief description of Irawati's writings in general, we would now like to discuss in detail two of her writings, namely,

(i) *Group Relations in Village Community* (1963), and (ii) *The Social Dynamics of a Growing Town and Its Surrounding Area* (1965).

### *Group Relations in Village Community*

Karve and Damle (1963) designed a methodological experiment to study group relations in village community. They collected both quantitative and qualitative data to test the hypothesis of the structuring of interpersonal and inter-group relations by the factors of kinship, caste and locality. The villages have been chosen on the east-west axis in western Maharashtra so as to represent three geographically distinct environments, namely, one is the village of *varkute* in north Satara district on the eastern famine tract, the second village Ahupe on the western edge of the Deccan plateau and the third village at the mouth of a small river on the west coast. The total number of families interviewed were 343, spread over 21 castes. Most of these people, except for Wadi, were residents of the village concerned for over two generations. Their educational attainments were very poor. The touchables were comparatively more literate than the untouchables and the tribals. The family type was more or less the same in all the villages.

The majority wanted their sons to follow the traditional occupation. The majority belonged to the farming castes, the next were servicemen and artisans. However, where change was desired, it was in favour of the white-collared occupation. In most of the villages, the landlord and tenant belonged to the same caste. Among those who borrowed money, the majority had to go outside their own caste to borrow money. The authors have seen the boundaries of kin and caste that were transcended in various types of interdependence entailed by economic relationships; still a considerable minority did not go outside the caste. Economic independence did not seem to imply social intercourse, like hospitality, etc., on a footing of equality. As regards hospitality, in almost all the castes, meals were given without any special occasion only to the kin. On some occasions, meals were served to the people of service castes. Occasional hospitality involving the receiving and giving of a cup of tea was also confined to the kin and caste. At the time of marriage, however, meals were served to almost the whole village by the agriculturists and professionals, while this activity was confined to kin and caste entirely among untouchables and the other service castes. This pattern was not significantly affected by factors like age, education, nearness to city and contact with the outside world.

The study reveals that the traditional values about the caste system, the system of age-grades, etc., by and large, continued to define the status system. It is true that among the many factors such as age, education and external influence sought to be correlated with behaviour and attitudes, only education seems to have some impact on behaviour, attitudes and opinions. Help as regards agricultural operations was generally received from people of one's own caste. There were few occasions of help outside the caste. Also, help during sickness and involving personal attendance was confined mostly to kin and sometimes to caste but medicines were given freely by other than the caste members. Help was given and received at the time of funeral in the traditional pattern. Even occasional help was confined to the caste. Most of the friendships were with persons of one's own caste, except extremely few genuine friendships across the caste. Almost every family had entertained guests. These were mostly relations by blood and marriage. Most of the villagers said that they would not like to leave the village, even if their children settled elsewhere due to their long association in the village. As regards factions and quarrels, involving inheritance, field boundaries, etc., were among kin. There were other quarrels about leadership, personal differences and trespassing. These, however, involved different castes.

As for the position of the Scheduled Castes (SCs), they did not have a place in the rural economy; and it was very difficult to uplift them. Even when certain public utilities were meant to be used by all, the untouchables were prevented from doing so. This of course was due to the stigma attached to untouchability. However, the fact that the untouchables had more or less ceased to be a functional element in the village system, cannot be ignored. For example, the untouchables had ceased to drag dead cattle of the farmers.

Thus, the authors find that most of the intercourse of an individual was confined to kin groups. And, the inter-group intercourse was regulated by the caste code. The attitudes and opinions confirm the behavioural pattern in terms of social distance and nearness dictated by the caste system. Of course, groups based on economic interdependence also bring about relationships and contact but such groups fail to bring about any significant personal and social intercourse. But, the system of social stratification defines and delimits personal and social intercourse. The exhaustive investigation made amply proves the point.

### *The Social Dynamics of a Growing Town and Its Surrounding Area*

Karve and Ranadive (1965) conducted a study on the social dynamics of a growing town and its surrounding area in the town of Phaltan of Satara district and 23 villages around Phaltan within a radius of less than seven miles in Maharashtra. This study was undertaken on behalf of the Research Programme Committee of the Planning Commission, Government of India, who bore its cost. The data was collected during the year 1961–62 and processed by the end of 1962. The type of survey which is presented here has two aspects, i.e., a theoretical one of trying to find out what is and a practical one of suggesting certain actions based on the findings.

As regards the first part of the work, it had set out to find what a small town is like and what its relationships are with the villages surrounding it. This was necessary to study because anthropologists have been working on the basis of two societies – an urban and a rural – of two cultural traditions – the great and small – as if there was nothing in between the two. In the fieldwork experience of one of the authors, the small town in India seemed to play a role between the two extremes, i.e., the crowded, impersonal, sophisticated city and the extremely isolated small and intimate society of the village. The town with its weekly market was the communication channel between the city and the village. To the city dweller, a small town is a backward place without economic, social or cultural opportunities. To the villager, it is exactly the opposite. Also, the city with its congestion and distances offers less and less amenities to a certain class, who may be attracted to a small town which might become the future city. The authors tried to assess this small town keeping in view the above considerations.

The authors tried to know the patterns of thought and behaviour of the small town and the villages as regards education, religion and economic activities. In the villages, there were more joint families than in the town but the difference was not too great. The new laws about ceiling area for land were leading to splitting up of the joint holdings both in the villages and in the town.

The immigration population of the town was drawn mostly from the neighbouring areas of the three districts of Poona, Satara and Sholapur. The town had not attracted people from places more than a hundred miles away but it was definitely a centre of attraction for the surrounding areas. The town had the rural character inasmuch as quite a good percentage of the people possessed land which they tilled themselves or got tilled by the hired labour. It differed in many respects from the villages. The difference was not due merely to being better off than the villagers; it was rather due to accepting new ways of life. This was revealed by the list of goods possessed by the sample families, by modes of dress, by modes using certain things and spending leisure hours. The difference in the behavioural pattern of the town and village sometimes seems to be due to education. Thus, schools and colleges, the dispensaries, the market yard, the weekly market, the tea shop, the cinema theatre, the cycle shop and the sugar factory in the town represent cultural amenities which had a significant place in the life of the village.

In the second part of the work, what the authors have seen in Phaltan and the surrounding villages suggested a model for building up of communities to which maximum cultural amenities can be provided by the government. This is necessary as the village is becoming a mere agricultural settlement. There is a need to form social engineering skills for the planning of a different sort. The first consideration will be how big such an area should be physically and in terms of population. The second consideration will again be a physical one of connecting the various villages with the town in the middle through all-weather roads. The third consideration would be to remodel, if possible, the existing habitation area so as to connect them easily through a sample design of roads with one another and with the centre. Also, at the centre itself should be concentrated services for education, medicine, recreation of many types and facilities for marketing and banking, etc. Lastly, the authority which would be set up to administer the existing amenities and to enhance the comforts and social intercourse should be made up equally by the town people and the village people.

In this respect, both social and political thinkers will have to discuss this model together with others. The authors think that such an experiment would provide goods and values to people at a cost which can be borne by the government and to which people can also contribute. The authors also suggest that more such studies in different regions of India might give a direction to social planning.

In the ensuing pages, emphasis will be on Karve's major writings on *Kinship Organization in India* (1953) and *Yuganta: The End of an Epoch* (1968).

### *Kinship Organization in India*

As stated at the outset, Karve had written the first draft of the book during her stay in England in 1951–52 at the invitation of the School of Oriental and African Studies of the University of London where she had the opportunity to discuss many points to Louis Haimendorf and Dumont. On her return, she thoroughly revised the first draft to bring in the form of the book. By this time, she had spent many hours of discussion with Drs John and Ruth who happened to be in Poona then. The study of kinship is based on personal inquiry supplemented by readings in Sanskrit, Pali, Ardhamagadhi, Hindi, Gujarati, Marathi and Maithili. Karve endeavoured to read Tamil too with her colleague, Professor C.R. Sankaran.

*Kinship Organization in India*, first published in 1953, has become the standard work on family structure in India. The book consists of nine chapters as follows:

1. Introduction

2. Kinship Usages in Ancient and Historical Periods: Data from the Vedas and Brahmanas
3. The Kinship Organization of Northern Zone
4. The Kinship Organization of the Central Zone
5. The Kinship Organization of the Southern Zone: General
6. The Kinship Organization of the Southern Zone: The Regions
7. The Kinship Organization of the Eastern Zone
8. Ownership of Property, Succession and Inheritance
9. Conclusion followed by Appendix I, II, III

Karve has presented the material on Indian kinship dividing the country into four different cultural zones in accordance with the marriage practices followed in each, i.e., (1) the northern, (2) the central, (3) the southern, and (4) the eastern. Three things are absolutely necessary for the understanding of any cultural phenomenon in India. These are configuration of the linguistic regions, institution of caste and family organization. Each of these three factors is intimately bound up with the other two and the three together give meaning and supply basis to all the other aspects of Indian culture.

(i) *Configuration of the linguistic regions:* A language area is one in which several languages belonging to one language family are spoken. For example, zones (1) and (2) comprise the language area of the Sanskritic or Indo-European languages; zone (3) is made up of the Dravidian language area while the zone (4) includes the scattered area wherein Austric or Mundari languages are spoken. Each of these language areas is further divided into different linguistic regions. In each of such regions, one language and its dialects are spoken. The linguistic regions possess certain homogeneity of culture, traits and kinship organization. The common language makes communication easy, sets the limits of marital connections and confines kinship mostly within the language region. Common folk songs and common literature characterize such an area. The kinship organization follows the linguistic pattern, but in some aspects, language and kinship pattern do not go hand in hand. Thus, though the Maharashtra region belongs to the area of Sanskritic languages but its kinship organization is to a large extent modelled on that of the Dravidian south – its southern neighbour.

(ii) *Institution of caste:* The second thing one must know if he/she wishes to understand any phase of the culture of any group of people in India is the caste system. The structure of the caste system has been well described by many Indian and foreign anthropologists and sociologists. Some important features about caste, however, need to be borne in mind to understand many features of kinship organization described by Karve. A caste is, with very few exceptions, an endogamous group, confined to one linguistic region (Karve, 1968). Endogamy and distribution over a definite area make caste members related to one another either by ties of blood or by marriage. Therefore, caste can be defined as an extended kin group (Karve, 1958–59). In Indian literature, both old and new, the various words for caste are *jati*, *jata* or *kulum*. Many castes having similar status and performing similar functions have names, one part of which may be common. Thus, the castes, engaged in the work of goldsmith, have Sonar (worker in gold) as the common part of their names. In Maharashtra, for example, there are following distinct castes doing work in gold: *Daivadnya Sonar, Ahir Sonar*, *Lad Sonar*, etc. Each of them is fully endogamous and occupies hereditary occupation within Maharashtra – a region slightly different from the others. Thus, endogamy, distribution over a definite region and a hereditary occupation are the characteristics of a caste. In addition, castes are also ranked in a certain order.

(iii) *Family organization:* The third important factor in Indian culture is the family and by family here is meant the joint family. In India, the joint family has endured for as long as the records exist. Even around 1000 B.C., at the time of the Mahabharata war, the joint family existed more or less as it exists today. Karve states:

> A joint family is a group of people who generally live under one roof, who eat food cooked in one kitchen, who hold property in common, participate in common family worship and are related to one another as some particular type of kindred.

The joint family has a seat, a locus, and is made up of a certain type of kin. In the book, Karve states the composition of joint family as there are three or four generations of males related to a male ego as grandfather and his brothers, father and his brothers, brothers and cousins, sons and nephews and wives of all these male relatives plus the ego's own unmarried sisters and daughters. Karve has followed the classical three or four generation formula but she does not include the generation of the common ancestor, the great grandfather, in the number of generations and does not mention unmarried males at all. This means that formula of the genealogical depth of the joint family is deeper than the classical formula. She mentions for the joint family of the formula almost all the functional characteristics generally mentioned in the description of the joint family household of the maximum depth and she also makes remarks about the general nature of life in such a household. She further mentions that every joint family has an ancestral seat or locus which some members may leave for an indefinite period.

Karve also refers to ten or twelve houses, each sheltering a joint family, altogether acknowledging common descent and capable of showing relationship through one line, i.e., lineage. She uses the term 'family' for many different kinds of kinship groups including lineage and clan. She states that when joint families of the two types split, they split into smaller joint families made up of a man, his wife, sons and daughters or a man, his sons and daughters and a couple of younger brothers. According to her method of counting generations, joint families of both these types would be two-generation units, whereas according to others, they would be three-generation units.

Thus, the linguistic region, the caste and the family are the three most important aspects of the culture of any group in India. This applies also to what are called the primitive tribes of India. These tribes have lived with the others for thousands of years. According to the Vedas, the difference between the cultural level of the conquering Aryans and the conquered Dasyus (forest dwellers) could not have been very great. Both were illiterate and polytheistic.

The present-day cultural problems before India largely revolve round these three entities – language, caste and family – as the following examples will show:

1. The tendency is to minimize the differences and establish uniformities. Some people would much rather have unitary states with one language than a federation with many linguistic states.
2. The new Indian State has abolished in law all privileges and discriminations connected with the caste system.
3. The establishment of a uniform civil code for all citizens is a directive principle of the Indian Constitution. So far a number of laws have been passed which, however, apply only to Hindus and not to others. The action is contrary to the professions about a secular state, which has the task of governing a multicultural, multi-religious society.
4. A state has a right to shape the lives of the individuals it governs. Welding of the Indian subcontinent into a nation is a great cultural task, but very often the urge for uniformity destroys much that from an ethical and cultural point of view can be allowed to remain. The need for uniformity is an administrative need, not a cultural one (Karve, 1961).

The Indian Parliament has during the past decade shown a tendency to legislate with the avowed purpose of changing ancient custom in the direction of uniformity. Thus, the Hindu Marriage Act of 1955 imposes a compulsory monogamy alien to Hinduism and disliked by many of both sexes; the Succession Act of 1956 likewise runs contrary to ancient custom in unnaturally barring the children of a concubine and their mother from any rights in the father's estate. There seems to be a number of Indian legislators who would like to forbid the practice of cross-cousin marriage so as to bring the marriage law in southern India into line with the north. But uniformity and unity are far from being the same thing, and before sacrificing the latter perhaps to achieve the former they would do well to consult sociologists like Karve (Hutton, 1965). 'If we assert that our society is multicultural, we must recognize that we are also a society with many alternative values and ways of life, and we must not destroy them under the pretence of building a nation. The path to uniformity is one tyranny and we shall lose our first cultural value if we make uniformity our goal' (Karve, 1968: 16).

In this book, Karve has discussed the kinship terminologies of all the three language areas. It would have been possible and might have seemed more logical to divide the book into three parts dealing with these areas separately as (1) Indo-European or Sanskritic, (2) Dravidian, and (3) Mundari organization of kinship. Instead, Karve presented the kinship organization in geographical sequence of (1) northern, (2) central, (3) southern, and (4) eastern zones. This procedure was adopted deliberately to emphasize the spatial pattern and interrelation of the kinship organization and the linguistic divisions. Since the geographical distribution of different language families in India is well known, here, she has only tried to relate this configuration with another cultural phenomenon – the kinship organization.

1. The description of the kinship organization of the northern zone is divided into two parts. The first is devoted to material found in ancient Sanskrit records with a short note which adds kinship terms in Pali found in Buddhist literature and in Ardhamagadhi found in Jain literature. These terms are useful for understanding the meaning of modern kinship terms used in Sanskrit and are briefly explained. The second part is devoted to a description of a generalized model for the whole of northern India called the northern zone and kinship terms in the northern languages (Punjabi, Sindhi, Hindi, Bihari, Bengali, Assamese and Pahadi) are given and briefly explained.
2. The central zone includes central India, i.e., Rajasthan, Madhya Pradesh, Orissa, Gujarat and Maharashtra. In this zone, people speak predominantly Sanskritic languages, though it also includes many tribes who speak Dravidian and Mundari languages. The kinship organization in the central zone, though modelled on the northern pattern, shows some very significant differences which can best be described as being due to culture contact with the other two zones, especially the southern zone of the Dravidian language area.

3. The description of the southern zone is given in two parts. The first part tries to give the whole Dravidian system and its differences from the northern system. In the second part, short description of the kinship system and terms of the linguistic regions of the Dravidian area are given. The author thinks that her interpretation of the southern system is of great significance for Indian cultural anthropology. The kinship organization in the various regions within this language area and of different castes and tribes within each region are presented as adjustments necessitated by cultural contact.
4. The eastern zone and its kinship organization are described in the next chapter. A new chapter has been added in the second revised edition (1965) dealing with inheritance and succession in the northern and southern zones. The concluding chapter indicates some important problems for research arising out of the present investigation. The third revised edition (1968) includes three new appendices which reflect the author's latest researches in the field.

The studies described in the book lead to further anthropological problems. Some of these are being investigated by Karve with the help of her colleagues but the field is so vast that a larger number of people getting interested in the same problems are always advantageous and so a few of these are indicated as follows:

1. How the kinship organization is influenced and strengthened by the caste system and how both of these conform to certain patterns found in wide geographical areas called linguistic regions? And, yet no linguistic region has the same kind of kinship pattern, no two castes possess identical relationship behaviour and no two families in a caste act exactly in the same way.
2. The rigidity or the elasticity of a social structure may depend either on the nature of a social structure or on the whole cultural fabric of a society. For example, in Maharashtra, some castes follow the northern type of kinship behaviour as regards marriage while the majority of castes allow the marriage of a man to his mother's brother's daughter.

3. Divorce is not tolerated by the Brahmanic law books and has not sanction of the priests. The Hindu law codified by the English with the help of the Brahmin savants and also withheld recognition of divorce. Thus, divorce is granted in the Indian law courts. The refusal to accept the existence of divorce has very far-reaching effects on kinship and caste organization.
4. The family in the majority of regions in India is an autonomous unit with its own gods, its own observances, its own economic organization, which is semi-independent of other similar units. The caste in its turn is also a closed autonomous unit which has certain limited contacts with other similar units and which controls the behaviour of families in certain respects.
5. The joint family provided economic and social security. The village where people spent all their lives was also the ultimate support of all the residents. The rise of industrial cities and the new opportunities of employment have resulted in loosening of the bonds of the joint family and of the village community.

The kinship organization described in this book presents different cultural zones with different modes of marriages. Marriage rules are rules about mating which must have an effect on the genetically make of a family or caste. Karve saw that in the north, the rules of marriage lay down that brides should be brought from families which are not related to blood; in other words, as far as possible one should not give a daughter into a family from which a girl is brought as bride and that in one generation more than one bride should not be brought from the same family. Her analysis of southern marriage pattern, based on the chronological division of the kin into older and younger kin, rather than on the principle of generations, is an important contribution to Indian anthropology.

Karve devotes an entire chapter to the comprehensive survey of property, succession and inheritance in the new edition (1965). She explains the differences between the *Dayabhaga* system of Bihar and Bengal and the *Mitakshara* system followed by the rest of Hindu India. She also deals with the system in matrilineal Kerala. She has succeeded in bringing out very clearly the contrast between the social system of northern India developed by a patrilineal and patrilocal society, probably associated primarily with a pastoral economy, and depending for its strength on external alliances and the incorporation of outsiders; and that of the south which has its strength in the internal consolidation of closely related kinship groups originally, no doubt, dependent upon agriculture. It is not, she concludes, through the association of exogamous moieties that reciprocal kinship terms and the obligations that go with them develop, but by the continuous exchange of daughters between two or more families, which may thus grow into a closely-knit kinship unit. It is perhaps characteristics of the author that she should tend to lay emphasis on the less obvious processes in the formation of social units. She has stressed a somewhat similar point elsewhere, when writing of caste, and in both cases has drawn attention to what Hutton (1965) perhaps may call the inductive method of group formation as contrasted with the deductive. Neither can be neglected of course in the study of Indian social organization, but the objectivity of her work, and her freedom from bias or dogmatism add to the weight of Karve's conclusions (Hutton, 1965).

Karve has not developed any theory but assumes that the theories of the other scholars, e.g., Levi Strauss, can be tried on the data presented by her. However, a few hypotheses are given in the last chapter. And, in the ultimate analysis, the problem of the greatest importance is to understand that the whole which is made up by the entire fabric of the social institutions, traditions and mental habits that goes under the name of a culture and is the foundation of the diverse personalities which one meets and which one is. A study of single social structure necessarily involves references to the whole culture without, however, carrying out a full analysis of it. In this sense, each study is incomplete and is doomed to remain ever incomplete.

### *Yuganta: The End of an Epoch*

*Yuganta* studies the principal, mythical heroic figures of the Mahabharata from historical, anthropological and secular perspectives. The usually venerated characters of this ancient Indian epic are here subjected to a rational enquiry that places them in context, unravels their hopes and fears, and imbues them with wholly human motives, thereby making their stories relevant and astonishing to contemporary readers. Irawati Karve, thus, presents a delightful collection of essays, scientific in spirit, yet appreciative of the literary tradition of the Mahabharata. She challenges the familiar and formulates refreshingly new interpretations, all the while refusing to judge harshly or venerate blindly.

### *Context of Mahabharata*

Anyone reading this book might well conclude that Karve's favourite Sanskrit work is the Mahabharata. For when she talks, she may recite long passages of the Mahabharata, launch upon analysis and discussion of personalities and deeds described in it, while her mind, which is constantly bursting with original and interesting ideas, often finds the stimulus for them in that gigantic work.

The Mahabharata has often been characterized by students of Indian civilization as the most informative work among all of the country's ancient literature. It is a growth over many centuries, which incorporates material of many varieties drawn from many sources – possibly a little history, certainly much myth, legend, fairy tale, fable, anecdote, religious and philosophical writing, legal material, even anthropological items, and miscellaneous data of other kinds. It is a genuine folk epic in basic character, which has been enlarged to a kind of Indian – at least Hindu – cultural encyclopaedia. But, it is not this quality of the Mahabharata that has made it so absorbing to Karve. She is attracted to it because it depicts a long roster of characters with all their virtues and their equally numerous faults, openly, objectively, even more, mercilessly displayed, especially when sought out by an inquirer like her, whose view of life is secular, scientific, anthropological in the widest sense, yet also appreciative of literary values, social problems of the past and present alike, and human needs and responses in her own time and in antiquity as she identifies them (Brown, 1968).

### *What is Mahabharata?*

*Mahabharata* is the name of a book in the Sanskrit language telling in very simple verse form the story of a family quarrel ending in a fierce battle. According to Karve and to Indians in general, this is not an imaginary, made up story, but represents a real event which took place about 1000 B.C. In the course of this narration, stories are given of the ancestors of the heroes who fought the battle. These were princes who ruled a city called Hastinapura situated somewhere near modern Delhi. The most illustrious king among these ancestors was the King Bharata (son of King Dushyanta or Dushmanta and Shakuntala). From the name Bharata is derived the word 'Bharata' which might mean: (1) any descendant of Bharata, or (2) any other thing about Bharata, as for example, a poem. 'Maha' means the big, the great. The word 'Mahabharata' lets us recognize stages in the making of this poem. Perhaps, there was a simple and less extensive story called Bharata and then by century long accretion it became a Maha (the big) Bharata (book about the descendants of Bharata).

The *Mahabharata* is supposed to have been composed by the sage Vyasa, who played a part in the events and who was an eyewitness of many of them. He is supposed to have told his stories to his disciples. The Mahabharata has had a peculiar history. The early Buddhist literature which followed within a few centuries of the Mahabharata has very few references to this story though it talks of the country of the Kurus and the excellent moral code of the land. The Jains made the Krishna story a part of their tradition and wrote on the Mahabharata incidents and stories. Apart from the peculiar sectarian bias in the Jain version of the Krishna story and the Mahabharata, it appears that there is also preserved in them some older stuff which, if systematically compared, may yield some older material on certain beliefs. In the Jain literature, Vasudeva, the father of Krishna, becomes a hero of an early book called *Vasudeva-hindi* (the wanderings of Vasudeva). The Bhagavad Gita which forms part of the Sanskrit Mahabharata became the most read religious book of the Hindus. Shankaracharya wrote the first commentary on it. It is being commented on and translated even in this century.

In *Yuganta* Karve does not retell the story of the Mahabharata. That has been done enough times. Instead, keeping it as a base, she delves into the human aspect of the epic. She dissects the various characters and keeping their very obvious strengths in mind, turns the spotlight on their weaknesses. Her approach is scientific, impersonal and anthropological. She does keep in mind the social and literary compulsions of the time in which it was composed. Gentle persuasion, rather than a frontal assault, is used to strip away layers of divinity that cloak what is a very human epic. Looking through her eyes, we can see that the Mahabharata is a remarkable mirror. It reflects accurately the different faces we wear.

The method Karve has chosen is to take it in parts. She has tried to place each character in context by narrating a brief part of the story that immediately precedes the character being studied. The reader need not be a scholar; thorough in all the labyrinthine plots and sub-plots that make up the monumental epic, but a broad familiarity with the main story is a must. Here, we have adapted the description of *Yuganta* in the narration of the characters of Mahabharata as reviewed by B.S. Keshav. The first character that Karve takes on is Bhishma, the patriarch.

(i) *Bhishma*: As we know, Bhishma was the last true heir to the Kuru throne. The bloodline, for all biological purposes, ended with him. He had taken the terrible vow of chastity so that his father Shantanu could marry Satyavati. When the children of Satyavati and Shantanu died without issue, the distraught queen approached him. She begged him to break his vow and marry the widows, but he did not relent. Maharshi Vyasa had to be approached to further the lineage through a social custom called 'niyoga'. Vyasa himself was the illegitimate son of Satyavati from a Brahmin sage. Bhishma remained a bachelor till the end of the Mahabharata as the eternal caretaker, the patriarch.

The author now questions, 'Was it really worth it?' Bhishma was the epitome of the cruel cliché, 'The road to hell is paved with good intentions'. To get wives for the sons of Satyavati, he abducted the three daughters of the Raja of Kashi. Amba, one of them committed suicide vowing to be reborn as the reason for Bhishma's death. He brought Gandhari as the wife of the blind Dhritarashtra and condemned her to a pitiful life. Likewise, he played hell with the lives of Kunti and Madri, getting them married to the impotent Pandu. Presiding all those years over the Kuru court as an elder, neither could he bring the warring princes together, nor could he prevent the fratricidal war. In the end, what did he really achieve?

(ii) *Gandhari*: Most versions of the Mahabharata leave one with a very one dimensional image of Gandhari. We only see the long-suffering woman who decided to join her husband in blindness. The author here brings to the fore other fascinating aspects of her character. We see glimpses of the shy bride, the tough queen, the doting and at times vengeful mother.

(iii) *Kunti*: The status of women in the society during the times of the Mahabharata can be perfectly seen in the life of Kunti. As a child, her father gave her away to his childless friend. Her stepfather asked her to serve the short-tempered sage, Durvasa. Stripped of politically correct delicacy, this 'service' could also mean getting into bed with him. Later, she was married to a king who was impotent. She spent the rest of her life trying to ensure that her sons got what was due to them. At each stage of her life, she really was not in control of the events as they unfolded. Her multifaceted character unfolds in the way she dealt with each of the calamities: childish and callous at the conception when she gave birth to Karna and abandonment of him; magnanimous when she allowed Madri to use the mantra she had got from Durvasa; mean when she reacted strongly to Madri's indiscretion with Pandu that led to his death; noble when she brought up Madri's children as her own; farsighted when she advised the brothers to marry a common wife; and calculative when she approached Karna on the eve of the battle. It is a brilliant analysis of a person's character. Throughout, as all the events flash past her, Kunti stands strong – very much human – but admirable.

(iv) *Father and Son*: This was the most fascinating of the essays. Here, the author explores the role of Vidura, the forgotten half-brother of Dhritarashtra and Pandu. He was also the son of Maharshi Vyasa and a maid – a fact that condemned him to secondary status throughout his life. Even though healthy of body and mind, he could not ascend the throne, as his mother was a maid. This brings up an analysis of the 'niyoga' system. Childless kings could ask their brothers to sleep with the queens to ensure continuation of the royal lineage. If a brother was not available, a learned Brahmin could do the honours. Adoption was not an option. Vyasa's role in the Kuru family was due to the refusal of Bhishma to break his vow. Vidura is considered to be an incarnation of Yamaraj, the God of Death, also known as Dharma Raj, the God of Justice. Yudhishthira, on the other hand, was known as the son of Yamaraj. The author gives a detailed analysis here of how Vidura could have been Yudhishthira's father by comparing the actions of the two at various situations in life. Though it may be repugnant to our 21st century eyes to imagine Vidura sleeping with Kunti, the way it is explained makes it very believable. The description of the death of Vidura is also hair-raising, to say the least.

(v) *Draupadi*: Before getting into the story of Draupadi, the author makes an interesting comparison between the Ramayana and the Mahabharata. Whereas the former was more idealistic, the latter was rooted in the chaos of human conflict. Whereas Sita, the only heroine of the Ramayana, had a pretty straightforward life; Draupadi, who could qualify as premier among many of the female characters in the Mahabharata, had a thornier path. Her courage and fortitude is equally complemented by her impetuousness and indiscretions. Her lifelong battle to remain true to all the brothers, equally, is evocatively brought out in their final journey to heaven. The author interpolates a small sequence here that is not a part of the Mahabharata, but should have been. She explores the relationship between Bhima and Draupadi. It is breathtaking in its clarity of vision.

(vi) *Paradharmo Bhayavahah*: *'Taking over another's Dharma is dangerous' – Bhagavadgita XVIII*

Here, the author has examined the role of the Brahmins in the Mahabharata. Two of the major characters are Drona and his son, Ashvatthama. She has gone into great detail about how Drona, despite his great learning, could not make a greater impact, while Ashvatthama failed totally and was cursed with eternal torture. What is interesting to note is that the caste system was not in a much evolved stage at that point in time.

(vii) *Karna*: Here, we come to the most enigmatic and tragic character in the Mahabharata. Cast away by Kunti at birth, Karna's entire life was a struggle to come to grips with his identity. This confusion led him to blunder after blunder. The author has taken great pains in analysing each action of his, whether it was the crude behaviour at the disrobing of Draupadi, the cruelty displayed in the killing of Abhimanyu, the innate generosity in his nature or the nobility to stick by Duryodhana's side even after knowing the truth. It is fascinating to get under the skin of this unsung hero and see what made him tick.

(viii) *Krishna*: The author grapples with the complexity of Krishna, the man and Krishna, the Godhead. After much research and analysis, she concludes that the deifying of Krishna as a God only happened after the Mahabharata. The story of his naughty childhood, the dalliances with gopis, etc., could only have been a later addition. During the epic, he was very much human. He is seen more as a close friend and contemporary of Arjuna. Rather than make a bald statement here and invite the wrath of a billion believers, the author refers and infers from myriad sources that reveal not only her scholarship, but also ability to sift through a mountain of information. He was intelligent, just, farsighted and brave, but no God, says the author. Later versions have parts inserted to reinforce the godly status.

### *The Palace of Maya*

One incident stands out and defies explanation. Krishna and Arjuna are said to have gone out for a hunt when the Pandavas were given the land called Khandavaprastha. It was a small village next to a jungle. The God of Fire, Agni appears and asks them to help him in burning the forest down. They do so, but in an unbelievably cruel manner, by cutting off the escape routes and ensuring that all the living beings in the forest are burnt. The only survivor, Maya went on to build the Palace of Maya for them. Such incidents are glossed over in most versions of the epic and provoke many questions.

### *Discourse*

Here, it is important to note that though the Mahabharata was composed and sung by Maharshi Vyasa, it was passed on to his disciples, who then took it forward by word of mouth, the only way possible at that point in time. By the time it was finally written down, many additions/interpolations were made. One version followed another till a critical version was widely accepted. The Mahabharata is said to have taken place at the end of the Dwapara Yuga. The Bhakti cult only started in later years, in the Kaliyuga, when the concept of gurus or prophets or messiahs began. Stories of a God that pardoned all began to take over, where a man had to behave piously and leave everything to an omniscient, omnipresent and omnipotent God, to be rewarded in the end. Most literature became sweet, sentimental and moralistic. Perversely, there were stories like that of Ajamila too. He lived a thoroughly wicked life, but on his deathbed said, 'Narayana'. It did not matter that Narayana was the name of his son; he was pardoned and given place in heaven. The Mahabharata, on the other hand, is all about the concept of dharma. Action by itself, according to one's dharma, is of prime importance. The fruits thereof do not dictate it.

Karve's *Yuganta* is a collection of essays on the Mahabharata and its characters. Karve's approach is very much that of an anthropologist. It is important to note that Karve's approach is a historical one, based on the belief that the seed of the story was an actual event that took place around 1000 BC; this is, of course, tempered by the idea that the epic in its original form was vastly different from the embellished, repeatedly reworked version, which we have today. Her thesis is that the original work was one of the last examples of pragmatism in Indian literature that was subsequently lost. In her essays, she does not deal at all with the religious aspects of the Mahabharata. Instead of treating them as a later interpolation, she makes the point that the Krishna of the original epic – a powerful and shrewd Yadava king who was indeed the prime mover for many of the key events in the story – bore little resemblance to the Krishna who emerged in subsequent centuries ('the flute playing lover of milkmaids, the divine child') as Indian literature became more sentimental and more centred around what she calls 'the dreamy escapism of the Bhakti tradition'.

Though Karve's essays are much more stimulating now, her treatment of two of the Mahabharata's esteemed characters is most complex, i.e., Bhishma and Karna. In the essay titled 'The Final Effort', she makes the provocative point that Bhishma, by sacrificing conjugal happiness and his rights to the throne, put himself in a position where he acquired moral superiority over the other characters (who led more conventional lives), so that it was never possible for them to question his actions. And that, under the pretext of being responsible for the house of the Kurus, he far overstayed his welcome, continuing to dodder about as a granddaddy/great granddaddy figure to generations of princes long after he should have properly given up worldly life and retired to the forest with his stepmother, Satyavati. 'That is what a Kshatriya was supposed to do...but this rule applied to ordinary family men immersed in their own affairs. Did Bhishma think he was immune because he belonged to that category of men who sacrifice the self and live only for others?... . In the last chapter his life it looks as if he deliberately sought out responsibilities that were not even his.'

In this context, Karve makes another astute observation:

> Bhishma was famed as a man who was completely unselfish ... a man who lived for the good of his clan, not himself. When a man does something for himself, his actions are performed within certain limits – limits that are set by the jealous scrutiny of others. But let a man set out to sacrifice himself and do good to others, and the normal limits vanish. He can become completely ruthless in carrying out his objectives. The injustices done by idealists, patriots, saints and crusaders can be far greater than those done by the worst tyrants.

In Karve's view, almost all the significant women characters in the epic are victims of Bhishma's injustices – notably Kunti,

Gandhari and Madri, princesses of noble houses, who were all married off to undeserving and/or cursed men and yoked to the house of Hastinapur where they found nothing but unhappiness. However, she is even harsher with poor Karna. Though she admits at one point that he appears to be 'a noble person and a true friend', she casually dismisses the episodes that most of his fame is built on, and which are such crucial parts of Indian folklore: when he promised Kunti that he would not kill any of his brothers except Arjuna, she says he was motivated not by generosity or love but by contempt; the giving away of his *kavacha* and *kundalas* to Indra was apparently nothing but a self-conscious attempt to prove himself better than others; and he was an overrated warrior and a poor military strategist, given to running away from the battlefield. Incidently, Karve treats Karna's tirade about the immorality of the Madarka women, mentioned in this post, as a later addition to the text. It makes no sense, she says, because people routinely ate beef in those days, and the standards of 'morality' in this passage is defined more by contemporary standards than those prevalent at that time of the epic.

The Mahabharata stands in contrast to the other great Sanskrit epic, the Ramayana. The latter the Hindus characterize as elegant poetry, high literary art (*kavya*), a court epic wherein the personalities are types illustrative of virtues and vices rather than emotionally complicated beings. To Hindu tradition, however, the Mahabharata is history (*itihasa*, a word which means literally 'thus it was'), and its characters are like that of the Iliad and other great folk epics.

Karve studies the humanity of the Mahabharata's great figures and no one of them emerges for her as wholly good or wholly bad, few as even prevailingly good or prevailingly bad. Duryodhana, the arch villain of the work, had been humiliated by the Pandava heroes and was filled with deep resentment. Arjuna, the great and noble warrior, was vacillating in purpose and also merciless, as in the slaughter of the Nagas (primitive non-Aryan folk) when he and Krishna and the God Agni burnt the Khandava forest. There was no ahimsa (non-violence) for those three! Bhishma, the wisest and most respected character in the epic, a peacemaker who tried to heal the factional strife in his family which is the theme of the work, nevertheless, when under the influence of his own sense of mission, wrought great injustices and had a large share in producing the fatal series of events that finally made the strife incurable and obliterated both the warring branches. Gandhari, generally admired for wifely devotion, who as a girl was deceitfully betrothed to a blind prince, and in consequence, to share her husband's misfortune, wore a bandage over her eyes by day and night until shortly before her death, is shown at the end of life to have inflicted the voluntary blindness upon herself not so much from an exaggerated sense of marital duty as to give her husband and his family a guilty feeling in retaliation for the deception practised upon her. Draupadi, heroine of the whole epic story, though the model of a good wife, was also an arrogant, opinionated, selfish, untrustworthy young woman, and an inveterate troublemaker throughout her life. The catalogue is endless. Even Krishna, reciter of the Bhagavad Gita and god incarnate, was a Machiavellian schemer, aiding his friends, the Pandavas, with shrewd counsel, though sometimes of dubious morality. All the great personages in the Mahabharata are cut down in her analysis to human size. Like the noble figures in the Greek epics and tragedies and in Shakespeare's chronicle plays, they exhibited a wide range of human feelings and passions – love, devotion, bravery, chivalry, and also hatred, envy, rage, violence, deceit, cowardice, unchivalry, injustice, censurable conduct even by the prevailing standards. This fact is what makes them interesting to Karve and her essays interesting to us. Seen through her eyes, the Mahabharata is more than a work which Hindus look upon as divinely inspired and venerate. It becomes a record of complex humanity and a mirror to all the faces which we ourselves wear. The Mahabharata, thus, becomes for us a work of high tragedy with 'the strange power' as Edith Hamilton puts it in speaking of Aeschylus, 'to exalt and not depress'. The royal house of the Kauravas and the Pandavas, rent by the violent passions of its factions, which were too great to be subdued by the virtues it possessed, like the house of Atreus came to inevitable, violent extinction. Though the Sanskrit drama does not know tragedy, the epic Mahabharata does the most genuine and deepest tragedy. This tragedy is what Irawati Karve has found and now shows us in this volume (Brown, 1968).

The *Yuganta* is a very informative book. It is amazingly written and one can understand the very epoch in a simple way. It also makes clear all the myths, the magic and godly activities which were not there in the true story and got interpolated in the later versions of the Mahabharata. It shows how Hindu culture evolved thereafter and perhaps, why such interpolations were done. Whether or not one may agree with Karve's interpretations. *Yuganta* is certainly a valuable book that shows how different the Mahabharata is when sentimentality/melodrama (of the sort that in Karve's view became popular long after the original epic was written) have been siphoned out of it.

This part of the book may not be palatable to all at first reading, but makes a lot of sense when we read it in her words. The author brings the book to a close on the premise that she started with, that the end of the Mahabharata was the end of an epoch, a Yuganta.

## Conclusion

Irawati Karve (1905–1970) was born in Burma and educated in Pune. A Master's degree in sociology from Mumbai in 1928 and a doctoral degree in anthropology from Berlin in 1930 marked the onset of a long and distinguished career of pioneering research. Karve, a researcher of international repute, known to have nurtured social sense in people and achieved supremacy in the fields of sociology, cultural and physical anthropology, was also an excellent author and a fine example of women's liberation.

Karve had knowledge of both social and physical anthropology – a combination which in these days of specialization only few of us can claim. Beyond that her acquaintance with Sanskrit and Pali literature enabled her to write on Indian kinship diachronically, particularly as she has gone to the trouble of learning to read Tamil for the sake of the light which early literature can through on South Indian systems.

She wrote in both English and Marathi, on academic subjects as well as on topics of general interest, and thus commanded an enviably wide circle of readership. Whether through her *Hindu*

*Society: An Interpretation*, a scholarly treatise in English, or through *Yuganta: The End of an Epoch*, her study in Marathi of the characters and society in the Mahabharata, we obtain ample illustration of the range and quality of her mind. But, at the international level, she is known for her study of various social institutions in India, and through her book on *Kinship Organization in India*, which first appeared in 1953 and marked a notable advance in our understanding of the structure of Indian society. It has not been superseded by any other general comparative treatment of Hindu kinship in India as a whole, and a reissue is more than overdue.

## Irawati Karve's Framework Summarized

### *Background*

1. Born in Myingyan, Burma to Ganesh Karmarkar.
2. Master's in Sociology from Bombay University and D. Phil from Berlin University, Germany.
3. A researcher of international repute in the fields of sociology and anthropology, excellent author and a fine example of women's liberation. Irawati was not just an armchair researcher, but she had traversed all over India, walked the Pandhari Wari (an annual walking pilgrimage of several days and kilometres) for several years and observed many fairs and pilgrimages from up close.

### *Aim*

To understand the social organization of Hindus.

### *Assumption*

To know the chances of losing our first cultural value if we make uniformity our goal.

### *Methodology*

1. Fieldwork method
2. Indological perspective
3. Inductive method
4. Diachronic approach

5. Archaeological and historical references

### *Typology*

1. Indological approach
2. Ethnological approach
3. Folk tradition
4. Anthropometric measurements
5. Serological and paleontological analysis

### *Issues*

Different aspects of Indian society, mainly

1. Hindu Society: Social organization of Hindus and their culture, religion, caste and kinship organization.
2. Yuganta: Historical understanding of Mahabharata's characters.

## Select Bibliography

Bose, N.K. (1969). 'Review of I. Karve's *Hindu Society*' (1962) (1st edition), *Man in India*, 42, 1: 11–13.

Brown, W. Norman (1968). 'Forward of the Book', Irawati Karve, *Yuganta*, Bombay: Orient Blackswan.

Cohn, Bernard (1990). *An Anthropologist Among the Historians and Other Essays*, Delhi: Oxford University Press.

Dumont, Louis and D.F. Pocock (1957). 'Review of I. Karve's *Kinship Organization in India'*, *Contribution to Indian Sociology*, 1: 43–64.

Hutton, J.H. (1965). 'Forward of the Bokk', Irawati Karve, *Kinship Organization in India*, Bombay: Asia Publishing House.

Kavadi, P.B. (1970). 'Irawati Karve: Portrait of Great Lady', *The Illustrated Weekly of India*, 13 September: 26–27.

Kalelkar, N.G. (1973). 'Irawati Karve', *Bulletin of Deccan College Research Institute*, 31–32, part 1 (1970–71) & part 2 (1971–72): 1–4.

Karve, Irawati (1953, 1965, 1968). *Kinship Organization in India*, Bombay: Asia Publishing House.

— (1958). *The Bhils of West Khandesh*, Bombay: The Anthropological Society of Bombay.

— (1958). 'What is Caste? (i) Caste as Extended Kin', *Economic Weekly*, 10, 4–6: 125–38.

— (1958). 'What is Caste? (ii) Caste and Occupation', *Economic Weekly*, 10, 12: 401–07.

— (1958). 'What is Caste? (iii) Caste as a Status Group', *Economic Weekly*, 10, 26–8: 881–88.

— (1959). 'What is Caste? (iv) Caste Society and Vedantic Thought', *Economic Weekly*, 11, 4–6: 149–63.

— (1961). *Hindu Society: An Interpretation*, Poona: Deccan College and in (1968). Poona: Deshmukh Prakashan.

— (2006). *Yuganta*, Bombay: Orient Blackswan.

Karve, Irawati and Yashwant Bhaskar Damle (1963). *Group Relations in Village Community*, Monograph Series 24, Poona: Deccan College.

Karve, Irawati and Jayant Sadashiv Ranadive (1965). *The Social Dynamics of a Growing Town and its Surrounding Area*, Poona: Deccan College.

Jai Maharashtra: Irawati Karve (2009). Maharashtra Navnirman Sena (MNS).

Sundar, Nandini (2007). 'In the Cause of Anthropology: The Life and Work of Irawati Karve' in Patricia Uberoi, Satish Deshpande and Nandini Sundar (eds), *Anthropology in the East: The Founders of Indian Sociology and Anthropology*, New Delhi: Permanent Black.

*Yuganta*. Reviewed by B.S. Keshav, sulekh.com, creative blog Chennai.

## Writings in Marathi

Karve, Irawati (1949). *Paripurti*. Pune: Deshmukh and Co.

— (1972). *Gangajal*. Pune: Deshmukh and Co.

— *Bhovara*.

— *Amachi Samskruti*.

— *Samskruti*.

— *Manavshastra va Samajshastra. In Sanshodhan-Karya*

# III

# Structural-Functional Perspective

Sociological functionalism is closely related to the structural-functionalist approach in anthropology, which tries to explain the various social forms found in tribal societies in terms of their contributions to social cohesion.

The followers of this perspective focus on the understanding of the 'ordering' and 'patterning' of the social world. Their focus of attention is mainly the 'problem of order' at a societal level. Their theoretical and empirical analyses have generally been based on the assumption that societies can be seen as persistent, cohesive, stable, generally inherited wholes differentiated by their culture and social structural arrangements. They even pose the questions: How did various institutions or customs originate? How does it fill in the broader context? How does the part relate to the whole? Regarding this perspective, A.R. Radcliffe-Brown says that the total social structure of a society, together with the totality of social usages, constituted a functional unity, a condition in which all parts work together with a sufficient degree of harmony or internal consistency, that is, without producing persisting conflicts which can neither be resolved nor regulated. Further, to explain any belief, rule, custom or institution demanded an analysis which linked the elements functionally with the structure of the culture as a system.

This perspective of society stresses the element of harmony and consistency not those of conflict and contradiction. The functional unity of a system is defined in terms of social order. In defining society in holistic terms, structural-functional implies that as everything within the system is necessarily functional for the whole. They are the believers of the fact that society is a relatively persisting configuration of elements and consensus is a ubiquitous element of the social system. It treats changes as a slow, cumulative process of adjustment to a new situation. Its explanation consists essentially of pointing out how the different types of activity fit on top of one another, and are consistent with one another, and how conflicts are contained and prevented from changing the structure.

M.N. Srinivas is to be credited for initiating the new line of structural-functional analysis in sociological and social anthropological research in India. Structural-functionalism is brought into sociology by borrowing concepts from biological sciences. Structure in biology refers to organisms meaning a relatively stable arrangement of relationships between different cells and the consequences of the activity of the various organs in the life process of the organism as their function. Spencer goes further and points out that not only analogy exists between the body social and body human but the same principle and the same definition of life is applied to both. Durkheim insisted on the importance of structure over elements. He has pointed to the importance of social morphology or structure. A new departure was marked in the thirties of the 19th century by the works of a number of British social anthropologists (Srinivas, 1964). Evans-Pritchard describes social structure in terms of persistent social groups and Radcliffe-Brown indicates that social structure is based on network of relations of person to person through genealogical connections. According to Srinivas, "In the recent British social anthropology, the two important concepts – structure and function – imply that every society is a whole and that its various parts are interrelated. In other words, the various groups and categories which are part of a society are related to each other" (Srinivas, 1964).

The structural-functional perspective relies more on the field work tradition for understanding the social reality so that it can also be understood as 'contextual' or 'field view' perspective of the social phenomena. The important followers of this perspective are M.N. Srinivas, S.C. Dube, McKim Marriott, I.P. Desai, D.N. Majumdar and others. In this section, we would discuss the structural-functional approach adopted by M.N. Srinivas, S.C. Dube and McKim Marriott in the study of Indian society.

# 8

# M.N. Srinivas

Mysore Narsimhacharya Srinivas (1916–1999) was born in a Brahmin family in Mysore on 16th November, 1916 and died at the ripe age of 83 at Bangalore on 30th November, 1999. Srinivas, who was himself from a Brahminic background, emerged as a breath of fresh air in the over-Brahminized world of Indian scholarship. Srinivas had initiated the tradition of basing macro-sociological generalizations on micro-anthropological insights and of giving a sweep and perspective to anthropological investigations of small-scale communities (Srinivas, 1996:22). He obtained MA, LLB and PhD from Bombay, and DPhil from Oxford. He was Professor of Sociology at Maharaja Sayajirao University of Baroda and University of Delhi; and Senior Fellow, Sociology Unit at Institute for Social and Economic Change, Bangalore; and J.R.D. Tata Visiting Professor, National Institute of Advanced Studies, Bangalore.

M.N. Srinivas, an internationally renowned scholar, was a student of G.S. Ghurye at the Department of Sociology of Bombay

University. He was an institution-builder, a creative researcher and a devoted teacher in a remarkable manner. He took up the challenge of building a Department of Sociology at M.S. University Baroda, which involved starting from scratch in every respect instead of choosing to be a lecturer at Oxford with all the prestige. Later on, he also helped in the setting of the Department of Sociology at Delhi University. However, he went to Oxford afterwards but he did not stay much and left in 1951. He joined the Institute of Social and Economic Change at Bangalore after leaving Delhi School of Economics. Srinivas was one of the few who preferred to be a professor and remained one all his life rather than accepting the offer of joining the powerful and prestigious post in the government.

## Theoretical and Methodological Perspectives

Srinivas has initiated the tradition of macro-sociological generalizations on micro-anthropological insights and of giving a sociological sweep and perspective to anthropological investigations of small-scale communities (Joshi, 2000). Srinivas wanted to understand his countrymen not on the basis of western textbooks or from indigenous sacred texts but from direct observation, field study and field experience. He made intensive field study of Coorgs between 1940–42. In his study, he describes the concept of functional unity by explaining the interaction in ritual context of different castes of Coorgs, mainly Brahmins (priests), Kaniyas (astrologers and magicians) and Bannas and Panikas (low castes). In the context of the study of Rampura also, he describes that the various castes in a village are interdependent.

Srinivas studies of caste and religion (1952, 1959, 1962, and 1966) highlighted not only their structural-functional aspects, but also the dynamics of the caste system in rural setting. He proposed conceptual tools like 'dominant caste', 'sanskritization-westernization' and 'secularization' to understand the realities of inter-caste relations and also to explain their dynamics. The concept of 'dominant caste' has been used in the study of power relations at the village level. Srinivas (1960) presents the results of a number of studies on the structure and change in the village society. Srinivas has written articles in the 1940s on Tamil and Telgu folk-songs.

Srinivas explains two basic concepts to understand our society. They are: (a) book view, and (b) field view.

(a) Book view (bookish perspective): Religion, *varna*, caste, family, village and geographical structure are the main elements, which are known as the bases of Indian society. The knowledge about such elements is gained through sacred texts or from books. Srinivas calls it book view or bookish perspective. Book view is also known as Indology, which is not acceptable to Srinivas and he emphasized to the field view.
(b) Field view (field work): Srinivas believes that the knowledge about the different regions of Indian society can be attained through field work. This he calls field view. Consequently, he prefers empirical study to understand our society. Srinivas took the path of small regional studies rather than the construction of grand theories. In this context, field work plays an important role to understand the nativity of the rural Indian society.

Srinivas also realized the need for a mathematical and statistical orientation in sociology. His self-analysis (1973) underlines this point. There are cogent reasons of both an ideological and a practical nature which explain why the secondary level of analysis described above is not usually pursued by scholars. The practical considerations are easy to detect. Perhaps, more in the past than at present, the fear of mathematics drive many brilliant and diligent scholars to the 'humanistic' disciplines like sociology.

## Writings of Srinivas

Srinivas has written on many aspects of Indian society and culture. He is best known for his work on religion, village community, caste and social change He was influenced by Radcliffe-Brown's notion of structure, who was his teacher at Oxford. He studied Indian society as a 'totality', a study which would integrate "the various groups in its interrelationship, whether tribes, peasants or various cults and sects" (Patel, 1998). His writings are based on intensive field work in South India in general and Coorgs and Rampura in particular (Shah, 1996). Srinivas produced outstanding works, for instance:

1. *Marriage and Family in Mysore* (1942)
2. *Religion and Society Among the Coorgs of South India* (1952)
3. *India's Villages* (1955)
4. *Caste in Modern India and Other Essays* (1962)
5. *Social Change in Modern India* (1966)
6. *The Remembered Village* (1976)
7. *India: Social Structure* (1980)
8. *The Dominant Caste and Other Essays* (1987)
9. *The Cohesive Role of Sanskritization* (1989)
10. *On Living in a Revolution and Other Essays* (1992)
11. *Village, Caste, Gender and Method* (1996)
12. *Indian Society through Personal Writings* (1996)

Srinivas has also written many other important essays including 'On Living in a Revolution' (1986), 'Some Reflections on Dowry' (1984), 'The Insider and the Outsider in the Study of Cultures' (1984) – all illuminating dimensions of ongoing social change in India. Thus, Srinivas' writings are interdisciplinary in nature. We would like to discuss here on the following themes of Srinivas' contribution:

1. Social change: Brahminization, sanskritization, westernization and secularization
2. Religion and society
3. Study of village
4. Views on caste
5. Dominant caste

### Social Change

'Social change' as a theme continues to be a significant concern of Indian sociologists and social anthropologists. This holds true not only for the pre-1950 phase but also for post-1950 period. Srinivas (1966) attempted to construct a macro-level analysis using a large number of micro-level findings on the processes of 'sanskritization', 'westernization' and 'secularization'. Interestingly enough, Srinivas returned to his micro-empirical setting – a village – after nearly a quarter of century and in a diachronic frame highlighted the nature of social change in that village over a period of time (Srinivas, 1977).

## *Religion and Society*

Srinivas' work *Religion and Society among the Coorgs of South India* (1952) led him to formulate the concept of 'Brahminization' to represent the process of the imitation of life-ways and ritual practices of Brahmins by the lower-caste Hindus. The concept was used as an explanatory device to interpret changes observed in the ritual practices and life-ways of the lower castes through intensive and careful field study. The notion of Brahminization, however, had implicit possibilities of further abstraction into a higher level concept, 'sanskritization', which Srinivas introduced because his own field data and those of many others indicated limitations of using only Brahminic model as frame of reference. Later, sanskritization, as a concept, thus, replaced Brahminization at a more abstract level.

Srinivas achieved this through enlarging the meaning of sanskritization and by distinguishing it from another concept, westernization, using both terms in a systematic manner to explain the processes of social change in India. This conceptual scheme, though referring mainly to the processes of cultural imitation, has a built-in structural notion, that of hierarchy and inequality of privilege and power, since the imitation is always by the castes or categories placed lower in social and economic status. We find a systematic formulation of the two concepts in Srinivas' *Social Change in Modern India* (1966), wherein he defines 'sanskritization' as the process by which a 'low' caste or tribe or other group takes over the custom, ritual, beliefs, ideology and style of life of a high and, in particular, a 'twice-born' (*dwija)* caste. The sanskritization of a group has usually the effect of improving its position in the local caste hierarchy. The major emphasis in study of social change through concepts of sanskritization and westernization and of the levels of traditions is on the changes in cultural styles, customs and ritual practices. There are, however, some presuppositions in the processes of both sankritization and westernization, which do imply precedent or concomitant structural changes, such as improvement in economic position of the sanskritizing caste, superiority and dominance of the caste being emulated and psychological disenchantment among the low castes from their own position in the caste hierarchy. Nonetheless, sanskritization brought changes within the framework of Indian tradition whereas westernization was a change resulting from the contact of British socio-economic and cultural innovations. Along with these concepts, Srinivas has used the term 'secularization' to denote the process of institutional innovations and ideological formulation after independence to deal with the question of religious groups and minorities. This became a national ideology.

Srinivas considers village as the microcosm of Indian society and civilization. It is the village, which retains the traditional composition of India's tradition. Srinivas occupies an eminent place among the first-generation sociologists of India. He belongs to the galaxy of G.S. Ghurye, R.K. Mukherjee, N.K. Bose and D.P. Mukerji. He conducted field work among the Coorgs and came out with his publication, *Religion and Society among the Coorgs of South India* (1952). Dumont and Pocock consider the book as a classic in India's sociology. It is in this work that Srinivas provides a basic structure of India's traditions. T.N. Madan hails the publication in these words:

> The strength of the *Coorgs* lies in its being firmly grounded in a clearly defined theoretical framework which happened to be essentially the one developed by Radcliffe-Brown who suggested the theme of the dissertation to Srinivas. *Religion and Society* is a very lucid exposition of the complex interrelationship between ritual and social order in Coorg society. It also deals at length and insightfully with crucial notions of purity and pollution as also with the process of incorporation of non-Hindu communities and cults in the Hindu social order and way of life.

In *Religion and Society*, Srinivas was concerned with the spread of Hinduism. He talked about 'Sanskritic Hinduism' and its values. Related to this was the notion of 'sanskritization' which Srinivas employed "to describe the process of the penetration of sanskritic values into the remotest parts of India. Imitation of the way of life of the topmost, twice-born castes was said to be the principle mechanism by which lower castes sought to raise their own social status". Curiously, Srinivas did not take up for consideration the phenomenon of the persistence of the masses of Hindus of low or no status within the caste system. For him, the most significant aspect of the history of the Coorgs, worthy of being recorded, was the history of this incorporation into the Hindu social order. Srinivas thinks that the only meaningful social change is that which takes place among the weaker sections for attaining higher status by imitating values of twice-born. And, those of the lower castes and tribal groups, who fail in this race of imitation, are doomed to remain backward. Srinivas spells the doom as below:

> Splinter groups like Amma Coorgs are decades, if not centuries, in advance of their parent groups; the former have solved this problem by sanskritizing their customs entirely while the latter are more conservative.

What Srinivas spells out about the imitating lower castes seems to be the announcement of a new age. If we attempt to identify traditions of Indian society, according to Srinivas, these are found among the higher castes – the twice-born. In other words, the traditions, rituals and beliefs, which are held and shared by the Brahmins, the Baniyas and the Rajputs, constitute Indian traditions. And, the beliefs of the lower sections of society, the untouchables and the tribals, do not have any status as tradition. For him, Indian traditions are high-caste Hindu traditions, lower-caste traditions are no Indian traditions. Obviously, but he anchors tradition into sanskritization, Srinivas was actually interested in caste. He considered it to be the 'structural bases of Hinduism'. He was not fascinated by Hinduism in its holistic form. He looked for it in the caste system. Thus, his thesis of Indian traditions runs something like this: "Indian traditions are Hindu traditions, and Hindu traditions are found in caste system. Holistic Hinduism is beyond his scope of discourse."

### *Study of Village*

Besides religion and caste, the third tradition component of Srinivas' study is village. Srinivas got the seed idea of studying India's villages from his mentor Radcliffe-Brown in 1945–46. When settled in India after his return from Oxford, he conducted the study of Rampur – a Mysore village – which gave him the concept of 'dominant caste'. The study has been contained in *The Remembered Village* (1976), it is here only that Srinivas takes some time to discuss social and economic changes, which have taken place in Rampura. He informs:

> Technological change occupied a prominent place in the life of the people of Rampura soon after independence. Technological change, of course, went hand in hand with economic, political and cultural changes.

The main aim of Srinivas has been to understand Indian society. And, for him, Indian society is essentially a caste society. He has studied religion, family, caste and village in India. He was a functionalist and was influenced by Radcliffe-Brown, Robert Redfield and Evans Pritchard. These anthropologists were functionalists of higher stature. Ideologically, they believed in status quo: let the Dalits survive and let the high castes enjoy their hegemony over subaltern. Srinivas' search for the identity of traditions makes him infer that the Indian traditions are found in caste, village and religion. For him, it appears that Indian social structure is on par with the advocates of *Hindutva*, say, the cultural nationalism.

Srinivas though talks about economic and technological development, all through his works he pleads for change in caste, religion and family. Even in the study of these areas he sidetracks lower segments of society. They are like 'untouchables' for him. Srinivas has extensively talked about the social evils of the caste society, he pleads for change in caste system and discusses westernization and modernization as viable paradigms of changes.

But his perspective of change is Brahminical Hinduism or traditionalism. In his zeal for promoting sanskritization, he has marginalized and alienated religious minorities. For him, Indian traditions are those, which are manifested in caste and village. His traditions are Hinduized traditions, and in no sense secular ones. Srinivas, in a straightforward way, rejects secularism and stands in favour of Hindu traditions. In his critique of Indian secularism, which appeared in a short article in the *Times of India* in 1993, he finds secularism wanting because he believes that India needs a new philosophy to solve the cultural and spiritual crises facing the country and that philosophy cannot be secular humanism. It has to be firmly rooted in God as creator and protector. Srinivas' construction of sanskritization and dominant caste put him closer to *Hindutva* ideology of cultural nationalism. At this stage of discussion, Doshi (2003) comments regarding India's traditions, it can be said that any tradition emanating from caste system cannot be nation's tradition as the constitution has rejected caste.

Srinivas' widely known classic, *The Remembered Village*, has all the qualities of a classic novel on changing village in a part of South India. Srinivas has portrayed the character types in 'Three Important Men of Village Rampura': the village headman and the landlord of the old type; the broker between village and the outside world, Kulle Gowda; and the powerful enterprising landlord of the new type, Nadu Gowda.

Srinivas concentrated on the study of some vital aspects of Hindu society and culture and his study did it explore the dimensions of interaction and interface between the Hindu and non-Hindu segments. The area that he studied did not have a large non-Hindu presence. He hoped that other sociologists would take up the study of the non-Hindu segments of Indian society and culture without which an Indian sociology, Indian in the sense of being comprehensive and authentic and hence truly representative of the plurality and complexity of India, would not emerge. In this context, Joshi (2000) viewed that Srinivas' self-definition and self-perception was never that of a Hindu sociologist but that of an Indian sociologist studying Hindu religion and its social institutions in a specific area through intensive fieldwork at the ground level.

### *Views on Caste*

Srinivas views caste as a segmentary system. Every caste, for him, is divided into sub-castes which are:

1. the unit of endogamy;
2. whose members follow a common occupation;
3. the units of social and ritual life;
4. whose members share a common culture; and
5. whose members are governed by the same authoritative body, viz., the panchayat?

Besides these factors of the sub-caste, for Srinivas, certain other attributes are also important. These are:

1. *Hierarchy:* To Srinivas, hierarchy is the core or the essence of the caste system. It refers to the arrangements of hereditary groups in a rank order. He points out that it is status of the top-most or Brahmins and the bottom-most or untouchables, which is the clearest in terms of rank. The middle regions of hierarchy are the most flexible, who may be defined as members of the middle ranks.
2. *Occupational differentiation:* Srinivas finds a close relationship between a caste and its occupation. He says that caste is nothing more the "systematization of occupational differentiation". Castes are known by their occupations and many derive their name from the occupation followed, e.g., Lohar, Sunar, Kumhar, Teli, Chamar etc. He also stresses that occupations are placed in a hierarchy of high and low.
3. *Restrictions* on commensality, dress, speech and custom are also found among castes. There is a dietic hierarchy and restrictions on acceptance of food.
4. *Pollution:* The distance between castes is maintained by the principles of pollution. Srinivas too argues that the castes must not come into contact with anything that is polluted whether an object or being. Any contact with polluted renders a caste impure and demands that the polluted caste undergo

purification rites. If pollution is serious such as when a high caste person has sexual relations with an untouchable, the person involved may be removed from his or her caste.

5. *Caste Panchayats and Assemblies:* Besides the above mentioned attributes of a caste, every caste is subject to the control of an order maintaining body or a Panchayat. Elder of each caste in a village together maintain the social order by exercising their authority collectively. Further, every caste member is answerable to the authority of its Caste Assembly. The authority of a Caste Assembly may extend beyond village boundaries to include in its jurisdiction of caste in other villages.

From the above, we can infer that the attributes of a caste definitely determined the nature of inter-caste relations. These attributes or customs of caste also determine the rank of a caste. This becomes obvious in the work of Srinivas on caste mobility or sanskritization.

### Sanskritization

We have seen above that how every caste is assigned in the caste rank order on the basis of the purity and impurity of its attributes. In his study of a Mysore village, Srinivas finds that at some time or the other, every caste tries to change its rank in the hierarchy by giving up its attributes and trying to adopt those of castes above them. This process of attempting to change one's rank by giving up attributes that define a caste as low and adopting attributes that are indicative of higher status is called 'sanskritization'. This process essentially involves a change in one's dietary habits from non-vegetarianism to vegetarianism, and a change in one's occupation habits from an 'unclean' to a 'clean' occupation. The attributes of a caste become the basis of interaction between castes. The creation of pattern of interaction and interrelations is best expressed in Srinivas' use of the concept of 'dominant caste'.

### Idea of Dominant Caste

Besides caste, Srinivas looks for yet another source or manifestation of tradition. He found it in the notion of 'dominant caste'. He first proposed it in his early papers on the village of Rampura. The concept has been discussed and applied to a great deal in work on social and political organization in India. He had defined dominant caste in terms of six attributes placed in conjunction:

(1) sizeable amount of arable land;
(2) strength of numbers;
(3) high place in the local hierarchy;
(4) western education;
(5) jobs in the administration; and
(6) urban sources of income.

Of the above attributes of the dominant caste, the following three are important: (i) numerical strength, (ii) economic power through ownership of land, and (iii) political power. Accordingly, a dominant caste is any caste that has all three of the above attributes in a village community. The interesting aspect of this concept is that the ritual ranking of a caste no longer remains the major basis of its position in the social hierarchy. Even if a caste stands low in the social hierarchy because of being ranked low, it can become the dominant ruling caste or group in a village if it is numerically large, owns land and has political influence over village matters. There is no doubt that a caste with relatively higher in ritual rank would probably find it easier to become dominant. But this is not the case always.

We take an example from the village Rampura in Mysore to illustrate the above. In this village, there are a number of castes including Brahmins, peasants and untouchables. The peasants are ritually ranked below the Brahmins, but they own lands and numerically preponderant and have political influence over village affairs. Consequently, we find that despite their low ritual rank, the peasants are the dominant caste in the village. All the other castes of the village stand in a relationship of service to the dominant caste, i.e., they are at the back of the dominant caste.

Srinivas was criticized for this concept with the charge that it was smuggled from the notion of dominance, which emerged from African sociology. Repudiating the critique, Srinivas asserted that the idea of dominant caste given by him had its origin in the field work of Coorgs of South India. His field work had impressed upon him that communities, such as the Coorgs and the Okkaligas, wielded considerable power at the local level and shared such social attributes as numerical preponderance, economic strength and clean ritual status. He further noted that the dominant caste could be a local source of sankritization, or a barrier to its spread. Sanskritization and dominant caste are therefore representation of Indian tradition. And, in this conceptual framework, the traditions of the lower castes and Dalits have no place, nowhere in village India; the subaltern groups occupy the status of dominant caste.

## Criticism

The life mission of Srinivas has been to understand Indian society. He though talks about economic and technological development but in the study of these areas sidetracks lower segments of society. In his endeavour for promoting sanskritization, he has marginalized and alienated religious minorities. For him, Indian traditions are those, which are manifested in caste and village. His traditions are Hinduized traditions and in no sense secular ones. The construction of sanskritization and dominant caste put him closer to *Hindutva* ideology of cultural nationalism. One can say that his understanding was more elitist or presents only upper caste view.

The indigenous concepts of social change prevailing among sociologists in the 1950s and, to a large extent also in the 1960s were formulated by M.N. Srinivas under the labels 'sanskritization' and 'westernization', which he regarded as "limited processes in modern India and it is not possible to understand one without reference to the other" (see *Caste in Modern India*, 1966: 8–9). Srinivas had evolved the concept of sanskritization while preparing his doctoral dissertation under the guidance of Radcliffe-Brown and Evans Pritchard at Oxford (1952). He finally formulated the concept as denoting the process by which a 'low' Hindu caste or tribal or other group, changes its customs, rituals, ideology, and way of life in the direction of a high and frequently 'twice-born caste'.

In 1956 Srinivas posited the concept of westernization as follows: "The British conquest of India set free a number of forces – political, economic, social and technological ... (which) affected the country's social and cultural life profoundly and at every point, and that the withdrawal of the British from India not only did not mean the cessation of these forces but, meant on the contrary, their intensification" (Srinivas, 1966: 53).

Now, as a summary of certain characteristics spontaneously observable in society, these concepts cannot claim any originality (Mukherjee 1979: 50). What Srinivas characterized as sanskritization in the idiom of sociology currently fashionable, had been described by the proto-sociologists Lyall and Risley as 'Aryanization' and 'Brahminization', as mentioned by Mukherjee in the first chapter of his book *Sociology of Indian Sociology* (1979). Possibly, sanskritization is a more precise expression of the process under reference, as is claimed by Srinivas who does not deny the antecedents to his concept (Srinivas, 1962: 42–43). Similarly, the process of westernization was noted by several proto-sociologists mentioned by Mukherjee (1979) and described in virtually the same manner as done by Srinivas.

The pioneers also were not unaware of the two processes and took particular note of them in the context of their respective value preferences, theoretical formulations and research orientation (e.g., Coomaraswamy and D.P. Mukerji). The two processes have, respectively, two levels of meaning – 'historic-specific' and 'contextual-specific', as Yogendra Singh has remarked regarding sanskritization (1973: 6) and Milton Singer had noted earlier (1959: 179).

## Conclusion

Srinivas occupies an eminent place among the first-generation sociologists of India. His focus on 'field view' over the 'book view' is a remarkable step in understanding the reality of Indian society. This reflects sociology of nativity. His field work among the Coorgs relates his approach as structural-functional and represents an exposition of the complex interrelationship between ritual and social order in Coorg society. It also deals with the crucial notion of purity and pollution as also with the process of incorporation of non-Hindu communities into the Hindu social order. This refers to the concept of 'sanskritization' which he used to describe the process of the penetration of Sanskritic values into the remotest parts of India.

## Srinivas' Framework Summarized

### *Background*

1. Educated and training in sociology.
2. Academic career at Bombay, Baroda, Delhi, Bangalore and Oxford.
3. His interest in understanding the rural social life.

### *Aim*

1. Dynamics of caste system in rural setting

### *Assumptions*

1. Structure and change.
2. The tradition of basing macro-sociological generalizations on micro-anthropological insights.
3. To understand his countrymen not on the basis of western textbooks or from indigenous sacred texts but from direct observation, field study and field experience.

### *Approach*

1. Structural-functional approach
2. Macro-micro perspective

### *Methodology*

1. Anthropological investigations of small-scale communities
2. Functional unity
3. Field investigations
4. Descriptive study

### *Typology*

1. Dominant caste
2. Brahminization
3. Sanskritization
4. Westernization
5. Secularization

### *Issues*

Different aspects of Indian society and culture:

1. Indian society and culture
2. Religion and society
3. Village study
4. Inter-caste relations
5. Social change

## Select Bibliography

Doshi, S.L. (2003), *Modernity, Postmodernity and Neo-Sociological Theories*, Jaipur: Rawat Publications.

Joshi, P.C. (2000), 'Remembering M.N. Srinivas', *Sociological Bulletin*, Vol. 49, No. 1.

Madan, T.N. (1994), *Pathways*, New Delhi: Oxford University Press.

Misra, P.K., K.K. Basa and H.K. Bhat, (2007), *M.N. Srinivas: The Man and His Work*, Jaipur: Rawat Publications.

Oommen, T.K. and P.N. Mukherji (1986), *Indian Sociology: Reflections and Introspections,* Mumbai: Popular Prakashan.

Patel, S. (1998), 'The Nostalgia for the Village: M.N. Srinivas and Making of Indian Social Anthropology', *South Asia*, Vol. 21, No. 1, pp. 49–61.

Shah, A.M. et al. (1996), *Social Structure and Change*, New Delhi: Sage Publications.

Singh, Yogendra (1986), 'Indian Sociology', *Current Sociology*, Vol. 34, No. 2.

—— (1994), *Modernization of Indian Tradition*, Jaipur: Rawat Publication.

Srinivas, M.N. (1952), *Religion and Society among the Coorgs of South India*, Oxford: Oxford Clarendon Press.

—— (1955), *India's Village*, Bombay: Asia Publishing House.

—— (1966), *Social Change in Modern India,* Bombay: Allied Publishers.

# 9

# S.C. Dube

Shyama Charan Dube (1922–1996) is a well-known anthropologist and sociologist in India. His application of the structural-functional approach for studying the Indian village community brought him in repute. Although he recognizes semi-autonomous character of the Indian village, he does not regard it as "static, timeless and changeless". He viewed that it is difficult to say any one village as representative of rural India as a whole; it cannot be representative in its cultural area. His study of Shamirpet provides description of social, economic and ritual structure, family level living etc.

S.C. Dube was born on 25th July, 1922 at Narsinghpur in Madhya Pradesh and passed away on 4th February, 1996 at the age of 73 years. Dube took his Master's degree from Nagpur University in Political Science and then proceeded to undertake research among the Kamar – a tribe of shifting cultivators in Madhya Pradesh. He has taught social anthropology and sociology at universities in India and abroad. He started his professional career as a lecturer at Bishop College, Nagpur, Maharashtra. Later, he joined the Department of Political Science in Lucknow University.

While teaching there, he got the book on *Kamar* published, and improved upon his anthropological readings through interactions with D.N. Majumdar, whom he assisted in the early stages of the publication of the journal *Eastern Anthropologist*. Then, he moved to Osmania University, Hyderabad as a reader to take the place of Von Furer Haimendorf in the Department of Sociology. He also went to the School of Oriental and African Studies (SOAS) and the London School of Economics. The interaction with academics including Raymond Firth who helped him in shaping the book on *Indian Village*. He was gifted speaker in English and Hindi.

Dube quit the Osmania University to become Deputy Director in the Anthropological Survey of India at Nagpur and later Professor of Anthropology in the University of Saugar in Madhya Pradesh. He had been very active on different positions. In the beginning, he was an advisor for National Institute of (Rural) Community Development. During 1972–1977, he was Director at Indian Institute of Advanced Studies, Shimla. In 1975–76, he was President of Indian Sociological Society. In 1978–80, he was also Vice-Chancellor of Jammu University. In 1980–93, he had been ICSSR National Fellow and also occupied important positions in UNESCO and UNO. He was also Chairman of Madhya Pradesh University Grants Commission.

## Theoretical and Methodological Approach

S.C. Dube, basically a product of Lucknow, played a key role in his study on India's Changing Villages. His later writings also maintained the same insight into India's social reality, gained from a macro-perspective, while simultaneously demanding precision in theoretical formulations and empirical verification of these propositions, e.g., *The Study of Complex Cultures* (1965), *Explanation and Management of Changes* (1971), *Contemporary India and its Modernization* (1974). Dube has all through been an ardent advocate of interdisciplinary orientation and a promoter of research interest. Thus, he had vision of looking things from different perspectives, which reflects his multidimensional personality. Commenting on the personality of Dube, Yogesh Atal writes: "Dube has constantly been on the move both geographically and intellectually. Rather than harping on the same theme and concentrating on a narrow speciality, he chose the challenging task of exploring new territory and extending the frontier of knowledge."

Dube (1965) proposed a more comprehensive frame of reference for the study of 'complex cultures' to understand Indian reality. He applied deductive-positivistic rather than inductive-inferential approach, based on null situation, like 'no change in modern India' or 'India's unchanging villages'.

Dube's *Indian Village* (1955) was a significant work in the post-1950 period in the sense that it was the first full-length account of a village social structure. Dube depicted rural social structure and institutions in his characteristically lucid style, and the work served as a model for descriptive-exploratory account of several other macro-settings that came to be studied later. But he did not offer any analytical insights, nor did he propose any alternative conceptual framework for studying Indian rural society (Dhanagare, 1993: 53–54).

Dube's interest in rural studies grew steadily largely because of the acceptance of the Community Development Programme (CDP) by the Government of India. This necessitated a shift from 'structure' to 'change' in India's villages as reflected in his other pioneering work, *India's Changing Villages* (1958).

## Works of Dube

S.C. Dube has contributed on a variety of themes including tribes, rural life, community development, modernization, management of change and tradition and development over the next 30 years. In a way, he has written on many aspects of Indian society and culture. The main works of Dube are as follows:

1. *The Kamar; Indian Village* (1955)
2. *India's Changing Villages* (1958)
3. *Institution Building for Community Development* (1968)
4. *Contemporary India and Its Modernization* (1974)
5. *Tribal Heritage of India* (1977)
6. *Understanding Society* (1977)
7. *Modernization and Development* (1988)

8. *Tradition and Development* (1990)
9. *Understanding Change* (1990)
10. *Indian Society* (1990)

He has also written some books in Hindi. They are *Manav evam Sanskrati, Bhartiya Gram, Vikas ka Samajshasta, and Sankraman ki Peera*. He was also the general editor of *Bhartiya Samaj Parichaya Mala*, etc.

Besides the above books, Dube contributed nearly two dozen papers in volumes edited by national and international sociologists and anthropologists. He has also published several research articles in renowned journals of the country and abroad.

Thus, Dube's works are multidisciplinary in nature. But, here, we would like to discuss the following themes:

1. Tribal society
2. Village study
3. Community development programme
4. Modernization and development
5. Political sociology
6. Indian society

### Tribal Society

Dube studied Kamar – a Scheduled Tribe of Madhya Pradesh – as part of his doctoral research. His first book on *Kamar* (1951) is a full-length study on one of the tribes of middle India.

### Village Study

Dube's another book on *Indian Village*, first published in 1955, was a milestone in the study of Indian society. In this book, he made a significant contribution in understanding the Indian society through structural-functional perspective. Writing in a lucid style, Dube brought out in this book the essence of life in an Indian village. While examining the village selected for his study he says that one must examine the various units through which the village community is organized.

The nature of study was interdisciplinary. It was sponsored and financed by the Social Service Extension Project of Osmania

University in 1951–52 which Dube directed. The study was conducted at the village *Shamirpet*, located at a distance of nearly 25 miles from Hyderabad. The village had a population of 2,494 including 340 Muslims and 19 ethnic groups belonging to Hindus. The field data were collected from historical, geographical, political and sociological perspectives on different aspects of social, economic and religious practices of village in India, which reflect an integrated picture of the village.

Dube describes a Deccan village in India in 1955 on the same lines which Robert Redfield conducted his first village study in Mexico in 1930. Many of his conclusions could provide the first insight into the complex web of Indian village life. He observes: "No village in India is completely autonomous and independent, for it is always one unit in a wider social system and is a part of an organized political society. An individual is not the member of a village community alone, he also belongs to a caste, religious group or a tribe with a wider territorial spread and comprises several villages. These units have their own organization, authority and sanctions."

The study presents a comprehensive picture of the functioning of village institutions although it is one of the earliest monographs on a village. Dube asserts that the economic system of rural India is founded mainly on caste's functional specialization, interdependence and occupational mobility. He also observes that the elements of classical Hinduism of an all-India spread are mingled with the regional religious beliefs and practices of Hindus of Deccan Plateau. Three major types of religious services and festivals are observed in the village. They are:

1. family ceremonies,
2. village familial and communal festivals, and
3. the Muslims and Hindus interaction with each other during festivals.

Dube provides a short account of worldview, inter-group relations, inter-caste attitude and stereotypes. He also discusses the three most significant stages of life, namely, childhood, youth and old age in a generalized biography.

### *India's Changing Villages*

As stated earlier, Dube's interest in rural studies grew steadily largely because of the acceptance of the Community Development Programme (CDP) by the Government of India. When the CDPs were launched in India, the book on *Indian Village* had become a landmark study. Then, Dube made the obvious choice to evaluate the CDP under the Cornell (India) Project in Saharanpur district of western Uttar Pradesh.

As Visiting Professor of Anthropology and Far Eastern Studies at Cornell, the next year, Dube wrote a book based on that study. This book, titled *India's Changing Villages: Human Factors in Community Development*, was published by a well-known publisher – Routledge and Kegan Paul in 1958. With this Dube became a recognized authority in planned change and development. In this book, Dube studied the impact of CDPs on Indian villages. He also pointed out the importance of human elements in community development. Simultaneously, he evaluated the changes and problems emerged from these programmes. He also described different traditions of India and their functional role in public life. He explained the meaning and characteristics of modernization.

### *Indian Village: Structure, Function and Change*

Dube conducted a descriptive study of the village Shamirpet, which is situated at a distance of about 25 miles from the twin cities of Hyderabad and Secunderabad in Andhra Pradesh in the Deccan Plateau of India. It is an outcome of the Social Service Extension Project, sponsored by the Department of Sociology and Anthropology. His aim has been to present a clear picture of an Indian village life and has basically used structural-functional approach. The book deals with the following aspects:

1. The setting, which includes the description of the village, the people, housing pattern, the neighbourhood etc.
2. Social structure, which includes:
   (a) Caste, inter-caste and inter-village organization. All the castes are endogamous and there is a permanent social

distance between them. In general, people on higher level refuse food from those on a lower level. Occupation of each caste is monopolized and sanctioned by religion. Dube found that persons belonging to different castes are united by common values and obligations.

(b) The Hindus and the Muslims constitute two distinct groups, who retain their own socio-religious identities.

(c) Internal organization of the village in terms of two different units, i.e., the socio-religious organization and administrative organization of government and semi-government officials. He observes women in terms of five activities, i.e., (i) domestic work, (ii) agriculture, (iii) festivals and ceremonies, (iv) birth, marriage and death, and (v) village administration and politics.

3. Economic structure: The main economic functions and activities of the major caste groups in the village are traditionally specified. However, agriculture is the main occupation of the villagers. They also keep cattle and domestic animals for their livelihood. For example, cows and she-buffaloes are kept for milk. Poultry is pursued by all sections of the village population except the Brahmins and the Komatis. Hunting, fishing, collection of fruits, medical herbs, roots, tubers and barks are the other pursuits. Villagers are also engaged in other non-agricultural occupations, which include the potter, the carpenter, the blacksmith, the barber, the washerman, and the menial servant etc.

4. Ritual structure includes folklore, myths, religious teaching of saints/poets and contacts with persons having knowledge of scriptures and popular religious books, animism, polytheism, and even monotheism also, beliefs, ghosts, demons, witches and magic. Dube describes: “The complex of these diverse factors constitutes the picture of the supernatural world ...”.

5. The web of family ties reflects the structure of the family. The patrilineal and patrilocal nuclear or joint family unit is the main aspect of the rural India. Dube also describes interpersonal relations within the family.

6. The Levels of Living: The levels of living of the people are discussed in terms of status differentiation in the community, standard of living, division of labour in terms of work and diet. He recognized that six factors contribute in terms of status differentiation: (i) religion and caste, (ii) landownership, (iii) wealth, (iv) position in government service and village organization, (v) age, and (vi) distinctive personality patterns.
7. Regarding *standard of living*, Dube categorizes people on the basis of their perception into four levels, which are recognized by people as (i) rich, (ii) well-to-do, (iii) average, and (iv) poor. Other ways through which one can differentiate between the standard of living of people such as type of dwelling and household possessions, clothing and ornament are also taken into account.

## Indian Society

Dube's book on *Indian Society* (1990) draws upon various sources in looking at the past and the present of Indian society. The growth of India's diversities and unities is traced through its complex history. The functioning, over the centuries, of *varna* and *jati* and of family and kinship is examined in urban and rural contexts, and gender relations are similarly treated. Naturally enough, this account of creation of today's India is followed by a brief assessment of ongoing and likely changes.

### *Trends and Change*

Contemporary Indian society has several contradictions with some extremely puzzling aspects. In a sea of mass poverty, it has some islands of dazzling prosperity. It boasts of its spirituality, but its elite – the rich and the powerful – set standards of ostentatious consumption that seem downright unethical.

In the pre- and early 'Jagir' period in Shamirpet, the contacts between village people and the state administration were on a very limited scale, and were confined mostly to payment of land revenue and settlement of land disputes. In the second half of 'Jagir' period these administrative contacts increased very considerably.

The police action undertaken by the Indian Union in 1948 changed the fortune and status of the state of Hyderabad. The first definite change is that Muslims who occupied a privileged position during the former regime now no longer do so. The second noticeable change is that under the administration, forced labour and forced extraction of hospitability by government officials have been prohibited. Thirdly, the abolition of feudal estates has been a big step in the direction of land reform. Fourthly, the government has intensified its welfare and nation-building activities. Finally, there has been considerable political activity in the rural areas by the political parties, culminating in the first general election of December 1951.

The state administration initiated some of its welfare and nation-building activities in the countryside. There has been very noticeable change in the dress and ornaments of the village people. There has also been much change in the list of articles of daily requirement. Several new varieties of entertainments are now available to the village people side by side with the traditional recreations of gossip, loafing and playing indigenous games.

The opening of small dispensary in the village and the availability of excellent facilities of modern medical treatment in the city have considerably changed the attitude of the people towards them and their treatment The social structure of the community is basically the same, although with every administrative or political change in the village.

### *Society: Continuity and Change*

The reason for change must be sought in a multiplicity of factors. So far state compulsion has been instrumental in bringing about little social and cultural change in the village community. The factors of utility, convenience and availability have played a more important role in bringing several new elements into the life of the community.

There were several organizational changes too. In the organization of the family, the changed conditions and changing attitudes of the people have brought about some significant variations. The caste system in the community presents only slight variations in some directions. Traditionally, the membership of the village council is hereditary and should be inherited by the eldest male child on the death of the father. At present, the government officials residing within the village discretely pull the strings and exert pressure on the council to secure favourable judgement in certain cases in which for some reason they happen to be interested. In place of their traditional occupations, people have started accepting other vocations.

The family has been under some stress and bonds of kinship are no longer as strong and cohesive as they used to be. However, what is often described as the 'joint family' was never the norm in Indian society: it was confined to some *jatis* in villages and small towns. Even among them, complete two-or-three-generation extended families were rare. But it is among these *jatis* that one finds a trend towards nuclearization of the family. Several factors account for the erosion of the family and kinship networks – modern education, new occupations, geographical mobility, impact of mass media, and so forth. Greater freedom of choice in marriage also makes living in large joint households non-viable. However, in important rituals and ceremonies, the extended family and kin groups demonstrate their solidarity and stand together.

Adoption of several new tools and instruments for occupational works, as well as of several other items of western technology, such as buses, railways, razors and electric torches introduced in the comparatively recent times which reflect their efficiency and utility. Communications too have now imported.

The influence of the city has brought about adjustment and modification in several spheres, but the need of balancing different extremes in the organization of the community has so far prevented any drastic structural change in village communities. Viewing the country broadly, we find three major trends:

(1) the regional culture, founded on the traditions, customs and life-ways of the culture area;
(2) the national culture, comprising some all-India traits inspired by the national renaissance, cemented by the struggle for

self-government as well as by social and economic reform and sustained by the will to find a rightful place in the community of nations; the elements in this category being partly revivalists and partly conscious innovations; and

(3) adoption of traits and elements from western technology and culture. Traditional social institutions and culture, traditions and life-ways are idealized: they originated long ago when man first appeared on the earth and the salvation of people lies in their faithful observation of these divinely ordained ways. The focus is local and regional, confined to family, kin, caste and some neighbouring village. The fundamental drive in the thought and activities of the group seems to be towards the goal of the adjustment of the individual to the universe. In interpersonal as well as inter- and intra-group relations, the people tend to view everything as hierarchically structured. The fundamental concepts of the rights and equality of men mean little to these people, whose visions are thus bounded by their own observation of the world.

## Caste Ranking

Besides books on Indian village, Dube has also written a few papers on the village studies among whom mention may be made of one "Thinking of Castes in Telangana Village" published in the book, *Rural Profiles of India* edited by late Professor D.N. Majumdar (1955). To Dube, the fundamental principle of caste ranking is a concept of ritual purity and pollution. The caste ranking in Shamirpet is also determined by traditions and myths since caste is based on an ascribed system of status. Dube establishes that the occupations allowed based on the daily practices such as rituals, hierarchy of food eaten, observance of rules connected with life cycle rituals etc. determined ranks. He puts great emphasis that the main criterion used for caste ranking in village is ritual and not economic.

## Dominant Caste and Village Leadership

In his paper entitled, 'Dominant Caste and Village Leadership' presented at a seminar on Trends of Change in Village India, organized by Central Institute of Study and Research in Community Development, Mussoorie, in 1961, Dube adds to the concepts and methods of study of pattern of rural leadership in India. He finds the political power concentrated in few individuals rather than diffused in caste. In each village, there are some dominant individuals, who have decisive say in political participation of the members of a village. They play a significant role in settling disputes, guiding the youth force for maintaining unity in the village, and organizing the village for common celebration of festivals. Their roles can also be observed at the time of elections of Gram Panchayat, MLA and MP.

## Youth Culture

In his paper on, "The Restive Students: Strands and Themes in Contemporary Youth Culture" (1972), Dube objects to term Indian students or contemporary youth as an 'undifferentiated mass'. In the light of the differences in their background, orientation and outlook, he identifies four sub-cultures of the contemporary youth. These are:

1. the Indian counterpart of the Hippies,
2. the models coming from the Westernized and alienated families,
3. youths of the medium to low privileged status of society, and
4. the largest group consists of first generation of literates and those whose parents have not had the benefits of higher education.

## Modernization

Modernization is an extremely complex phenomenon, which involves a large number of interrelated changes of many different kinds. Dube deals with some of these in a sociological perspective. He considers the actual structural implications of change as well as the nature of some of the processes of change. Obstacles in the way of modernization, such as ill-balanced changes and rigid social norms, are given social attention.

India has been trying to modernize for the first twenty-five years of its independence and has had successes as well as failures. In his book on *Contemporary India and Its Modernization* (1974), Dube deals with subjects as diverse as bureaucracy, leadership, education, planning, and secularism. These perceptive essays have in common the fact that they attempt to analyse critically the country's successes and failures. The criticism is constructive since Dube follows an approach that is diagnostic and prescriptive.

Modern society is a rational and scientific. Dube identifies several components for constructing an adequate national framework for modernization. These are as follows:

1. The cohesive bonds of society must be strengthened. This can be done by encouraging consciously planned inter-regional and inter-ethnic interdependence, by secularizing political and economic participation, and by working for increasing acceptance of the legitimacy of the established authority. In this context, the close connection between legitimacy and credibility must be emphasized; the latter is determined in a substantial measure by visible performance.
2. Social restraint and social discipline are important. These depend partly on the credibility of the established authority and partly on the latter's capacity to deal effectively with economic trends of different types. Everyone, from the highest to lowest, should be subjected equally to the norms of restraint and discipline. Differential application of these norms causes distrust and often leads to an ambivalent attitude to authority.
3. The need for expertise, both in policy making and implementation, cannot be overemphasized. The administrative structures should be visualized as a series of independent and interpenetrating but specialized and differentiated roles. These considerations apply equally to the political sector.
4. The reward system should be structured that it encourages excellence of performance and curbs inefficiency and corruption. The cannons of public morality should be applied with equal rigour to politicians, to bureaucrats, and in fact everyone else.

Judged by these criteria, what has been India's performance after independence as viewed by Dube. There certainly has been a change in the structure of values and generally in the personality system, but this change is characterized by ambivalence both to tradition and modernity. Education and mass communication have played their part in promoting new values. A small section of India's population – the small elite and its satellites – which was more equipped to take advantage of the new opportunities and had the manipulative skills to make them more or less their preserve, profited from them, whereas poverty in the rural and urban areas has been constant over the years with 40 per cent of the population remaining below the poverty line.

The policy processes of the country are in a state of total disarray for want of expertise. Democracy, socialism and secularism have been adopted as the objectives of the state policy, but no plan with careful specification has been formulated. However, in many ways, the contemporary predicament of India can be attributed to certain global trends.

## Development

Dube, in his book *Modernization and Development* (1988), has divided the growth and diversification or specification of the concept of development into four phases.

In the first phase, development essentially meant economic development and economists focused their attention exclusively on economic growth.

In the second phase, the relationship between economic development and social change was more keenly realized and its consequences emphasized. Economic development and technological change was hindered by institutional factors. Thus, modification in the institutional framework of society and alternatives in the attitudes and values were to be contemplated to facilitate and accelerate the process of economic development. This revolution gave birth to modernization paradigm.

The third phase may be described a reactive and responsive one. It was born out of a strong reaction in the inadequate paradigm of development and modernization and responded positively to more successful praxis of development.

The fourth phase is a reflexive phase. One has to understand the world order and also the national orders. Both have to be altered if human social survival is too ensured.

The distributive aspects of economic growth and the diffusion of the benefits of modernization reflect the development. In fact, development that makes no visible change in the degraded lot of the common man – the majority in the country's population – is no development. Growth that permits a small segment of the society to wallow in vulgar high living is immoral. No country permitting 60 million children to remain undernourished can justifiably register the claim that it is modernizing. Then, there is a runaway unemployment. Fourteen million people are on the roster of the unemployed today. An estimate suggests that 8,000 persons are added to it every day. Despite all efforts, there is little evidence of our capacity to arrest population explosion. Inflationary pressure is increasing and prices cannot be held in check as viewed by Dube in 1973.

## Conclusion

Dube highlighted the role of various social structures like social, economic, ritual and political to help in shaping the village. Further, the elements of various social structures are interlinked at the individual level as well as the higher order to bring about solidarity and consensus among the villagers. Attempt has been made to understand the factors which led to the changing scenario of village Shamirpeth (Hyderabad) in Andhra Pradesh. In his book, *India's Changing Village* (1958), Dube deals with the changes brought about in Indian villages by initiation of CDPs in India. The book discusses the human factors' responsibility in bringing changes in villages of India through CDP.

## Dube's Framework Summarized

### *Background*

1. Education and training in Political Science
2. Academic career at Nagpur, Hyderabad, Lucknow, Saugar, London etc.
3. His interest in understanding the rural and tribal social life.

### *Aim*

1. To give clear picture of social, economic and religious aspects of rural life.

### *Assumptions*

1. India's diversities and unities traced through its complex history.
2. 'Structure' to 'change'.

### *Methodology*

1. Structural-functional approach
2. Deductive-positivistic method
3. Diagnostic and prescriptive
4. Interdisciplinary orientation

### *Typology*

1. Macro perspective
2. Field investigations
3. Descriptive exploratory accounts

### *Issues*

Different aspects of Indian society and culture:

1. tradition and change
2. complex culture
3. rural sociology
4. community development
5. modernization and development
6. sociology of economic development
7. explanation and management of changes

## Select Bibliography

Doshi, S.L. (2003), *Modernity, Post-Modernity and Neo-Sociological Theories*, Jaipur: Rawat Publications

Dube, S.C. (1955), *Indian Village*, London: Routledge and Kegan Paul.

—— (1958), *India's Changing Villages*, London: Routledge and Kegan Paul.

—— (1973), *Contemporary India and its Modernization*, Delhi: Vikas Publishing House.

—— (1974), 'Sociology of Economic Development' in *ICSSR: A Survey of Research in Sociology and Social Anthropology*, Vol. II.

Sharma, S. (1985), *Sociology in India*, Jaipur: Rawat Publications.

Singh, Yogendra (1986), 'Indian Sociology', *Current Sociology*, Vol. 34, No. 2.

# 10

# McKim Marriott

McKim Marriott (b. 1 February 1924), PhD in Anthropology (Chicago, 1955), is Professor in the Department of Anthropology in Social Sciences Collegiate Division of the University of Chicago. He served as Assistant Professor, Department of Anthropology and Social Science, College Division University Chicago, 1957–1960; Associate Professor, 1960–1964; Professor, 1964–1998; Professor Emeritus, since 1998. He was also Fellow, Center for Advanced Study Behavioral Sciences, Stanford, California, 1961–1962 and Lewis Henry Morgan lecturer, University Rochester, New York, 1967. He has done field work in Uttar Pradesh and Maharashtra, edited Village India, and authored varied studies on rural social organization and change. He is concerned with formulating and simulating indigenous sociologies and psychologies in India, Japan, and other countries.

## Works of Marriott

1. *Village India: Studies in the Little Community* (1955)

2. *Caste Ranking and Community Structure in the Five Regions of India and Pakistan* (1960)
3. *India through Hindu Categories* (1990)

## Methodology

Marriott used the structural-functional approach in his study of village India. Influenced by the model of Robert Redfield and Milton Singer, Marriott had conducted some studies on social change in India utilizing this conceptual framework. The basic ideas in this approach are 'civilization' and 'social organization of tradition'. It is based on the evolutionary view that civilization or the structure of tradition (which consists of both cultural and social structures) grows in two stages: first, through orthogenetic or indigenous evolution, and second, through heterogenetic encounters or contracts with other cultures and civilizations. In this context, we would like to discuss the writings of Marriott in the following paragraphs:

### *Communities and Traditions*

The discussion on relationship between communities and traditions has a history in the emergence of adequate concepts for the study of a social phenomenon. Redfield had propounded the idea of 'folk culture', relying largely on the distinctions put forward earlier by the European sociologists, such as those of Gemeinschaft and Geselschaft (Tonnies) and mechanical and organic solidarity (Durkheim). Redfield (1955) formalized his ideas in the concept of 'little community' with its four characteristics of smallness, distinctiveness, homogeneity, and self-sufficiency. Marriott saw the interplay among the communities of rural and urban centres. In his essay on "Little Communities in an Indigenous Civilization", (1955) Marriott explicitly indicates the relationship between the local caste system and the larger order of state and civilization.

### *Village India*

Marriott's edited *Village India: Studies in the Little Community* (1955) is one of the most well-known collections of village studies in the fifties, and even today it could be considered eminently relevant. It includes contributions by both foreign and Indian anthropologists. The book aims at looking Indian villages from the complexity of Indian civilization. The methodology, however, is structural-functional. The contributors have re-examined the concept of caste. It has been the effort of the editor to make caste more precise, and less open textured.

Our main concern here is to discuss the Marriott's paper entitled "Little Communities in an Indigenous Civilization" (1955), which is contributed in *Village India*. Marriott conducted his study at the village of Kishan Garhi in Aligarh district of Uttar Pradesh from December 1950 to April 1952. Kishan Garhi is not like an isolate whole, but a world in itself. It has internal divisions of economic interest groups. It grows crops, which are sold outside the village. There are many external economic relationships. Internal divisions are also in matters of marriage and kinship. The village is divided politically too in terms of factions. Marriott observes: "These structural facts make Kishan Garhi seem very much less than an isolated whole in the primitive sense" (1955). However, Kishan Garhi is 'isolable'. Marriott further writes: "But still I am compelled to go on to say that the village of Kishan Garhi is like a living thing, has a definable structure, is conceptually a vivid entity, is a system – even if it is one of many subsystems within the larger socio-politico-religio-economic system in which it exists. Especially am I so compelled if I look at the concerns and emphases that the people of the village express and if I try to evaluate the structural aspects of their lives as they evaluate them" (ibid.). Marriott relies on certain cultural practices, norms and etiquettes etc. for considering Kishan Garhi as an 'isolate'. The question is: How far these notions and practices are the core of the village life? Are they not peripheral aspects of social structure? To us, Marriott's phenomenological anthropology looks somewhat superficial as a methodological device.

In his paper, Marriott directly raises questions of interrelation of an Indian village with the larger society and with the civilization of which it is a small and local part. The balanced account of the village in Aligarh district both as a unified world in itself and also as part of communities outside itself treats more fully than do earlier papers this question, recurrent for the book as a whole. But, the topic is only introductory here. To Lewis' characterization of types of village organization and of countrywide networks Marriott adds a greatly expanded historical dimension: he treats Kishan Garhi as an element in the development of native Indian civilization. Government and culture alike have grown upward from Kishan Garhi and thousands of other villagers. And, the government and the reflective thought of India have influenced the development of all these Kishan Garhis. Upward from the village to the institutions and ideas of the state and the civilization, and the downward from the civilization and the state to the village, his mind runs in his efforts to identify some of the characteristic historical processes by which a native civilization, seen through the life of a village, may be understood.

In this paper, Marriott sees historical interaction in relation to little community and greater community. Government and land tenure and then caste organization, as products of interaction over many generations, are looked in. Native Indian government is in part a growth upward from the institutions of the local community. On the other hand, features of the village that appear at first as local developments – elements of kinship structure, village layout, and typical modes of conflict – turn out to be "reflexes of general state policy". And caste relationships too are in part reflexes of institutions of the wider community, "degradations of the royal style". The conclusion is reached that "both little communities and greater communities are mutually necessary conditions of each other's existence in their present forms". Besides the role of state and caste, Marriott has analysed festivals and deities in great detail with a view to understand the nature of the village community in India.

Marriott also makes the same point in terms of culture and content of ideas. To little and great communities correspond little and great traditions. The religious life of Kishan Garhi is examined in historical depth. It is asked: "What elements of ritual and belief represent contributions from village life upward to the formation of India's great Sanskritic tradition? What elements are local modifications of elements of that great tradition communicated downward to it?" To the two aspects of the double process of this interaction between little and great traditions Marriott gives names: universalization and parochialization. We are being helped to a viewpoint, a set of concepts, and a way of work that will allow anthropologists to study a village in its generic historic processes of interaction with the civilization of which it is a part. Marriott's work combines "a focus upon the small half-world of the village" with a "perspective upon the universe of Indian civilization".

In this very well-argued essay, Marriott discusses the small world of a village within the universe of Indian civilization. He also asks two questions: (1) Can such a village be satisfactorily comprehended and conceived as a whole in itself? (2) Can understanding of one such village contribute to understanding of the greater culture and society in which the village is imbedded? To provide answers to these questions, Marriott discusses certain aspects of social structure and religious culture of Kishan Garhi. The paradox is that if 'yes' is given in the case of the first question, then 'no' is given in regard to the second. Thus, there is an inverse relationship between the two questions. Marriott explains this problem as follows: "We cannot say both that an Indian village is comparable with a primitive isolate and also that it is dependent upon and part of a system that is outside itself. We cannot claim simultaneously that the great tradition of Indian civilization is relevant and that it is irrelevant to the understanding of peasant life."

Marriott writes: "In India, we are on middle ground". The village reaches beyond its central locus far into the outside world, and the outside world in turn reaches into the most central core of the village society. The following observation of Marriott may be referred: 'Although Kishan Garhi is a conservative and a relatively traditional village, I cannot say it is self-contained, complete little community comparable with primitive little communities. Nor, on the other hand, can I doubt that it is a community, and a clearly isolable community for its residents. So how am I to conceive it within its larger universe?' He accepts the notions of 'levels of socio-cultural integration', 'active fields', 'the folk-urban continuum' and 'levels of communal relations' for analysing relations between 'primary civilization' and 'secondary civilization'. An indigenous great tradition remains in constant communication with its own little traditions. The processes of 'universalization' and 'parochialization' facilitate interaction between the great and little traditions. Therefore, Marriott constructs the concepts of 'universalization' and 'parochialization'. These two concepts have been explained with the concepts of great and little traditions.

### *Little and Great Traditions*

A few of the concepts, which have emerged from the village studies made during 1950s, are considered to be significant for analysing change in rural society. Most of these concepts are cultural in nature and evolved out of caste in rural India. The concepts of little and great traditions also stand for change in rural caste system. Both of these concepts are constructed by Milton Singer and McKim Marriott.

The origin of little and great traditions is from Robert Redfield, who conducted his studies in Mexican communities. It was Redfield who talked about little community. For him, little community was a village that had smaller size, self-sufficient and relatively isolated. Redfield did not mention anything about little traditions or great traditions. Singer and Marriott, who were influenced by the studies conducted by Redfield for their intensive study of India's villages, elaborated the original model of Redfield in the light of data generated from Indian villages. Yogendra Singh (1994) has commented upon the construction of little and great traditions in Indian villages by these two anthropologists.

### *Parochialization and Universalization*

Marriott (1955: 197–200) envisaged two concepts, namely, 'parochialization' and 'universalization' with the two poles having been defined as the great and the little traditions. Thus, Marriott characterizes the mode of interaction between the 'little' and 'great' traditions in the Indian village as 'parochialization' and 'universalization'. The first is when elements of the 'great' tradition percolate downward and become organic part of the 'little' tradition losing thereby their original form. The second process operates when elements of the 'little' tradition (deities, customs, rites, etc.) circulate upward to the level of the 'great' tradition. Marriott gives many examples of such circular processes of change from his observations in India. Sanskritization, according to him, does not proceed as an independent process; it is superimposed on non-sanskritic cultural forms through accretion rather than simple replacement.

*Parochialization* refers to the manner in which the elements of the great tradition shed off some of their pure form and add local colour instead. Marriott presented the complementary concept of 'universalization' indicating an upward mobility of local tradition until it begins reaching the regional or the national level. The possibility of styles of life moving upward can be seen in social context when Brahmins migrating to remote areas appear to take over some of the local customs. He argues that there is a constant interaction between the great and little traditions.

## Social Stratification

Rural stratification, according to Marriott, is closed rather than open; there are limited sets of inter-group ties and in this context the reference group behaviour often tends to be dysfunctional. In urban areas, not only the stratification system relatively open but its character is 'attributional' and 'interactional'. In other words, if a certain individual group or family is able to acquire high status attributes such as education, wealth, or better occupational position in the cities, the individual or group may be able to pass as a member of higher social rank. In the villages, on the other hand, the ranking depends more on the traditional evaluation of caste status. This is reflected in most forms of inter-group or inter-individual interactions. Mere acquisition of higher status attributes may not be sufficient here for the evaluation of the caste status.

Moreover, in the metropolitan settings, the principle of 'corporate ranking' does not operate as it does in the rural system of stratification. In corporate ranking, status is attributed to the entire group or even if individuals or families in the group are able to acquire status-enhancing attributes, the status of the group as a whole is not changed. The status is collectively defined on cultural criteria. In the rural caste system principles of purity and pollution, hereditary occupation and kinship relations which are more binding factors in social stratification, render the ranking system corporate. The process of status mobility through sanskritization, in a way, manifests this corporateness in the rural ranking system. This explains the tendency in the rural areas to mobilize caste, tribe or ethnic groups as a whole for advancement of social status. Compared to this, in urban centres, non-corporate mode of status mobility is quite common.

The above distinction between the rural and urban systems of social stratification highlights only the main characteristic of structural pattern.

Thus, Marriott (1968) points out the complexity of India's system of stratification and stresses the need for a number of new analytic notions in order to understand what any given effort at caste mobility is about. First of all, the contrast between closed, interactional rural system of stratification and the open, attributional urban system should be taken into consideration. Further, he distinguishes the ranking and mobility of castes as corporations concerned with ritual dominance and pollution from the ranking and movements of individuals and groups concerned with wealth, power or prestige. Finally, he refers to the felt locus of each caste and specified to which of the several possible relevant hierarchies and audiences – local, regional, sectarian, civilizational, or national – its behaviour is referred to by itself and by others.

### *Specialized Study of Caste Ranking*

Marriott, in his path-breaking work on *Caste Ranking and Community Structure in Five Regions of India and Pakistan* (1960), takes the position that in terms of stratified structural relationship, the Muslim operate within the framework of the caste system. He develops a rigorous, comparative method for studying 'elaborateness' of caste ranking based on a notion of demographic factors of ethnic diversity in social ecology. He locates the factors causing elaboration in the social ecology and in the pattern of inter-ethnic interaction (Marriott, 1959). He further develops a matrix analysis of caste ranking and food transactions. One may also mention here to his publication on *Hindu Caste Ranking: The Lewis Henry Morgan Lectures* (1967).

In his article, "Multiple Reference in Indian Caste System" Marriott (1968: 103) suggests reference group approach to the study of caste stratification system in India. He refers to 'multiple reference' in the caste system. He argues that in order to gain fuller understanding of the stratification system in India, its processes should be observed at various levels. These levels are: rural as different from metropolitan system of ranking, individual, group and corporate units in ranking and finally, "a series of successively wider zones of reference for the units in any local system, the several zones being distinctively characterized by distinctive values".

At an another level, according to Marriott (1968: 109), caste stratification reflects its structural features in India that of zones. He mentions three zones: (1) the zone of the village community and its directly connected parts in the countryside; (2) the zone of the recognized cultural or linguistic region; and (3) the zone of whole civilization. In the village, zone, castes or sub-castes are the most relevant category for ranking is class. Classes manifest themselves through categories like 'lord' or 'servant' in northern India, or the 'waterbearing' or 'non-waterbearing' in Bengal or 'light people' or 'dark people' in Gujarat. In the civilizational zone, however, the more inclusive categories those of *varna*, ethnic origin or the cosmopolitan scheme of gradation according to Marriott offer a framework for understanding social stratification.

The conflicts in the system of social stratification emerge from the changing frames of reference in the ranking of castes from one level of categories to another. This process has also contributed to the crystallization in favour of any one of these three levels of ranking systems and Marriott says that all of them are operating in a 'multiple reference model'.

Marriott's analysis does not indicate the complexity of the social stratification system in India, but it offers us an insight into the mechanisms by which stratification process at one level, such as rural or metropolitan, interacts with that of other levels such as those of the three zones of the village, region and civilization.

An understanding of the dialectical relationship between the stratification mechanisms at different levels can be had only through the analysis of the various social forces that operate in social stratification. Marriott's scheme offers categories for the description of the pattern of stratification in India, but is limited in theoretical validity and power. It does not offer theoretical codes for transcription of data from one level of observation to another and finally, it fails to indicate how the scheme of categories of ranking suggested by him constitute or do not constitute a logically interrelated set of status ranking principles through which the dynamics of social stratification could be understood and analysed (Singh, 1974: 322–23).

### *Hierarchical Order*

The stratification of society is also maintained through the customs and traditions advocated by religion. The caste system, despite the efforts made by secular forces, continued to survive because of the values inherent in caste system. Marriott has identified the ritual and religious aspects of hierarchical relations in the village life. The commensual relations in the village are even today regulated by the concept of purity and pollution. In the cities there are no taboos so far as commensality is concerned.

### *Social Mobility*

Marriott (1968), reviewing a number of studies on social mobility, finds relevant distinctions at three levels in the ranking system related to the Indian mobility pattern. These are based on distinctions between: (1) rural from metropolitan types of ranking system, (2) individual or group from corporate units in ranking, and (3) a series of successively wider zones of reference for the units in any local system, the several zones being characterized by distinctive values. The zones, according to him, are the village, the linguistic, region and the whole civilization.

### *Hindu Cultural Categories*

It is an anomalous fact that social sciences in India have developed from western rather than Indian cultural realities. As a result, western disciplines often do not recognize and, therefore, cannot deal with realities reflected in many Indian social institutions. In his volume on, *India through Hindu Categories* (1990), Marriott explores social science ideas which can be developed from the realities known to Indian people. These ideas are drawn from the Hindu cultural categories, not merely because they offer coherent and comprehensive systems of thought, but especially because they illuminate variations, which escape the notice of conventional social science.

## Marriott's Framework Summarized

### *Background*

1. Educated in USA.
2. Academic career in USA.
3. Interests in India, Japan, and other countries.

### *Aims*

1. To formulate indigenous sociologies and psychologies in India, Japan, and other countries.

### *Assumption*

1. Evolutionary view of civilization or the structure of tradition

### *Methodology*

1. Structural-functional

### *Typology*

1. Little and great traditions
2. Parochialization and universalization

### *Issues*

1. Rural social organization
2. Social stratification and social mobility

3. Caste
4. Hindu cultural categories
5. Communities and traditions

## Select Bibliography

Desai, A.R. (1969), *Rural Sociology in India*, Bombay: Popular Prakashan.

Doshi, S.L. and P.C. Jain (1999), *Rural Sociology*, Jaipur/New Delhi: Rawat Publications.

Marriott, McKim (1959), 'Interactional and Attributional Theories in Caste Ranking', *Man in India*, Vol. 39, pp. 127–147.

— (ed.) (1961), *Village India*, Bombay: Asia Publishing House.

— (1965), *Caste Ranking and Community Structure in the Five Regions of India and Pakistan*, Poona: G.S. Press.

— (1968). 'Multiple Reference in Indian Caste system' in James Silverberg (ed.), *Social Mobility in the Caste System in India*, Mouton: The Hague.

— (1968). 'Caste Ranking and Food Transactions: A Matrix Analysis' in Milton Singer and Bernard S. Cohn (eds), *Structure and Change in Indian Society*, Chicago: Aldine Publishing Co.

Marriott, McKim (ed.) (1990), *India through Hindu Categories*, New Delhi: Sage Publications.

Sharma, Surendra (1985), *Sociology in India: A Perspective from Sociology of Knowledge,* Jaipur: Rawat Publications.

Singer, Milton (1964). "The Social Organization of Indian Civilization", *Diogenes*, Vol. 45, Winter.

Singh, Yogendra (1977). *Social Stratification and Change in India*, New Delhi: Manohar.

— (1994). *Modernization of Indian Tradition*, Jaipur: Rawat Publications.

# IV

# Marxist Perspective

The dialectical-historical orientation is related primarily to Marxist methods and propositions for the analysis of social reality. Yogendra Singh (2004) has used the term dialectical and not Marxist because in Indian sociology, Marxist approach comprises several adaptive models; many innovations have been made on classical Marxist formulations for the study of Indian society. Also, among Indian sociologists, there is a growing awareness that Marxist categories and paradigms will have to be reformulated and tested against societal realities of various historical origins to validate them as universal or particular categories in sociology. In this perspective, when we look at the growth of dialectical-historical orientation in theory, we find that comparatively it is a less developed branch of Indian sociology. Most basic Marxist thinking in India was done in the forties and fifties by non-sociologists (Singh, 1973, 1977).

The study of Indian social reality from the Marxian perspective has been conducted by scholars such as, M.N. Dutta,

S.A. Dange, D.D. Kosambi, A.R. Desai, D.P. Mukerji, P.C. Joshi, R.S. Sharma, Irfan Habib, D.P. Chattopadhyay and others. Among the early sociologists who emphasized the significance of the dialectical model were D.P. Mukerji, A.R. Desai and Ramkrishna Mukherjee. In this section, we would concentrate on the dialectical-historical approach adopted by D.P. Mukerji, A.R. Desai, Ramkrishna Mukherjee and D.N. Dhanagare in the study of Indian society.

# 11

# D.P. Mukerji

Dhurjati Prasad Mukerji (1894–1961), popularly called as DP, was one of the founding fathers of sociology in India. He was born on 5 October 1894 in West Bengal in a middle class Bengali family that had a fairly long tradition of intellectual pursuits. According to Satyen Bose, the famous physicist, when DP passed the entrance examination of Calcutta University, he, like Bose, wanted to study the sciences, but finally settled for economics, history and political science. He got MAs in economics and history, and was to have proceeded to England for further studies, but the outbreak of the First World War precluded this.

DP began his career at Bangabasi College, Calcutta. In 1922 he joined the newly founded Lucknow University as a lecturer in economics and sociology. He stayed there for a fairly long period of thirty-two years. Radhakamal Mukerjee, the first professor in the department, had been responsible for bringing DP to Lucknow. He retired as Professor and Head of the Department in 1954. For one year (1953) he served as a Visiting Professor of Sociology at the International Institute of Social Studies, The Hague. After his retirement from the University of Lucknow, he was invited to the Chair of Economics at the University of Aligarh, which he occupied with great distinction during his last five years of active academic life. He was the first President of the Indian Sociological Conference. He also remained the Vice-President of the International Sociological Association.

DP was an outstanding Indian whose versatile interests have made landmarks not only in the field of sociology but also in economics, literature, music and art. Yet, sociology has been benefited most from his erudite contributions. DP, besides being a scholar, was an extremely cultured and sensitive person. His personality was remarkable for its power in influencing and moulding the young people who came in touch with him. He was a Marxist but preferred to call him a Marxiologist, i.e., a social scientist of Marxism. He analysed Indian society from Marxian perspective of dialectical materialism.

### *As a Scholar*

Perhaps of much greater importance than his writings were his lectures, discussions and conversations. It was through these that he shaped the minds of youth and trained them to think for themselves. "Shaping men is enough for me", he often told his students.

His command over diverse fields of knowledge was incomparable; he talked with equal facility on the subtleties of systems of philosophy, history of economic thought, sociological theories, and theories of art, literature and music. He combined in a unique manner a profound scholarship with an extremely well-developed critical faculty, which enabled him to relate all scholarly details to the problems facing men and culture today. In acuteness of thought and brilliance of expression, he had no peer. These qualities of DP have inspired innumerable students and in whatever they do they carry his deep impress.

DP was a pioneer in the field of sociology of culture. This work is an endeavour to focus upon an area, which was dear to his heart. It is only a modest attempt and it may have many deficiencies but we feel that there is a convergence of ideas that make a unified theme. It is hoped that this work will elicit interest among sociologists and scholars in the related fields.

In his work on *Indian History: A Study in Method*, DP discusses the relevance of Marxist method to understand history. He also emphasizes the need for philosophy and historical matrix as essential for understanding any society. He fails to examine the major philosophical dialectical materialist premises about human beings, which distinguished Marxist approach from the idealist, biological or mechanistic postulates about what man is.

### *As a Teacher*

DP's career as an intellectual included, most prominently, his contributions as a teacher. He had a much greater and abiding influence on others through the spoken, rather than the written, words. The freedom that the class room, the coffee house, or the drawing room gave him to explore ideas and elicit immediate response was naturally not available via the printed page. Moreover, the quality of his writing was uneven, and not all that he wrote could be expected to survive long. Therefore, he loved to be a teacher and was very popular amongst his students. He encouraged dialogue and interchange of ideas with his students. Thus, he was a co-student, a co-enquirer, who never stopped learning. He had such an influence on his students that he lives in the minds of his students even today.

### Methodology

D.P. Mukerji was perhaps the most popular of the pioneers in Indian sociology. Like all of them, he resisted any attempt at the compartmentalization of knowledge in social science. He came to sociology more as a social philosopher. However, he ended up more as an advocate of empiricism, involving spiritual feelings.

He was deeply interested in understanding the nature and meaning of Indian social reality rooted in the Indian tradition. He was equally interested in finding out the ways of how to change it for promoting welfare of the common people by adapting the forces of modernity to the specificity of Indian tradition. He was acknowledged to be a Marxist. Nevertheless, he introduced himself as from the doctrinaires or dogmatic Marxist. It implied that he followed Marxism as a method of analysis, rather than a political ideology. His dialectical analysis of Indian history suggested that tradition and modernity, colonialism and nationalism, individualism and collectivism could be seen as dialectically interacting with each other in contemporary India.

DP contributed the perspective of Marxian sociology in India. He was tolerant of western ideas, concepts and analytical categories. He viewed that there is a need for an indigenous sociology and social anthropology, but he certainly did not want to insulate these disciplines in India from the western social traditions.

As we have mentioned above, DP preferred to call himself 'Marxologist' rather than 'Marxist' and attempted a dialectical interpretation of the encounter between the Indian tradition and modernity which unleashed many forces of cultural contradictions during the colonial era (Singh, 1973: 18–20). He focused more on the historical specificity of India's cultural and social transformation, which was characterized less by 'class struggle' and more by value assimilation and cultural synthesis that resulted from the encounter between tradition and modernity (see Madan, 1977: 167–68).

Apart from the broad perspective, Radhakamal Mukerjee and DP had little in common as intellectual. DP's contribution to sociology and social anthropology in India differs significantly from those of Radhakamal Mukerjee and D.N. Majumdar who were his contemporaries in Lucknow. DP was never involved in any empirical exercises of data collection of surveys. Not that, he did not believe in the inherent value of empiricism. It was just that temperamentally he preferred to be an armchair social critic, social philosopher and culturologist. His academic interests were diverse: they ranged from 'music and fine arts as peculiar creations of Indian culture' to the 'Indian tradition in relation to modernity' (Mukerji, 1948, 1958). He was not a prolific writer like his contemporaries in Lucknow. Yet, as an intellectual and an inspiring teacher, he left behind a powerful legacy that influenced the later generation of Indian sociologists in no small measures.

Concerning DP's approach to the understanding of Indian society, culture and change, two points need to be stressed. First, like Radhakamal, he was very much against maintaining rigid barriers between one social science discipline and another, and both shared historical perspective in their studies. However, although both, like Ghurye, had an abiding interest in the study of structure and change in Indian society, in their works, we do not find a new conceptual framework as such (Unnithan et al., 1965: 15–16).

## Writings

DP was a versatile scholar. He wrote nineteen books, including *Diversities* (1958); ten in Bengali and nine in English. His early publications include: *Basic Concepts in Sociology* (1932) and *Personality and the Social Sciences* (1924). Some of the other publications are: *Modern Indian Culture* (1942, revised enlarged edition in 1948), *Problems of Indian Youth* (1942), and *Views and Counterviews* (1946). *Modern Indian Culture* (1942) and *Diversities* (1958) are known as his best works. His versalities can be seen from his other contributions such as *Tagore: A Study* (1943), *On Indian History: A Study in Method* (1943), and *Introduction to Music* (1945). Apart from these, he also enjoys a unique place in Bengali literature as a novelist, essayist and literary critic.

## Perspective

DP was one of the very few social scientists in the academic world who recognized the importance of Marxism to analyse socio-economic forces operating in human society. He considered Marxism as a theory, which was founded on the priority of society and group which are separate and exterior to man, the individual a sort of environment to facilitate and hinder unfoldment of the capacities of the autonomous individual isolate.

DP's deepest interest was in the Marxian method rather than in any dogmas. In a short paper entitled, 'A Word to Indian Marxists', included in his *Views and Counterviews* (1946: 166), he had warned that the 'un-historically minded' young Marxist ran the risk of ending up as a 'fascist', and Marxism itself could 'lose its effectiveness in a maze of slogans'. Nevertheless, it would not be misleading to say that DP did not indeed embrace Marxism in various ways, ranging from a simple emphasis upon the economic factor in the making of culture to an elevation of practice to the status of a test of theory. It was a close but uncomfortable embrace.

In his basic two books on *Personality and the Social Sciences* (1924) and *Basic Concepts in Sociology* (1932), DP considered 'personal documents' products of his endeavour to formulate an adequate concept of social sciences. From the very beginning, he organized his ideas around the notion of personality. He took up the position that the abstract individual should not be the focus of social science theories. He pleaded for a holistic, psycho-sociological approach. It was this synthesis of the double process of individuality and the socialization of the uniqueness of individual life, that a personality could be understood (Mukerji, 1924).

Looking back to the work of his lifetime, DP said in his presidential address to the first Indian Sociological Conference in 1955 that he had come to sociology from economics and history because he was interested in developing his personality through knowledge (1958: 228). The office of a comprehensive social science, transcending the prevailing compartmentalization of social sciences, was conceived by him to be the development of an integrated though many faceted personality. This is an idea, as A.K. Saran (1962: 167) has pointed out, in some ways parallel to the ideal suggested by Moore in his *Principia Ethica*.

DP asserts that knowledge and knower ought to be seen together. Knowledge has to be philosophic, albeit based on empirical data. It has transcendent disciplinary boundaries. The Indian intellectuals had borrowed worldview, based on western liberal outlook. The element of 'purpose' has been stressed as 'progress' is not a stage in automatic self-generating evolution. Progress is a movement of freedom. For DP progress involves balancing of values and he draws from religious scriptures to identify the hierarchy of values.

Here, we would like to highlight DP's contribution to the following:

1. Personality
2. Modern Indian Culture
3. Traditions
4. Nature and Method of Sociology
5. Role of New Middle Classes
6. Making of Indian History
7. Modernization
8. Music

### *Personality*

DP once told with a sense of humour that he propounded the thesis of 'purusha'. The 'purusha' is not isolated from society and individual. Nor is he under the hold of group mind. The purusha establishes the relationship with others as an active agent and discharges responsibilities. His argument is that the 'purusha' grows as a result of his relations with others and, thus, occupies a better place among human groups.

DP admits that the Indian social life is like the life of bees and beavers and the Indians are almost a regimented people. But "the beauty of it" is that the majority of us do not feel regimented. DP doubts whether the western individual man dominated by the market system has any freedom at all. He is exposed to the manipulation of advertisements, press-chains, chain stores and his purse is continuously emptied. All this does not leave much scope for individual's right of choice and consumer's sovereignty. Contrastingly, the low level of aspiration of an average Indian, which is moderated by group norms, results into greater poise in life. This should not be missed in our urge for uplifting the level of wants. The Indian sociologist thus will have to accept the group as his unit and eject the individual. For that is the tradition of India. The Indian sociologists will have to understand the specific nature of this tradition.

### *Modern Indian Culture*

Emphasis in his works has changed through passage of time. DP was very sensitive and was influenced by environment around him.

He drew from traditional culture as well as modern. *Modern Indian Culture: A Sociological Study* was first published in 1942 and its revised edition in 1947 – the year of partitioned independence. Synthesis has been the dominant organizing principle of Indian culture. The British rule provided a real turning point to the Indian society. The middle class helped in the consolidation of British rule in India, but later challenged it successfully. DP's vision of India was a peaceful, progressive India born out of 'union' of diverse elements, of distinctive regional cultures. Reorientation to tradition was an essential condition of moving forward. DP denied that he was Marxist; he claimed to be only a 'Marxologist'.

The national movement was anti-intellectual, although it generated idealism and moral fervour. He concluded: "Politics has ruined our culture." DP believed that no genuine modernization is possible through imitation. He feared cultural imperialism. Modernization is a process of expansion, elevation, revitalization of traditional values and cultural patterns. Tradition is a principle of continuity. It gives us freedom to choose from different alternatives. Modernity should be defined in relation to, and not in denial of, tradition.

DP's arguments have been criticized. Saran has pointed out that DP does not subject the socialist order itself to analysis and takes its benign character on trust. He fails to realize that a technology-oriented society cannot easily be non-exploitative and not anti-man; and the traditional and the modern worldviews are rooted in different conceptions of time. DP's concern is seen as that of westernized Hindu intellectual. There is a need to read DP, reprint his works and examine his ideas (Madan, 1993).

### *Tradition*

What is meant by tradition? DP points out that tradition comes from the root 'tradere', which means "to transmit". The Sanskrit equivalent of tradition is either *parampara*, that is, succession or *aitihya*, which has the same root as *itihasa*, or history.

Traditions are supposed to have a source. It may be scriptures, or statements of stages (*apta vakya*), or mythical heroes with or without names. Whatever may be the source, the historicity of traditions is recognized by most people. They are quoted, recalled, esteemed. In fact, their age-long succession ensures social cohesion and social solidarity.

### *Dynamics of Tradition*

Tradition, thus, performs the act of conserving. But it is not necessarily conservative. DP asserts that traditions do change. Three principles of change are recognized in Indian tradition: Sruti, Smriti, Anubhava. It is *anubhava* or personal experience, which is the revolutionary principle. Certain Upanishads are entirely based on it.

But it did not end there. Personal experience of the saint-founders of different sects or *panths* soon blossomed forth into collective experience producing change in the prevailing socio-religious order. The experience of *prem* or love and *sahaj* or spontaneity of these saints and their followers was noticeable also in the *Sufis* among the Muslims. The traditional system gradually accommodated the dissenting voices. Indian social action has given latitude to align rebel within the limits of the constitution. The result has been the caste society blunting the class-consciousness of disadvantaged.

### *Dialectics of Tradition and Modernity*

The strength of the Indian tradition lies in its crystallization of values emerging from past happenings in the life-habits and emotions of men and women. In this way, India has certainly conserved many values: some good and others bad. The point, however, is that of utilizing the forces, which are foreign to Indian traditions, e.g., technology, democracy, urbanization, bureaucracy, etc.

DP is convinced that adjustments will certainly occur. It is almost guaranteed that Indians will not vanish, as primitive tribes have done, at the touch of western culture. They have sufficient flexibility for that. Indian culture had assimilated tribal culture and many of its endogenous dissents. It had developed Hindu-Muslim cultures and modern Indian culture is a curious blending, *varansankara*. "Traditionally, therefore, living in adjustment is in India's blood, so to speak".

DP does not worship tradition. His idea of "complete man" or "well-balanced personality" calls for a blend of (1) moral fervour and aesthetic and intellectual sensibility with (2) the sense of history and rationality. The qualities of the second category are emphasized more by modernity, than by the Indian tradition. Hence, the dialectics between tradition and modernity herein lies in the need for understanding the tradition. DP observes that "the knowledge of traditions shows the way to break them with the least social cost".

DP's most popular and significant writings on 'tradition and modernity' help us in understanding the authentic measuring of these two bipolar concepts. He argued that there is dialectical relation between India's tradition and modernity, British colonialism and nationalism and individualism and collectivity, i.e., Sangha. His concept of dialectics was anchored in liberal humanism. He argued all through his works that traditions are central to the understanding of Indian society. The relations between modernization which came to India during the British periods and traditions are dialectical. It is from this perspective of dialectics that, DP argued, we shall to define traditions.

The encounter of tradition with modernization created certain cultural contradictions, adaptations and in some cases situations of conflict also. Describing the consequences of the tradition-modernity encounter, Yogendra Singh (1986) writes:

> In D.P. Mukerji's writing we find some systematic concern with analysis of Indian social processes from a dialectical frame of reference. He mainly focuses upon the encounter of the tradition with that of the west which, on the one hand, unleashed many factors of cultural contradictions and, on the other, gave rise to a new middle class. The rise of these forces, according to him, generates a dialectical process of conflict and synthesis which must be given a push by bringing into play the conserved energies of the class structure of Indian society.

The encounter between tradition and modernity, therefore, ends up in two consequences: (1) conflict, and (2) synthesis. Indian society, as DP envisages, is the result of the interaction between tradition and modernity. It is this dialectics, which helps us to analyse the Indian society.

DP's concept of tradition appeared for the first time in the year 1942 when his book *Modern Indian Culture: A Sociological Study* was published. His characterization of tradition in the context of Indian culture runs as below:

> As a social and historical process.... Indian culture represents certain common traditions that have given rise to a number of general attitudes. The major influences in their shaping have been Buddhism, Islam, and western commerce and culture. It was through the assimilation and conflict of such varying forces that Indian culture became what it is today, neither Hindu nor Islamic, neither a replica of the western mode of living and thought nor a purely Asiatic product (1948: 1).

The central thesis of the book was that the key to the history of India was cultural synthesis – creative response to the internal and external political and cultural challenges – and that the history of India was more than its past notwithstanding the views of Hegal and Marx on the subject. DP did not regard the disruptiveness of the British rule as a permanent injury: it was only an interruption. He recognized that the Hindu-Muslim cultural synthesis was the weakest at the level of cognitive categories, but stressed shared economic interests, and applauded achievements in music, architecture and literature. DP did not consider the partition of the sub-continent as more than an event in its geopolitics. The future, he was almost confident, would transcend the present in a true dialectical movement. Let us not politicize culture, he used to say.

The Tagore study restates DP's thesis about the importance of roots. Comparing Tagore with Bankimchandra Chatterji, he writes: "His [Tagore's] saturation with Indian traditions was deeper; hence he could more easily assimilate a bigger dose of western thought." And again: "The influence of the West upon

Tagore was great ... but it should not be exaggerated.... At each stage in the evolution of his prose, poetry, drama, music and of his personality we find Tagore drawing upon some basic reservoir of the soil, of the people, of the spirit, and emerging with the capacity for larger investment" (Mukerji, 1972: 50).

### *Composition of Traditions*

Indian tradition is the resultant of certain historical processes. They actually construct the structure of Indian culture. These traditions belong to several ideologies such as Buddhism, Islam, Christianity, tribal life and western modernity. The process of synthesis has, therefore, constructed these traditions. In this respect, it would be mistaken to believe that traditions are Hindu only. In fact, they combine traditions of various ethnic groups of the country. How the principles of various religious ideologies shaped the Indian traditions has been interpreted by T.N. Madan as under:

> In this historical process, synthesis has been the dominant organizing principle of the Hindu, the Buddhist and the Muslim, who had together shaped a worldview in which according to D.P., 'the fact of being was lasting significance'. His favourite quotation from the Upanishads was charaivati, keep moving forward. This meant that there had developed an indifference to the transient and the sensate and a preoccupation with the subordination of the 'little self' to the ultimately its dissolution in the 'supreme reality' (1948: 2).

DP tried to provide a classification of Indian traditions under three heads, viz., primary, secondary and tertiary. The primary traditions have been primordial and authentic to Indian society. The secondary traditions were given second ranking, when the Muslims arrived in the country. And, by the time of the British arrival, Hindus and Muslims had yet not achieved a full synthesis of traditions at all levels of existence. There was a greater measure of agreement between them regarding the utilization and appropriation of natural resources and to a lesser extent in respect of aesthetic and religious traditions. In the tertiary traditions of conceptual thought, however, differences survived prominently.

### *Sources of Traditions*

Indian sociologists have talked enough about traditions but little effort has been made to identify the sources and content of traditions. And this goes very well when we talk about D.P. Mukerji. Admittedly, traditions occupy a central place in any analysis of India's traditions and modernization. But DP has not given the contents of these traditions. The major sources of traditions are Hinduism, Buddhism, Islam and western culture, but what traditions, for instance, of Hinduism or Islam constitute the broader Indian traditions has not been made specific by DP. His weakness in this respect has been identified by T.N. Madan who says that the general make up of Indian traditions according to DP could be a synthesis of Vedanta, western liberation and Marxism. But, what about the synthesis of Islam and Buddhism? DP fails to provide any such synthesis of other major traditions. Madan (1993) comments on this failure of DP as under:

> An equally important and difficult undertaking would be the elaboration and specification of his conception of the content of tradition. Whereas he establishes, convincingly I think, the relevance of tradition to modernity at the level of principle, he does not spell out its empirical content except in terms of general categories.... One has the uncomfortable feeling that he himself operated more in terms of institution and general knowledge than a deep study of the texts. A confrontation with tradition through field work in the manner of the anthropologist was, of course, ruled out by him, at least for himself.

### *Nature and Method of Sociology*

DP was by training an economist. He was, however, aware of the limitations of the practices of other economists. They were interested in mastering and applying sophisticated techniques and abstract generalizations following the western model. They failed to view the economic development in India in terms of its historical and cultural specificities. He noted with concern that our progressive groups failed in the field of intellect and also in economic and political actions, "chiefly on account of their ignorance of and unrootedness in Indian social reality".

Social reality has many and different aspects and it has its tradition and future. To understand this social reality, one should have a comprehensive and synoptic view of (i) the nature of interactions of its various aspects, and (ii) the interplay of its tradition and the forces leading to a changed future. Narrow specializations in particular disciplines cannot help this understanding. Sociology can be great help here. "Sociology has a floor and a ceiling like any other discipline." However, the speciality of sociology "consists in its floor being the ground floor of all types of social disciplines and its ceiling remaining open to the sky". Neglect of social base often leads to arid abstractions as in recent economics. On the other hand, much of empirical research in anthropology and psychology has been rendered useless because of its narrow scope. Sociology helps us in having an integral view of life and social reality. It will look into the details but it will also search for the wood behind the trees. DP learnt from his teachers and peers the need for a synoptic view of the vast canvas of social life. He, therefore, consistently harped on the synthesis of social sciences. Sociology might help this attempt at synthesizing.

The first task of sociology is to understand the specific nature of forces that sustain a particular society over the time. For this reason, DP stresses that sociologists of India must understand the nature of tradition, which has conserved Indian society for centuries. But sociology is never defence of the status quo. DP asserts that "sociology should ultimately show the way out of the social system by analysing the process of transformation". DP's sociological analysis of the Indian society has the merit of showing that the Indian society is changing, but without much disintegration. He was, therefore, aware that the study of the Indian social system requires a different approach to sociology because of its tradition, its special symbols and its special patterns of economic and technological changes in culture and symbols follows thereafter. DP observes: "In my view, the thing changing is more real and objective than change per se."

DP declares that "it is not enough for the Indian sociologist to be sociologist. He must be an Indian, that is, he is to share in the folkways, mores, customs and traditions for the purpose of understanding this social system and what lies beneath it and beyond it".

The Indian sociologist will try a synthesis of two approaches: He will adopt a comparative approach. A truly comparative approach will highlight the features shared by the Indian society with other societies and also the specificity of its tradition. For this reason, the sociologist will aim at understanding the meaning of the tradition. He will carefully examine its symbols and values. At the same time, he will also take a dialectical approach to understand the conflict and synthesis of the opposing forces of conservation and change.

### *Marxism and Indian Situations*

DP had a great faith in Marxism. Marxism gives an idea of a desirable higher stage in the development of human society. In that higher stage, personality becomes integrated with the others in society through a planned, socially directed, collective endeavour for historically understood end, which means a socialist order. But, he expressed doubts about the efficacy of the analysis of the Indian social phenomena by the Marxists. He gave three reasons for it: (1) The Marxists would analyse everything in terms of class conflict. But, in our society, class conflict has for a long time been covered by the caste traditions and the new class relations have not yet sharply emerged. (2) Many of them are more or less ignorant of the socio-economic history of India. (3) The way economic pressures work is not that of mechanical force moving a dead matter. Traditions have great powers of resistance. Change of modes of production may overcome this resistance. A speed change of this nature may be achieved by violent revolutions only. But, if a society opts for revolution by consent and without bloodshed, it must patiently work out the dialect of economic changes and tradition.

DP's emphasizes that it is the first and immediate duty of the Indian sociologists to study Indian traditions. And, it should precede the socialist interpretations of changes in the Indian traditions in terms of economic forces.

### *Rejection of the Positivism of Western Social Sciences*

DP was against the positivism of western social sciences. For it reduced individuals into biological or psychological units. The industrial culture of the west had turned individuals into self-seeking agents. The society in the west had become ethnocentric. By emphasizing individuation, i.e., recognition of the roles and rights of the individual, positivism had uprooted man from his social moorings. DP observes, "our conception of man is purusha and not the individual or vyakti". The word *vyakti* rarely occurs in our religious texts or in the sayings of the saints. *Purusha* or person develops through his co-operation with the others around him, through his sharing of values and interests of life with the members of his group. India's social system is basically a normative orientation of group, sect or caste action, but not of voluntaristic individual action. As a result, a common Indian does not experience the fear of frustration. DP makes no difference between the Hindu and the Muslim, the Christian and the Buddhist in this matter.

### ***Role of the New Middle Classes***

The urban-industrial order, introduced by the British in India, set aside the older institutional networks. It also discovered many traditional castes and classes. It called for a new kind of social adaptation and adjustment. In the new set-up the educated middle classes of the urban centres of India became the focal point of the society. They came to command the knowledge of the modern social forces, that is, science, technology, democracy and a sense of historical development, which the west would stand for. The new society of India calls for the utilization of these qualities and the services of the middle classes have been soaked with the western ideas and lifestyles. And they remained blissfully, and often contemptuously, ignorant of Indian culture and realities. They are oblivious to the Indian traditions. But traditions have "great powers of resistance and absorption". Even "on the surface of human geography and demographic pattern, traditions have a role to play in the transfiguration of physical adjustments and biological urges".

In India, for example, things like city planning and family planning are so tied up with traditions that the architect and the social reformer can ignore them only at the peril of their schemes. India's middle classes, thus, would not be in a position to lead the masses to build India along modern lines. They were uprooted from their indigenous traditions. They have lost contact with the masses.

India can move on to the road of modernity only by adapting it to her traditions if the middle classes re-establish their link with the masses. They should not be either apologetic for or unnecessarily boastful of their traditions. They should try to harness its vitality for accommodating changes required by modernity. A balance between individuation and association will be achieved thereby. India and the world will be enriched with the new experience.

### Making of Indian History

At this point it seems just pertinent enough to point out that, while DP followed Marx closely in his conception of history and in his characterization of British rule as uprooting, he differed significantly not only with Marx's assessment of the positive consequences of British rule, but also with his negative assessment of pre-British traditions. It is important to note this because some Marxists have claimed on their side, despite his denials that he was a Marxist; he jestingly claimed to be only a 'Marxologist' (Singh, 1973: 216). Some non-Marxists also have, it may be added, described him as Marxist.

It will be recalled that Marx had in his articles on British rule in India asserted that India had a strong past but "no history at all, at least no known history"; that its social condition had "remained unaltered since its remotest antiquity"; that it was 'British steam and science' which "uprooted, over the whole surface of Hindustan, the union between agriculture and manufacturing industry". Marx had listed England's 'crimes' in India and proceeded to point out that she had become 'the unconscious tool of history' whose action would ultimately result in a 'fundamental revolution' (see Marx, 1853). He had said: "England had to fulfill a double mission in India: one destructive and the other regenerating – the annihilation of old Asiatic society, and the laying of the material foundations of western society in India (1959: 31).

Thus, for Marx, as for so many others since his time, including intellectuals of various shades of opinion, the modernization of India has to be its westernization.

As has already been stated above, DP was intellectually and emotionally opposed to this view about India's past and future whether it came from Marx or from liberal bourgeois historians. He refused to be ashamed or apologetic about India's past. The statement of his position was unambiguous:

> Our attitude is one of humility towards the given fund. But it is also an awareness of the need, the utter need, of recreating the given and making it flow. The given of India is very much in ourselves. And we want to make something worthwhile out of it (1945: 11).

Indian history could not be made by outsiders; it has to be enacted by the Indians themselves. In this endeavour, they not only had to be firm of purpose but also clear headed. He wrote:

> Our sole interest is to write and enact Indian history. Action makes making; it has a starting point – this specificity called India; or if that be too vague, this specificity of contact between India and England or the West. Making involves changing, which in turn requires (a) a scientific study of the tendencies which make up this specificity, and (b) a deep understanding of the crisis (which marks the beginning no less than the end of an epoch). In all these matters, the Marxian method ... is likely to be more useful than other methods. If it is not, it can be discarded. After all, the object survives (1945: 46).

'Specificity' and 'crisis' are the key words in this passage: the former points to the importance of the encounter of traditions and the latter to its consequences. When one speaks of tradition, or of 'Marxist's specification', he/she means in DP's words, "the comparative obduracy of the culture pattern". He expected the Marxist approach to be grounded in the specificity of Indian history (1945: 45; 1946: 162ff), as indeed Marx himself had done by focusing on Indian capitalism, the dominant institutions of western society in his times. Marx, it will be said, was interested in precipitating the crisis of contradictory class interest in capitalist society (1945: 37). DP, too, was interested in the study of tradition and modernity in India. This could be done by focusing first on tradition and then only on change.

> The first task for us, therefore, is to study the social traditions to which we have been born. This task includes the study of the changes in the traditions by external and internal pressures. The latter are most economic.... Unless the economic force is extraordinarily strong – and it is only when the modes of production are altered – traditions survive by adjustments. The capacity for adjustment is the measure of the vitality of traditions. One can have full vitality of this treasure only by immediate experience. Thus, this is that I give top priority to the understanding (in Dilthey's sense) of traditions even for the study of their changes. In other words, the study of Indian traditions ... should proceed the socialist interpretations of changes in Indian traditions in terms of economic forces (1958: 232).

He hovered between Indian traditions and Marxism and his adherence to Marxist solutions to intellectual and practical problems gained salience in his later work, which was also characterized by heightened concern with tradition.

### *Modernization: Genuine or Spurious?*

For DP the history of India was not the history of her particular form of class struggle because she had experienced none worth the name. The place of philosophy and religion was dominant in his history, and it was fundamentally a long-drawn exercise in cultural synthesis. For him, "Indian history was Indian culture" (1958: 123). India's recent woes, namely, hatred and partition, had been the result of arrested assimilation of Islamic values (ibid.: 163); he believed that history halts until it is pushed (ibid.: 39).

The national movement had generated much moral fervour but DP complained, it had been anti-intellectual. Not only had there been much unthinking borrowing from the west, there had also emerged a hiatus between theory and practice as a result of which thought had become impoverished and action ineffectual. Given his concern for intellectual and artistic creativity, it is not surprising that he should have concluded: "politics ruined our culture" (1958: 190).

What was worse, there were no signs of this schism being healed in the years immediately after independence. When planning arrived as state policy in the early 1950s, DP expressed his concern, for instance, in an important 1953 paper on 'Man and Plan in India' (1958: 30–76), that a clear concept of the new man to formulate a negative judgment about the endeavours to build a new India, and also diagnosed the cause of the rampant intellectual sloth. He said in 1955: "I have seen how our progressive groups have failed in the field of intellect, and hence also in economic and political action, chiefly on account of their ignorance of and unrootedness in India's social reality" (1958: 240).

The issue at stake was India's modernization. DP's essential stand on this was that there could not be genuine modernization through imitation. A people could not abandon their own cultural heritage and yet succeeded in internalizing the historical experience of other peoples; they could only be ready to be taken over. He feared cultural imperialisms more than any other. The only valid approach, according to him, was that which characterized the efforts of men like Ram Mohan Roy and Rabindranath Tagore, who tried to make "the main currents of western thought and action ... run through the Indian bed to remove its choking weeds in order that the ancient stream might flow" (1958: 33).

DP formulated this view of the dialectics between tradition and modernity several years before independence, in his study of Tagore published in 1943, DP views the nature and dynamics of modernization. It emerges as a historical process which is at once an expansion, an elevation, a deepening and revitalization – in short, a larger investment – of traditional values and cultural patterns, and not a total departure from them, resulting from the interplay of the traditional and the modern. From this perspective, tradition is a condition of rather than obstacle to modernization; it gives us the freedom to choose between alternatives and evolve a cultural pattern which cannot but be a synthesis of the old and the new. New values and institutions must have a soil in which to take root and from which to imbibe character. Modernity must, therefore, be defined in relation to and not in denial of tradition. Conflict is only the intermediate stage in the dialectical triad: the movement is toward coincidentia oppositorum.

Needless to emphasize, the foregoing argument is in accordance with the Marxist dialectic which sees relations as determined by one another and therefore bases a 'proper' understanding of them on such a relationship. Synthesis of the opposites is not, however, a historical inevitability; it is not a gift given to a people consciousness (1958: 189); it is a "dynamic social process and not another name for traditionalism" (ibid.: 100–2). History for DP was a going concern (1945: 19), and the value of the Marxist approach to the fully awakened endeavour. The alternative to self-conscious choice-making is mindless imitation and loss of autonomy and, therefore, dehumanization, though he did not put it quite in these words.

Self-consciousness, then, is the form of modernization. Its content, one gathers from DP's writings in the 1950s, consists of nationalism, democracy, the utilization of science and technology for harnessing nature, planning for social and economic development, and the cultivation of rationality. The typical modern man is the engineer, social and technical (1958: 39–40). DP believed that these forces were becoming ascendant:

> This is a bare historical fact. To transmute that fact into a value, the first requisite is to have active faith in the historicity of the fact.... The second requisite is social action ... to push ... consciously, deliberately, collectively, into the next historical phase. The value of Indian traditions lies in the ability of their conserving forces to put a brake on hasty passage. Adjustment is the end-product of the dialectical connection between the two. Meanwhile (there) is

> tension. And tension is not merely interesting as a subject of research; if it leads up to a higher stage, it is also desirable. The higher stage is where personality is integrated through a planned, socially directed, collective endeavour for historically understood ends, which means ... a socialist order. Tensions will not ease there. It is not the peace of the grace. Only alienation from nature, work and man will stop in the arduous course of such high and strenuous endeavours. (1958: 76)

In view of this clear expression of faith (it is what, not a demonstration), it is not surprising that he should have hold Indian sociologists (in 1955) that their 'first task' was the study of 'social traditions' (1958: 232), and should have reminded them that traditions grow through conflict.

It is in the context of this emphasis on tradition that his specific recommendation for the study of Mahatma Gandhi's views on machines and technology, before going ahead with 'a large scale technological development' (1958: 225), was made. It was not small matter that from the Gandhian perspective, which stressed the value of wantlessness, non-exploitation and non-possession, the very notions of economic development and underdevelopment could be questioned (ibid.: 206). But, this was perhaps only a gesture (a response to a poser), for DP maintained that Gandhi had failed to indicate how to absorb the new social forces which emerged from the West"; moreover, "the type of new society enveloped in the vulgarized notion of *Ramarajya* was not only non-historical but anti-historical" (ibid.: 38). But he was also convinced that Gandhian insistence on traditional values might help to save Indians from the kind of evils (for example, scientism and consumerism) to which the west had fallen prey (ibid.: 227).

The failure to clearly defined the terms and rigorously examine the process of synthesis, as already noted above, re-appears here again and indeed repeatedly in his work. The resultant 'self-cancellation', as Gupta (1977) puts it, provided certain honesty and certain pathos to DP's sociology. In fact, he himself recognized this when he described his life to A.K. Saran as a 'series of reluctances' (Saran, 1962: 162). Saran concludes: DP did Vedanta, western liberalism, Marxism – which all beckoned to him 'do not mix'.

## *Music*

DP's *Introduction to Music* (1945) is a sociological piece which can be compared with *The Rational and Social Foundations of Music* by Max Weber (tr. and ed. by Don Martindale, London, 1958). DP's work even today remains only of its kind. It shows that "Indian music, being music, is just an arrangement of sounds; being Indian, it is certainly a product of Indian history". He further shows both the similarities and differences between Indian music and western music. In both regions, religious and folk music had been the inevitable context of classical music. In both, classical music at moments of crisis had drawn from people's music for fresh life, elaborated its leisure, and imposed sophisticated forms upon it in return. Music was equally intimate with functions of collective living and equally susceptible to the genuine influences that worked upon the culture pattern. So long as the princely courts, the priestly dignitaries and strongly entrenched guilds fixed the rule of living, Indian and European music alike betrayed the rudiments of melody and harmony. Since then, the tempo of change has been slower in India than in Europe, according, partly, at least, for the so-called 'spiritually' of her music. In fact, the community and the homogeneity of Indian music are astonishing (1945: 8).

## Conclusion

Dhurjati Prasad Mukerji was one of the founding fathers of sociology in India. He had fairly long tradition of intellectual pursuits. Being an intellectual meant two things to DP. First, discovering the sources and potentialities of social reality in the dialect of tradition and modernity, and, second developing an integrated personality through pursuit of knowledge. Indian sociologists, in his opinion, suffered from a lack of interest in history and philosophy and in the dynamism and meaningfulness of social life. Paying attention to specificities in a general framework of understanding was the first principle derived from Marx. DP developed this methodological point in an important essay on the Marxist method of historical interpretation. He embraced Marxism in various ways, ranging from a simple emphasis upon the economic factor in the making of culture to an elevation of practice to the status of a test of theory.

In this chapter, we found an explanatory exposition of a selected aspect of D.P. Mukerji's sociological writings, using as far as convenient to his own words. The theme of 'tradition' and 'modernity' occupies an important place in his work and also survives as a major concern of contemporary sociology. Taking DP's work as a whole, one soon discovers that his concern with tradition and modernity, which became particularly salient during the 1940s and remained so until the end, was in fact a particular expression of a larger, and it would seem perennial concern of westernized Hindu intellectuals. This concern manifested in a variety of ways. There is an urge for a synthesis of Vedanta, western liberalism and Marxism.

The work of D.P. Mukerji is quite significant in building sociology of India. He was deeply influenced by Marxian thought as is evident in his emphasis on economic factors in the process of cultural change. We find that how he looks at the impact of the west on the Indian society as a phase in the social process of cultural assimilation and synthesis. In his view, Indian culture has grown by a series of responses to the successive challenges of so many races and cultures, which has resulted in a synthesis.

Mukerji's basic ideas remain relevant for sociology in India even today. He showed that development of man or person is conditioned by the social milieu. Therefore, national independence, economic development and the resolutions of class contradiction within society are necessary conditions for human development in countries like India. Nevertheless, they are not sufficient conditions. Appropriate values for integrating autonomy of the self with collective interests, rationality with emotionality and care for tradition will have to be created. A study of Indian tradition and its dialectical relation with the forces of modernity may suggest how such values are generated. DP's greatest contribution lies in his theoretical formulations about the role of tradition in order to analyse social change. He reminded us that the Indian social reality could be properly appraised only in terms of "its special traditions, special symbols and its special patterns of culture and social actions".

## D.P. Mukerji's Framework Summarized

### *Background*

1. Education and training in economics at Calcutta.
2. Academic career at Calcutta and Lucknow.
3. Interest in understanding the nature and meaning of Indian social reality rooted in the Indian tradition and also to find out the ways of how to change it for promoting welfare of the common people by adapting the forces of modernity to the specificity of Indian tradition.

### *Aim*

1. The role of tradition in order to analyse social change

### *Assumptions*

1. Development of man or person is conditioned by the social milieu.
2. Marxism as a method of analysis rather than a political ideology.

### *Methodology*

1. Marxian perspective of dialectical materialism
2. Trans-disciplinary approach.

### *Typology*

1. Armchair social critic.
2. Marxian framework of analysis.

### *Issues*

Different aspects of Indian society, namely,

1. Indian Tradition
2. Tradition and Modernity
3. Personality
4. Role of New Middle Class
5. Music

## Select Bibliography

Avasthi, Abha (1997), *Social and Cultural Diversities*, New Delhi: Rawat Publications.

Bhattacharya, S.K. et al. (2003), *Understanding Society*, New Delhi: NCERT.

Doshi, S.L. (2003), *Modernity, Post-modernity and Neo-Sociological Theories*, Delhi: Rawat Publications.

Madan, T.N. (1993), "Dialectic of Tradition and Modernity in the Sociology of D.P. Mukerji", in N.K. Singh (ed.), *Theory and Ideology in Indian Sociology*, Jaipur: Rawat Publications.

— (1994), "D.P. Mukerji: A Centenary Tribute", *Sociological Bulletin*, Vol. 43, No. 2, September.

Mukerji, D.P. (1924), *Perspectives and the Social Sciences*, Calcutta: The Book Company.

— (1932), *Basic Concepts in Sociology*, London: Kegan Paul, Trench, Trubner & Co.

— (1942, 1948), *Modern Indian Culture*, Bombay: Hind Kitab.

— (1943, 1972), *Tagore: A Study*, Calcutta: Manisha.

— (1945), *On Indian History: A Study in Method*, Bombay: Hind Kitab.

— (1945), *An Introduction to Indian Music*, Bombay: Hind Kitab.

— (1946), *Problems of Indian Youth*, Bombay: Hind Kitab.

— (1946), *Views and Counterviews*, Lucknow: Universal.

— (1955), "Indian Tradition and Social Change", Presidential Address to the First All India Sociological Conference.

— (1958), *Diversities*, Delhi: Peoples Publishing House.

Oommen, T.K. and P.N. Mukherji (1986), *Indian Sociology: Reflections and Introspections*, Mumbai: Popular Prakashan.

Saran, A.K. (1962). "D.P. Mukerji 1894–1961", *The Eastern Anthropologist*, 15 (2): 167–69 An Obituary.

Singh, Yogendra (1986), "Indian Sociology", *Current Sociology*, Vol. 34, No. 2.

Venugopal, C.N. (1998), *Religion and Indian Society: A Sociological Perspective*, New Delhi: Gyan Publishing House.

# 12

# A.R. Desai

Akshay Ramanlal Desai (1915–1994) was born on April 16, 1915 at Nadiad in Gujarat and died on November 12, 1994 at Baroda in Gujarat. In his early years, he was influenced by his father Ramanlal Vasantlal Desai, a well known litterateur who inspired the youth in Gujarat in the thirties. A.R. Desai took part in student movements in Baroda, Surat and Bombay. He graduated from the University of Bombay, and also obtained a law degree and a PhD in sociology under G.S. Ghurye from the same university in 1946. Later on, he taught at the Bombay University and also became head of the department. In 1947, he got married to Neera Desai, who has done pioneering work in the field of women's studies. In 1953, he took the membership of the Trotskyites Revolutionary Socialist Party and resigned from its membership in 1981.

## Methodology

Among Indian sociologists one who has consistently advocated and applied dialectical-historical model in his sociological studies is A.R. Desai. Desai closely studied the works of Marx and Engels and the writings of Leon Trotsky by whom he was very much influenced. He may be regarded as one of the pioneers in introducing the modern Marxist approach to empirical investigations involving bibliographical and field research.

In the above context, Desai alone among Indian sociologists has consistently applied Marxist methods in his treatment of Indian social structure and its processes. He is a doctrinaire Marxist. He rejects any interpretations of tradition with reference to religion, rituals and festivities. It is essentially a secular phenomenon. Its nature is economic and it originates and develops in economics. He finds it in family, village and other social institutions. He also does not find the origin of tradition in western culture. His studies mainly of nationalism and its social configuration (1966), his examination of community development programmes for economic development in villages (1959), his diagnosis of the interface between state and society in India or the relationship between polity and social structure (1975), his treatment of urban slums and their demographic problems (1972), and finally his study of peasant movements (1979) are all based on a Marxist method of historical-dialectical materialism. He considers that the emerging contradictions in the Indian process of social transformation arise mainly from the growing nexus among the capitalist bourgeoisie, the rural petty-bourgeoisie and a state apparatus, all drawn from similar social roots. This thwarts the aspirations of the rural and industrial working classes by sheer of its power and of its skilful stratagems. The contradiction, however, is not resolved. It only takes new cumulative forms and re-emerges in the form of protests and social movements. The social unrest is rooted in the capitalist path of development followed by India, bequeathed to it as a legacy of the national movement.

## Writings of Desai

A refreshingly new perspective to evaluate changes in Indian society was brought about by a few Marxist sociologists. A.R. Desai, a student of Ghurye, stands out in this respect with his devoted and sustained endeavours to understand the diverse aspects of Indian social reality: *The Social Background of Indian Nationalism*

(1948); currently operating (1973); and immanent features of Indian nationalism (1975); the issue and problems of *Rural Sociology in India* (1969); *Slums and Urbanization of India* (1970, 1972); and the implications of the modernization of Indian society in the world context (1971), *State and Society in India* (1975), *Peasant Struggle in India* (1979), *Rural India in Transition* (1979), and *India's Path of Development* (1984). Desai also developed the field of political sociology in 1960s. In an anthology, Desai (1979) included the studies on peasant struggles, which have also been carried out by historians and social scientists of diverse orientations.

Like D.P. Mukerji (1958), A.R. Desai (1976) studied Indian society from Marxian perspective and also used history fruitfully. Desai and Pilllai (1972) conducted a study of slums, which constitutes a separate category within the area of city studies. In 1969 Desai published an edited volume on *Rural Sociology in India*, which was a major turning point and pacesetter in the field of agrarian studies.

Closely related to the new trend in agrarian sociology has been the trend of studying social movements, particularly among the peasantry. Sociology and social movements remained for a long time a neglected area. Desai's (1948) study of the Indian National Movement – its class character and inherent contradictions – was of course a noteworthy and pioneering contribution of the pre-1950 era. Here, in this chapter, we would discuss the important contributions of Desai on major themes as follows:

1. Village structure
2. Transformation of Indian society
3. Social background of Indian nationalism
4. Peasant struggles
5. State and society

### *Village Structure*

It is viewed that Indian village was a self-sufficient unit in pre-British period. The village population was mainly composed of peasants. The peasant families enjoyed traditional hereditary right to possess and cultivate his holding from generation to generation.

Therefore, village was based on agriculture carried on with the primitive plough and bullock-power and handicraft by means of the primitive equipment.

The village council was the *de facto* owner of the village land, which represented the village community. All exchange of products produced by the village workers was limited to the village community. The village did not have any appreciable exchange relations with the outside world. Further, the pre-British Indian society almost completely subordinated the individual to the caste, family and the village *panchayat*. The culture of pre-British India was feudal in nature, which was predominantly mystical in character. This was due to the fact that the society was economically on a low level, stationary and socially rigid. Whatever changes occurred were quantitative and not qualitative in character.

### Transformation of Indian Society

The transformation of the pre-British India from feudal economy to capitalist economy was a result of the British conquest of India. The British government adopted the capitalist path of development in their political and economic policies at three levels, viz., trade, industry and finance.

The introduction of new economic reforms of the British government disrupted the old economic system. Consequently, it decayed the old land relations and artisans with the emergence of new land relations and modern industries. In place of village commune appeared modern peasant proprietors or *zamindars*, as private owner of land. The class of artisans disappeared with modern industry. New classes like the capitalist, industrial workers, agricultural labourers, tenants, merchants etc. emerged. Thus, the British impact not only led to the transformation of the economic anatomy of Indian society, but also its social physiognomy. Further, the new land revenue system, commercialization of agriculture, fragmentation of land etc. also led to the transformation of Indian village.

At higher level, this resulted in growing polarization of classes in agrarian areas, poverty in rural areas and exploitation by the owners of land. It gives rise to new class structure in agrarian society with categories like *zamindars*, absentee landlords, tenants, peasant proprietors, agricultural labourers, moneylenders and merchant class. Similarly, in urban society, there were capitalist industrial working class, petty traders, professional class like doctors, lawyers, engineers etc.

The British government also introduced railways, postal services, centralized uniform law, English education, modern industry and many more, which brought qualitative change in Indian society. It is said that although the British government had various exploitative mechanisms in India, but unintentionally these efforts led to unification of Indian society. The role of railways and press is significant in this direction. It has brought the scattered and disintegrated Indians into the mainstream. The implication was social movements, collective representations, national sentiments, and consciousness among Indian people and formation of unionism at various levels. Such a social infrastructural set-up gave rise to nationalist freedom movement and awakening of Indian nationalism.

### *Social Background of Indian Nationalism*

Desai applies the Marxist approach to the study of 'nationalism' in India during the British rule. He spells out historical-dialectical materialism and applies it to the study of various types of movements – rural and urban, caste and class structure, social mobility, education and other aspects of Indian society. Though Desai's book was published in 1948, it became more popular in the late sixties and the seventies perhaps due to the increased consciousness of Indian social scientists towards social self-consciousness.

Desai's first full-length work *The Social Background of Indian Nationalism* was a trendsetter not only for its Marxist academic orientation, but also for the way in which it cross-fertilized sociology with history. Quite like other Marxists, he employs production relations for the explanation of traditional social background of Indian nationalism in his classical work.

The book is an excellent effort to trace the emergence of Indian nationalism from dialectical perspective. According to

Desai, India's nationalism is the result of the material conditions created by the British colonialism. The Britishers developed new economic relations by introducing industrialization and modernization. This economic relationship is predominantly a stabilizing factor in the continuity of traditional institutions in India, which would undergo changes as these relations would change. Desai thinks that when traditions are linked with economic relations, the change in the latter would eventually change the traditions. It is in this context that he thinks that caste will disintegrate with the creation of new social and material conditions, such as industries, economic growth, education, etc.

Desai's definition of tradition is a watershed. He does not trace it from caste, religion or ritual. The dialectical history of India that he presents very clearly shows that traditions have their roots in India's economy and production relations. Despite merits of the dialectical approach applied by Desai in the definition of tradition, Yogendra Singh argues that the merits are not without weaknesses. What is wrong with Desai is that he was very profound when he applies principles of Marxism in analysing Indian situation but fails at the level of empirical support. In other words, his theoretical framework can be challenged by the strength of substantial data. The critique of Yogendra Singh runs as under:

> The important limitation of the dialectical approach for studies of social change in India is the lack of substantial empirical data in support of his major assertions, which are often historiographic and can easily be challenged. In theoretical terms, however, this approach can be more visible for analysis of the processes of change and conflict in India provided it is founded upon a sound tradition of scientific research. Despite this limitation, some studies conducted on this model offer useful hypotheses, which can be further tested in course of the studies on social change.

The large amount of work produced by Desai is testimony to the missionary zeal with which he carried on his endeavour. He authored, edited and compiled a large number of books. His pioneering studies were *Social Background of Indian Nationalism*

(1948) and *Recent Trends in Indian Nationalism* (1960). In these works, he developed the Marxian framework to outline the growth of capitalism in India. He provided an analysis of the emergence of the various social forces, which radically altered the economy and society in India within the context of colonialism. The state which emerged in India after independence, he postulated, was a capitalist state. The theme of the relation between the state and the capitalist class was explored in his writings. To him, the administrative level apparatus of the state performed the twin functions of protecting the propertied classes and suppressing the struggles of the exploited classes. In *India's Path of Development* (1984) he took on the traditional communist parties and the Marx scholars who spoke of the alliance with the progressive bourgeoisie, of semi-feudalism, of foreign imperialist control over Indian economy, and who postulated a 'two-stages theory of revolution' or accepted a 'peaceful parliamentary road to socialism' in India. Desai's works include a number of edited volumes on rural sociology, urbanization, labour movements, peasant struggles, modernization, religion, and democratic rights. They are a rich source of reference material for students, researchers and activists.

### Peasant Struggles

In his two volumes entitled *Peasant Struggles in India* (1979) and *Agrarian Struggles in India after Independence* (1986), Desai has complied excellent material on peasant struggles in India during colonial rule and after independence. The difference in the character of struggles then and now is highlighted. Agrarian struggles, at present, Desai suggests, are waged by the newly-emerged propertied classes as well as the agrarian poor, especially the agrarian proletariat, whereas the former fight for a greater share in the fruits of development. The poor comprising pauperized peasants and labourers belonging to low castes and tribal communities struggle for survival and for a better life for themselves. Thus, Desai maintained, progress could be achieved only by radically transforming the exploitative capitalist system in India. The theme of the state was explored in several of his studies.

## *State and Society*

In *State and Society in India* (1975), Desai provided a critique of the theories of modernization accepted by a large number of academic establishments. He clearly stated that in reality the concept assumed "modernization on capitalist path a desirable value premise". It, however, served as a valuable ideological vehicle to the ruling class pursuing the capitalist path. Desai remarked on the absence of a comprehensive analysis of the class character, class role and the economic, repressive, ideological functions of the post-independence Indian state by Marxist scholars. In many of his later works he pursued the theme of the repressive role of the state and the growing resistance to it. In *Violation of Democratic Rights in India* (1986), *Repression and Resistance in India* (1990), *Expanding Governmental Lawlessness and Organized Struggles* (1991) and *State and Repressive Culture* (1994), jointly with Wilfred D'Costa, he highlights the violation of the democratic rights of minorities, women, slum dwellers in urban India, press and other media by the state (Munshi and Saldanha, 1994).

In his studies of nationalism, analysis of rural social structure, the nature of economic and social policies of change in India and the structure of state and society, he has consistently tried to expose the contradictions and anomalies in policies and process of change resulting from the capitalist-bourgeoisie interlocking of interest in the Indian society (Desai, 1959, 1966, 1975). According to Desai, the polarization of class interest, especially of the bourgeoisie, is the foundation of modern society in India. It has thus inherent in it the class contradictions and the logic of its dialectics. This has been thoroughly exposed by Desai in his several writings.

## Relevance of Marxist Approach

In the fifties and early sixties, American structural-functionalism and British functionalism dominated social sciences in general and sociological researches in particular. However, Desai undeterred by these imperialistic influences continued to write on Indian society and state from the perspective of an involved scholarship.

In his presidential address to the XV All India Sociological Conference, Desai narrates about twenty-seven points referring to the assessment of Indian sociology. He finds that the dominant sociological approaches in India are basically non-Marxist, and the Marxist approach has been rejected on the pretext of its being dogmatic, value-loaded and deterministic in nature. The relevant approach, according to Desai, is the Marxist approach as it could help to study of government policies, the classes entrenched into state apparatus and India's political economy. Desai writes: "I wish the social science practitioners in India break through the atmosphere of allergy towards this profound and influential approach and create climate to study the growing body of literature articulating various aspects of Indian society, the class character of the state and the path of development."

Thus, in his presidential address, Desai focused on the relevance of the Marxist approach to the study of Indian society. According to him, the Marxist approach helps one to raise relevant questions, conduct researches in the right direction, formulate adequate hypotheses, evolve proper concepts, adopt and combine appropriate research techniques and locate the central tendencies of transformation with its major implications.

Desai highlights certain crucial aspects of Marxist approach to the study of Indian society. The Marxist approach helps to understand the social reality through the means of production, the techno-economic division of labour involved in operating the instruments of production, and social relations of production or what are more precisely characterized as property relations. Thus, the Marxist approach focuses on understanding the type of property relations which existed on the eve of independence in India. These are being elaborated by the state as the active agent of transformation of post-independent India. Hence, the Marxist approach will help the Indian scholars to designate the type of society and its class character, the role of the state and the specificity of the path of development with all the implications.

Desai argues that property relations are crucial because they shape the purpose, nature, control, direction and objectives underlying the production. Further, property relations determine the norms about who shall get how much and on what grounds. For understanding the post-independence Indian society, the Marxist approach will focus on the specific type of property relations, which existed on the eve of independence and which are being elaborated by the state as the active agent of transformation both in terms of elaborating legal-normative notions as well as working out actual policies pursued for development and transformation of Indian society into a prosperous developed one.

In brief, the Marxist approach gives central importance to property structure in analysing any society. It provides "historical location or specification of all social phenomena". Moreover, "this approach recognizes the dialectics of evolutionary as well as revolutionary changes of the breaks in historical continuity in the transition from one socio-economic formation to another". In this context, Desai tried to understand the Indian society which also reflects in his works. Desai not only did give notice to the mainstream that Marx has a place in sociology, but also, he provided a forum for radical-minded scholars to broaden their horizon of research.

## Analysis of Indian Society through Marxist Approach

Marx pointed out that different sub-formations within a society could not be understood adequately if seen in the context of the historical level. Thus, the Marxist approach endeavours to locate, within a specific society, the forces which preserve and forces which prompt it to change, i.e., the forces driving to take a leap into a new or a higher form of social organization, which would unleash the productive power of mankind to a next higher level. Further, Desai argues that the methodology adopted by social scientists is apt to understand social reality from the ideology of capitalism. But that is a false finding. He further argues that changes need to be interpreted from the perspective of production relations. And it is precisely the method he has applied.

The Marxist approach further considers that focusing on the type of property relations prevailing in the Indian society as crucial-axial element for properly understanding the nature of transformation that has been taking place in the country. This approach does not demand crude reducing of every phenomenon to economic factor; it also does not deny the autonomy, or prevalence of distinct institutional and normative features peculiar to a particular society. For instance, according to Desai, it does not deny the necessity of understanding the institution like caste system, religions, linguistic or tribal groups or even specific cultural traditions which are characteristics of the Indian society. The Marxist approach, in fact, endeavours to understand their role and the nature of their transformation in the larger context of the type of society, which is being evolved, and understand them in the matrix of underlying overall property relations and norms implicit therein, which pervasively influence the entire social economic formation. Desai feels that adoption of the Marxist approach will be helpful in studying the industrial relations, not merely as management-labour relations, but as capital-labour relations, and also in the context of the state wedded to capitalist path of development, shaping these relations. Similarly, it will help understand the dynamics of rural, urban, educational and other developments, better as it will assist the exploration of these phenomena in the larger context of the social framework, which is being created by the state shaping the development on capitalist path of development. The Marxist approach will also assist in understanding why institutions generating higher knowledge-products, sponsored, financed and basically shaped by the state, pursuing a path of capitalist development, will not basically allow the paradigms and approaches to study, which may expose the myth spread about state as welfare neutral state and reveal it as basically a capitalist state. The constitution evolved its bourgeois constitution and the leadership is representing capitalist class and is reshaping the economy and society on capitalist path. The slogan of socialistic pattern is a hoax to create illusion and confuse the masses. The real intentions and practices are geared to the development on capitalist lines.

According to Desai, the bourgeoisie is the dominant class in India. The Indian society is based on the capitalist economy. The dominant culture in our country is therefore the culture of the dominant capitalist class. Indian capitalism was a by-product of imperialist capitalism. Indian capitalism was born during the declining phase of world capitalism when, due to the general crisis of capitalism, even in advanced capitalist countries, the ruling bourgeoisie, not cognizant of the cause of the crisis, have been increasingly abandoning rationalism and materialist philosophies and retrograding to religio-mystical world outlooks. Desai argues that Indian bourgeoisie built up a fundamentally secular bourgeois democratic state, which has been imparting modern scientific, technological and liberal democratic education. This class and its intelligentsia have been, in the cultural field revivalist and more and more popularizing supporting and spreading old religious and idealistic philosophic concepts among the people. The idealistic and religio-mystical philosophies of the ruling bourgeois class, further reinforced by crude mythological culture rampant among the masses, constitute the dominant culture of the Indian people today. The social role played by this culture is reactionary since it gives myopic picture of the physical universe and the social world, a misexplanation of the fundamental causes of the economic and social crises, opiates the consciousness of the masses and tries to divert the latter from advancing on the road of specific solutions of their problems.

## Conclusion

In this chapter, we have tried to focus upon the works of A.R. Desai, which show that how Marxist approach can be applied in understanding Indian social reality. The *Social Background of Indian Nationalism* reflects on the economic interpretation of Indian society. Desai applies historical materialism for understanding the transformation of Indian society. He explains that how the national consciousness emerged through qualitative changes in Indian society. It must be observed by the concluding words that in all his writings Desai has examined the usefulness of Marxian framework to understand Indian's reality. Desai's all other writings also reflect the Marxist approach to understand the Indian society.

## Desai's Framework Summarized

### *Background*

1. Educated at Baroda and Bombay.
2. Academic career in Gujarat and Bombay.
3. Interests in social movements, Indian National Movement, agrarian system etc.
4. Active in student movements in Vadodara, Surat and Bombay.

### *Aim*

Analyse the emerging contradictions in the Indian process of social transformation.

### *Assumption*

Social unrest is rooted in the capitalist path of development.

### *Methodology*

Marxist method of historical-dialectical materialism.

### *Typology*

Dialectical-historical model.

### *Issues*

Different aspects of Indian society, namely,

1. National movement
2. Peasant struggles
3. Slums and urbanization
4. State and society
5. Democratic rights

## ■ Select Bibliography

Desai, A.R. (ed.) (1959), *Rural Sociology in India*, Bombay: Popular Prakashan.

— (1966), *Social Background of Indian Nationalism*, Bombay: Popular Prakashan.

— (1971), *Essays on Modernization of Underdeveloped Societies,* Bombay: Thacker.

— (1975), *State and Society in India: Essay in Dissent*, Bombay: Popular Prakashan.

— (1979), *Peasant Struggles in India,* Delhi: Oxford University Press.

— (1979), *Rural India in Transition,* Bombay: Popular Prakashan.

— (1981), 'Relevance of the Marxist Approach to the Study of Indian Society', *Sociological Bulletin*, 30 (1):1–20.

Doshi, S.L. (2003), *Modernity, Postmodernity and Neo-Sociological Theories*, Jaipur: Rawat Publications.

Nagla, Madhu (2005), 'Approaches to Indian Sociology', unpublished paper.

Oommen, T.K. and P.N. Mukherji (1986), *Indian Sociology: Reflections and Introspections,* Mumbai: Popular Prakashan.

Singh, Yogendra (1986), 'Indian Sociology', *Current Sociology*, Vol. 34, No.2.

# 13

# Ramkrishna Mukherjee

Ramkrishna Mukherjee has been a distinguished scientist of the Indian Statistical Institute, Calcutta, and an adjunct Professor of Sociology at the State University of New York, Binghamton. Born in 1919, he was educated at Calcutta University (M.Sc., 1941) and at Cambridge (PhD, 1948). He then moved to London to become the Chief Research Officer to his Majesty's Social Survey, London (1948–49) after which he went to Ankara as Consultant, Government of Turkey (1949), and also as Consultant to London School of Economics (1952). He began his career as guest Professor of Indian Studies at the Humboldt University in Berlin (1953–57). From 1957 through 1979, he functioned as Research Professor at the Indian Statistical Institute, Calcutta.

Mukherjee has also been a member of the Indian Council of Social Science Research (1974) and advisor to many institutions and the journals in the social sciences in India and abroad. He was the President of the Indian Sociological Society (1972–74) and the member of the Executive Committee of the International Sociological Association (1974–78). His research experience includes work in India as well as Bangladesh, UK, France, Germany, Sweden, Czechoslovakia, Turkey and Uganda.

## Methodology

Mukherjee's main concerns are systematic and inductive sociology, diagnostic research and related methodology. He recommends the use of the diagnostic mode to get the best possible explanation of social reality. Among the Indian sociologists, like D.P. Mukerji, Ramkrishna Mukherjee also emphasized the significance of dialectical model for the study of Indian society. In his later works, Ramkrishna has changed from dialectical-historical to a probabilistic nomological approach for the study of social reality (Singh, 2004). He calls his approach 'inductive inferential' which is neutral to the type of propositions, Marxist or non-Marxist, that one chooses to test and verify. The role of history and dialectics in the sociological thinking and research, according to Mukherjee, stops at the level of formulation of proposition; these may help in even a taxonomic formulation of categories (see Mukherjee, 1970, 1975) or social indicators, but beyond this the logical principles of test and verification would have to operate independently.

In his rigorous study, Mukherjee (1972, 1977) used systematic quantitative methodology to measure kinship distance and extent of change in family structures in West Bengal.

## Works

Mukherjee's research interests include historical sociology, studies in the classification of families and rural society, problem of acculturation and social indicators. He wrote more than a dozen books and over hundred research papers for internationally reputed journals. His major publications include: *The Problem of Uganda* (1956), *The Dynamics of a Rural Society* (1957), *The Sociologist and Social Change in India Today* (1965), *Six Villages of Bengal* (1971), *The Rise and Fall of the East India Company* (1958), *Social Indicators* (1975), *Family and Planning in India* (1976), *West Bengal Family Structure: 1946–66* (1977), *What will it be? Explorations in Inductive Sociology* (1978), *Sociology of Indian Sociology* (1979) etc.

In this chapter, we discuss the following major aspects, which have been highlighted in the writings of Ramkrishna Mukherjee:

1. Agrarian social structure
2. The sociologist and social change in India today
3. Trends in Indian sociology
4. Studies in Indian sociology

## Agrarian Social Structure

Mukherjee's (1949, 1957, 1958) initial works on rural Bengal – its economic structure and dynamics – could be partly attributed to K.P. Chattopadhyay's initiative in portraying that side of Indian social reality of which sociologists and social anthropologists coming from urban middle class background were likely to lose sight. At the Indian Statistical Institute, Calcutta, agrarian class structure, class relations and agrarian social change were given priority in large scale sample surveys. Mukherjee conducted a series of studies on agrarian structure in Bengal in the 1940s. The theme of agrarian social structure and change was to re-appear in Indian sociology only after a gap of nearly two decades in the late 1960s and in the 1970s.

Ramkrishna made systematic historical as well as empirical studies using dialectical model. His book on *The Rise and Fall of the East Indian Company* (1958) is a contribution to economic and social history of the institutionalization of colonialism in India through stabilization of economic policies, disintegration of feudalism and aristocratic despotism, and the rise of new middle classes. In his *The Dynamics of Rural Society* (1957), Mukherjee studies social and economic changes in a set of villages through changes in the structure of classes. He emphasizes the necessity to grasp the systematic and organic character of Indian society for understanding of its social processes. In this study of rural society, Mukherjee makes use of statistical data from various sources to generate conceptual categories of the class structure in villages and analytically posits them to unravel the problem of rural social structure and development from a quasi-Marxist perspective. The use of statistical data makes this study comparable to those in other regions and states of India, although Mukherjee confines his attention to West Bengal.

## The Sociologist and Social Change in India Today

The book entitled, *The Sociologist and Social Change in India Today* (1965) contains six main chapters. These are revised or enlarged versions of six papers which Mukherjee had written between 1961 and 1964. In the equal numbers, they can be classified under the category of "fallacies and facts" and of "focus and orientation", as has been done in the following with the chapter 4 and the chapter 8 summarizing the discussions contained in the two respective parts of the book.

Facts are many; fallacies are countless. The focus of attention also need not be the only one that has been demonstrated here; and orientation towards further research must cover further grounds than those indicated in this book.

### *Social Change*

'Change' to a sociologist is a mater of inference. What we deduce actually is 'difference' within a 'society' from the analysis of a set of observations. And, we may interpret those 'differences' as *change* in reference of an assumed *point of departure.* Also, we may not do so, and interpret the 'differences' as causal fluctuations. So, the task we should undertake centres round the questions: (i) what is the point of departure? (ii) what are the 'differences'?; (iii) how are these differences effected, and what pattern emerges thereby?; and (iv) why does such a pattern emerge?

These questions follow in a chronological order, while to answer them unequivocally is virtually an impossible proposition. But, we may approximate reality with successive precision provided we steer our activities in right times. Therefore, a discussion on fallacies and facts may logically precede that on "focus and orientation". This is how the contents of the book have been arranged.

### *Two Fallacies: Concept of Rural-Urban Dichotomy or Rural-Urban Continuum*

According to Mukherjee, two major fallacies commonly found in India today, namely, urban and/or industrial development bring in 'new values' in society commensurate with the social transformation we desire in our country. Cities and towns are growing or emerging. Also that increasingly improved means of transport and communication are bringing the villages nearer the urban centres is an accepted phenomenon. Therefore, at whatever pace it may be, urban development and urbanization are gathering momentum in India. But, what is their effect on the social transformation of the people involved?

### *On Urbanization and Social Transformation*

This is a moot question. Because, in whichever way the process and the degree of urbanization may be interpreted, the underlying assumption is that: "The differences between rural and urban populations represent contrasts between the old and the new, and in a sense they provide us with insights into the character of man's social and cultural life prior to urbanization" (Gibbs, 1961). How far, and in what manner, then, the rural-urban differences and inter-relations can be so explained in India? The question implies an examination of two aspects of the problem, which may appear to have no conception between them but are in fact closely associated: (1) as a consequent to the process and degree of urbanization, whether changes in the social organization and/or in the ideological orientation of the people are evident, incipient, or absent; (2) in the first two of the three enumerations, whether the course of changes conforms to the concept of *rural-urban dichotomy* or of *rural-urban continuum.*

If a particular course of urbanization is to be nurtured or destroyed, how is it taking place in society has to be ascertained beforehand, namely, as between two conceptually exclusive entities of urban and rural? or, in terms of a spectrum, which registers the influence of the urban sector on the rest of the country in a gradient of physical distance, transportation time and cost, etc., as "city-large towns-small towns-neighbouring village-remote villages"?

The first process would subscribe to the concept of rural-urban dichotomy, whereas the second to that of rural-urban continuum. And, the respective process would have an important bearing on the strategy and tactics of implementing any planned programme for India's social development.

Mukherjee has done his study in the state of West Bengal and Giridih sub-division of the district Hazaribagh in the adjoining of Bihar. He has examined the pattern of migration to urban areas so as to ascertain whether it would facilitate the operation of the concept of rural-urban dichotomy or rural-urban continuum or none. Therefore, an examination of exact process at work with respect to rural-urban differences and relationships has been looked in.

### *Focus on Social Organism: Diagnosis of Soft Spots*

Mukherjee found that the social development of the people cannot be answered in terms of rural-urban differentials, or for that matter, from a formal examination of various forms of social stratification. It requires looking into the *soft spots* in the social organism, irrespective of its rural-urban or other forms of formal stratification. Such as, if the educated persons are to be the torchbearers of progress in this respect, the content of the education offered to them and their consequent reactions would require examination so as to determine the soft spots through which the desired course of change may be implemented in the society under reference. Or, if the Hindu high caste people are to be the precursors of a new way of life, to take another hypothetical case for purpose of illustration, the potentiality of germination of such a life among them would require careful investigation with the same aim in view. Either way, or in more ways than the above two, the soft spots in the social organism require careful and sustained exploration. After that, their relative occurrence in, and/or their relative importance to, city-town-village stratification of society may decide whether rural-urban dichotomy or rural-urban continuum would be the suitable concept to formulate and execute relevant policies for social development and whether the small towns would have a role to play in that context. The examination of formal associations between patterns of migration, administrative and political divisions, cross-cultural factors, and occupational and industrial profiles of settlement of social groups and individuals, etc., does not lead us to a fruitful inference; although this is undoubtedly the primary stage in the course of our researches into the problem under reference. Mukherjee concludes that (1) there is not yet any evidence of social development, and (2) a causal or concomitant relation between cultural changes sue to urban living or urbanization and 'social' development cannot be legitimately deduced, and so (3) the concept of rural-urban dichotomy or rural-urban continuum need not be meaningful in the context of urbanization and social transformation in India at the moment.

## Trends in Indian Sociology

According to Mukherjee, an assessment of the development of sociology and social anthropology in India cannot be attempted without examining the overlapping of the various theoretical, methodological and ideological influences on the growth of these twin disciplines, sociology and social anthropology. In a comprehensive review of "Trends in Indian Sociology", Mukherjee (1979) discusses diagnostic perspective about Indian sociology. The main questions are:

(1) What is it (enumeration of the phenomenon)?
(2) How is it (classification)?
(3) Why is it (causality)?
(4) What will it be (possibility)?
(5) Why should it be (desirability)?

These five questions should interact in sequential manner with a dialectical appreciation having both positive and negative points in regard to reality of phenomena. Mukherjee sharply focused on the links between theory, ideology and praxis or between the questions: what is it? How is it? Why is it? And, what will it be and why should it be? (Mukherjee, 1977b: 2–4).

The perspective related to these questions has been discussed by Mukherjee in *What will it Be?: Explorations in Inductive Sociology* (1978). Since that perspective is applied here to the phenomenon of

Indian sociology which has been entitled, *Sociology of Indian Sociology.*

Mukherjee employed in a paradigm these fundamental questions in order to distinguish three modes of social research, viz., descriptive, explanatory and diagnostic. He has shown that the three modes are sequentially related, and that the crucial demand of contemporary social research is to adopt the diagnostic mode. This will lead to evaluation of the best possible explanation of social reality at the existing state of knowledge and thus, social research will proceed from description, and beyond explanation, towards prediction.

He also discuses the principles of the three modes of social research and drawn a systematic relation among them. Basically, he has distinguished diagnostic research as *inductive-inferential* from the descriptive and explanatory research as *deductive-positivistic.* Because of this fundamentally different perspective, diagnostic research calls for concept formation in a different manner, and requires an appropriate methodology. Therefore, Mukherjee has discussed how mutually distinguished but homologous phenomena of *social change*, *social development* and *nation-building* should be conceived, giving indication to their appropriate methodology.

He has also discussed the most crucial aspect of contemporary social research, viz., the treatment of the objective 'information' and the subjective 'value' as confounded variables to denote facts, and how this can be efficiently done by diagnostic research in contradistinction to the descriptive and explanatory research.

## Studies in Indian Sociology

In a 1979 publication, *Sociology of Indian Sociology*, Mukherjee identified growth points in terms of its practitioners who he classified as pioneers, modernizers, insiders, and pace makers and non-conformists. He has made by scholars belonging to these categories, and identifying the 'insiders' emerging in the late sixties and seventies as those who were the product of the system rather than entrants from other disciplines.

Studies in Indian sociology, as it is for similar place- and people-bound studies, are usually oriented towards recording the topic-wise proliferation of the subject and its specialization and diversification, with some relative comments on the nature and direction of changes in the thematic field. While these essentially descriptive studies are necessary to take stock of the current stage of development of the discipline in one place and in the world perspective, they cannot fully explain the reasons behind the changing course of the discipline in the given societal context. A search for this explanation would not only diagnose the soft and hard spots in the discipline towards further changes but also provide the base to predict its course in the immediate future. Mukherjee has tried to examine the development of Indian sociology systematically. He also suggests "what should it be" of Indian sociology in the contemporary Indian and world perspectives.

According to Mukherjee, from the very beginning, sociology as a body of knowledge has been founded upon a deductive and positivistic basis; inductive sociology has made little headway too far on both the ideological grounds and due to practical considerations. And, while lately mathematical reasoning and statistical principles are employed more and more as the building bricks of sociology, its foundation is not affected thereby; eventually, social causation is explained in terms of one or another 'theory' whether or not this theoretical orientation – be it Weberian, Durkheimian, Marxists or any other – its distinctly spelt out. The concern for a meta-theory is of course noticeable in present times but since its methodological requirements are not usually given adequate attention, it is still thought to consist of another theory rather than of a transmission engineered through the consolidation of all available and possible theories which is its objective.

It may not be fortuitous, therefore, that 'research methodology' is thought of as a distinct aspect of sociology in particular, and of the social sciences in general, but is not regarded as being an independent element for, say, physics in particular, and the natural sciences in general. It may also be of significance that while value is regarded to be an inextricable component of sociology and, at the same time, that an objective appreciation of the 'social facts' is seen to be of the supreme objective of sociology, the two are seldom treated as confounded variables – conceptually and methodologically. Hence, it is readily accepted for sociology as a 'social' or 'humanistic' science that "there appears to be an inherent gap between the language of theory and research which can never be bridged in a completely satisfactory way" (Blalock, Jr., 1961).

The above statement, of course, acquires a substantive meaning in relation to conceptualization for, ultimately, knowledge forms an asymptotic relation with reality, so that, we may continually advance our understanding of social reality but can never comprehend it fully and finally. Nevertheless, the scope and the course of comprehension of reality are spread out in an infinite but enumerable space. Therefore, a cautionary note is in order: "there are no limits on the non-scientific use of mathematics in sociology, unless it be the reluctance of its scientifically minded to tolerate pseudo mathematics as well as the metaphysics which would reject mathematics in principle" (Martindale, 1963). Also, in the course of continual advance in sociological knowledge, it is not less relevant to bear in mind that none of methodological difficulties often alleged to confront the search for systematic explanations of social phenomena is unique to the social sciences or is inherently insuperable (Nagel, 1961).

## Mukherjee's Framework Summarized

### *Background*

1. Educated at Calcutta University and Cambridge.
2. Academic career at Berlin (Germany), London (UK), Ankara (Turkey), and Calcutta (India).
3. His interests include historical sociology, studies in the classification of families and rural society, problem of acculturation and social indicators.

### *Aim*

Main concerns are systematic and inductive sociology.

### *Assumption*

To get the best possible explanation of social reality through the diagnostic mode of investigation.

### *Methodology*

1. Historical sociology
2. Marxism: Dialectical approach
3. Inductive sociology

### *Typology*

Historical/Dialectical Approach

### *Issues*

Different aspects of Indian society, namely,

1. Rural society
2. Family structure
3. The rise and fall of the East India Company
4. Social indicators
5. Sociology of Indian sociology
6. Explorations in Inductive sociology
7. Sociologists and social change

## Select Bibliography

Blalock, H.M. Jr. (1961), *Casual Inferences in Nonexperiment Research*, Chapel Hill: The University of Carolina Press.

Madan, G.R. (1972), *Western Sociologists on Indian Society*, Mumbai: Allied Publishers.

Martindale, D. (1963), 'Limits to the Use of mathematics in the Study of Sociology', in Charlesworth, J.C. (ed.), *Mathematics and the Social Sciences*, Philadelphia: The American Academy of Political and Social Sciences.

Mukherjee, Ramkrishna (1957), *The Dynamics of a Rural Society: A Study of the Economic Structure in Bengal Villages*, Berlin: Akademie-Verlag.

— (1958), *The Rise and Fall of the East India Company*, Berlin: Verlag der Wissenschaften.

— (1965), *The Sociologists and Social Change in India Today*, Delhi: Prentice-Hall of India.

— (1974), 'The Sociologist and the Social Reality', *Sociological Bulletin*, 23 (2):169–92.

— (1975), 'History and Tradition in Indian Society: Null and Alternate Hypotheses', *Sociological Bulletin*, 24 (1): 95–107.

— (1979), *Sociology of Indian Sociology*, New Delhi: Allied publishers.

Nagel, E. (1961), *The Structure of Science*, London: Routledge and Kegan Paul.

Oommen, T.K. and P.N. Mukerjee (1986), *Indian Sociology: Reflections and Introspections,* Mumbai: Popular Prakashan.

Singh, Yogendra (1986), *Indian Sociology: Social Conditioning and Emergent Concerns,* New Delhi: Vistaar.

# 14

# D.N. Dhanagare

Dattatreya Narayan Dhanagare (1936–2017), like A.R. Desai, has also consistently applied Marxist approach to understand the Indian society. In this context, we have tried to focus upon the works of Dhanagare which show that how Marxist approach can be relevant in understanding Indian social reality through historical and comparative methods. Unlike ethnographic-cultural and structural-functional traditions, Dhanagare emphasizes class analysis in the study of social movements particularly peasant movements in India which was challenged by the western theorization of peasant movements and gave a new twist to the global discourse.

Dhanagare was born in Washim in Vidharbha region of Maharashtra on 11 June 1936 and passed away on 7 March 2017 at the age of 81 years after suffering a cardiac arrest, at Aditya Birla Hospital, Pimpri-Chinchwad, Pune, his granddaughter Sneha Dhanagare said. Aditya Birla Hospital, where Dr Dhanagare was undergoing treatment, in a statement said, 'Dr Dhanagare was on a regular dialysis. He was suffering from triple vessel disease, known case of hypertension and severe left ventricular dysfunction. He came for routine dialysis, during which sudden fall in BP was noticed. He was immediately attended and shifted to ICU but due to acute cardiac event, the coronary syndrome and comorbidities, he succumbed to death'. Dr Dhanagare is survived by his sons Shridhar, married to Mona, and Gouranga, married to Shilpa; he also has one granddaughter Sneha. Maharashtra Education Minister, Vinod Tawde in his condolence message said, 'Dhanagare sir was a true academician, who always worked for students. With his demise, we have lost a true teacher', Sneha Dhanagare said.

Hailing from a small town in Maharashtra, Dhanagare came from a lawyer's family. Though Dhanagare obviously got the social and cultural capital of an upper caste, educated, highly respected family background, affordability was an issue as far as his educational choices were concerned. He was 'sent' to arts stream, he stated. He was a school child during the Second World War period. He attended a municipal school for six years. Around 1942, even in a small town called Washim, most of his teachers came from the non-Brahmin background. The social ambience was plural and diversity was experienced in the rural and semi-urban areas of Vidarbha – the ex-Nizam ruled territory (Berar), quite contrary to the mainstream beliefs about those times. He completed his high school education at the government high school, which was co-ed. Up till the high school level, there were no tuitions. He said, 'In fact it was not seen as desirable to attend tuitions unlike today. However, at the intermediate level, I earned a gold medal in civics. This proved to be a turning point for my academic life as the Principal advised my father to send me to Hislop College at Nagpur' (Tambekar, 2017).

After completing his school education, when he reached Nagpur for higher studies, there were multiple challenges awaiting him. He had to orient himself to English language training. Since he was good at languages, he stood first in Marathi language in his B.A. examination. Following the common understanding that there was no future for literature or language studies he decided to choose Sociology. He certainly wanted to avoid law as it was his father's profession. At Hislop College he was then allowed entry in M.A. Sociology after his teachers vouched for his ability to study

Sociology and to study in English medium. Also he was admitted only due to his high rank in B.A. to choose Sociology, which was taught in English alone, for post-graduation.

Dhanagare was a brilliant student who had his education in Nagpur University during 1955–59 where he received his Bachelor of Arts (B.A.) in First Class, sixth in order of merit and silver medal in Marathi literature in 1957 and Master of Arts in Sociology in First Class, first in order of merit in 1959. He received a Fellowship to pursue further higher studies in social sciences at the University of Massachusetts, USA in 1965–66. Dhanagare developed research papers during his stay at the university in the USA, which were eventually published in research periodicals, such as *India Quarterly, Sociological Bulletin* and *Indian Psychological Review.* After coming back to India, Dhanagare prepared a paper on electoral violence during the fourth general election in India in 1967 and presented it at the All India Sociological Conference which was subsequently published in the *Economic and Political Weekly.*

Dhanagare was awarded the prestigious Commonwealth Scholarship for 1970–73 by the UK to pursue doctoral research at the University of Sussex where he received Doctor of Philosophy (D.Phil/Ph.D) in 1973 from University of Sussex, England (UK) in the supervision of Zevedie Barbu. He acquired a lot of lessons by attending the seminar courses of Tom Bottomore, Zevedie Barbu and Berry Willium in the University of Sussex which helped him to select the issue of peasant movements in India for his Ph.D research work. Therefore, he has done his doctoral work on *Peasant Movements in India, 1920–50.* His association with Sussex University offered him an opportunity to gain deeper insights into the sociological tradition that were rooted in history and philosophy on the one hand and permitted freedom of conceptual innovation on the other. The association brought a major shift in his academic orientation from fieldwork-based research to research in historical sociology with comparative perspective. His stay in Sussex not only earned him some life-long intellectual friends but also made him aware of the enormous scholarly material, manuscripts and documents (Sahay, 2017). His doctoral thesis (OUP, 1983, four reprints thereafter) proved to be a pace-setting work in the study of social movements and in comparative social history and sociology.

Immediately after doing M.A. at Hislop, as a topper of Nagpur University, Nagpur, Dhanagare first joined S.S. College, Amravati, as a lecturer to teach sociology in both Marathi and English languages. At S.S. College he met his life partner, Nisha. He was also selected for government service in revenue department and he even worked for a very short while as a bureaucrat. He shifted to the Institute of Social Sciences in Agra University as a faculty member in 1961. He developed a sustained academically fruitful relationship through his works and teachings with notable sociologists, such as R.N. Saxena, Brij Raj Chauhan, S.K. Srivastava, B.D. Soni and Yogesh Atal who were his colleagues in the institute. Dhanagare moved to the Indian Institute of Technology (IIT), Kanpur, in 1968 as a lecturer. Dhanagare's research work in the University of Sussex which was published initially in the form of papers in the journals, such as *Past and Present, Journal of Peasant Studies, Contribution to Indian Sociology, Sociological Bulletin, South Asia* and *Australian Journal Politics and History* elevated him to the position of Reader in IIT, Kanpur. Dhanagare accepted an offer of chair professorship in the Department of Sociology from the University of Pune (now Savitribai Phule Pune University) in 1977 where he remained till his retirement in 1995. He contributed a lot in making the department one of the best in the country.

Dhanagare had also remarkable administrative skills and was a great institution builder. As the Vice-Chancellor of Shivaji University, Kolhapur, Member Secretary of the Indian Council of Social Sciences Research (ICSSR) and the President of the Indian Sociological Society, he contributed a lot to the betterment of these institutions and has left an inconceivable mark on these institutions. He did not succumb to political pressure and foul play in Shivaji University, Kolhapur, and retained the autonomy of the University. To him, institution building was equally important and challenging as research, teaching and supervision.

Dhanagare won several awards such as Commonwealth Scholarship, ICHR Fellowship, and Visiting Asian Scholar at

Scandinavian Institute of Asian Studies, Copenhagen, Denmark (1983), UGC National Lecturer, Visiting Research Professor, Tokyo University of Foreign Studies and Shastri Indo-Canadian Institute's Visiting Fellowship in Canada. Besides teaching in Agra University, IIT Kanpur and Pune University, he has also held such important positions as Member-Secretary of the Indian Council of Social Science Research, New Delhi on deputation from 1991–93, and as Vice-Chancellor, Shivaji University, Kolhapur between 1995–2000. He has also done work on 'Populism and Power: Farmer's Movement in Western India' (1980–2014) during his Fellowship at the IIAS, Shimla (February 2012 to July 2014). He received the 2011 Indian Sociological Society Lifetime Achievement Award. He was a Life Member of the Indian Sociological Society, Indian Institute of Public Administration, Marathi Samajshastra Parishad, People's Union of Civil Liberties, Indian Association of Social Sciences and a Member of International Sociological Association.

Dhanagare was also a columnist in a leading weekly magazine *Saadhana*, which is published from Pune. Vinod Shirsath, editor of *Saadhana* said, 'Dr Dhanagare was not only a popular professor in Pune, but when he got selected as the VC of Shivaji University, he laid foundation to many systems and developments, which are still in practice. His contribution in building an institution and making in pro-student is immense'. Though Dhanagare's tenure as Vice-Chancellor of SUK was controversial as he locked horns with local satraps on various issues. In 2000, 75 professors from Pune as well as teachers from different colleges in the city supported his efforts to usher in a clean administration at the university.

## Theoretical Insights of Dhanagare

When Dhanagare started his career as a teacher in the early 1960s, Marxist social thought was not popular in teaching and research in sociology in India. Mostly sociologists were conducting village studies based on Parsonian Functionalism. Dhanagare was among earliest sociologists in India who introduced alternative perspectives, particularly, Marxist perspective in teaching and research. He began with quantitative methods, but went beyond it to use comparative and historical methods. He made historical and comparative methods as important source of knowledge in sociology in India. He undertook analysis of texts – newspapers, archives or other sources. As far as theoretical perspectives are concerned, he was not dogmatic. He began with the Marxist theory. Later, he pursued neo-Marxist writings like that of Laclau and Mouffe while analysing the Farmers' Movement.

His most recent book *Populism and Power*, is a brilliant critique of the rise and fall of farmers' movements, particularly the Shetkari Sanghatana movement in Maharashtra in the context of neoliberal reforms based on structural Marxist approach. He was one of those rare Indian sociologists who constantly engage with historians, economists and political theorists. He had an uncommon grasp of Marathi, English and Sanskrit literature; he used to read a great number of books covering the expanse of literature, philosophy and even art, music and sports (Mohanty, 2017). He belonged to the Yogendra Singh tradition. He was against regionalization of sociology. He thought of sociology as a general science with a specific take on the tussle between tradition and modernity. Recently, Mohanty (2017), Sahay (2017), Tambekar (2017) and Nagla (2017) have given reminiscences and written about the life and works of Dhanagare.

## Themes and Perspectives of Dhanagare

Dhanagare went on experimenting in terms of themes, theoretical perspectives or conceptual schemes. He was not caught in the label called 'Rural Sociology' or 'Sociology of Social Movements'. Dhanagare discourses in sociology, keeping in view of the context and situation of Indian society. First, his discourse was on democracy as a political system and as a democratic way of life and whether the Indian social structure would allow democratic way of life to survive and sustain in India or not. The second was of course the discourse of development in a 'developing society'. Having studied paths of development analysed by Barrington Moore (Jr.), he began contemplating on the theme of sociological connotations of development, which were many a times, quite different and sometimes, diametrically opposite to, what was popularly understood as 'development'. The third discourse was that of innovative development of agriculture, particularly, the Green Revolution. Among all his books, *Peasant Movements in India* is by far the most popular one. In this work, he engaged with the Marxist perspective critically. In the period after the New Economic Policies were passed in early 1990s, the new coinage 'Non-Governmental Organizations' became very popular. Dhanagare analysed this phenomenon of expansion of voluntary organizations in their new *Avataar* – NGOs.

He analysed the relationship between globalization and wide expansion of non-governmental organizations. Dhanagare has written repeatedly on the field of higher education in India. Higher education in India has expanded considerably since independence. He has attempted to understand the dimensions of this change in the post-liberalization period. Mere expansion without a commitment to quality is an empty promise. As ex-Vice Chancellor of Shivaji University, Kolhapur, he could see the advantages and disadvantages of liberalization and privatization of education on ground.

## Major Areas of Research of Dhanagare

Dhanagare's major areas of research are social movements, sociology of development, agrarian sociology in India, education and society, peasant movements (Maharashtra in particular), regionalism-regional identity formation in India (Vidarbha in particular), structure and dynamics of rural society in India, and environment and development. He introduced courses mainly focusing on social movements, sociological theory and Indian sociology with particularly Marxist perspective.

## Writings of D.N. Dhanagare

D.N. Dhanagare's area of specialization was rural sociology and farmers' movements. He is the author of 26 works, in 51 publications, in two languages. The bibliography compiled at the end of this chapter shows extraordinary range of his writings. His major works are as follows:

1. *Agrarian Movements and Gandhian Politics* (1975), Extension Lecture Series 1. Institute of Social Sciences, Agra University, Agra.
2. *Rural Transformation in India: Challenges and Prospects* (1982), Hukerikar Memorial Lecture Series 5, J.S.S. Institute of Economic Research, Dharwad.
3. *Peasant Movements in India, 1920–1950* (1983), Oxford University Press, Delhi.
4. *Themes and Perspectives in Indian Sociology* (1993), Rawat Publications, Jaipur.
5. *Joint Forest Management: A Study of Uttar Pradesh* (2001), 14th G.B. Pant Memorial Lecture Series, G.B. Pant Social Science Institute, Allahabad.
6. *The Writings of D.N. Dhanagare: The Missing Tradition – Debates and Discourses in Indian Sociology* (2014). Orient Blackswan, New Delhi.
7. *Populism and Power: Farmers' Movement in Western India, 1980–2014* (2016). Routledge, London.

Besides his above major books, Dhanagare has also published several research and review articles in journals and edited volumes of national and international repute. Besides English, he has also published in Marathi, including his notable work *Hirave Anubandha*. His range of writing covers areas like peasant movements, farmers' movements, globalization, commercialization of higher education in India, democracy and civil society, and critique of sociology in India. We would like to discuss here briefly some of the writings of Dhanagare as follows:

1. *Peasant Movements in India, 1920–1950*
2. *Themes and Perspectives in Indian Sociology*
3. *The Writings of D.N. Dhanagare: The Missing Tradition – Debates and Discourses in Indian Sociology*
4. *Populism and Power: Farmers' Movement in Western India, 1980–2014*
5. *Practicing Sociology through History: The Indian Experience*
6. *Relevance of Sociology: Some Determinants*
7. *Joint Forest Management in UP: Mismanagement of Water Resources*

8. *Drought in Maharashtra: Misplaced Priorities, Mismanagement of Water Resources*
9. *Learning–Teaching Paradigm*

## Peasant Movements in India 1920–1950

Dhanagare's book on *Peasant Movements in India, 1920–1950* (1983), is the most important analysis of the role of the peasantry in revolutionary or near-revolutionary movements in India. It also establishes the sorts of social structure and historical circumstances that are conducive to peasant revolts and movements. The main purpose of this important study is to analyse the role that different classes of the peasantry play in revolutionary or near-revolutionary movements in India, and the kinds of social structure and historical circumstances that are conducive to peasant revolts and movements. The book is a pathway for people who wish to learn about movements such as Tebhaga and Jharkhand as well as about peasant politics in India.

Dhanagare formulates his problem of enquiry taking as point of departure from Barrington Moore's view of the role of peasantry, but still within the Marxian frame of reference. He also explores three questions after observing that is less pertinent to know whether or not the peasantry has revolutionary potential:

1. What roles do different classes of peasantry in a society play in revolutionary movements?
2. What kinds of social structure and historical circumstances are conducive to peasant revolts or movements?
3. Why the mobilization of peasant at one time and place leads to peaceful or constitutional agitations, but assumes an insurrectionary or rebellious form in another place and time (Dhanagare, 1983: 6).

Dhanagare makes explicit the underlying assumptions of these questions. Dhanagare chose thirty years of 20th century (1920–1950) to study five peasant movements spread over Malabar, Bardoli, Oudh, Bengal and Telangana. Two chapters – Agrarian Structure and Peasant Revolts in India before 1920, and Peasant Organizations and the Left Wing in India 1925–1947 – provide the background and the linkage respectively. All the essays which have been included in the book were earlier published in different journals between 1974 and 1980.

Dhanagare characterizes the 1921 Moplah rebellion as an expression of long-standing agrarian discontent among tenants, labourers and agriculturists, which was intensified by the religious and ethnic identity of the Moplahs, majority of them were Muslims (Dhanagare, 1983: 82). The rebellion, which was pre-political in nature and lacked systematic organization, effective leadership and ideology, targeted the upper class peasants belonging to upper Hindu castes, such as Kshtriya, Nayar and Nambudari. By the end of December 1921, the rebellion was completely suppressed with killing of 2,337 Moplahs.

The Bardoli movement of 1928 was a movement of the class of rich and middle-class peasants (Patidar peasants) against the method of revenue assessment and revision. Patidar peasants made a tactical alliance with poor sections of peasantry, such as Dublas and other tribal groups. The movement was encouraged by Mahatma Gandhi or the Congress Party because it did not give rise to consciousness along class lines and did not disturb the traditional social structure. The Bardoli Satyagraha succeeded politically by espousing the cause of the better-off sections of the Indian Peasantry but it did not arouse class consciousness among poor peasants. The Congress party assumed the mask of working for the masses, but it actually worked for middle and rich peasants. The poor peasants were left estranged as usual (1983: 125).

The 1920–1922 peasant movement in Oudh, was a spontaneous violent struggle by poor peasants due to a steep increase in prices of goods and rent and insecure rights in land by tenants. It increased income to the rich and middle-class peasants but it spelt deepening distress for the poor peasants who were unable to grow enough for subsistence. In 1930–1932, circumstances had changed. The agrarian distress during the depression was felt more by rich and middle strata of peasantry. Accordingly, they launched a movement under the leadership of the Congress Party. The Congress Party persuaded a sizable poor tenants and landless labourers to participate in the 1930–1932 movement. However, when the prices recovered and stabilized, the rich and middle peasants gave up the struggle. In 1920–1922, movement was local and religion was used to mobilize poor peasants at the grassroots. In 1930–1932, the Congress Party mobilized peasantry without arousing political consciousness along class lines as a part of nation-wide struggle for freedom.

The All India Kisan Sabha, a farmer organization affiliated to the Communist Party of India, staged two Left-wing peasant movements in India: the Tebhaga struggle in Bengal and Telengana revolt in Andhra. The Tebhaga movement in Bengal in 1946–1947 was a struggle by sharecroppers, who were mostly Muslims, tribals and Harijans, to retain a two-thirds share of the agricultural produce for themselves and thereby reduce the rent paid by *Jotedars* – a class of rich farmers belonging mainly to upper Hindu castes – from one-half to one-third of their produce. The movement was led by educated people mostly from the urban middle class. It was the first consciously attempted revolt by a politicized peasantry in India. The Tebhaga movement would not have happened without CPI and Kishan Sabha activity.

Telengana peasant revolt which happened in the erstwhile Hyderabad state was launched by the Communist Party of India in the middle of 1946 and lasted till October 1951. Hyderabad state was a feudal or despotic state under the Nizams. There were two major agrarian classes: upper class consisting of landlords, Jagirdars, Deshmukhs and Sahukars and the lower class consisting of poor peasants, tenants, sharecroppers and agricultural labourers. The communist organizations such as the Kishan Sabha and Andhra Conference voiced the peasants' grievances and successfully launched a movement to abolish landlordism and *vetti* system, prevent rack-renting and eviction of tenants, reduce taxes, revenues and rents, and confirm occupancy rights of cultivating tenants. The poor peasants and the landless labourers began to seize lands from landlords and deshmukhs. This enlarged the scope of the movement but the leaders belonging to upper class and castes started deserting the movement. In 1948, the Nizam, the Muslim nobility, and also the Majlis-i-Ittehad organized a paramilitary voluntary force consisting of 1,00,000 razakars to fight against the peasant movement. It is the merger of Hyderabad state into India in 1948 that led to decline of Telengana movement. The Indian army suppressed the communist squads by killing over 2,000 peasants and party workers and by arresting 25,000 communists.

M.S.A. Rao in his review of the Dhanagare's book raises basic questions about the validity of perspectives and methodology of the study and Dhanagare responded to the points of substance in *Sociological Bulletin* (1983). However, the book reflects on the role of different agrarian classes in peasant movements using Marxian conceptual framework. It observes that India during this period of history witnessed a plethora of peasant organizations. These organizations drew their ideological orientation either from the congress or from the left-wing political parties. Dhanagare examines Bardoli Satyagraha, and other agrarian agitations in the context of national Congress politics in Oudh. In the two essays, he generally considers peasant agitations led by Gandhi and the Indian National Congress. He is highly critical of Gandhian ideology and strategy in these movements such as the Champaran, Kheda and Bardoli.

## Themes and Perspectives in Indian Sociology

The book of Dhanagare (1993) on *Themes and Perspectives in Indian Sociology*, is a collection of the essays published in different periodicals from 1980 to 1990. These essays, written by Dhanagare since 1980, embody his reflections on the growth of sociology as an intellectual discipline in India. These are addressed not only to the sociology profession but also to social sciences in India in general. While attempting to trace the entire development of sociology, the essays also try to bring out the dominant themes and perspectives that were mirrored in the way craft of sociology was put to sue by professional practitioners. The book consists of eight chapters. Dhanagare thought that it would be worthwhile to provide some background details of the context in which these essays were written instead of giving summaries of the contents of each article in the introduction of the book.

The essay on 'Search of Identity' was written on an invitation from late Romesh Thaper to contribute to *Seminar's* monthly symposium on 'Understanding Society'. The second article is in the nature of a status-report on sociology and social anthropology in India commissioned by the Bangkok office of the UNESCO. What appears in this volume as the essay, 'Towards an Integrated Approach to Social Reality', is the reinterpretation of a paper Dhanagare presented on 'Interdisciplinary Approach of Social Reality in Social Sciences' at a seminar on the same at Pune. The next essay on Kosambi's 'Dialectical Materialism' first emerged in the form of Dhanagare's lecture notes. The essay's on 'Subaltern Consciousness and Populism' has an equally fascinating origin. A part of this article was first drafted in the form of a review article on Ranajit Guha's (1983) seminar work which was a precursor of what later developed into a major theoretical, almost paradigmatic orientation in 'the other history' known as the 'Subaltern Studies' approach (Guha, 1982–87). The theme of the next essay happens to be 'Action Groups and Social Transformation'. The last essays in this volume are about the 'Relevance of Sociology', in the Indian context.

Throughout the essays, we find 'sociology in India' and 'Indian sociology' as two expressions used interchangeably. The latter according to Louis Dumont (1970: 1–32), is that specialized branch which stands at the confluence of Indology and sociology and which he advocates as the right type of 'mix' prerequisite to the understanding of Indian society. However, this specificity of usage is not subscribed to in these essays. Quintessentially, the essays are about 'sociology in India', the way it came to be institutionalized as an academic discipline and the phases of creative tension and joy it has gone through. In this sense, this collection of essays could be seen as a study in the broad arena of 'history of ideas, and sociology of knowledge', though basically the essays are about the course of development of sociology (and social anthropology to a certain extent) in India.

The essays in Dhanagare's volume on, *Themes and Perspectives in Indian Sociology,* (1993) critically review the development of sociology in India which has established itself in the world of scholarship. Taking the position of an 'outsider within' the author has surveyed the themes and perspectives that dominated sociological concerns reflected in the literature produced by Indian sociologists from 1950s to late 1980s. Without concealing his own value-preferences, the author has offered a critique of the prevailing theoretical and methodological orientations, the cognitive structures in which they are embedded as well as the shifting research interests within the sociology scholarship in India. The most striking feature of the essays is these are written in a style that blends objectivity with empathy and intellectual sensitivity. Throughout these essays the author stresses the need to preserve scientific outlook in sociological task and still synthesize it with value commitments of sociologists.

About theoretical and methodological shifts, Dhanagare reiterated his position that he had articulated in his book titled, *Themes and Perspectives in Indian Sociology*. 'Following Karl Popper, he believed that sociology did not have paradigm shift. Marxist perspective was always the weakest in Indian sociology. However, some exemplary studies on agrarian relations and change have been successfully conducted redefining western concepts. Similarly in social movement studies, a couple of good studies with Marxist scheme were undertaken across India. Considering influence of British anthropology, the tradition of empirical work from functionalist perspective remained very strong. Though statistical techniques, and survey method is still taken very seriously by many, case studies and life history and oral history method have now gained importance in recent times' (Tambekar, 2017).

## The Writings of D.N. Dhanagare: The Missing Tradition – Debates and Discourses in Indian Sociology

D.N. Dhanagare has been an inspirational figure for students and scholars of sociology for over four decades now. His seminal writings on peasant movements, farmers' issues, state, civil society, Green Revolution, to name a few, are notable contributions to the discipline. Dhanagare's *Peasant Movements in India, 1920–1950*, first published in 1983, turned out to be one of the most incisive analysis on the various instances of peasant revolts in the larger context of the struggle for freedom in India. Located firmly in the Marxist tradition, Dhanagare did set a trail that provoked numerous studies on the peasantry, contributing to knowledge. All these changed the way in which peasant struggles were seen; it also influenced the approach to the study of the national movement in India.

The *Writings of D.N. Dhanagare* (2014) appeared in the couple of decades after the 1980s. It is a definitive collection of essays illuminating his range of interests. But none of them deals with peasantry in as direct a manner as his 1983 work. Indeed, it is reflective of the shift away from such concerns as peasant studies or labour studies in the decade beginning 1991; the time when Nehruvian socialism (for whatever it meant) was abandoned in preference to the market economy (again, whatever it means). If Dhanagare, along with others like A.R. Desai, lent a historical frame to concerns in sociology, the liberalization era witnessed scholarly works that critiqued the policies of the government. More than half the essays in this collection reflect this shift.

Apart from an 'Introduction', discussing the debates and discourses in Indian sociology, the collection is divided into four sections: 'Sociology under Global Regime', 'State and Civil Society', 'Discourses on "Revolution"' and 'Controversies in Indian Sociology'. All the essays in the four sections are essays or papers presented by Dhanagare at various points of time, between 1987 and 2012. There is a method behind the selection. As for instance, in the essay titled 'Green Revolution and the Social Inequalities' the style is scholarly and incisive, rather than rhetorical. In other words, attempts have been made to explain the post-liberalization experience in terms of aspects of the lives, struggles and travails of those opposed to the regime.

Globalization, according to Dhanagare, is only another word to describe capitalism. This, however, is a calculated attempt to gloss a fact where 'systems of formal governance are relegated to the status of subordinate partners while the business, dominated by MNCs and their managerial class, controls decision-making process and occupies a pre-eminent position in the global economy' (Ananth, 2015).

In the ten essays of the volume, Dhanagare analyses his views and positions on issues such as globalization, neo-liberal capitalism, transnational corporations, state, civil society and university as an important forum for civil society. The introductory chapter begins with a biographical narrative of Dhanagare's own evolution as a sociologist, which indigenously blends with the elaborate exposition on the 'Debates and Discourses in Indian Sociology'. However, he opines that sociology in India has been considerably deficient in engaging in discourses and has neglected some crucial areas like nationalism and communalism.

In the above context, the book starts with a long insightful commentary on the nature of sociology in India. First, it observes that Indian sociologists run the risk of degenerating into 'academic narcissism', as they tend to advance their truth claims with complete indifference to truth claims of others. In doing so, they display an aversion to sustained involvement in dialogues, debates and discourse analysis. Second, there is an absence of true dialogues and debates in Indian sociology. So, discourses are neither initiated nor continued. Many themes that sociologists raise in their studies are not followed or continued. Finally, whatever meaningful discourses that have taken place have remained confined to the miniscule elite minority. So, the gap between elite and masses in Indian sociology is widening. The elites look down upon vernacular grassroots level practitioners of sociology in India (Sahay, 2017).

The essays in the first section consists of three chapters revolve around the theme of 'Sociology under the Global Regime' and analyse how without de-linking the Indian economy from the global capitalist regime it is possible for the country to put forth a viable alternative, provided the political class has the will to implement the right policies. Two chapters in this section deal with the phenomenon of globalization. This section contains an interesting chapter on the problems of urban fringe that illuminates the politics of urban development and the encounter of fringe areas with neo-liberal capitalism.

The second section discusses the uneasy relationship between the state and civil society. The two essays included in this section have emerged out of the author's deep involvement in studies in agrarian social structure and transformation in India and also in the study of social movements in general. In continuation of the first one, in the second essay, Dhanagare introduces university as a forum of civil society and submits that Indian universities can be centres of discourses.

The two chapters in section three delve on 'Revolution'. The first chapter looks at the notion of revolution with reference to agriculture and social inequality. Second chapter examines its conceptual ramifications in terms of its usage as a scientific concept, as an ideal type and as a metaphor. In his analysis on the agrarian revolution, Dhanagare poignantly reveals how agricultural development is accompanied, quite ironically, by growing social inequalities in rural India.

The three essays in the final section express everyday concerns of practicing sociologists in India. Resonating with his distinctive style and verve, the introduction charts the important debates and discourses in Indian sociology, apart from reflecting this erudite academic's passionate journey within the sociology discipline. In the chapter on 'Schools of Sociology', with special reference to Bombay School, Dhanagare, while trying to understand the failure in India to produce schools of sociology with its emulative 'distinct theoretical approach and perspective', distinguishes between schools of having a 'legacy' of their own, with no rigour, and schools having 'rigour' in research but leaving no legacy behind. In this context, he challenges the 'quasi-feudal atmosphere' that prevails in most of the departments of sociology in India where 'networks of patronage operate in all spheres, so that scholarship is undermined' (Dhanagare, 2014: 336).

Besides, the so-called schools in Indian sociology neither developed a distinct theoretical approach or perspective of its own nor were able to engage in paradigmatic research. They were isolated academic institutions without commanding followings in the domain of sociology. Social policy has not been a major concern in sociology in India. But there are sociologists who lobby vigorously with the government officials to bring to their notice the utility of their research and their policy implications. They also involve themselves in evaluating existing social policies in order to contribute to effective governance.

At the end of the introductory chapter, Dhanagare states, 'to the best of my ability I have taken positions on issues and debates discussed in these essays, Dhanagare has taken a firm stand in favour of the reality at the 'grassroots' and the 'below' as against the 'elites' and the 'above'. Be it in critiquing global order, neo-liberal capitalism, or Green Revolution, or in analysing civil society, state, and democracy, or examining controversies in Indian sociology, Dhanagare unambiguously remains at the side of the masses and the subaltern. Therefore, the motif of 'discourse from below' may be seen as a thread with which these essays are woven together (Palackal, 2014: 471).

The volume is a compilation of essays that D.N. Dhanagare has delivered on different occasions (from 1987 to 2012) either as memorial lectures or as presidential addresses of the Indian Sociological Society, besides a couple of papers presented in symposiums and seminars. Though eclectic in nature justifiably, the essays display a compelling class of sociological discourse, wherein Dhanagare discusses the views on the subject from multiple angles, at the same time expressing his own views 'without fear or fervour' (Palackal, 2014: 469–71).

The Foreword by Partha Nath Mukherji is a fitting tribute from a well-known scholar, colleague and friend. Mukherji writes, 'He (Dhanagare) introduces his book with a masterly commentary virtually on the evolution of sociology in India – an attempt that is far from essays, given the vast array of scholars and their contributions and the limitations of space'.

## Populism and Power: Farmers' Movement in Western India, 1980–2014

In *Populism and Power: Farmers' Movement in Western India*, D.N. Dhanagare comprehensively traces the farmers' movement in Maharashtra over three decades. This is the final work by prominent Indian sociologist D.N. Dhanagare, which covers the strategic and structural aspects of peasants' movements in India. It explores in detail the rise and fall of the peasants' movements in Maharashtra between 1980 and 2014, taking on a variety of fundamental issues like populist movements and their relevance to India; the conditions that enable Indian farmers to mobilize; the relationships between leaders and followers/activists, and between movements and class interests; and the nature of class hegemony. In addition, the book looks at the failure of populism to get electoral support, or of succeeding in the cases it does get power. Khurshed Alam finds the book addresses a wide range of fundamental issues relating to populism and peasant mobilization in India.

The book defines farmers as those cultivators who are, unlike peasants, not dependent on the landlords but on the market. It argues that when government introduced Green Revolution, all stakeholders in agriculture were hoping to benefit from it because the stated target was all round development of rural India. It was believed that substantial growth in food production during 1970–1990 because of the Green Revolution would eventually generate employment and remove the spectre of poverty, hunger and malnutrition among the millions of the rural poor. However, the ensuing reality turned out to be contradictory. In fact, the benefits (in context to subsidies and advantages) were grabbed and monopolized by rich farmers, belonging to dominant castes, using their political linkages, patronage and protection.

The first chapter of the book offers an excellent theoretical review which covers both western and Indian perspectives and develops a framework of analysis for the movements under study. The second chapter covers the farmers' movement in Maharashtra, drawing on both fieldwork and secondary sources. He also outlines some of the historical context, building on his earlier book, *Peasant Movements in India, 1920–1950* (1983). In this chapter, Dhanagare introduces Shetkari Sanghatana, a leading farmers' organization which led the peasant movement in Maharashtra during the period under analysis. The third chapter covers the class character of peasants' movement in Maharashtra, 1980–2011. Dhanagare critically examines the emergence of rich farmers as a class, and questions whether economic populism or class is the key driver. He also explores the link between the farmers' movements and politics.

The fifth chapter looks at participation of women, who were voluntarily involved from the first agitation in 1980. It explores the social background of female activists and women's mobilization in other states, and theorizes women's oppression.

Other chapters explore the farmers' movement response to new economic reforms, the electoral politics of farmers' movement and how it damaged the peasant movement in Maharashtra, and the decline of the farmers' movement as a result of the structural changes that have taken place in Indian economy. A strange feature of the book is that it adopts the neo-Marxist analytical approach without fully subscribing the associated ideas.

The book also consists of a paper on the farmer movement in Meerut, UP, by the Bhartiya Kisan Union (BKU) under M.S. Tikait's leadership. Most of the BKU's demands were the same as had been raised by other farmer organizations in other states of India, such as their remunerative prices for sugarcane and reduction in electricity/canal water charges. The BKU proudly declared itself to be a purely non-political forum. Throughout the 25-day agitation in Meerut in 1988, the BKU's indifference and hostility towards the mainstream political parties was visible. Though the BKU mobilized farmers in large numbers belonging to rich, middle and poor peasants using populist ideology but it withdrew agitation unconditionally without gaining much from the government.

In brief, 'This book traces the entire trajectory of the farmers' movement in Western India, especially Maharashtra, from the 1980s to the present day. It reveals the fundamental contradictions between populism as an ideology and as political power within the democratic state structure. The volume highlights the ideologies of the movement; its emergence in the wake of a perceived agrarian crisis; how it conflates economics and populism; the role of leadership; stages of development from grassroots agitations rooted in civil society to the attempts to create space within structures of democratic politics; the eventual formation of a separate political party and consequent implications. It maps the linkages between populist ideology and mass participation, and their contested successes and failures in the domain of electoral politics. Further, the author underlines the effectiveness of the movement in addressing class and gender equations in the region' – Publisher's description.

Dhanagare was the writer in India's intellectual magazine *Economic and Political Weekly (EPW)*. We are giving some of the ideas presented in the different *EPW* issues. In his special article, he views: Social movements that succeed in mobilizing the masses subsequently attempt to institutionalize themselves. Moving from the domain of civil society into the realm of state politics, the leadership can change its goals and transformative priorities. This paper examines what happened to the farmers' movement (Shetkari Sanghatana) in Maharashtra between 1980 and 2014, especially after it decided to enter electoral politics and set up its own Swatantra Bharat Party. Probing its electoral performance, the paper tries to find out what happened to the mass movement, and explains why the farmers' movement that succeeded in mass mobilization failed to convert mass support into electoral votes (*EPW*, Vol. 49, issue No. 49, 6 December 2014).

## Practicing Sociology through History: The Indian Experience

Quite a few social science disciplines in India – more specifically, anthropology, sociology, and political science have chosen to remain estranged from history in the course of their development and institutionalization for quite some time. The reasons are not far to seek. Barring some notable exceptions, most Indian sociologists preferred to distance themselves from historical analysis during the 1930s to 1960s or so. In recent decades, however, in the study of both the existing structures and the processes of social change, professional sociologists in India have been increasingly reaching out to history and trying to rediscover historical connections of their discipline.

The real purpose of historiography is to offer an image of the past in order to unravel the forces that underlie the present. It is a method of doing comparative history and sociology whereby the past is reconstructed in order to understand and, if possible, explain the present. It would be quite instructive to see the extent to which practitioners of sociology in India have worked their way through history. The exercise here is only illustrative and not exhaustive. It is naturally restricted to Dhanagare's familiarity with relevant sociological literature, which he delivered at the I.P. Desai memorial lecture 18, at Centre for Social Studies, Surat on, 'Practising Sociology through History: The Indian Experience'. Later on this lecture was published in *EPW* in 2007.

In his paper on, 'Practicing Sociology through History', Dhanagare (2007) examines, in two parts, the extent to which Indian sociologists have creatively engaged themselves in systematic use of history for understanding and explaining social phenomena. It also critically assesses the rigour with which a reconstruction of past events and experiences has been attempted so as to understand and explain the present in sociological studies in India. While reviewing seminal writings of scholars who used Indology extensively, as also those of sociologists who have attempted systematic use of history in macro-analysis, this paper focuses attention on contributions of Indian sociologists who have used the historical method rigorously in rural studies, as also in studies of social movements, agrarian structure and change, caste and analysis of industrial and urban settings. Finally, it distinguishes between 'metaphoric' and 'substantive' use of history and opines that the real potential of historical sociology lies in the latter. It also expresses optimism that despite the initial indifference of Indian sociologists towards history, they are now rediscovering their discipline's roots in history and are also realizing its intrinsic value in generating, what Ernest Nagel (1961) called, 'historical explanation' (*EPW*: Vol. 42, Issue No. 33, 18 August 2007 – The second and concluding part was published in *EPW*: Vol. 42, Issue No. 34, 25 August 2007).

In the first part of the paper on 'Practicing Sociology through History', Dhanagare (2007) considered those sociologists who used classical texts, i.e. Indological sources, with a view to understanding contemporary social structures, institutions, and cultural practices. Part II looks at the work of later sociologists, who make up a different category: Those who take into account and narrate the historical background of the social reality that constitutes their research. This paper lays stress on the necessity of a 'substantive' use of history for sociological purposes. It takes particular note of those sociologists who have used history rigorously to arrive at broader levels of explanation, generalization and theoretical abstraction, in the process thereby ensuring a 'completion' of their sociological mission. It is this process that needs to be further exploited by present day sociologists. (*EPW*: Vol. 42, Issue No. 34, 25 August 2007 – This is the concluding part of the paper; the first part was published in *EPW*: Vol. 42, Issue No. 33, 18 August 2007).

While summing up this somewhat elaborate review it is necessary to highlight the main tendencies among historically oriented sociologists and the way they view the relevance of history in their sociological studies. The first category of sociologists consists of those who have used classical texts, i.e. Indological sources in understanding contemporary social structures, institutions, statuses, roles, values, and cultural practices by tracing their origins to one or more Sanskrit texts and then reinterpreting or rationalizing them in the present day context. In the second category we find those sociologists, not few in number, who narrate historical background of social reality, either of the past or contemporary one, which they are researching for. In some cases such a historical account is given as a routine matter to assure readers that relevant past has not been ignored. However, neither such a historical account forms a part of researcher's explanatory scheme nor is it integrated with their sociological analysis. In some cases, though, researchers do believe that the historical background given in great detail deepens their understanding of the research problem or may help them to search appropriate answers to their research questions. In the second category, what is involved is mostly a *metaphoric* use of history. What is, however, important is the *substantive* use of history for sociological purposes. Among Indian sociologists there are some who have used historical analysis and method substantively, in the sense that they have deployed it as an explanatory device, or to test a hypothesis. It is immaterial whether they have used primary archival sources or secondary sources. A.R. Desai, Yogendra Singh, P.C. Joshi and a few others have attempted macro-analytical exercises primarily with the help of reliable secondary source material. Ramkrishna Mukherjee, however, used both. Significantly enough, quite a few Indian sociologists have tried their hand at historical reconstruction by using or consulting primary archival sources that they thought was necessary for their sociological inquiry. They include A.M. Shah, M.S.A. Rao, Anand Chakravarti, D.N. Dhanagare, Ramchandra Guha, Hetukar Jha, Gail Omvedt, Sujata Patel, P. Radhakrishnan, Hira Singh, and Rajendra Singh. It is even more heartening to see that some of the younger sociologists, like P. Abbasi, Sharit Bhowmik, C.B. Damle, Surinder Jodhka, D. Parthasarathy, Virginius Xaxa and a few others have further enriched this tradition of substantive use of history in their sociological studies. All of them have displayed remarkable sense of commitment and discipline in using history rigorously to arrive at broader level of explanation, generalization and theoretical abstraction wherever possible without which, they thought, their sociological mission would have remained incomplete.

Dhanagare's argument is that it is the potential of the substantive use of history, whether for a macro or for a micro-analysis, whether by consulting secondary or primary archival sources, that needs to be fully exploited further by Indian sociologists. Over three decades ago, A.M. Shah (1974: 454) had suggested that 'sociologists should not depend entirely on historians for historical knowledge but they should go into historical research'. His suggestion has not been taken seriously enough. It is high time that Indian sociologists rediscover the intrinsic value of history and historical method by creatively using it in their researches and by using them in their pedagogic practices.

## Relevance of Sociology: Some Determinants

Drawing upon Peter Berger's five 'images' of sociology, in his paper, 'Relevance of Sociology: Some Determinants' Dhanagare attempts to develop an argument that relevance of sociology can be decided only on the basis of the image/s that practitioners of the discipline carry in their minds. Going beyond these popular images, he highlights three major determinants of 'relevance' *viz.* (i) methodology, (ii) theory and (iii) ideology, and argues that both positivist and praxiological overtones are embedded in all the paradigms ranging from functionalism to Marxism. Moreover, the understanding of the 'relevance' question itself tends to shift the ground within a disciplinary discourse as it did in Indian sociology. In the final analysis, the paper stresses that the question of relevance is a value or a moral question. It is only when the nature of these values is utilitarian that positivist science could mediate; otherwise, 'relevance' is determined primarily by the 'voice of conscience'.

The synthesis of the scientific spirit and social criticism, which Dhanagare advocated in the paper, presupposes that in the ultimate analysis, the question of 'relevance' cannot be settled purely in the arena of 'science' as such. It is quintessentially a 'value' question, a moral question and, as such, a matter of praxis – the only determinate one as such, because it is only when the nature of these values is utilitarian that 'science' (its positivist canons and spirit) can mediate. On the 'basic' moral question, praxis would have to be guided by blind intuition – or what is often called the 'voice of conscience'. In this sense the issue of the relevance as well as the accountability of sociology will always be settled in the minds of the analysts, i.e. the practitioners of sociology (Dhanagare, 1990).

### Joint Forest Management in UP: People, Panchayats and Women

In his special article on 'Joint Forest Management in UP', Dhanagare (2000) reports the experience of joint forest management (JFM) initiatives in Uttar Pradesh. Sustainable use of land and forest produce requires a change in attitudes both of government departments and the people. 'Joint' in JFM remains on paper as forest department's work for, rather than with, the people. The initiative also needs to be integrated with other rural development programmes and to give women a larger role (*EPW*: Vol. 35, Issue No. 37, 9 September 2000).

### Drought in Maharashtra: Misplaced Priorities, Mismanagement of Water Resources

In his special article on, 'Drought in Maharashtra: Misplaced Priorities, Mismanagement of Water Resources' Dhanagare (1992) examines: Why is it that conditions of water and food scarcity have become a recurrent historical pattern in Maharashtra, particularly in the less developed regions of Vidarbha and Marathwada? Why does this progressive and industrially advanced state have to suffer such an ignoble water scarcity after four decades of planned development? And, above all, why is it that chief ministers and ministers come and go, and political fortunes of parties too rise and fall, often dramatically, but the non-availability of safe and adequate drinking water to the common man and woman in rural Maharashtra continues unabated? (for more details about this situation, one may read the full paper in *EPW*, Vol. 27, Issue No. 27, 4 July 1992).

## Learning–Teaching Paradigm

In the ensuing paragraphs, I am using excerpts drawn from the interview of Dhanagare taken by Shruti Tambekar (2017) for *Bhartiya Samajshastra Sameeksha*. The descriptions are as follows:

> Dhanagare struggled during his post-graduate studies. He was determined student and worked very hard. The classes did not have any room for discussion or expressing one's own thoughts in the classroom. As two American Professors on their sabbatical were teaching us at Hislop, he received training that could be called unique. Dr Richard Taylor, an Anthropologist from California taught us Cultural Anthropology. Dr Edwin Driver, who cast deep influence on him, was a specialist in methodology and demography. The assignment completed by Dhanagare, however, proved to be more profitable as Dr Driver, later recommended and facilitated admission to the University of Massachusetts, Amherst, USA in 1965–66 due to his insightful contributions to the research project.

At Agra, Dhanagare had period with great joy and gratitude for both stalwarts like R.N. Saxena and contemporaries like Brij Raj Chauhan, B.D. Soni and Yogesh Atal. It was at Agra that he taught papers in research methodology and criminology for the first time. At the Agra Institute, he had informal discussions with colleagues on sociological issues and he had experienced that such discussions clarify and illuminate many nuances of theoretical or methodological issues. He first encountered the writings of classical thinkers, including Marx, Weber and Durkheim which helped in the discussions in theoretical frameworks.

From Agra Institute, Dhanagare went to University of Massachusetts, USA for two years. The exposure at UMass was excellent in terms of a reading, new courses and writing skills. He studied one paper on ancient theory, one on race relations, another course on group dynamics, a compulsory course on statistics and a paper taught by Richard Park, the Korean faculty member, on methodology. This two-year stay introduced Dhanagare to the latest trends in sociology teaching and exposed him to a new teaching-learning paradigm based on intensive training in term paper writing, initiative in learning and self motivated criticality of students.

Dhanagare regretted returning to Agra without a doctoral degree, he decided to make the most of his learning in the USA and published five articles based on the learning, research and thinking while in the USA. After two years he moved to IIT, Kanpur. Teaching at IIT, according to Dhanagare, 'was very rewarding and challenging at the same time. The classes were very big comprising of more than 150 students and these students could challenge the teacher as they were well read and some of them were brilliant. These students were never after grades. It was here that I consciously started publishing my research based articles in reputed journals like *Sociological Bulletin, Past and Present, Contributions to Indian Sociology* and *Journal of Peasant Studies* (Tambekar, 2017). Dhanagare introduced a course on 'Gandhi and Indian Politics' at IIT, Kanpur. Till very recently, many of his IIT students remember how that course cast everlasting influence on them even after 40 odd years.

In 1970, after being selected for the Commonwealth Fellowship, Dhanagare went to University of Sussex for a D.Phil., where he stayed till 1973. 'My Sussex years transformed me completely. British system of education encouraged self-motivated training. There were some seminar courses, where the students are expected to have read prescribed texts and beyond and classes are only discussion oriented. Z. Barbu, my supervisor, had come to

England after fleeing from Romania. He was responsible for getting Professor Tom Bottomore to Sussex. Bottomore was my mentor, and I imbibed the principles of historical and comparative sociology during my three year stay there. At Sussex, in those days a galaxy of great scholars was around. Ranajit Guha was arguing about new themes in South Asian history. Hamza Alavi was pursuing his work on Colonial Capitalism. Visiting Indian scholars of all hues were an additional attraction. I spent those three years working on my thesis arguing against Barrington Moore's very famous argument about passivity of the Indian peasants. Kothari had suggested to me that I should look at peasants, but with a long review article on Barrington Moore's chapter on India, my proposal was endorsed by my supervisor, Barbu. I questioned his prototype of revolution and the book based on D.Phil. work on "Peasant Movements in India" is still taken seriously by the old and the young!' (Tambekar, 2017).

Dhanagare spent his long span of time at University of Pune, Pune. After his D. Phil. in University of Sussex, he joined Department of Sociology at University of Pune. He spoke at length very fondly about his Pune years. 'As I have stated in the introduction of book *The Missing Tradition*, I feel I am an 'Outsider Within'. Not being a product of the Lucknow School or the Bombay School or the Calcutta School, I was free to pursue ideas that emerged from my field work or my insights about social reality. I was not bound by a certain theoretical line or a fixed methodological trajectory. This freedom allowed me to exercise creativity all these years.

Explaining about the background of the Pune Department, he stated, 'The Department of Sociology at Pune was a reputed centre of learning with Professor Irawati Karve as its founder and Professor Damle as the Parsonian sociologist heading it. When I came to Pune, Irawati Karve's school of physical anthropology and Professor Y.B. Damle's Functionalist School were reigning in Pune. The department, however, had a liberal ethos. I must say that there was complete freedom to pursue my own kind of sociology at Pune. Though initially I taught a course on methodology and a course on classical thinkers, later on I taught courses designed by me, namely, 'Agrarian Structure and Change' and 'Sociology of Development'. I conducted research based on my theoretical and methodological convictions and choices. I still appreciate this space given to me at Pune by colleagues, authorities and students. I enjoyed teaching at Pune as a result' (Tambekar, 2017).

D.N. Dhanagare unlike Herbert Marcus and Tom Bottomore always glowed with robust optimism regardless of whether he was interpreting a line of theoretical development or evaluating current political trends or organizing international sociology conferences. His analysis was always backed by historical awareness, careful scrutiny of data and serious reflection. And his commitment to his distinctive version of Marxism as a form of social theory and to socialism as a political project never wavered.

One day when Dhanagare was frequently going to the hospital for dialysis, he talked to me on phone about his critical condition. I made up my mind to meet him. Just few days before he died, I met him at his residence at Pune while going to Kolhapur University for an academic assignment. He took snack with me and talked for a long time in happy mood sharing professional experiences. We were together at many times at different places particularly I had a chance to visit Pondicherry University as visiting professor where he also used to visit every year for about a week. We used to deliver talks to the students of sociology and also to other subjects in social sciences. During our stay, I found that he was very dedicated scholar and committed to the profession with his high integrity. He used to deliver talks with full preparation having systematic notes. He was very inspiring person to everyone. After every lecture he was always surrounded by the students outside the classroom for further discussions related to the teaching and research. He also encouraged me and praised about my book on *Indian Sociological Thought*. This reflects his simplicity. As a reputed teacher Dhanagare is well known throughout the country. We always dearly miss him.

Professor Dattatreya Narayan Dhanagare was a towering figure of Indian sociology. With his passing away, an era of scholarship in the history of the agrarian and development studies in

India has come to an end. He has guided 13 students for their doctoral works. Among them most notably are Virginius Xaxa (Tribal Expert), Raka Saran (Industrial Sociologist), Binay Kumar Patnaik (Sociology of Science and Technology, Sociology of Development, Social Movements) and late Sharmila Rege (Feminist Scholar) who extended glory of Dhanagare. Teacher, sociologist, institution builder, D.N. Dhanagare leaves behind a rich legacy of research, learning and inspiration. A scholar of his calibre is rare indeed. His death has caused a big vacuum in social sciences in general and sociology in particular. However, his works will continue to inspire and guide generations of scholars to come. Today, he is not among us but his reminiscences will always be with us.

## D.N. Dhanagare's Framework Summarized

### *Background*

1. Dhanagare was born in Washim in Vidharbha region of Maharashtra on 11 June 1936.
2. Education in Nagpur University during 1955–59 for Bachelor of Arts (B.A.) in First Class, and Master of Arts in Sociology in First Class, first in order of merit in 1959.
3. Received Doctor of Philosophy (D.Phil/Ph.D.) in 1973 from University of Sussex, England (UK) in the supervision of Zevedie Barbu.
4. Professor at the Department of Sociology, University of Pune (now Savitribai Phule Pune University) in 1977 where he remained till retirement in 1995.
5. Member-Secretary of the Indian Council of Social Science Research, New Delhi on deputation from 1991–93, and as Vice-Chancellor Shivaji University, Kolhapur between 1995–2000.

### *Aim*

Experimenting in terms of themes, theoretical perspectives or conceptual schemes to understand rise and fall of farmers' movements.

### *Assumptions*

Establishes the sorts of social structure and historical circumstances that are conducive to peasant revolts and movements.

### *Methodology*

Used historical and comparative methods as important source of knowledge in sociology in India.

### *Theoretical Perspective*

Analysed Marxist perspective critically.

### *Typology*

Analysis of texts – newspapers, archives or other sources.

### *Issues*

1. Social Movements, Sociology of Development,
2. Agrarian Sociology in India,
3. Education and Society,
4. Peasant Movements (Maharashtra in particular), Regionalism-Regional Identity Formation in India (Vidarbha in particular),
5. Structure and Dynamics of Rural Society in India,
6. Environment and Development.

## Select Bibliography

Ananth, N. (2015), 'Global Economy' in World Bank Group (2015), *Global Economic Prospects: The Global Economy in Transition*, Washington D.C. World Bank.

Dhanagare, D.N. (1963). 'On Sutherland's Theory of Differential Association,' *The Journal of Social Sciences*, 3 (2), 31–39.

— (1964). 'Theoretical Formulations in Contemporary Criminology', *Indian Journal of Social Research*, 5 (2), 289–298.

— (1967). 'Delinquency and Opportunity Theory in the Context of Justification', *Sociological Bulletin*, 16 (2), 39–59.

Dhanagare, D.N. (1967). 'Apartheid: Its Theory and Practice in South Africa', *India Quarterly, A Journal of International Relations*, 23 (4), 338–361.

—— (1968). 'Violence in the Fourth General Elections: A Study in Political Conflict', *Economic and Political Weekly*, 3 (1&2), 151–156.

—— (1968). 'Perception of Leader's Competence and the Rates of Positive Negative Reactions in Work-Groups: A Proposal for Small Group Experiment', *Indian Psychological Review*, 4 (2), 126–133.

—— (1968). 'Urban-Rural Differentials in Election Violence', *Political Science Review*, 7 (3&4), 747–759.

—— (1968). 'Political Elites and Caste Association: A Critique', *Economic and Political Weekly*, 3 (48), 1852.

—— (1969). 'The Problems of the Visually Handicapped and Their Rehabilitation', *The Social Science Review*, 11 (1), 22–38.

—— (1969). 'Urbanism and Crime', *Economic and Political Weekly*, 4 (28–30), 1239–1242.

—— (1974). 'Social Origins of the Peasant Insurrection in Telengana, 1946–1951', *Contributions to Indian Sociology* (New Series), 8, 109–34. Reprinted in Desai A.R. (ed.). (1979). *Peasant Struggles in India* (pp. 486–516). Bombay, India: Oxford University Press.

—— (1975), *Agrarian Movements and Gandhian Politics* (Extension Lecture Series: 1), Agra: Institute of Social Sciences, Agra University.

—— (1975). 'The Politics of Survival, Peasant Organisations and the Leftwing in India, 1925–46', *Sociological Bulletin*, 24 (1), 29–54.

—— (1975). 'Congress and Agrarian Agitation in Oudh 1920–22 and 1930–32', *Journal of South Asian Studies*, 5 (1), 67–77.

—— (1976). 'Peasant, Protest and Politics: The Tebhaga Movement in Bengal 1946–47', *The Journal of Peasant Studies*, 3 (3), 360–378.

—— (1977). Agrarian Conflict, Religion and Politics: The Moplah Rebellions in Malabar in the Nineteenth and Early Twentieth Centuries. *Past and Present*, 74 (1), 112–141.

—— (1979). The End of the Congress Hegemony: The Sixth Lok Sabha Elections in UP, 1977. *Political Science Review*, 28 (1), 28–51.

—— (1979). Prosperity and Debt in Rural Punjab. *Sociological Bulletin*, 28 (1&2), 120–130.

—— (1980). Literacy and Structural Change in Rural Society in Colonial India. *The Journal of Social Studies*, 7, 45–65.

Dhanagare, D.N. and Sharan, R. (1980). Trade Unionism Among the Women Workers of Kanpur. *Indian Journal of Industrial Relations*, 15 (3), 447–458.

Dhanagare, D.N. (1980). Search for Identity. *Seminar,* 254, 23–26.

— (1980). Agrarian Structure, Social Change and Peasant Revolts in India. *The Journal of Development Studies*, 17 (1), 98–106.

— (1980). Myth and Reality in the Bardoli Satyagraha–1928: A Study in Gandhian Politics. *Australian Journal of Politics and History*, 26 (2), 265–278.

— (1981). Interdisciplinary Approach to Social Reality. *Journal of Higher Education*, 7 (1), 97–109.

— (1981). *Violence and Politics: A Trend Report. In ICSSR, Political Dynamics – Survey of Research in Political Science* (pp. 93–125) 3. New Delhi, India: Allied Publishers.

— (1982), *Rural Transformation in India: Challenges and Prospects*, Hukerikar Memorial Lecture Series 5, Dharwad, India: J.S.S. Institute of Economic Research.

— (1982–1983). Urbanism and Crime, 1976–78. *International Journal of Critical Sociology*, 6, 14–22.

— (1983). *Peasants Movements in India, c.1920–1950,* New Delhi: Oxford University Press. Reviewed by: M.S.A. Rao in *Sociological Bulletin*, Vol. 32, No. 2 (September 1983), pp. 235–240.

— (1983). Rejoinder. *Sociological Bulletin*, 32 (2), 240–244.

— (1984). Equality in the Indian University. *Minerva: A Review of Science Learning and Policy*, 22 (3–4), 388–403.

— (1984). 'Agrarian Reform and Rural Development in India: Some Observations'. *Research in Social Movements, Conflicts and Change: A Research Manual*, 7, 177–201.

— (1984). Prospects of an Integrated Approach to Social Reality. In Kumar R. (ed.). *Philosophical Theory and Social Reality* (pp. 168–183). New Delhi, Allied Publishers.

— (1985). Sociology and Social Anthropology in India. In Atal Yogesh (ed.). *Sociology and Social Anthropology in Asia and the Pacific* (pp. 313–360). New Delhi, Wiley Eastern.

— (1985). Social Tensions and Protest Movements in Maharashtra. *Economic and Political Weekly*, 20 (24), 1030–1031.

— (1985). Peasant Movements in India, 1920–50. In Nakamura H. (ed.). *Transformation and Peasant Movement in Contemporary Asia* (pp. 5–31). Tokyo: Tokyo University of Foreign Studies.

— (1985). Rural Development, Poverty and Protest. *Contributions to Indian Sociology* (New Series), 19 (2), 349–358.

— (1986). Vidarbha's Separate Identity: Historical Background. *State and Society*, 6 (2), 16–29.

Dhanagare D.N. (1986). D.D. Kosambi: Dialectical Materialism and the Structure and Dynamics of Indian Society. *Sociological Bulletin*, 35 (2), 33–54.

— (1987). Green Revolution and Social Inequalities in Rural India. *Economic and Political Weekly*, 22 (19–21), AN137–AN144.

— (1988). Political Economy of Farmers' Movements in India. *Prajnan – Journal of Social and Management Sciences*, 17 (2), 245–251.

— (1988). Nine Theses on Social Movements: A Critique. *Economic and Political Weekly*, 23 (21), 1089–1092.

— (1988). Action Groups and Social Transformation in India. *Indian Journal of Social Sciences*, 1 (4), 413–433.

— (1988). An Apoliticist Populism. *Seminar*, 352, 24–31.

— (1988). Subaltern Consciousness and Populism: Two Approaches in the Study of Social Movements in India. *Social Scientist*, 16 (11), 18–37.

— (1989). 'Peasant and Politics: Strategies of Farmers' Movement', *The Times of India*, (Bombay edition), p. 12.

— (1990). Relevance of Sociology: Some Determinants. *Indian Journal of Social Work*, 51 (1), 1–13.

— (1990). Shetkari Sanghatana: The Farmers' Movement in Maharashtra: Background and Ideology. *Social Action*, 40 (4), 347–369.

— (1992). Drought in Maharashtra: Misplaced Priorities, Mismanagement of Water Resources. *Economic and Political Weekly*, 27 (27), 1421–1425.

— (1992). Sustainable Development, Environment and Social Science Research in India. *IFSSO: Bulletin of the International Federation of Social Science Organisations*, 27–28, 38–50.

— (1993). *Themes and Perspectives in Indian Sociology*, Jaipur: Rawat.

— (1993). Tradition and Modernity as Paradigms of Social Change: A Critical Overview. *The Loyola Journal of Social Sciences*, 7 (1), 18–35.

— (1993). NGOs and Foreign Funding. *Man and Development*, 15 (2), 133–146.

— (1993). Remembering Tom Bottomore. *Economic and Political Weekly*, 28 (48), 2581–2583.

— (1993). Three Constructs of Hinduism. *Seminar*, 411, 23–27.

— (1994). The Class Character and Politics of the Farmers' Movement in Maharashtra During the 1980s. *The Journal of Peasant Studies*, 21 (3–4), 72–94.

— (1997). Transnational Corporations and Their Role in the Indian Economy. In Yamaguchi H. et al. (eds). *Tradition and Modernity* (pp. 163–182). New Delhi: Munshiram Manoharlal.

Dhanagare D.N. (1999). The New Farmers' Movement in Maharashtra and its Response to New Economic Reforms. In Oshikawa F. (ed.). *South Asia under the Economic Reforms* (pp. 247–261). Osaka, Japan: The Japan Centre for Area Studies.

—— (2000). Joint Forest Management in UP: People, Panchayats and Women. *Economic and Political Weekly*, 35 (17), 3315–3324.

—— (2001). *Joint Forest Management: A Study of Uttar Pradesh*, 14th G.B. Pant Memorial Lecture Series, G.B. Pant Social Science Institute, Allahabad.

—— (2001). Towards an Anthropology of Nation-States. *Journal of Indian School of Political Economy*, 13 (2), 367–372.

—— (2001). Civil Society, State and Democracy: Contextualising a Discourse. *Sociological Bulletin*, 50 (2), 167–191.

—— (2003). Globalisation: Towards an Alternative View. *Sociological Bulletin*, 52 (1), 4–31.

—— (2004). Social Policy Concerns in Indian Sociology. *Sociological Bulletin*, 53 (1), 4–30.

—— (2007). Practising Sociology Through History: The Indian Experience – I. *Economic and Political Weekly*, 42 (33), 3414–3421.

—— (2007). Practising Sociology Through History: The Indian Experience – II. *Economic and Political Weekly*, 42 (34), 3499–3508.

—— (2009). Social Integration: Role of the State and Civil Society. In Dubey, Muchkund, Jabbi M.K. (eds). *A Social Charter for India: Citizens' Perspective of Basic Rights* (pp. 160–170). New Delhi, India: Pearson.

—— (2011). On Encounter Between Urban Fringe and Neo-Liberal Capitalism. In Dikshit, J.K. (ed.). *The Urban Fringe of Indian Cities* (pp. 24–31). Jaipur: Rawat Publications.

—— (2011). Legacy and Rigour: The Bombay School of Sociology and its Impact in Universities in Maharashtra. In Patel Sujata (ed.). *Doing Sociology in India: Genealogies, Locations and Practices* (pp. 127–157). New Delhi: Oxford University Press.

—— (2013). Understanding the New Farmers' Movement in Maharashtra: Towards an Analytical Framework. *The Eastern Anthropologist*, 66 (2–3), 163–217.

—— (2014). *The Writings of D.N. Dhanagare: The Missing Tradition – Debates and Discourses in Indian Sociology.* New Delhi: Orient Blackswan Private Limited.

—— (2014). Negative Returns of Ambivalence Electoral Politics of the Farmers' Movement, 1980–2014. *Economic and Political Weekly*, 49 (49), 40–50.

Dhanagare D.N. (2016). *Populism and Power: Farmers' Movement in Western India, 1980–2014*. London: Routledge.

— (2016). Declining Credibility of the Neoliberal State and Agrarian Crisis in India: Some Observations. In Mohanty B.B. (ed.). *Critical Perspectives on Agrarian Transition: India in the Global Debate* (pp. 138–163). London: Routledge.

Dumont, Louis (1970). *Homo Hierarchicus: The Caste System and Its Implications*, London: Weidenfeld and Nicolson.

Guha, R. (ed.) (1982–87), *Subaltern Studies: Writings on South Asian History and Society*, Vols. I and V, New Delhi: Oxford University Press.

Mohanty, B.B. (2017). 'Reminiscences of D.N. Dhanagare', *Economic and Political Weekly*, Vol. 52, No. 11, 18 March.

Nagel, Ernest (1961), *The Structure of Science: Problem in the Logic of Scientific Explanation*, London: Routledge.

Nagla, B.K. (2017). 'D.N. Dhanagare: Ek Bhartiya Marxvadi Samajshastri', *Bhartiya Samajshastra Sameeksha* (A Hindi Journal of Indian Sociological Society), Vol. 4, No. 2, July–December, pp. 26–33.

Palackal, Antony (2014). Book Review of *The Writings of D.N. Dhanagare: The Missing Tradition* in *Sociological Bulletin*, Vol. 63, No. 3, September–December and also reviewed by, V. Krishna Ananth (2015) in *Indian Historical Review*, Vol. 42, Number 2, 1 December.

Sahay, Gaurang R. (2017). 'Life and Works of Dattatreya Narayan Dhanagare: An Introductory Account', *Sociological Bulletin*, 66 (2), 223–236.

Shah, A. M. (1974). 'Historical Sociology: A Trend Report', in M.N. Srinivas et al. (eds) *Survey of Sociology and Social Anthropology*, (Sponsored by ICSSR, New Delhi), Bombay: Popular Prakashan, pp.432–59.

Tambekar, Shruti (2017). 'D.N. Dhanagare: Bharat Main Prasangik Samajshastra', *Bhartiya Samajshastra Sameeksha* (A Hindi Journal of Indian Sociological Society), Vol. 4, No. 2, July–December, pp. 54–63.

# V

# Stratification Perspective

## What is Social Stratification?

Stratification is a system of social ranking involving relations of superiority and inferiority. The relations of superiority-inferiority between the units of ranking are governed by a set of norms. These relations are essentially social relations. Parsons (1954: 69) calls 'patterning' or 'ordering' of social relations a stratification system of society. 'Ordering' or 'patterning' of social relations would involve the value system, the power structure, the role of ascriptive and achievement aspects, the pattern of conformity and deviance and reward and punishment attached with them.

According to Tumin (1969), "social stratification is the arrangement of any social group or society into a hierarchy of positions that are unequal with regard to power, property, social evaluation, and/or psychic gratification." *Power* refers to the ability to secure one's ends in life, even against opposition. *Property* may be defined as rights over goods and services. *Evaluation* refers to a societal judgement that a status or position is more prestigious and honourable than others are, or more popular, or preferable for one or another reason. *Psychic gratification* includes all sources of pleasure and contentment that are not otherwise classifiable as property, power or evaluation. Tumin further describes five basic characteristics of social stratification as follows:

1. It is social, i.e., patterned in character.
2. It is ancient, i.e., it has been found in all past societies.
3. It is ubiquitous.
4. It is diverse in its forms.
5. It is consequential, i.e., the most important and most desired.

## Key Concepts of Stratification

Before we discuss the theories of social stratification, it is essential to know the key concepts of stratification. Gupta (1991) explains two general terms as key concepts of stratification. They are: (i) hierarchy, and (ii) difference.

(i) According to Dumont (1988), *hierarchy* implies the regular ordering of a phenomenon on a continuous scale in such a manner that the elements of the whole are ranked in relation to the whole. Height, weight, income and even power (once it has been quantified) can be arranged in a hierarchical order. Tall and short people can be arranged in a hierarchy of height. Hierarchy is one form of stratification. But not all systems of stratification are hierarchical. Some are, but many, are not. In the latter case 'difference' is valorized, and notions of hierarchy may or may not surface.

(ii) *Difference* rather than hierarchy is dominant in some stratification systems. In other words, the constitutive elements of these differences are such that any attempt to see them hierarchically would do offence to the logical property of these very elements. The layers in this case are not arranged vertically or hierarchically, but horizontally or separately. Such an arrangement can be easily illustrated in the case of language, religion or nationalities.

Sharma (2010) discusses some basic concepts relating to stratification such as equality, inequality, hierarchy, exclusion, poverty and deprivation. Among them, the concepts of 'equality' and 'inequality' are basic to modern social sciences and the capitalist system. Politically speaking, equality may be a genuine expression, but economically, differential access to societal resources seems to be a stark reality. Such an inequality is rationalized and justified as an essential and inevitable phenomenon. The term 'hierarchy' is used for ordering of social units as superior and inferior or higher and lower. Race and caste are considered as natural hierarchies as both imply an ordering of endogamous groups having unchanging hereditary membership. *Social exclusion* implies social relations. There are different forms of social exclusion in India, namely, caste, religion, gender, disability, etc. For instance, the basis of caste system is the principle of inclusion and exclusion or pure and impure to define superior and inferior positions and access to power and privilege. In an another important example, social exclusion is a cause of poverty or poverty causes social exclusion. This is a vexed issue. Poverty and inequality go together and co-exist, though in different measures, in different societies. In his book, *Development as Freedom*, Amartya Sen clearly exposes "poverty as capability deprivation". He observes that poverty can be sensibly identified in terms of deprivation. Age, sex, illness or some disability can impede capability building of a person. Keeping in view these issues, there is one important thing to consider and evaluate public action in reducing inequality or poverty or depreciation.

## Theories of Social Stratification

The theories of social stratification have been discussed in a number of ways. However, three main approaches occupy a place of prominence in social stratification theory (Sharma, 1974; 2010). These are: 1. Functional Approach, 2. Marxian (Dialectical) Approach, and 3. Weberian Approach.

### *Functional Approach*

The keynote of the functional approach to study the social stratification is the functional differentiation as an inevitable phenomenon. One person cannot perform all or most of the functions in a society. For different functions, persons of different intent and ability are required. The persons are rewarded according to the value attached to the functions they perform. This differential reward pattern gives rise to stratification and hierarchy. The functional theory of stratification advanced by Davis and Moore conforms with this analysis of functional approach to the stratification. Most of the studies on the caste system in India were conducted from the functionalist perspective in the first half of the 20th century, and even after this, in the decades of sixties and seventies. From H.H. Risley to J.H. Hutton, and then to G.S. Ghurye, M.N. Srinivas, Louis Dumont – all enumerated positive functions of the caste system. Yogendra Singh observes that the basic premises of structural-functional studies on social stratification have implied a systematic teleology on the 'hierarchical' model of caste society, harmony or consensus.

### *Marxian (Dialectical) Approach*

Karl Marx is the principal architect of the dialectical approach to the study of social stratification. Here, it would be quite relevant to mention that Marx did not propound a simple theory of technological or economic determination. He propounded a wide structural theory of society. However, Marx equates class stratification with all other types of stratification systems. He considered power and status stratification as the products of class stratification. Thus, to Marx, all other aspects of the society are subordinate to the economic aspect, as he considered the latter as 'deterministic' or 'fundamental' and the former as the 'by-products', 'secondary' or 'super-structure'. According to Marx, 'stratification' is determined, therefore, by the system of relations of production, and 'status' is determined by man's position in this very system in terms of ownership and non-ownership of the means of production. Under the labels of 'class' and 'class struggle' Marx propounded not one theory but a galaxy of theories. He does not make a distinction between 'class' and 'status' or between 'class hierarchy' and 'social stratification'. He, however, makes it explicit that 'production' is by 'social individuals' and, therefore, it should be understood in 'social context'. The assertions of such a nature make it clear that the Marx's theory of class could be understood and sociologically examined as a system of stratification in terms of 'domination' and 'subjection' or 'effective superiority-inferiority relationships'.

Dahrendorf regards the 'functional' and 'conflict' theories as complementary to each other for understanding social stratification. These theories, according to Dahrendorf, cannot be combined into an integrated theory of stratification. In fact, society has two faces, namely, conflict and integration. Therefore, they could be looked at from different perspectives. Lenski (1966) is, however, optimistic about the combination of the two theories. His observation is that the distinction between the two is basically of approach. The process of synthesis is already underway as he feels. This synthesis is 'analytical', and it has been possible through the result of the application of the scientific method of stratification. Whatever may be the extent of combination between the two approaches, the controversy between the 'functional' and the 'conflict' schools today still remains as lively as before.

The Indian academia has been actively debating on Marxism as an ideology and as a practice since 1940s. Marx described India as an example of "Asiatic mode of production". Under such a system, Marx imagined absence of private property in land. However, he also mentioned that later on private property in land emerged. India has also been viewed as a pre-capitalist economic formation. But it was neither classless nor static. It means that the Asiatic mode does not deny the role of class contradictions and class structures. Karl A. Wittfogel, Eric Hobsbawm and D.D. Kosambi have upheld the view that India was never a static formation. According to Kosambi, caste- and class-based stratification and exploitation existed side by side in India. Similarly, different forms of slavery and bondage, and feudal relations, have also existed in different combinations in the same areas and at the same time.

### *Weberian Approach*

Weber makes a clear distinction between class, status and power. Power is the key to the Weberian theory of social stratification. Class is an economic category, a product of the 'market situation'. Status is determined by 'honour'. 'Status groups' constitute the social order based on honour. The way in which 'status honour' is distributed is important in the understanding of social stratification. Weber makes it clear that classes and status groups are not necessarily independent phenomena. His theory of 'class, status and party' corresponds with the three orders of society, namely, economic, social and political. However, the three orders are not identical or independent; one can be influenced by the other. Thus, striving for power is not always for economic prosperity. It may be for its own sake or for social owner. All power does not provide social honour, and power is not the only source of social honour. Thus, status is determined by the social honour one enjoys, and the latter is expressed through different styles of life. The Weberian theory of social stratification is based on his classic essay "Class, Status, Party" (Weber, 1948). It has influenced several scholars in India, including André Béteille, Anil Bhatt, P.C. Aggrawal, K.L. Sharma, etc. Caste was taken as a singular institution of social ranking by M.N. Srinivas, Louis Dumont and several others in the fifties and sixties.

On the whole, the debate on the functional approach to social stratification was initiated by Davis and Moore (1945) by way of inevitability of functional differentiation and corresponding intent and ability for different tasks, values and rewards. Along with the lively debate on the functional approach, the impact of Max Weber's view of social stratification, in terms of "class, status and party", as three orders, has been immense. The Marxian view on class and class conflict has also inspired studies of agrarian and industrial relations in India.

The main approaches to the study of social stratification are the Marxian, Weberian, functional, socio-psychological and structuralist. Each of these approaches refers to a specific viewpoint by which structures and processes of social stratification are viewed and patterns of hierarchic social relations are ascertained (Sharma, 1997). Singh (1977) finds systematic theories such as functionalism and Marxism more powerful than the conceptual schema. Singh classifies all approaches as universalistic-particularistic and cultural-structural specific. Singh analyses caste as a universal reality and not as a typical Indian social reality on the one hand, and as a cultural/ideological system versus a system of relationships, on the other. The conceptual schemes like the closed and open and segmentary and organic systems of the caste stratification (Bailey, 1963; Béteille, 1966) also fall under this broad rubric of the functionalist analysis. Studies of class stratification in particular have used the Marxist models employing interactional categories and concepts. Ramkrishna Mukherjee (1957), Daniel Thorner (1976), D.N. Dhanagare (1991) and several others have studied agrarian relations in interactional terms focusing upon the nature of mode of production in Indian agriculture.

## Studies on Social Stratification in India

A number of books and articles were published on social stratification during the second half of the 20th century. It is difficult to mention all the major writings of the scholars who have studied on stratification in India. Therefore, I am referring here some of the trend reports and edited volumes which highlighted the different issues of stratification in India. These would be helpful to researchers for doing further studies on stratification in India. Yogendra Singh (1974, 1977, 1985) prepared an Indian Council of Social Science Research (ICSSR) trend report on social stratification, in which he has highlighted many important theoretical and substantive issues. He discusses the nature of social order, social equality, social justice and the nature of man. K.L. Sharma (1980, 1994) has also published two volumes which focus on the study of social stratification in terms of theoretical approaches, ideological underpinnings, and methodological orientations in the studies of caste, tribe, ethnicity, class, power, social mobility, etc. Sharma (1977) also prepared the third trend report of the ICSSR. In this report, the focus was on the understanding of culture, rural-agrarian setting, urban-industrial stratification, weaker sections, gender, caste, class, ethnicity and power. Surendra Sharma (1985) provides a comprehensive review of the studies of social stratification in India mainly focusing upon theory, ideology and method from the viewpoint of the sociology of knowledge. K.L. Sharma (1986) edited a volume incorporating sixteen contributions, of which seven are on caste and related aspects, such as class power, social mobility, estate, etc. The remaining nine articles are on stratification in ancient India, political power, agrarian classes and mobilization, rural development, professions, industrialization, ethnicity, etc. In Dipankar Gupta's edited volume *Social Stratification* (1991), barring some contributions in section three on "class", all articles are on caste and related issues. The contributions in Sharma's volume (1986) are based on field studies comparable with the "caste profiles" as reported in the volume edited by Dipankar Gupta. However, the difference between the two volumes lies in the fact that Gupta's volume is caste-centric, whereas Sharma's volume provides a semblance of caste, ethnicity, class and power (Sharma, 2010). However, no book on social stratification in India can ignore the subject of caste and class. For a long time caste and class were considered synonym for social stratification. Caste was so in India, and class was equated with stratification in the Western countries. Though, there are some other domains of social stratification such as power, gender, ethnicity and race. Another volume edited by K.L. Sharma (1999) includes articles on historicity of social stratification, occupation, caste and family, elite, *varna* and caste, division and hierarchy, caste and class, class conflict, mobility, etc. Recently, a volume edited by Modi, Nagla and Agrawal (2009) on *Themes in Social Stratification and Mobility* offers an insightful understanding and analysis of issues related to social stratification, mobility, village community, urban life, tribal and peasant movements, gender relations, etc. in India in a broad theoretical and empirical perspective.

However, more than these edited volumes and books, the studies have been done by a number of scholars in India, mainly, F.G. Bailey (1963), André Béteille (1966, 1969), Anil Bhatt (1975), Victor S. D'Souza (1969), Louis Dumont (1972), G.S. Ghurye (1950, 1961), Dipankar Gupta (1991), K.L. Sharma (1974, 1980, 1986, 1994, 1997, 1999), Yogendra Singh (1974, 1977, 1985), etc. In this section, we are particularly concerned with the writings of André Béteille who tries to analyse different dimensions of social stratification in India linking theory with empirical data.

## References

Bailey, F.G. (1963). "Closed Social Stratification in India", *European Journal of Sociology*, Vol. IV, No.1.

Beeghley, Leonard (1978). Social Stratification in America, California: Goodyear Publishing Co.

Béteille, André (1966). *Caste, Class, and Power: Changing Patterns of Stratification in a Tanjore Village*, Bombay: Oxford University Press.

Béteille, André (ed.) (1969). *Social Inequality: Selected Writings*, Harmondsworth: Penguin Books.

Bhatt, Anil (1975). *Caste, Class and Politics*, Delhi: Manohar Book Service.

Dhanagare, D.N. (1991). 'The Model of Agrarian Classes in India' in Gupta, Dipankar (ed.) *Social Stratification*, Delhi: Oxford University Press.

D'Souza, Victor S. (1969). *Social Structure of a Planned City: Chandigarh*, Delhi: Orient Longman.

Davis, Kingsley and Wilbert Moore (1945). "Some Principles of Stratification", *American Sociological Review*, Vol. 10, No. 2, pp. 242–249.

Dumont, Louis (1972). *Homo Hierarchicus: The Caste System and its Implications*, London: Granada Publishing Ltd. and also published in 1988, Delhi: Oxford University Press.

Ghurye, G.S. (1950). *Caste and Class in India*, Bombay: Popular Prakashan.

— (1961). *Caste, Class and Occupation*, Bombay: Popular Prakashan.

Gupta, Dipankar (ed.) (1991). *Social Stratification*, Delhi: Oxford University Press.

Lenski, Gerhard (1966). *Power and Privilege: A Theory of social Stratification*, New York: McGraw-Hill.

Modi, Ishwar, Nagla, B.K. and Agrawal, Arvind Kumar (2009). *Themes in Social Stratification and Mobility*, Jaipur: Rawat Publications.

Mukherjee, Ramkrishna (1957). *The Dynamics of Rural Society*, Berlin: Academie Verlag.

Parsons, Talcott (1954). 'An Analytical Approach to the Theory of Social Stratification', *Essays in Sociological Theory*, Glencoe: The Free Press.

Sharma, K.L. (1974). *The Changing Rural Stratification System*, New Delhi: Orient Longman. See also by K.L. Sharma (1980). *Essays on Social Stratification*, Jaipur: Rawat Publications; (ed.) (1986). *Social Stratification in India*, New Delhi: Manohar Publications; (1994). *Social Stratification and Mobility*, Jaipur: Rawat Publications; (1997). *Social Stratification in India: Issues and Themes*, New Delhi: Sage Publications; (1999). *Social Inequality in India: Profiles of Caste, Class and Social Mobility*, Jaipur: Rawat Publications; and (2010). *Perspectives on Social Stratification*, Jaipur: Rawat Publications.

Sharma, Surendra (1985). *Sociology in India: A Perspective from Sociology of Knowledge*, Jaipur: Rawat Publications.

Singh, Yogendra (1974). "Sociology of Social Stratification: A Trend report", in *A Survey of Research in Sociology and Social Anthropology*, ICSSR Vol. I, Bombay: Popular Prakashan. See also by Yogendra Singh (1977). *Social Stratification and Change in India*, Delhi: Manohar Publications; (1985). "Sociology of Social Stratification in India: A Trend Report", in *A Survey of Research in Sociology and Social Anthropology*, ICSSR Vol. II, New Delhi: Satvahan Publications.

Thorner, Daniel (1956). 'Feudalism in India', in Rushton Cioulborn (ed.) *Feudalism in History*, Princeton: Princeton University Press.

— (1976). '*Agrarian Structure*', *The Agrarian Prospect in India*, Delhi: Allied Publishers.

Tumin, Melvin M. (1969). *Social Stratification*, New Delhi: Prentice-Hall of India.

Weber, Max (1948). 'Class, Status and Party', Gerth, H.H. and Mills, C.W. (eds), *From Max Weber: Essays in Sociology*, London: Routledge and Kegan Paul.

# 15

## André Béteille

André Béteille is a Professor Emeritus of Sociology at Delhi School of Economics in University of Delhi. In his long and distinguished career, he has taught at Oxford University, Cambridge University, the University of Chicago and the London School of Economics. He has also been Professor Emeritus of Sociology in the University of Cambridge, the London School of Economics, the Erasmus University of Rotterdam, the University of California at Berkeley, and the Institute of Advanced Study, Berlin. He even at an early age received numerous awards and fellowships from a number of universities both in India and abroad. He was the first Nehru Fellow. One may also add that in 1992 in recognition of his high scholarly contributions to the field of sociology he was elected as a Fellow of the British Academy – a distinction that rarely comes to an Indian and that too to a sociologist. Professor Béteille has worked as Chancellor, North-Eastern Hill University and Chairman, Indian Council of Social Science Research. In 2005, in recognition of his work in the field of sociology and his distinguished service to the nation, he was awarded the Padma Bhushan by the President of India. The same year he was appointed as a member of the Prime Minister's National Knowledge Commission which he quit in protest in 2006, following a proposal for increasing caste-based reservations. The same year, he was made National Professor, and is currently Chairman of the Centre for Studies in Social Sciences, Kolkata.

Béteille was born in September 1934 in the town of Chandannagore, then under French rule – the youngest of three brothers and a sister. His father was French and mayor of the Chandannagore Municipality. Thus, he is a French parentage and in many ways a quintessential Bengali *Bhadralok* who has Bengali mother and grandmother. They left a deep impression on him. Moreover, he grew up in Bengal, spent a part of his school years and all his college and university days in Calcutta. He is equally comfortable with Bengali as in English. He has profound knowledge of European, particular English, literature. Few people know that Béteille is also a good singer of Rabindranath Tagore's songs.

Béteille studied at Chandannagore and at a boarding school in Patna, before moving to Calcutta in 1946. He has had his higher education in Calcutta where the family shifted after independence. He graduated from St. Xavier's College, Calcutta. He started his studies as a student of physics but halfway switched to anthropology, inspired in part by N.K. Bose, who later became his first intellectual mentor. He did honours in anthropology at University of Calcutta and had also completed M.Sc. from the same university. After a brief stint at the Indian Statistical Institute as a research fellow, he started teaching degree courses and shortly after the Department of Sociology opened in Delhi and was emerging as a premier department so Béteille moved there as a lecturer in sociology and began research for Ph.D. under M.N. Srinivas who was then heading the department.

Béteille began his career as a specialist in social stratification and questions of equality and universality. From 1990, he has started taking deep interest in liberal philosophy and issues arising from poverty and social injustice. He is the first Indian sociologist who saw the relevance of the theories of John Rawls and creatively applied his thought to sort out the tangle that policies on positive discrimination. However, all this is still in the realm of social stratification. Béteille was influenced by N.K. Bose. He has memories of Srinivas who stressed on the importance of fieldwork. The important work of Bose on 'The Structure of Hindu Society' foreshadows much of the work of Dumont and Pocock; he was a great fieldworker and lived with tribal people and showed the value of ethnographic observation combined with classical texts. Béteille also spotted differences between Bose and Srinivas.

Among British anthropologists, Béteille was most influenced by Evans-Pritchard through his writings and his influence on M.N. Srinivas and Max Gluckman. During the Simon Fellowship at Manchester he had an impact of Gluckman's contributions to anthropology and John Barne's idea of social networks. He has also memories of Meyer Fortes and his influence on Srinivas (a craftsman) and Edmund Leach and his writing on 'Political Systems of Highland Burma' which shook British anthropology out of its complacency but avoided the role of a guru.

Béteille had natural inclination to compare ways of life because of his own mixed background and prompted orientation towards anthropology. He had first intended to work with Tamil speakers in Delhi. Srinivas insisted him to work in an area very different from the one in which he had grown up and which was unusual for social studies in India.

## Theoretical Perspective

Béteille's critical contribution has been contextualizing local concepts and understandings, such as caste and class, hierarchy and equality, and in more universal and generalized theories of inequality, stratification and justice. His works draw upon universal categories and concepts. He always places them in the context of empirical ground realities. Béteille closeness to Weber naturally also signalled his distance from Marx – a scholar whom he respected but from afar. He is the best known scholar in India on liberal theory and its application in social policy. Aware as he is, of the difficulties and limitations of the comparative method, he still manages to use it effectively.

Béteille uses Weberian categories and mode of analysis. Thus, he refines the conceptualization of 'ideas and interests', and analyses the similarities and interdependence of tribe and caste through intermediary category of the 'peasant'. He uses gender and its implication for 'blood' and hereditary to make an incisive comparison of race and caste.

## Writings of André Béteille

André Béteille is one of India's leading sociologists and writers. He is particularly known for his studies of the caste system in South India. He has authored many books. In the words of historian Ramchandra Guha, Béteille has written insightfully about all the major questions of the day: India's encounters with the West, the contest between religion and secularism, the relationship between caste and class, the links between poverty and inequality, the nurturing of public institutions, the role and responsibilities of the intellectual, etc. He also worked on backward classes and their position in Indian society based on Smut's lectures given in Cambridge in 1985.

- His publications include:
- Caste, Class and Power: Changing Patterns of Stratification in a Tanjore Village (1965)
- Castes: Old and New, Essays in Social Structure and Social Stratification (1969)
- Inequality and Social Change (1972)
- Studies in Agrarian Social Structure (1974)
- Six Essays in Comparative Sociology (1974)
- Inequality among Men (1977)
- The Idea of Natural Inequality and Other Essays (1983)
- Society and Politics in India: Essays in a Comparative Perspective (1991)
- The Backward Classes in Contemporary India (1992)
- Antinomies of Society: Essays on Ideologies and Institutions (2000)
- Sociology: Essays on Approach and Method (2002)

- Chronicles of Our Time (2000)
- Equality and Universality: Essays in Social and Political Theory (2002)
- Ideology and Social Science (2006)
- Marxism and Class Analysis (2007)

Besides the above books, Béteille also wrote a number of essays mainly on Secularism Re-examined, Race and Caste, Teaching and Research, Government and NGOs, The Indian Middle Class, etc.

In this chapter, we would discuss the following issues which emerge from the writings of Béteille:

1. Civil Society
2. Social Stratification in India
3. The Idea of Equality and Inequality
4. Studies in Agrarian Social Structure
5. Society and Politics in India
6. Backward Classes in Contemporary India
7. Ideologies and Institutions
8. Religion and Secularism

## Anti-Utopia: Essential Writings of André Béteille

In a career spanning over decades known for its robustness and versatility, André Béteille's contribution and his influence on the way of sociology is researched, studied and taught in India has been immense. Béteille's work is characterized by a single openness to diverse upon universal theories and concepts. Béteille's is always rooted in the context of empirical studies. He believes that the research for exotica in Indian society has led to an intellectual overemphasis on caste and a subsequent neglect of class characteristically. His own study of the caste system reflects his commitment to the comparative method and not to ideology or the book-view.

Bringing together the essence of the Béteille's ideas and writings, the collection of 19 essays, introduced by Dipankar Gupta, has been especially selected. The book is divided into five sections, each of which is devoted to Béteille's varied intellectual interests. The essays range from the significance of the comparative method to ideas of equality and inequality and finally to issues regarding civil society and institutional well-being. In each instance,

Béteille's characteristic significance of blending theory to Indian reality is clearly evident. It is because of his erudition that he is, unarguably, one of the most quoted scholars in India. This collection is also evident of Béteille's political position which is the result of deep intellectual scrutiny and why utopian visions are unappealing to him. Béteille's ability to utilize his academic prowess to comment on popular contemporary issues makes him a happy anti-utopian for he envisions progress and is ever hopeful.

## Civil Society

Béteille's writings on civil society convey the clear impression that if India can realize citizenship substantially by pressing on with the potentialities within liberal democracy, then that alone would be worthy of many a revolution. In the section on 'civil society and institutional well-being' he contextualizes secularism in an understanding of the 'citizen' and 'civil society' and urges the autonomy of public institution.

In the section dealing with 'stratification in India', Béteille explores the dynamics of class, status and political mobilization. Here, he does not accept Marx's economic reductionism, even as he unmasks the ideological totalities of Louis Dumont's structuralism.

Dipankar Gupta (2011) analyses the different meanings of the concept of 'civil society' in the West and in India. He identifies two major strands in this debate in India. One seeks to 'valorize' tradition against an oppressive and homogenizing state. The other represented by Béteille seeks instead to nurture modern institutions intermediate between the individual and the state, such as universities, hospitals and law courts. Béteille's is a lonely voice against the neo-rationalists, engaged not in a hopeless harking back to the past but in securing the autonomy from the state and sectarian politics of intermediate institutions. Gupta suggests that in this otherwise laudable task Béteille has committed the error of ignoring the necessary functions of the democratic state. The exclusive focus on intermediate institutions lets the state off the hook, so to say, allowing it to abdicate its role in creating the conditions for effective citizenship.

## Antinomies of Society

This collection on 'Antinomies of Society: Essays on Ideologies and Institutions' brings together some of the Béteille's recent works on institutions, civil society and democracy – all viewed in a comparative perspective but with India at the centre of attention.

The essays in this volume are devoted to changing norms and values with special emphasis on the tensions, oppositions and contradictions inherent in them. In exploring various facets of contemporary social and political life, Béteille reveals the stresses and strains of democracy in India and the difficulties of transforming a hierarchical society into an egalitarian one. In so doing, he exposes the disjunction between political ideals and social constraints. These and other antinomies are discussed in a set of essays that focus on a range of ideologies and institutions. Marxism, nationalism and secularism are among the ideologies discussed, along with the university, the civil service and other major institutions.

## Equality

More controversial is his discussion of 'equality and individualism: the tension between fact and value', and its implication for affirmative action and reservation quotas. The paradox of modern societies, so acutely evident in India, is not equality in principle but inequality in practice. Privileging competition accentuates natural inequalities of endowment and endeavour, and overlays these further with socially constructed ones. For no matter, how fair the competition and equal the opportunity may be, this does not, and cannot, lead an equality results.

Following Ronald Dworkin, Béteille makes a subtle and complex argument that is not easily accepted in the heat of political debate over reservations in this country. Thus, equality as a right is fundamental for all citizens. It implies 'equal respect' and 'treatment as equals' before the law. But, it does not imply 'equal treatment' since treating un-equals as equals only perpetuates inequalities, for it does not level the playing the field.

The privileges of nobility and caste once perpetuated such inequalities. Today, for real, not just formal equality of opportunity and fair competition, a reverse discrimination is needed before these can be a level playing field. This is what 'equality of policy' must bring about, and it is less a matter of individual rights as of rightly advantaging now groups that were unfairly unadvantaged before. This is not a matter of historical redress so much as one of the social egalitarianism a civic imperative today.

Heredia (2005), reviewing the Béteille's *Anti-Utopia,* said that it is not my intention here to close this debate or settle the other controversies that this volume *Anti-Utopia* raises, but rather to invite the readers to engage with the issues. Gupta's presentation of Béteille's *Anti-Utopia* is a good place to start on this, and other such contested issues. The essays in the collection are categorized thematically and the two appendices help to contextualize Béteille more personally: one on his 'Two grandmothers' and the other a recent interview he gives to the editor Professor Gupta.

## Social Stratification In India

### *Caste, Class and Power*

In *Caste, Class and Power,* which was a slightly revised version of a Delhi University Ph.D. thesis written under the supervision of M.N. Srinivas, Béteille followed the established convention of the anthropological research, based on intensive fieldwork, long stay in a community and detailed observation of its everyday life. But, instead of focusing on problems that were then central to anthropology such as kinship, marriage, religion and ritual, he chose class and stratification which were central to the concerns of sociology. The book was written with the conviction that the convergence of sociology and social anthropology was a distinct and exciting possibility, and that Indian sociologists could contribute something to its realization. The book had a mixed response. Béteille was sharply criticized by some anthropologists in Europe for trying to introduce class and stratification into a domain where they did not fit. On that point he believes he has prevailed over his critics.

The choice of Tanjore for the study was mainly of Béteille's own idea. He had intended to study temples and how they worked. He had first impressions of Tanjore, Tamil speakers, living with Brahmins and he could understand their ritual language. He had background of his mother's family who were orthodox Brahmins and grandmother particularly religious. He links his impressions with memories of his childhood in Calcutta and the contrasts between Brahmin behaviour in cities and countryside in India. He noted similar behaviour among widows in Tanjore. He surprised by relations between castes which were much more formal than in Calcutta or Delhi. Béteille talks about his fieldwork in Tanjore, India, and the things which most surprised and interested him.

Béteille conducted his study on 'caste, class and power' at a Tanjore village (Sripuram, not a real name of the village) of Tamilnadu in South India in 1961–62. He did fieldwork in the village for about ten months. This was a micro-empirical study which generated many discussions after its publication entitled *Caste, Class and Power* in 1971. Previous books of village studies by F.G. Bailey, Adrian Mayer and McKim Marriott were based on caste structure whereas Béteille's work added class and power structure and he examined the changing relationship between the three and the forces that brought about the change in rural stratification system in India.

As has been emphasized from the beginning, change is a fundamental feature of the social structure of Sripuram today. Béteille tries to understand this process of change in the three systems, namely, caste, class and power. In reality, caste, class and power are closely interwoven. They can be treated separately, and particularly the last two, only by a process of abstraction. Caste, class and power refer in different ways to the phenomenon of social stratification. Caste and class resemble each other in some respects and differ in others. Let us first note these points of similarity and difference before seeing how the two systems are interrelated in their actual working.

### *Caste*

Several scholars have considered Indian society as "caste society". In his study, Béteille also emphasizes the caste structure of the Sripuram village of Tanjore district which was traditionally very complex and conservative district. The whole village is divided into different castes comprising three main segments, namely, Brahmins, non-Brahmins and Adi-Dravids (Untouchables). Caste system is a continuous process and is identifiable too. It enjoys both legal and religious sanctions in traditional Indian society. Different castes are assigned different roles, not only in economic matters, but over a wide range of social phenomena. In traditional society, punishment differs not only according to the nature of the offence committed, but also according to the caste of the offender.

Béteille has outlined the basic features of the "caste" model of Indian society while examining its usefulness as a scheme of analysis. These features are: (1) it is based on ideas and not on the actual behaviour of the people; (2) these ideas are found in the classical texts; (3) the system is based on "rules of the game"; and (4) different castes fulfil complementary functions, and their mutual relations are "non-antagonistic". Béteille comments that this model does not explain specific society and particularly its economic and political life. This model could apply to any system of religious beliefs as it reflects in the rituals which divide people of the Sripuram. This also exhibits the interests of the people. Béteille remarks that the study of "interests" is quite necessary to understand political and economic problems.

### *Class*

Classes, in contrast, are *de facto* categories. Classes are in principle and, to some extent, in practice open; castes are not open. Classes do not enjoy the kind of legal and religious sanctions which were associated with castes (or, for that matter, with estates in feudal society). It is true that inequalities before law, which were associated with the different castes, have been completely removed, or almost so, in course of the last hundred years. Nonetheless, old habits of mind, conditioned by a legal and religious structure which for centuries upheld these inequalities, continue to play a part in the relations between castes in contemporary society.

Social classes, defined in terms of ownership or non-ownership of the means of production, tend to be reduced to a few broad divisions. In the context of the agrarian social structure of Sripurum classes are hierarchically arranged social categories, based broadly upon ownership or non-ownership of the means of production. Classes are sub-divided in terms of (i) the types of ownership and control, and (ii) the types of services contributed to the process of production. Thus, a distinction is made between sharecroppers and agricultural labourers. Further, rentiers, farmers, cultivators, share-croppers and agricultural labourers constitute distinct categories only at the conceptual level. They do not, in reality, comprise discrete groups, since it is frequently found that a single person is a rentier and a farmer, a sharecropper and an agricultural labourer.

### *Power*

After discussing caste and class, Béteille analyses the system of power in Sripuram village. The village has both caste and class. The distribution of power, again, creates a hierarchy which is different from the hierarchies of caste and class. The system of caste and class has also some sort of power. One of the aspects of power is institutional and formal which is achieved through political parties and panchayats. For example, the political party which is in government wields more power. Power of caste, class and groups of village transcends also beyond the village. Béteille looks social stratification of the village in context to caste, class and power of the village.

The distribution of power has acquired a very dynamic character after independence. In some ways the traditional relationship between caste and power has been reversed. Whereas power in the past was concentrated in the hands of Brahmins, today, the village panchayat is controlled by non-Brahmins and the traditional elite is being pushed into the background. Power has also become independent class to a greater extent than in the past. Ownership of land is no longer a decisive factor in acquiring power. Numerical support and a strategic position in the party machinery play an important part. Adult franchise and Panchayati Raj have introduced new processes into the village society. The struggle for power has become a pervasive phenomenon. This may partly be due to the fact that today much more power is accessible to the common man than was ever in the case in the past (Béteille, 1991b).

### *Analytical Perspective of Caste, Class and Power*

As discussion of the structure of Indian society must begin with a consideration of inequalities that are to be encountered in almost every sphere of life, particularly in context to caste, class and power. In his book *Caste, Class and Power* (1965), Béteille wrote: "there was much greater consistency between the class system and the caste system in traditional society and even sixty years ago". More recently, land had begun passing out of Brahmin hands, while their tenants now had much stronger rights – they could no longer be evicted so easily. Brahmins' pre-eminent position continued to operate in the ritual sphere, but here too challenge was not unknown. For instance, the day India became a republic on 26 January 1950, a group of non-Brahmins and Adi-Dravidas (the erstwhile untouchables) marched through the agraharam till the gates of its main temple – an act that "was not only ritually polluting, but (which) brought social humiliation of the Brahmins" (ibid.: 152). The most decisive shift was in the realm of political power. Till 1946 a Brahmin ran the village panchayat. But with adult suffrage numbers had become more important than ritual status. Now, many physically powerful non-Brahmin castes such as the Kallars had come to dominate village politics. Thus, power has shifted much more decisively from the traditional elite of the village into the hands of the new popular leaders (ibid.: 172, 199).

Béteille worked for his thesis with M.N. Srinivas but there was a significant departure in his theoretical orientation. Srinivas made a difference to the way social anthropology was researched in India through his emphasis on in-depth fieldwork. Béteille acknowledged the importance of fieldwork but was conceptually in another league – that of Weberian sociology. Functionalism was the order of the day. Orientalism and English empiricism were also in fashion. Hermeneutics structuralism and interpretative sociology and phenomenology were not in vogue. But Béteille was open to those sociological theories and his major contribution to actually use the Weberian mode of analysis in his doctoral thesis on caste, class and power in a South Indian village. He used Weber's concept of class, status and power in the context of Indian ground realities. Till then, village studies were their documentary in character, governed by functionalism, or romanticized generalization. Béteille criticizes Dumont's *Homo Hierarchicus* for portraying the Indian caste system as a ubiquitous totality whereas caste in India is neither uniform nor continuous.

Béteille's work on *Caste, Class and Power: Changing Patterns of Stratification in a Tanjore Village* (1966) departs significantly from the writings which equate caste with stratification. Following Weber's dictum of "class, status and party", Béteille describes "caste, class and power". He places caste before class, whereas Weber puts status (caste) after class. Power remains at the third place after class and status or caste and class in both Weber and Béteille, respectively. Béteille mentions 'stratification' in a somewhat frivolous manner. For example, he states that caste, class and power relate in different ways to the broader phenomenon of social stratification. Again, Béteille considers caste hierarchy as representing only one aspect of social stratification, but in the same vein he also states that inter-caste relations are related with the economic and political organization as if caste is independent of inter-caste relations or as if caste is an encompassing system. There is anomaly and contradiction because Béteille treats caste as one of the three dimensions of social stratification, and he also incorporates economic and political aspects in its orbit. The same logic he applies to the phenomenon of class and power (Sharma, 2010).

Béteille's enchantment with Weber's triology of "class, status and party" is clearly evident in his *Caste, Class and Power*. Béteille justifies differentiation of statuses and roles (structures) as the basis of distinct orders such as caste, class and power. However, the basis of Weber's thesis lies in the recognition of individual, his behaviour (action) based on subjectivity, and objectification. Weber understands individual and his action(s) through *Verstehen*. Methodological appreciation provided by Weber is not visible in

Béteille's study of a village in South India. Béteille's method of study is in tune with 'functionalism', which is a characteristic feature of British Anthropology as advanced by A.R. Radcliffe-Brown, B. Malinowski, Evans-Pritchard, etc. (ibid.).

### *Race and Caste*

Béteille article, "Race and Caste" (*The Hindu*, 10 March 2010 and A Response to Béteille – by Kalpana Kannabiran) is useful in that it provides us with an excellent opportunity to broaden the national debate on the issue of race and its relevance to an understanding of caste, particularly in the context of the UN Convention on the Elimination of Racial Discrimination (CERD).

This debate, which has been initiated by Dalit human rights groups across the country and by the National Federation of Dalit Women, has, till now, been restricted to rights-based struggles in the country, and the Dalit intelligentsia. The debate, therefore, has centred on the articulation of caste as discrimination, and the various forms of that discrimination – exclusion, untouchability, denial of constitutional rights and guarantees, violent subjugation and [histories of] slavery – as resonant of internationally recognized forms of racism. This articulation of caste has its intellectual history, not in the 'scientific' work of anthropologists of European origin and their 'native' heirs, but in the political work of Indian ideologues who were committed to the establishment of an egalitarian social order, and who in that endeavour saw caste as the single most powerful obstacle to the realization of that commitment – Jotiba Phule, Savitribai Phule, Pandita Ramabai, Periyar and Ambedkar, to name the most influential ones.

Although Béteille argues that "[b]y treating caste discrimination as a form of racial discrimination and, by implication, caste as a form of race, the U.N. is turning its back on established scientific opinion" and further that the very analogy is "scientifically nonsensical", anthropology tells us that the word 'caste' is derived from the Portuguese 'casta', an early sixteenth century word which embraced several meanings, not the least significant of which was "purity of blood". Scientific opinion has not to date refuted the interpretation of the word 'casta'. The science of anthropology has also actively applied this term to describe the specific form of institutionalized discrimination and its application to the two levels of groups in the Indian sub-continent: the jatis, roughly about 3,000 or more and the four varnas. Debate on caste in anthropology has focused primarily on whether one should use it to designate the first, more local category, or more effectively signified varna, while the term 'sub-caste' described the jati more closely. But there was no disagreement on the use of the word 'caste' itself. The debates on race with reference to the Indian sub-continent that Béteille speaks about are predicated on an unquestioned acceptance of caste as a social group. Not jati or varna, but caste as the quintessentially Indian social grouping.

Setting caste aside for the moment, how 'scientific' is the notion of race? Referring to the shifts in the semantic field of race in eighteenth and nineteenth century Europe, Colette Guillaumin argues that Gobineau's work [which Béteille alludes to in passing] on race not only does not define race, but also "makes no attempt to establish any causal link whatsoever between physical phenomena and mental or social ones". Brain weights of blacks and whites, for instance, she says, are equated with the degree of intelligence. Even prior to its use, alongside caste, race theory was part of a larger exercise of domination – cultural, political, hence natural – with the dispenser of scientific judgments inevitably belonging to cultures of dominance, race and racism constantly fusing into one another, the former in fact deriving from the latter.

The contentious area clearly is the application of the term 'race' to 'caste'. Problematic for Béteille ["scientifically nonsensical", "politically mischievous", "moral irresponsibility"], and also for the Indian government, which is resisting the analogy along curiously similar lines. India's Report on the CERD of 29 April 1996, while celebrating racial diversity as the quintessence of Indian society, states that "the term 'caste' denotes a 'social' and 'class' distinction and is not based on race. It has its origins in the functional division of Indian society during ancient times ... Measures of positive discrimination have been incorporated into the Indian Constitution to enable Scheduled Castes (SCs) and Scheduled Tribes (STs), who tend to be among the economically underprivileged classes, to enter the mainstream of national life and to facilitate their intermingling with the rest of the Indian population." Further, the Report states that although Article 1 of the CERD includes the term 'descent' in the definition of racial discrimination and although both castes and tribes are descent based systems, "[i]t is obvious ... that the use of the term 'descent' in the Convention clearly refers to 'race'. Communities which fall under the definition of Scheduled Castes and Scheduled Tribes are unique to Indian society and its historical process." Both Béteille's dismissive condemnation and the Indian government's attempt to remove caste from the broader matrix of descent based systems are unexplained and unsubstantiated [unscientific, if you like].

The analogy between race and caste, which does not date back to Ashley Montague or to Franz Boas, as Béteille argues, but more than a couple of centuries earlier to the original application of the term 'casta' itself – a term that recognized the kinship between race and caste. The word 'asprsya' [literally, untouchable] was first used in the Visnusmrti, which prescribes death for any member of these castes who deliberately touches a member of a higher caste. However, the sexuality of untouchable women belonged to the upper caste men, and was an indispensable part of the labour provided by slave women. Romila Thapar argues that although Brahmanism was constantly challenged by the heterodox traditions, and metaphysical ideals of rights did make their appearance intermittently in legal codes two thousand years ago, these rights were extended only to elite groups. Slaves, Sudras and serfs did not enter the account. Phule's accounts of caste in the nineteenth century are even grimmer. Ambedkar's concerns in the twentieth century centred on finding ways in which independence could bring freedom to the oppressed: affirmative action and positive discrimination being an important first step.

At the time when Phule, Ambedkar and Periyar were articulating an understanding of caste in terms of lived experience and political reality, Risley and Guha were attempting, in their own ways, a 'scientific' racial classification of caste, from their respective locations within colonial administration. The application of race as a category to understand social reality within the Indian sub-continent came much after its use in colonization. No social group is completely homogenous across region and time. SCs are no exception. However, it is perfectly legitimate to assert the commonality of experience across cultural, linguistic, regional, national and ethnic diversity. Ambedkar's coining of the word 'Dalit' was part of this exercise in unifying the oppressed and forging a common cause. The current move to bring caste within the ambit of the CERD is not a move by the United Nations alone. It is far more importantly an assertion by Dalit groups across the country, part of an effort to realize the visions of anti-caste movements in the earlier part of this century.

Is it political mischief to say that Blacks and Dalits share a history of subjugation, slavery and social exclusion, that has changed only in form and continues untrammelled even today and that both must have recourse to common instruments of redress? Or is it invidious neo-conservatism to say that the assertion by Dalit groups to bring caste-based discrimination under the ambit of international instruments is no different from the assertion of superior rights by some groups claiming Aryan blood? As to what makes scientific sense and what non-sense, surely we know by now that science itself is a deeply ideological enterprise, and both the practices of science and its uses are far from neutral and objective.

## The Idea of Equality and Inequality

Béteille's interest reflects in equality and inequality in human societies in his book entitled *The Idea of Natural Inequality and Other Essays* (1983). After the publication of this book he pursued work on caste in larger context than one village which appeared as *Castes: Old and New* (1969) and moved on to study class through agrarian relations and only after that to the more general theme of inequality.

The essays in this volume examine various aspects of inequality with special reference to contemporary India but viewed in a comparative perspective. They deal with different forms and dimensions of inequality and with alternative conception of equality. The work as a whole seeks to combine social analysis with social criticism, directing the critical approach to traditional hierarchical orders as well as modern systems of inequality generated by the market and the state. It is part of an effort to develop a common language in which the sociologist can address himself not only to his fellow sociologists, but also to other social scientists as well as the general reader. Some of the essays deal with equality and hierarchy as alternative designs for society while other focus on specific domains of society such as the legal order or the educational system. The essays are all based on lectures delivered in universities and other institutions of higher learning in places as far apart as Bombay, Cambridge, Sydney and London.

## Studies in Agrarian Social Structure

*Studies in Agrarian Social Structure* (1974) was the fruit of work done while Béteille was a Jawaharlal Nehru Fellow. It contains essays on two topics, namely, class formation and class consciousness. According to Béteille, when sociologists spoke of differentiation in a village, they generally meant the ranking of castes, not the differential access to land or its products.

According to Béteille, our concern is with the phenomena of caste, class and power and with their changing relations. He refers to the agrarian classes, namely, landowners, peasants and agricultural labourers. In Bengal, the agrarian classes include landowners, Jotedars, Bargardars and Adhiyars and Khet-Majurs as mentioned by Béteille. In other study, Béteille refers to five agrarian classes. All these classifications are arbitrary as neither they are based on attributional criteria nor on interactional approach. But these classifications do not go along with the Marxian perspective. For example, the classes of landowners, moneylenders and labourers are mentioned by Thorner. Kotovsky mentions bourgeoisie capitalist-type landowners, rich peasants, landless or land-poor peasantry and agricultural labourers. In all these class categories, the emphasis is on the process of class interaction, dependence-independence and conflict as observed by Singh.

Béteille also observes quite similar a situation like that of Bailey. He explains that "differentiated institutional structures of various kinds" have emerged. These structures are: (1) the growth of money economy as opposed to inherited status; (2) a new caste-free occupational structure; (3) a new kind of educational system; and (4) the development of differentiated political structures. The writings of Béteille are indicative of the shift from caste-oriented studies to class-oriented studies of rural stratification. He pinpoints that a number of intensive studies of village communities do not always give a clear idea of changes in the association between caste and landownership because of the dominance of the caste frame of reference to the relative neglect of the agrarian class structure comprising landowners, tenants and agricultural labourers as a system of relationship itself. Béteille's analysis suffers from methodological and conceptual weaknesses. Béteille has made use of the participant observation technique for studying class relations and has adopted Weberian conceptual trichotomy of "class, status and party" to investigate "caste, class and power" without examining its relevance to Indian situation. The concepts which are germane to history and experience of Indian reality would be appropriate to understand social stratification in village India. Like Bailey, Béteille also suffers from the fallacy of structural shifts from one structure to another (Sharma, 1980: 35). The differentiation of the class system has been brought about by the introduction of caste-class nexus and the development of market mechanism.

## Society and Politics in India

Like his first work, *Caste, Class and Power*, this latest book is rooted in the ethnography of the present. The volume on *Society and Politics in India: Essays in a Comparative Perspective* (1991) brings together some of the most important essays written over the past two decades by Béteille. He focuses upon the relationship between various forms of inequality and distinction (race, caste, tribe, ethnicity and gender) and on the relationship between the values of equality and individualism; and on the ambivalent role of the modern Indian state as the guarantor of these values. Béteille displays his command of the history of modern thought. However, he does not neglect theory or comparison. These essays seek our connections between seemingly disparate elements of public life. They examine the agenda that

India set for itself at independence and the many social and cultural obstacles that still stand.

The essays brought together in this collection were written or published between 1964 and 1990. Society and politics are subjects of continuous and animated discussion in contemporary India. The essays presented in this volume have the extensive use of the comparative method. Béteille also tried to make use of the concept of social structure. The volume consists of ten essays besides an introduction. The first two essays deal with race and caste, but not quite the same way. They are both comparative in outlook: 'race, caste and gender' being more self-consciously so than 'race, caste and ethnic identity'. Both can be deepened by a consideration of gender and its place in societies divided by race or by caste. Both are also about collective identities. Similarly, in the essay on 'The Concept of Tribe', Béteille examines the special significance of collective identities in the social morphology of India – past and present. 'Caste and Politics in Tamilnadu' is an attempt to interpret regional political processes in the light of fieldwork experience. 'The Politics of "Non-antagonistic Strata"' sought to challenge the view that castes ceased to be castes when they organized themselves for competitive politics. The essay, 'Networks in Indian Social Structure' examines the limitations of a morphological approach wherein attention was confined exclusively to enduring groups and relations between them. Furthermore, two essays included in this selection on the backward classes reflect vast literature on the subject – descriptive, analytical and prescriptive. These essays deal with the issues of social stratification and social mobility respectively. The approach is directly sociological showing in particular the influence of Max Weber. The last two essays deal more with ideas, beliefs and values than social structure in the morphological sense. Equality is more an ideal than a fact; or rather, it is a social fact in so far as it is collectively acknowledged as an ideal and a value. In the last, Béteille writes: "I end as I began with the plea for a differentiated view of each and every society as a basis for the comparisons and contrasts we make between them."

## Backward Classes in Contemporary India

*The Backward Classes in Contemporary India* (1992) is a set of essays on the backward classes in contemporary India by Béteille who has devoted thirty years to the study of the subject. The essays written for scholars as well as laypersons deal primarily with the issues of public policy and, as such, have topical value in view of the importance assumed by the problem of reservations.

Béteille begins with a critique of the equality provisions in the Constitution of India. He argues that the problem is not simply that of the contradiction between the principle of the equality and the practice of inequality, but also of the tensions between divergent concepts of equality. He deals in particular with the problem of balancing the principle of equal opportunities with the principle of redress.

The discussion dwells on the disparities between groups that were such a striking feature of traditional India. An analysis of the structure of Indian society shows that the social situation of the SCs/STs has been and continues to be markedly different from that of the OBCs, which means that measures to redress that are appropriate to the former are not appropriate to the latter.

The author argues that reservations in education and employment should be treated as matters of policy and not of rights. In our society, the individual, and not the caste or the community, is the fundamental bearer of rights and capacities. If caste quotas are treated as matters of right and extended indefinitely, there will be irreparable damage to institutions such as universities, hospitals and banks which are governed by principles that are radically different from those governing the relations between castes.

## Ideology and Social Science

Ramachandra Guha, one of the pioneers of sociological studies in India said, '(Amartya) Sen has recently given us *The Argumentative Indian;* and now, in your hands, is (André) Béteille's equally compelling collection of essays on Indian ideas, themes and debates.' André Béteille has, over the past four decades, contributed a series of topical and stimulating articles to various newspapers. Some of these articles were collected in the book *Chronicles of Our Time*, published a few years ago. *Ideology and Social Science* is a new and rivetting collection of Béteille's writings on Indian society, politics and culture. The fifty articles in this book cover a very wide range of subjects: from the practice of sociology to the prospects of political liberalism, from contemporary debates about caste and caste quotas to old and still persisting myths about what is said to constitute the essence of Indian culture. Béteille's ambit includes the relevant and important themes of secularism, diversity and unity in cultures, the culture of tolerance, discrimination at work, value systems in the changing Indian family, and caste practices in village communities. Steering clear of passing intellectual trends as well as partisan politics, Béteille reaches his conclusions based on a careful examination of the evidence, not on a search for facts that fit a pre-conceived theory. Through his writings, he makes a cogent and passionate appeal to separate sociological theory from the frameworks of social activism. For students of sociology as well as the general reader, this is a book that will stimulate thought and generate interest in social and political issues that are at the core of India's modernity and tradition.

## Sociology: Essays on Approach and Method

For forty years, Béteille taught sociology at Delhi School of Economics. His collection *Sociology: Essays on Approach and Method* (2002) brings together some of his basic concerns as a teacher and a scholar. They include the nature and scope of sociology, and its relations with other disciplines such as anthropology, economics and political science. The book as a whole is animated by a very distinctive conception of sociology as an intellectual pursuit.

## Sociology and Social Anthropology

Béteille discussed the relationship between sociology and social anthropology first in his book on "Six Essays in Comparative Sociology" published in 1974. Later on, again, he presented the same issue in his book *Sociology* published in 2004. To Béteille, sociology and social anthropology are interwoven in such a manner that it is very difficult to detract them from each other. However, Béteille did some exercise which reflects in the following aspects:

1. The distinction between sociology and social anthropology (or cultural anthropology, or ethnology) thrives on a dichotomous view of the world: Whites and natives, civilized and primitive, us and they. This, historically, has been the basis of distinction made in the West between the two. But, given the way in which Indian society is constituted, it provides very little basis for generating or sustaining this kind of dichotomous distinction.
2. The relationship between sociology and social anthropology in India is not the same as in France or Britain. The division of labour between sociology and social anthropology emerged in Britain or United States under specific historical conditions. The division of labour among scholars should be governed ultimately by academic and not by administrative considerations.
3. Karl Mannheim (1953) wrote two essays, one on American sociology and the other on German sociology, in which he contrasted that the American sociology emphasizes on empiricism whereas German sociology gives importance to philosophical aspect. After the revolution, sociology is understood as "bourgeois sociology" in Russia (Osipov, 1969).
4. In India, the first university department of sociology started at Bombay University in 1919 and of anthropology at Calcutta University in 1922. It is interesting to note that eastern India gives priority to anthropology whereas western India to sociology. Today, we have large number of sociology departments as compared to anthropology in India.
5. As is well known, Radcliffe-Brown enjoyed great prestige among social anthropologists in the English-speaking countries who emphasizes to do study of social structure in anthropology. This is the scope of anthropology. In Europe, social anthropology has very limited scope where it is considered in terms of physical anthropology. In America, anthropology means a study of culture which is called social

and cultural anthropology in Europe. However, American calls it a study of human beings or ethnology.

6. Gradually, it has become such a trend in social sciences that sociologists started doing study of industrial societies and social anthropologists engaged them in the study of tribes. This was the start for the distinction in both the subjects.
7. Sociologists adapted to survey methods and social anthropologists used fieldwork for longer period. Even Béteille himself spent ten months in Sripuram and Srinivas spent fifteen months in Rampur village.
8. Radcliffe-Brown's idea that there can be only one science of comparative sociology embracing the study of all societies. He calls up to the extent that comparative sociology in fact is a social anthropology.

Béteille tried to differentiate sociology and social anthropology in an Indian context. According to him, both the subjects are the same. Earlier, the two disciplines had marked out distinct, overlapping domains, with sociology studying 'us', the advanced industrial societies of the West, and anthropology studying 'them', or the rest. Now, there is no difference in their study of societies. Therefore, sociology and social anthropology are one in that direction.

## Comparative Method

For Béteille, like Weber, the comparative method is the essence of sociological research. But comparison, according to him, should not be a compulsive search for difference and exotica a search for similarities is an equally rigorous analytical pursuit. His essay on the comparative method attacks those who study other societies only to seek out differences. According to him, the search for similarities is also a legitimate pursuit and one that requires great analytical rigour. Sociologists do the study of their own culture whereas anthropologists do the study of other cultures. Thus, according to Béteille, anthropology is a comparative and objective social science. However, Béteille also views that it is difficult to differentiate between sociology and anthropology. This itself is a paradox. For example, in India, when an Indian does study of

Mumbai, he is called a sociologist whereas, when a British scholar does so, he is known as an anthropologist.

For Béteille, the comparative method is the essence of sociological theory. While it might appear to a facile observer that sociology is a fairly easy subject, in fact, he contends, it is very difficult to pursue. The questions of sociology can only be focalized in a comparative framework and the answers are never the ones that are near at hand. The comparative method must constantly tilt at common sense that is essentially unreflective. That common sense and popular values are also facts of sociology that make the task of the intellectual that much more difficult. In general, Béteille believes that people do not want to hear about general concepts. As intellectual judgement is constantly threatened by personal predilections and preferences, it is all the more necessary to employ the comparative method to get rid oneself of biases so as to be able to come to more general formulations. It is not just Weber here, but Béteille also finds Durkheim a great inspiration, particularly in the context of the comparative method.

Unlike others who commend the comparative method because sociology does not have laboratory, Béteille believes that without it sociology and social anthropology would have little to say in terms of enlarging the frontiers of theory. Durable knowledge comes from comparison over space and time. Over and above that, the comparative method not only brings out the biases in others, but also makes aware of one's own prejudices. In that sense, Béteille's advocacy of the comparative method is also an exercise in hermeneutic – all the down from Max Weber to Hans Georg Gadamer.

Two of Béteille main concerns are with the comparison of societies and the social significance of tradition. He engages with the ideas of a variety of sociologists ranging from Emile Durkheim and Max Weber to N.K. Bose and M.N. Srinivas, and argues that the study of Indian society has something important to contribute to the development of sociology as a general and comparative discipline. This is an important contribution towards advancing our critical understanding of the social framework within which we live.

## Criticism

Guha and Parry (1999: 26) point out: "a criticism that can be made of André Béteille's career is that he has not devoted sufficient attention to the institutional reproduction of his brand of sociology. In part, because his personal style is not that of the assertive academic patron, he has not built a formal, easily identifiable 'school', a group of disciples who would take forward his methodological focus on the field-view and comparative analysis, and develop his theoretical insights on such questions of absorbing interest and continuing political importance as patterns of inequality and the fate and functioning of institutions." However, Guha and Parry's volume shows that the intellectual influence of Béteille can work in ways other than the 'guru-chela' parampara.

## Conclusion

André Béteille, a sociologist par excellence, has produced works of consistent eminence for the past four and half decades. In terms of theory, methodology and application in social policy, Béteille has taken Indian sociological studies to a new height. Dipankar Gupta has brought together the essence of Béteille's writings by selecting and compiling his essays in a book. It comes as an introduction by Gupta and the essays range from the conceptual understanding of sociology, the significance of comparative method and ideas of inequality to concrete issues of Indian society such as caste, class, civil society and distributive justice.

During Béteille's college and university years in Calcutta and even till date, Marxism has been the most dominant intellectual force, but he found himself unsympathetic to it on account of the utopian promise the Marxist theories made. According to Béteille, social inequality can be tamed, even controlled, by the interventions of various kinds, but cannot be done away with. To this end, he proposes various social policies, including those of positive discrimination. Classless society is utopian; a stratified society with social inequality as well as intervention is the best possible bargain any society can have.

Béteille worked for his thesis with M.N. Srinivas but there was a significant departure in his theoretical orientation. Srinivas made a difference to the way social anthropology was researched in India through his emphasis on in-depth fieldwork. Béteille acknowledged the importance of fieldwork but was conceptually in another league – that of Weberian sociology. Functionalism was the order of the day. Orientalism and English empiricism were also in fashion. Hermeneutics, structuralism and interpretative sociology and phenomenology were not in vogue.

But Béteille was open to those sociological theories and his major contribution to actually use the Weberian mode of analysis in his doctoral thesis on caste, class and power in a South Indian village. He used Weber's concept of class, status and power in the context of Indian ground realities. Till then, village studies were either documentary, in character, governed by functionalism, or romanticized generalizations. Béteille criticizes Dumont's *Homo Hierarchicus* for portraying the Indian caste system as a ubiquitous totality whereas caste in India is neither uniform nor continuous.

For Béteille, like Weber, the comparative method is the essence of sociological research. But comparison, according to him, should not be a compulsive search for difference and exotica a search for similarities is an equally rigorous analytical pursuit. Sociology is a systematic study of the nature and forms of social life with special emphasis on social institutions and groups like caste, class and so on. Comparative analysis by placing all societies on the same plane of enquiry should be the starting point. Sociology seeks to understand desirable ways of living as well as how people actually live. It is a descriptive and interpretative rather than being idealistic and prescriptive in nature.

Béteille's study of caste reflects his commitment to the comparative method and his distaste for utopian thinking. Caste for him is not timeless, static phenomenon binding all Hindus unequivocally. The British rule, along with the impetus from Indian scholars and social reformers, and opportunities used by Indian trading and artisan classes, made transformations in the caste system possible. Most importantly, caste has lost most of its ritual purity. Constitutionally backed positive discrimination and affirmative action for the backward castes and classes have increased. This is surely the result of active participation and support of intellectuals and civilians belonging to the more privileged castes. Political activism in democratic India has come a long way.

With modernity and the emergence of strong public opinion, the individual has gained recognition, with concomitant undermining of traditional group loyalties. Béteille places his futuristic vision in the establishment of a civil, secular and open society, where citizens are on an equal platform with the state. Béteille's contribution to the way sociology researched and thought in India has been immense (Saha, 2006).

## André Béteille Framework Summarized

### *Background*

Béteille received his undergraduate and graduate degrees in anthropology from the University of Calcutta. Thereafter, he received his doctorate from the University of Delhi.

*Aims:* Béteille speaks of his childhood and natural inclination to anthropology, his training, fieldwork in Delhi and the influence of his supervisor, M.N. Srinivas. His work reflects on equality and inequality in human societies and publications on such, especially the caste system. He analyses the work of Dumont, as well as Marxism, Hinduism and Islam. He cites those who have influenced him and his work, and closes with an overview of his current interests in nationalism and tribal identities in India, as well as his lectures on backward classes.

*Assumptions:* To contextualize local concepts and understandings, such as caste and class, hierarchy and equality, in more universal and generalized theories of inequality, stratification and justice.

### *Methodology*

The separation of the field from the book view was of great importance for Béteille. He uses comparative method effectively.

### Theoretical Perspective

Béteille's works draw upon universal categories and concepts; he always places them in the context of empirical ground realities. Béteille closeness to Weber naturally also signalled his distance from Marx – a scholar whom he respected but from afar. He is the best known scholar in India on liberal theory and on its application in social policy.

### Typology

1. Weberian categories and mode of analysis: Béteille refines the conceptualization of 'ideas and interests', and analyses the similarities and interdependence of tribe and caste through intermediary category of the 'peasant'. He uses gender and its implication for 'blood' and hereditary to make an incisive comparison of race and caste.
2. Ethnographic analysis of a Tanjore village: It pays close attention to patterns of dress, housing, occupations, food, language, worship and above all social relation.

### Issues

1. Social Stratification in India
2. The Idea of Equality and Inequality
3. Studies in Agrarian Social Structure
4. Society and Politics in India
5. The Backward Classes in Contemporary India
6. Ideologies and Institutions
7. Religion and Secularism
8. Civil Society

## References

Béteille, André (1965). *Caste, Class and Power: Changing Patterns of Stratification in a Tanjore Village*, Berkeley: University of California Press.

—— (1969). *Castes: Old and New, Essays in Social Structure and Social Stratification*, Bombay: Asia Publishing House.

— (ed). (1969). *Social Inequality: Selected Readings.* Harmondsworth: Penguin Books.

— (1972). *Inequality and Social Change.* New Delhi: Oxford University Press.

—.(1974). *Studies in Agrarian Social Structure,* New Oxford University Press.

— (1974a). *Six Essays in Comparative Sociology,* Oxford University Press (enlarged edition published as *Essays in Comparative Sociology,* Oxford University Press, 1987).

— (1975). *Essays in Comparative Sociology,* New Delhi: Oxford University Press (expanded edition in 1987).

— (1977). *Inequality Among Men.* Oxford: Basil Blackwell. (Italian edition published as La diseguaglianza fra gli uomini, Il Mulino, 1981).

— (1980). *Ideologies and Intellectuals.* New Delhi: Oxford University Press.

— (1983).*The Idea of Natural Inequality and Other Essays,* Oxford University Press, (new, enlarged edition, Oxford University Press, 1987).

— (ed.) (1983a). *Equality and Inequality,* New Delhi: Oxford University Press.

— (1985). 'Stratification', in Adam Kuper and Jessica Kuper (eds), *The Social Science Encyclopedia.* London: Routledge and Kegan Paul.

— (1989). 'Are the Intelligentsia a ruling Class?', *Economic and Political Weekly,* 24(23).

— (1990). 'Some Observations on the Comparative Method', *Economic and Political Weekly,* 25(6).

— (1991). *Society and Politics in India: Essays in a Comparative Perspective,* London: Athlon Press (L.S.E. Monographs in Social Anthropology, No. 63).

— (1991a). *'Society as Critical Understanding: An Interview with André Béteille by Stefan Molund', Anthropological Studies,* No. 48.

— (1991b). 'Caste, Class and Power', in Dipankar Gupta (ed.), *Social Stratification,* New Delhi: Oxford University Press.

— (1992). *The Backward Classes in Contemporary India,* New Delhi: Oxford University Press.

— (1992a). 'Religion as a Subject for Sociology", *Economic and Political Weekly,* 27(35).

— (1993). 'Sociology and Anthropology: Their Relationship in One Person's Career', *Contributions to Indian Sociology,* n.s. 27 (2): 291–304.

— (1994). 'Inequality and Equality', in Tim Ingold (ed.), *Companion Encyclopedia of Anthropology.* London: Routledge.

— (1994a). 'Secularism and Intellectuals', *Economic and Political Weekly*, 29(10)

— (1995). 'My Formative years at the Delhi School of Economics (1959–74)', in Dharma Kumar and Dilip Mookerjee (eds), *D School: Essays on the Delhi School of Economics*, New Delhi: Oxford University Press.

— (1996). *Civil Society and Its Institutions* (the First Fulbright Memorial Lecture), Calcutta: United States of Educational Foundation for India.

— (1996a). *Caste, Class and Power: Changing Patterns of Stratification in a Tanjore Village*. Delhi: Oxford University Press (2nd edition).

— (1996b). 'Sociology and Common Sense', *Economic and Political Weekly*, 31(35–37).

— (1996c). 'Inequality', in Alan Barnard and Jonathan Spencer (eds), *Encyclopedia of Social and Cultural Anthropology*. London: Routledge.

— (1997). 'Newness in Sociological Enquiry', *Sociological Bulletin*, 46(1).

— (1997a). *The Place of Tradition in Sociological Enquiry* (the Fourth Radhakrishnan Memorial Lecture), Shimla: Indian Institute of Advanced Study.

— (1997b). 'My Two Grandmothers', *Civil Lines*, No. 3.

— (1998). 'Science and Tradition: A Sociological Enquiry', *Economic and Political Weekly*, 33(10).

— (1999). 'Sociology and Area Study', *Journal of the Japanese Association for South Asian Studies*, pp. 124–137.

— (2000). *Antinomies of Society: Essays on Ideologies and Institutions*, New Delhi: Oxford University Press.

— (2000a). *Chronicles of Our Time*, Penguin Books.

— (2002b). *Sociology: Essays on Approach and Method*, New Delhi: Oxford University Press.

Bose, N.K. (1967). *Culture and Society in India*, Bombay: Asia Publishing House.

Gerth, H.H. and C. Wright Mills (eds) (1946). *From Max Weber: Essays in Sociology*, New York: Oxford University Press.

Guha, Ramchandra and Jonathan P. Parry (eds) (1999 and paperbacks in 2011). *Institutions and Inequalities: Essays in Honour of André Béteille*, New Delhi: Oxford University Press.

Gupta, Dipankar (ed.) (2005). *Anti-Utopia: Essential Writings of* André Béteille, New Delhi: Oxford University Press.

Gupta, Dipankar (ed.) (1991). *Social Stratification*, New Delhi: Oxford University Press.

Heredia, Rudolf C. (2005). Book Review of *Anti-Utopia: Essential Writings of* André Béteille in *The Hindu*, Tuesday, November 08.

Kannabiran, Kalpana (2010). Béteille article, "Race and Caste" (*The Hindu*, 10 March 2010 and A Response to Béteille). [The author works with Asmita Resource Centre for Women and teaches Sociology and Human Rights at NALSAR University of Law, Hyderabad].

Osipov, G. (1969). *Sociology*, Moscow: Progress Publishers.

Macfarlane, Alan interviewed André Béteille On 1st June 1986, filmed by Julian Jacobs.

Molund, Stefan (1961). 'Sociology as Critical Understanding: An Interview with André Béteille, *Anthropologic Studies*, 48: 31–47.

Saha, Suhrita (2006). Book Review of *Anti-Utopia: Essential Writings of André Béteille*, The *Telegraph*, Calcutta (India), Friday, November, 03.

Sharma, K.L. (1980). *Essays on Social Stratification*, Jaipur-Delhi: Rawat Publications.

Shils, Edward (1961). *The Intellectual Between Tradition and Modernity: The Indian Case*. The Hague: Mouton and Co.

# VI

# Cultural Perspective

Sociologists and anthropologists use 'culture' as a collective noun for the symbolic and learned aspects of human society, including language, custom and convention, by which human behaviour can be distinguished from that of other primates. Cultural anthropology (as distinct from physical anthropology) takes as its special province the analysis of the culture of human societies. Anthropology recognizes that human behaviour is largely culturally, not genetically, determined. This has given rise to debates about cultural diffusion and the uniqueness of cultures and cultural relativity.

The most important landmark in the beginning of what we have heuristically called 'culturological orientation' in the theoretic nature of sociology is Srinivas' work *Religion and Society Among the Coorgs of South India* (1952). The conceptual schemes that Srinivas has formulated to analyse the phenomenon of social and cultural change have made the outstanding impact on Indian sociology. It offered an analytic frame to many village studies conducted from

1952 to 1968 particularly (cf. Srinivas, 1955; Marriott, 1955; Majumdar, 1955, 1958; Chauhan, 1974) and later on in the discursive treatment of Indian sociology.

Here, we are specifically concerned with the writings of Yogendra Singh who tries to analyse both of modernization and traditionalization processes of cultural analysis through conceptual categories based on sociological and historical data.

# 16

# Yogendra Singh

Yogendra Singh was Professor Emeritus of Sociology at the Centre for the Study of Social Systems, Jawaharlal Nehru University, New Delhi. He was also its founder. He was born on 2 November 1932 in a Jamindar family of a village in the Basti district of Uttar Pradesh. He passed away on 10 May 2020 at Delhi. He obtained his Master's and PhD degrees from Lucknow University. He had the privilege of being taught by eminent teachers like Radhakamal Mukerjee, D.P. Mukerji, D.N. Majumdar, Baljit Singh and A.K. Saran. After attaining his doctorate, Singh taught for a period of three years at the Institute of Social Sciences, Agra, and later on joined Rajasthan University to start a new Department of Sociology along with T.K.N. Unnithan and Indra Deva. He also taught at the University of Jodhpur for some time. After spending a decade in Rajasthan, Singh was invited to establish the Centre for the Study of Social Systems at Jawaharlal Nehru University, New Delhi in 1971. He has guided more than thirty students for doctoral research.

Yogendra Singh is very simple, creative and humanist in his real life, which also reflects in his writings.

A distinguished scholar-theoretician, Singh has taught at various universities in India and abroad. He has also conducted significant fieldwork in several South Asian countries. He has been very actively engaged in the profession of sociology in India and held responsible positions on various academic as well as government committees concerned with the formulation of social policies. He is member of the research advisory committee of the Planning Commission and the ICSSR and also convener of the UGC national panel of sociology. He has also been the President of Indian Sociological Society. He is the recipient of several awards for his contributions to sociology and social anthropology.

## Methodology

Yogendra Singh is neither functionalist nor Marxist but he emphasizes theory in relation to context. Therefore, he relates structural-functional, structuralism, structural-historical, culturalism and Marxist orientation and constructs in the study social stratification. He applied integrated approach for his analysis of social stratification, modernization and change in Indian society.

## Writings

Singh has published extensively in national and international scholarly research journals. He is also author of many books. His main works are:

1. *Modernization of Indian Tradition* (1973)
2. *Essays on Modernization* (1977)
3. *Social Stratification and Social Change in India* (1978)
4. *Image of Man: Ideology and Theory in Indian Sociology* (1984)
5. *Indian Sociology: Social Conditioning and Emerging Concerns* (1987)
6. *Social Change in India: Crisis and Resilience* (1993)
7. *Culture Change in India: Identity and Globalization* (2000)
8. *Ideology and Theory in Indian Sociology* (2004)
9. *Social Aspects of Scientific and Technological Revolution* (co-author) (1978)
10. *Sociology of Non-Violence and Peace* (co-author) (1968)

11. *Traditions of Non-Violence* (co-author) (1972)
12. *The Sociology of Culture* (co-author) (1991)
13. *Towards a Sociology of Culture in India* (co-editor) (1965)
14. *For a Sociology of India* (co-editor) (1967)

In his studies, Singh has concentrated his focus on the following aspects of Indian society:

1. Social stratification
2. Social change
3. Modernization
4. Indian sociology
5. Culture change

## Social Stratification

Stratification is the social process through which rewards and resources such as wealth, power and prestige are distributed systematically and unequally within are among societies. The sociology of social stratification inheres many basic and complex theoretical issues. These relate to the nature of social order, social equality and inequality, social justice, power and the nature of man. In sociology, these issues relate to questions of theory, structure and process of social stratification. The three are organically interrelated, though heuristically distinct. In this context, Singh offers a basis for the analysis of substantive as well as theoretical issues in social stratification.

Singh has analysed the studies on social stratification and social change conducted in the 1950s and in the 1970s. In his ICSSR Trend Report on the Sociology of Social Stratification, Singh (1974) comments: "Theoretically, most studies of social stratification calls first for answers to the 'what' and 'how' questions about pertinent phenomena with reference to the structural units of the entity; secondly, it requires answers to the 'why' questions with reference to the need in society for ranking the roles and statuses of its members and/or to provide the media for the flow of 'institutional power'; and, thirdly, it leads to the 'what will it be' and 'what ought it to be' questions with reference to the changing process of entity." But, he noted after reviewing the relevant works in Indian sociology in this context, that researches have been preoccupied with (1) 'what' and 'how' questions, (2) that consideration of caste hierarchy has predominated with 'class' considered occasionally as another aspect of this phenomenon, and (3) that the whole subject has largely been considered at an impressionistic level in lieu of an analysis, in real terms, of the relative relevance of the various aspects of social stratification in India.

As a result, far from answering the question, 'what will it be' on the basis of valid and efficient theories, these studies cannot even answer the 'why' question by generating appropriate hypotheses or propositions regarding social stratification:

> Theoretically, as we have discussed above, most studies of social stratification in India have focused on caste and social mobility in this system; sometimes occupational strata have been analysed or class stratification has been formulated on the basis of the census data through a set of attributes for classification. In theoretical terms most such studies of caste or class stratification operate at the level of nominal scales. One major limitation that such studies suffer from is their inadequacy for generating general or even middle-range hypotheses or propositions regarding social stratification. This is true not only for the caste studies but also for most efforts for classification of classes on the basis of ad hoc sets of attributes. Such studies add to our insight into the nature of some problem and trends of change at an impressionistic level, but are devoid of 'theoretical power'. There is need, therefore, to undertake studies in social stratification having macro-sociological perspective. Such studies may use 'real' definitions of caste, class and other categories and be conducted through a systematic research design with a battery of significant assumptions and hypotheses. The results of such studies could be tested and compared for precision and relevance at cross-regional or cross-national levels (ibid.).

The book entitled, *Social Stratification and Change in India* (1977) carries a new and updated introduction on the two substantive themes in a conceptual-theoretical perspective, which was originally prepared as a trend report on concepts and theories of social stratification and change in India. It reviews critically the studies conducted following independence up to the end of the sixties on the themes of social stratification and social change in India. Its focus is on the adequacy of concepts and theoretical schemes in these studies, but in course of this examination the dilemmas and structural contradictions in the processes of social stratification and change in India have also been exposed. It links them to their social and historical context. It highlights their achievements, and shows up the gaps yet to be bridged by Indian sociology.

How could one formulate sociology of social stratification in India? Theoretically, how is such an endeavour made possible by developments in stratification and social change, theory and its structure and process analysis? How have been Indian sociologists blended the uses of 'category' and history in their analysis of social stratification and change? These, and scores of other issues in sociology of stratification and change, have been examined in this volume.

Concepts, particularly examined in the analysis of social stratification, are those of 'caste', 'class' and 'peasantry' and 'elites' and the process include 'social mobility', 'structural differentiation' and its consequent social contradictions. The sociology of change in India has similar been reviewed in terms of theoretic-adequacy and relative power of the evolutionary, nominalist (sanskritization-westernization), structuralist, dialectical, cognitive, historical and institutional approaches employed in various studies. Thus, Singh (1977) reviews the trend of sociology of social stratification on India focusing upon some of these specific structural units of stratification. These are mainly:

(i) caste system and social stratification, and
(ii) class structures and social stratification.

### *Caste System and Social Stratification*

The theoretical position of caste in the analysis of Indian social system is highly complex. It constitutes both a structural unit of social stratification as well as a system. The distinction between the two would depend upon the level of analysis involved. Sociologists who look across the cultural view of caste have, right from the beginning, associated it with an autonomous principle of stratification. The bases of this view are: institutionalized inequality (scheduled caste), closure of social system in respect of social mobility, an elementary level of division of labour legitimized on ritual basis of reciprocity, and emphasis on quality (ritual purity or racial purity) rather than performance. In other words, caste is associated with an autonomous form of cultural system or worldview.

Singh (1969) conducted a study of caste and power structure in rural society. His study of caste and its changing forms and functions refers to the implication of the system for Indian social stratification. It is not meant to be a review of caste studies as such. Caste system is seen here as a status principle of social stratification, for sociology of social stratification in India, the treatment of caste becomes unavoidable as a standard to measure changes with reference to other principles of stratification such as of wealth (class) and power (elite). These new principles only sometimes operate autonomously; more often they operate contingently together with the caste principle of social stratification.

### *Class Structures and Social Stratification*

The class element in the social stratification in India is organically connected with the caste stratification although for heuristic purposes a conceptual distinction should be made. An important theoretical issue that arises in this context is of the nature of class, whether it is a universal or particularistic category. In Marxist as well as non-Marxist sociology, class is viewed as a universalistic phenomenon. The substance of class is assumed to be uniform for all societies, irrespective of their historical and cultural differences of discontinuities. This assumption may not always be well founded and there is need to examine it in the Indian context. Singh (1977) finds that a series of overlapping or intermediary structural forms exist in India that range from caste, ethnic group to class without having been individually crystallized.

In India, the analysis of class stratification has been undertaken both of the Marxist and non-Marxist theoretical dispositions. The class categories employed in the census documents and other socio-economic survey agencies are mainly based on attributional criteria of income, occupation or agricultural or non-agricultural modes of earning the livelihood. The term 'maliks', 'ryots' or even orthodox Marxist categories such as 'bourgeoisie', etc., are used by social scientists of specific theoretical dispositions (see Thorner, 1956; Pavlov, 1964). Compared to the studies on caste, the literature on class is, however, not substantial. The reason is partly historical, and more importantly it is because of the continued overlaps between the caste and class status situations or interaction in the Indian system of social stratification. Often, it is difficult to draw a sharp line where the caste principle of stratification ceases and the class principle begins. Sometimes, this peculiar inter-mixture of status principles in India leads social scientists to make simplistic statements. For instance, caste stratification is associated with the rural and class stratification with the urban situation (see, Rosen, 1966). It is, however, overlooked that caste and class are two principles of stratification, which have persisted in the Indian social systems in a dialectical relationship.

## Social Change

Singh (1973) labels social change as 'ideology'. If the relevance of the concepts of sanskritization and westernization is not as analytical proposition but 'truth asserting concepts' as Singh has aptly characterized them – sanskritization, westernization, parochialization, universalization, little and great traditions, rural-urban dichotomy or continuum, etc. enriched the body of sociology of knowledge.

At the very beginning of re-emergence of the cognitive-historical trend, some of its proponents, who later made a significant contribution to the development of Indian sociology, were still strongly influenced by the prevailing trend of the structural-functional approach and the behaviour outlook. As a result, their efforts to Indianize Indian sociology were hesitant and their attempt to cut across the overpowering dominance of the 'western' viewpoint was not altogether successful. A notable example in this context may be Yogendra Singh's monograph on the *Modernization of Indian Tradition* (1973), which was written during 1966–67. It contains many insights into the Indianization of Indian sociology.

The Trend Report on the Concepts and Theories of Social Change further substantiates it. Singh (1974) viewed that studies on social change in India have been fragmentary. These studies usually refer to isolated aspects such as caste, family, occupation, etc., and these elements themselves are usually found to have been studied in a local setting – at most at a regional level, and not for India as a whole. However, it was by an impressionistic amalgamation of these separate factors and their placement on the axis of the twin social processes of sanskritization and westernization (or, modernization) that social change in India has predominantly been interpreted, with the 'dominant caste' serving as the lever of change.

Singh found that the process of sanskritization is not merely a positional change in the caste hierarchy but a strategy on the part of those in the lower echelons to challenge the status of those in the higher echelons by adopting their 'way of life' (Singh, 1968). To Singh (1994: 6), "The specific sense of sanskritization lies in the historicity of its meaning based on the Hindu tradition. In this respect, sanskritization is a unique historical expression on the general process of acculturation as a means of vertical mobility of groups.... We may call them 'historical specific' and 'contextual specific' connotations of sanskritization."

The Indian sociological formulations of the concept of social change find a beginning in the writings of the British and Indian scholars following the last quarter of the nineteenth century and onwards. Gradually, these concepts and formulations got differentiated and a variety of approaches emerged. For a brief survey, Singh (1977: 95) classifies these approaches into the following types:

1. Evolutionary approaches
2. Cultural approaches: sanskritization-westernization; little and great tradition, and multiple traditions
3. Structural approaches: differentiation and mobility analysis
4. Dialectical-historical approaches

This classification is purely heuristic. It represents the dominant theoretical or conceptual orientation found in the writings of the sociologists concerned.

Traditionally, social change in India was very slow but it accelerated after independence due to democratic system, secularism, economic development, social justice and socialism. To Singh, social change has been observed much more in social, cultural, political and economic fields. Singh (1993: 12) discusses two types of tendencies of social change in modern India: "First, there has taken place a substantial change in the social structure without simultaneously bringing about a structural change in the society. It results into tensions and often builds up social crisis. Secondly, there has taken place a sea-change in the subjective domain or the consciousness of the people in respect of social change." In his book on *Social Change in India: Crisis and Resilience* (1993), Singh discusses social change in India on following aspects:

(1) Contradictions and challenges of social change,
(2) Social transformation of the Indian society,
(3) Contemporary social crisis and its dimensions,
(4) Economic development and changing family system,
(5) Law and social change,
(6) Structure, traditions and Indian societal resilience,
(7) Ethnicity, unity and Indian civilization,
(8) Social processes and dimensions of Indian nationalism,
(9) National integration of Indian society,
(10) Concept of social structure, and
(11) Social stratification.

In all the essays, Singh adapts western theories in terms of historicity of Max Weber, functionalism of Parsons, dialectic of Marx and social processes such as cooperation and conflict but he tries to understand in context to the Indian society and culture. Singh is also influenced by the ideology of Gandhi and Nehru. He studies both stability and change in India. He applies integrated approach and explains structural rationalization and functional specificity of Indian society.

The contours of emerging social contradictions become visible as Singh's review (1977) reflects broadly the process of social stratification and change in Indian society. The class structure is slowly but steadily moving towards polarization. The upper and middle classes, both in rural and industrial sectors, have gained maximum benefits and have expanded their base of social, economic and political power. Despite the recent events leading to the breakdown and restoration of democracy in India, this stark structural reality of the Indian social system has not changed. The poor and the have-nots, the Harijans and the backward tribes remain at the bottom of the social hierarchy. With the power of the middle classes having increased, their plight has also become more poignant. This process breeds tension, organized resistance and motivates people towards the search for ideologies, which may not always be consistent with the ideology of the dominant sections of the Indian upper and middle classes. It would increasingly generate conflicts and contradictions. To grasp this reality of the Indian social system, a dialectical model of reasoning is assuredly more effective and offers greater promise. But, it has to a dialectic informed with the historicity of societies which would render it more creative and innovative.

### Toward an Integrated Approach

According to Singh (1973), some major concepts and approaches about social in India can be grouped as: (i) sanskritization and westernization; (ii) little and great traditions consisting of (a) processes of parochialization and universalization, and (b) cultural performances and organization of tradition; (iii) multiple traditions; (iv) structural approach, based on (a) functional model, and (b) dialectical model; and (v) cognitive historical or Indological approach. Singh (ibid.: 5–22) reviews each of them to find common grounds for a conceptual integration.

After the evaluation of these approaches, Singh finds that each one of them has advantages of its own for the study of social change, but these advantages are limited as none of them provides a comprehensive perspective on social change in India. Therefore, a series of concepts related to social change could be integrated into a logical system on the basis of similarities in theoretical formulations. Singh (ibid.: 22–27) presented a paradigm for an integrated approach to analyse social change in India as given on the next page:

The paradigm is a logical corollary of Singh's analysis about the levels at which an integrated view on social change in India can be achieved. According to Singh, this approach can be seen in the following theoretical perspectives:

1. The causation of social change is to be sought both from within and without the social system or the tradition. For this we find the concepts employed by Redfield and Singer as being particularly useful and make a distinction between the heterogenetic or exogenous and orthogenetic or endogenous sources of change.
2. A distinction between cultural structure and social structure is also made to focus upon the need to observe changes at the level of these two relatively independent *substantive domains*. Again, following Redfield, cultural structure has further been sub-divided into the categories of the little tradition and the great tradition. Similarly, the social structure is divided to form categories of micro-structure and macro-structure.
3. These distinctions follow from the need to focus upon the *contexts*, as discussed above, through which processes of change could be evaluated in matters of spread and depth.
4. Finally, the *direction* of change is represented in a linear evolutionary form from 'traditionalization' toward 'modernization'. Traditionalization comprises the total range of changes governed by orthogenetic patterns in the cultural and social structures. Modernization similarly represents the net balance of changes following from heterogenetic contacts.

The causal forces, substantive domain, contexts and direction of change provide us the logical boundaries within which the more specific processes of social change in India could be observed and described. These specific processes and the relevant concepts describing them have been noted in the paradigm in each appropriate cell. Singh examines the significance of the specific concepts in course of the analysis of change pertaining to the relevant

**Paradigm for an Integrated Approach**
**Modernization**

| *Sources of Changes* | *Cultural Structure* | | *Social Structure* | |
|---|---|---|---|---|
| Heterogenetic changes | Little Tradition | Great Tradition | Micro-structure | Macro-structure |
| | Islamization | Secondary-Islamic Impact | Role-Differentiation | Political-Innovations |
| | Primary-Westernization | Secondary-Westernization or (modernization) | New-Legitimization | New Structures of Elite, Bureaucracy, Industry, etc. |
| Orthogenetic Changes | Sanskritization or Tradtionalization | Cultural Renaissance | Pattern – Recurrence, Compulsive Migration or Population shift | Elite Circulation, Succession of Kings,' Rise and Fall of Cities and Trade Centres |

**Traditionalization**

substantive domain. For instance, in the cultural structure of India, the Islamic impact constitutes an important heterogenetic source of cultural transformation and synthesis and its significance can be seen at the levels of both of the little and great traditions. This has been followed by westernization as a major form of exogenous cultural impact on India, and its ramifications also have relevance for the little and great traditions.

The changes in social structure could also be discussed more fruitfully when a distinction is made between the macro- structures and micro-structures. The instances of macro-structures are: bureaucracy, industry, market, leadership, political parties, etc. These consist of role relationships, which have a pan-Indian extension of boundaries. In contrast, the micro-structures, such as kinship, family, caste and sub-caste and tribe, etc., have limited boundaries for extension of role relationships and their obligations.

The integrated approach, as offered by Singh through a schematic arrangement of concepts of change, has the advantage of being comprehensive as well as theoretically consistent.

### Modernization in India

Modernization is a composite concept. It is also an ideological concept. The models of modernization co-vary with the choice of ideologies. The composite nature of this concept renders it pervasive in the vocabulary of social sciences and evoke its kinship with concepts like 'development', 'growth', 'evolution' and 'progress'. The basic problematic of modernization in the Third World nations is ideological, particularly when we examine the modernization ideology in India.

In the book on *Essays on Modernization in India* (1977), Singh has analysed the varied and complex processes involved in the modernization in India, the forces released by it and their bearing on the stability, creativity and development in India as a dynamic nation and composite civilization. The essays, included in this volume, deal both with conceptual and substantive issues in the process of modernization in India. Each essay offers a treatment of this process in both contexts on a selected theme, be it political structure and process, academic role structures, industrialization or contemporary cultural patterns. The emphasis on historicity in preference to universality defining the context of modernization, the pre-eminence of structural changes in society to render the adaptive process of modernization successful in the developing countries particularly India and the eclectic nature of cultural and ideological response of India to the challenges of modernization, represent some of the unifying principles that bind these essays into a composite cognitive approach to modernization. Offering an integrated perspective, Singh portrays the challenges and contradictions that India encounters in the course of its modernization.

The idea of modernization evokes ambivalent feelings, even sharp reactions among thinking people – laymen and scholars alike. It has many facets and as a process its ramifications are varied and complex. The search for clarity on this concept often stops with study of its superficial symptoms. And, to understand this in a country of India's historical depth and cultural and social pluralism can be all the more challenging.

The relevance of essays on modernization contained in Singh's book (1977) can be seen in the above context. Can modernization be treated as a universalistic process or does it have its own historicity? What are the essentially cognitive and cultural correlates of modernization? Can it be looked upon as a scientific and operational notion in social science and can its magnitude empirically tested on a sub-structure of society? What are the processes involved in political, cultural, social and educational modernization in India? And, what new faces of social, political and cultural contradictions are released while these processes are on? And, how do these forces account for the future stability, sustained creativity and development of India as a dynamic nation and composite civilization?

The book examines all these questions in social, structural and comparative historical perspectives. And, this integrated approach has led the author to demonstrate how specious and spurious can be the hypothesis of modernization that detaches the forces of history and ideology from its framework of analysis.

## Indian Sociology

The writings of Yogendra Singh are in many ways sociology of Indian sociology. They offer a profile of Indian sociology exposing the foundations of concepts and theories on which most Indian studies on social stratification and change are based. Here, we are concerned to the Singh's important work on *Indian Sociology* (1987) which was published synchronizing with the 11th World Congress of Sociology held at New Delhi in August 1986. It exposes the foundations of concepts and theories. It is a comprehensive review-essay, commissioned by the International Sociological Association. It provides us with an excellent framework for analysing the trends in Indian sociology over the years.

## Images of Man

The book *Images of Man: Ideology and Theory in Indian Sociology* (1984) is a critique of sociology, its changing theoretical orientations and philosophical concerns. Taking the notion of 'man' as its central focus, it counter-poses the tendency in the nature of sociology towards instrumental perfection for becoming a 'science' as against the projection of a 'worldview' for man in society. It examines the linkages between sociology and philosophical anthropology.

Image of man is a basic theme in the worldview of sociology. The emergence of sociology as new discipline was deeply influenced by the technology and industrial revolution and the impact of science on the culture of the western society. The growth of humanism, rationalism and secularism as new values, which also implied a new moral order of society, the principles of civic liberty and social justice, had deeply shaken the traditional worldview of the medieval West. Indeed, as Max Weber has shown, basic changes were already going through in the ethics of Christianity. These changes were promoting an image of man, which was ethically more responsible, more individualized (free from the organic bondage with the church and clergy) and more 'this worldly'.

Sociology emerged probably as a result of the convolution of these two worldview systems: the scientific and religio-ethical.

Indeed, as the subsequent individual tensions in sociological theory and method reveal, its worldview has been continually oscillating between the pulls of science, which emphasized formalism, rationalism and instrumental orientation and that of ethics, which was deeply conjoined with questions of moral status or image of man, problem of 'alienation' and the linkages between man and society, the normative basis of 'community' and 'social order' and structure of power. The interplay of intellectual and historical forces in the western society, which defines the variations between those two tendencies in sociology, also offer the material basis for objective understanding of the ideological basis of sociology and its concept of man. This subject forms the theme of the first essay in this volume, *The Concept of Man in Sociology*.

The two essays that follow it "Ideology, Theory and Method in Indian Sociology" and "Functional Metaphor in Indian Sociology" are treatments of the ideological, theoretical and methodological elements in the growth of Indian sociology in contradistinction with the first essay, which deals exclusively with the variations in the ideological orientations of western sociology. These two essays deal with the patterns of theoretic differentiation in Indian sociology, its 'metaphoric' rather than formal character, and its evolution in methodological and normative directions. The distinguishing feature of Indian sociology here turned out to rest in its essential historicity, its colonial heritage and its consequent cognitive hiatus. It leaves the imprint on the main theoretic and operational choices of Indian sociologists. The ideology in Indian sociology is broadly defined in terms of this dialectic between historical and cognitive forces.

An issue related both to the nature of theory and methodology is that of relevance. It can be formulated both in normative and operational terms. It also involves the role of extra-cognitive forces in the development of cognitive systems or concepts and theories in sociology. The centrality of this dilemma of Indian sociology has been analysed in the essays "The Relevance of Social Science in India" and "The Role of Social Sciences in India: A Sociology of Knowledge." The last essay of this volume on "Some Reflections on Indian Sociology" focuses upon the historical conditioning of

Indian sociology, its value frames and impending problems of theory and methodology.

The book historically surveys the growth of Indian sociology since independence, especially its changing theoretical concerns. The urge for indigenization of Indian sociology has been examined in the perspective of its professional growth and concern for social change. What is the meaning of 'relevance', in social science? How could one separate the epistemic connotation of 'relevance' that is, relevance of categories and scientific operations, from a meaning of 'relevance' that measures it only in terms of instrumental efficiency for bringing about a desired social change? The book makes an excellent attempt to deal with this complex and baffling problem. Furthermore, the book offers sociology of knowledge perspective for evaluation of the growth of Indian sociology and social science. Looking into the colonial antecedent of sociology, it endeavours to explore the extra-academic factors and forces which contributed in the popularization of certain sets of concepts and theoretical preferences in the analysis of Indian social reality.

In fact, in an important sense, the book deals with the very nature of sociological theory itself in terms of its logical structure and content. Does the usage of 'theory' in Indian sociology indicate a growing process of logical systematization, or mere 'metaphoric' content in analytical reasoning? Could the debate between the 'functional' and 'dialectical' orientations in Indian sociology be sustained on logical grounds? These issues and their moorings in ideology have thoroughly examined with illustrations from empirical studies.

## Ideology and Theory in Indian Sociology

Sociology, like most social sciences, is embedded in ideology. *Ideology and Theory in Indian Sociology* (2004) is a collection of essays, which offers insight into the normative and ideological underpinnings of the Indian sociology in the context of its growth and the challenges that it has encountered in the realms of theory and methodology. These issues have been analysed in the perspective of the western sociology and its own theoretical and methodological evolution.

The book highlights how Indian sociology, despite its deeper linkages with the theoretical and methodological traditions of the West, has in the ideological and normative domains evolved successfully its own discourse. The volume also illustrates the nature of the inner epistemological tensions, which continue to dominate the debates on how to ground the Indian sociology and its paradigm into the Indian philosophical traditions. This epistemic tension is also reflected in the manner that the crisis in the western sociology's philosophical moorings continues to cross-mirror in the Indian sociology as well. An instance in this context, which this volume has analysed, is that of the philosophy of 'post-modernity' and its challenge to the theories and methods of the Indian sociology. Thus, this volume offers a perspective to the sociological studies of these problems. The volume includes the following essays:

1. Worldview of Sociology and the Challenge of Post-Modernity
2. The Concept of Man in Sociology
3. Ideology, Theory and Methods in Indian Sociology
4. Indian Sociology: Retrospect and Prospect
5. Functional Metaphor in Indian Sociology
6. The Relevance of Social Sciences in India
7. Challenges of Globalization, Identity and Economic Development: An Indian Perspective

Here, we refer to an important essay on ideology, theory and method in Indian sociology by Singh (1979), which covers a period of a quarter century of sociology in India from 1952 to 1977 as under:

(i) 1952 to 1960 – a period of adaptive changes and innovations;
(ii) 1960 to 1965 – a period of significant shifts in theoretic priorities and beginning of some critical tensions in theory and ideology of Indian sociology;
(iii) 1965 to 1970 – a period of marked sociological self-awareness and growth of new directions in theoretical and substantive contributions; and
(iv) 1970 to 1977 – a period of new maturity and new horizons of knowledge.

The four periods correspond with four theoretic developments in Indian sociology. These theoretic orientations are:

(i) philosophical theoretical orientation
(ii) culturological orientation
(iii) structural theoretic orientation
(iv) dialectical-historical orientation

The *philosophical orientation* in Indian sociology is associated with the contributions of Radhakamal Mukerjee, D.P. Mukerji and A.K. Saran. This orientation has not made a significant impact on the theoretical nature of the Indian sociology according to Singh (1983). It is interesting to note that despite the profoundness of scholarship of these scholars, the impact is minimal. The impact of western sociology was becoming more and more enveloping and empirical bases of societal understanding looked simpler than the rigour of philosophy.

The *culturological orientation* begins with the work of Srinivas, *Religion and Society among the Coorgs of South India*. Brahminization, sanskritization and westernization were major concepts derived from this study. Sanskritization characterized a change within the framework of Indian tradition.

The *structural theoretic orientation* focuses on power structure, social stratification, family structure, demography and similar aspects which reveal patterns, arrangements and repetitiveness. The empirical aspects are converted into abstracted concepts, models and categories. The structural studies have also taken comparative framework.

The *dialectical-historical orientation* is primarily on Marxist approach and method for the analysis of social reality. The dialectical method has not been termed as Marxist as adaptations have been made keeping in view the Indian social reality. It is, however, a less developed branch of Indian sociology. D.P. Mukerji and Ram Krishna Mukherjee emphasized the significance of dialectical model. A.R. Desai had consistently used dialectical-historical approach with ideological fervour and commitment. He has consistently exposed contradictions in policies and programmes of change. The dialectical-historical theoretic orientation grew rapidly in the seventies, when micro-empirical realities were subjected to class observation along with macro-structural social and economic processes in India (Singh, 1983).

Singh's typology of four major theoretic orientations is significant and logically coherent. According to Singh (1993), these theoretical orientations basically have implicit or explicit ideological connotation. The implications can be discerned at the level of analysis, which as a critique rejects the way social reality is managed or justifies the formation of social reality as it has come to be, manipulated and constructed. At other level, they imply need for alternatives, modifications and corrections. Knowledge-neutrality is contradictions in terms. Evaluation and analysis of social reality reveals systematic formulation of scattered, diverse and immediate impressions, which are mediated through common man's impressionistic perceptions and views. At the third level, dominance of theoretical orientations generated institutionally tends to lead to negation and blinding of our own intellectual traditions.

## Culture Change in India

The study of culture changes has not drawn the attention of sociologists in the same measure as that of the changes in the social structure and its processes. The compilation of essays by Yogendra Singh on *Culture Change in India: Identity and Globalization* (2000) is an effort to focus upon some of the significant processes of changes in the domain of culture in India. To begin with, the first chapter, "The Significance of Culture in the Understanding of Social Change in Contemporary India" deals with various orientations in the work of Indian sociologists in their study of culture, the new challenges that such study may now encounter due to the new processes of culture changes through the emergence the 'information society' and its consequences leading to the resurgence of the consciousness of the identity among ethnic groups, minorities and weaker sections of society. It also refers to various facets of relationship between culture, its patterns and the processes of economic and political institution building in the Indian society.

The other essays in this volume focus primarily on the contemporary themes of culture changes in India. These changes could be divided into two categories: first, those which concern the substantive structures of culture and its relationship with social institutions; and secondly, those which refer to the processes of change in culture, specially engendered by the forces of globalization, telecommunication revolution and the emergence of market economy in a qualitative new form. The structural issues of change refer to the impact of globalization upon local cultures in India (chapter 2), the nature of cultural identities at the local, regional, and national levels and the extent of their inner resilience to withstand the forces of globalization (chapter 3), and the emerging popular culture in India, its impact upon the styles of life of the youth and other social categories in rural and urban population and the extent to which the western impact upon the changes in lifestyle threatens the cultural identity of persons exposed to popular culture (chapter 4).

The other substantive issues, such as the process of nation-building (chapter 5), language as the marker of cultural identity (chapter 6), the desired role of political leadership in economic development (chapter 7), the relationship between modernity and ethnicity(chapter 8), the changes in community structures and its cultural implications (chapter 9), and the impact of changes in social structure upon leisure activities and its institutions in rural and urban India (chapter 10) have been examined in the context of their significance to culture changes – both institutional and ideological. Finally, Singh has analysed the implications of the globalization of cultures and of the emerging global market economy upon the teaching and research in sociology. Thus, he has discussed the changes in culture in the context of factors, which are social, psychological and ideological in nature, and also influence the formation and crystallization of cultural identities.

Singh views that globalization expands the scope and speed of cultural interaction across societal boundaries; the incidence of migration and emergence of cultural diaspora bring about intense cultural, social and economic interaction. This is made possible due to the telecommunication revolution but the cultural processes that it sets into motion acquire significance, related as these are to the possibilities of cultural assimilation, adaptation, integration or conflict in course of such cultural contacts.

### *Culture Change and the Analytical Categories*

The choice of analytical categories or concepts circumscribes the scope of thematic treatment of a problem. It also defines the premises and assumptions, which underly the treatment of the cultural phenomena. The preference for a particular set of concepts for analysis of culture has also latent in its epistemological structure and the choice of ideologies. On this basis, the value-neutrality of 'scientific categories' for analysis of phenomena has been widely challenged.

### *Issue of Identity*

The issues of cultural identity in the process of globalization derive from their legitimation from the complexity, which is inherent in the rational utilitarian foundation of choices of values and life goals in our contemporary life. It is imperative that we come to terms with this reality while analysing the nature of culture change, as also the questions of new resurgence of the consciousness of cultural and social identities based on micro-situations, whether of locality, region or religion etc. The process of cultural globalization and its myriad challenges should be observed and analysed in the context of substantive and methodological problems which recognize this reality.

The volume offers a critical evaluation of changes in cultural values, institutions and ideologies, which constitute India's response to the contemporary challenges from the forces of cultural and economic globalization. In the backdrop of discussions of conceptual and theoretical issues in the study of culture and its processes of change, it evaluates the significance of the present social structure of the Indian society, its historical past and contemporary processes in defining the boundaries and directions of the changes in its cultural systems, whether at the level of locality, region, nation or civilization. It is argued that the unique of this relationship between culture and social structure in India, and its adaptive dynamism to meet with new cultural challenges, has provided its resilience to preserve its cultural identity.

The book mainly concerns with changes in cultural styles through exposure to global cultural patterns. It also examines the impact of electronic media, migration and increased pace of inter-cultural interactions upon local, regional and national levels of culture. It deals with how these processes have led to the rise in popular culture, changes in the form and style of leisure activities, given rise to new normative standards for defining community relationships, political leadership and generally how it reflects upon India's ability in the future to maintain cultural and social resilience to face up the new challenges of modernization and globalization.

## Yogendra Singh's Framework Summarized

### *Background*

1. Educated and trained in economics and sociology at Lucknow.
2. Academic career at Institute of Social Sciences, Agra; University of Rajasthan, Jaipur, University of Jodhpur, Jodhpur; McGill University, Montreal (Canada); and JNU, New Delhi.
3. Interest in understanding the nature and meaning of Indian social reality.

### *Aim*

To offer a profile of Indian sociology exposing the foundations of concepts and theories.

### *Assumption*

Theory should be related to the context.

### *Methodology*

Integrative approach

### *Typology*

1. Structural-functional
2. Structuralist

3. Structural-historical
4. Marxist orientation

### *Issues*

Different aspects of Indian society, namely,

1. Social stratification
2. Social change
3. Modernization
4. Indian sociology
5. Culture change

## Select Bibliography

Singh, Yogendra (1965), co-editor, *Towards Sociology of Culture in India*, New Delhi: Prentice Hall of India.

— (1967), co-editor (with T.K.N. Unnithan et al.), *For a Sociology of India*, New Delhi: Prentice Hall of India.

— (1968), co-author (with T.K.N. Unnithan), *Sociology of Non-Violence and Peace*, New Delhi: Council for Social Development.

— (1972), co-author (with T.K.N. Unnithan), *Traditions of Non-Violence*, New Delhi: Heinmann.

— (1973), *Modernization of Indian Tradition*, Delhi: Thomson Press (India) Ltd.

— (1977), *Essays on Modernization*, New Delhi: Manohar.

— (1978), co-author (with Ralph Dahrendorf, et al.), *Social Aspects of Scientific and Technological revolution*, London: Sage Publications.

— (1978), *Social Stratification and Social Change in India*, New Delhi: Manohar.

— (1984), *Image of Man: Ideology and Theory in Indian Sociology*, Delhi: Chanakya Publications.

— (1987), *Indian Sociology: Social Conditioning and Emerging Concerns*, New Delhi: Vistaar Publications.

— (1991), co-author (with Boris Erasov), *The Sociology of Culture*, Moscow: Progress Publishers.

— (1993), *Social Change in India: Crisis and Resilience*, New Delhi: Har Anand Publications.

— (2000), *Culture Change in India: Identity and Globalization*, Jaipur: Rawat Publications.

— (2004), *Ideology and Theory in Indian Sociology*, Jaipur: Rawat Publications.

# VII

# Civilizational Perspective

Civilizational perspective refers to understand a society from its civilization. A civilized society is that whose relative freedom from the struggle for mere survival enables it to become more complex in its culture and structure. Civilization is most often distinguished from *hunter-gatherer* and *horticultural* societies, which are often referred to as "primitive" by those who count themselves among the civilized. The civilizing process explains changes in the structure and culture of a society.

Civilizational perspective stresses on complex structure of great and little traditions. It includes the studies on the tribal, rural and urban culture. This perspective also views civilization as an organization of specialists in functional relation to folk societies. Thus, the civilizational perspective involves study of a combination of many subjects like analysis of classical and medieval texts, administrative records, village, caste and its wider network and ultimately the issue of unity and diversity. It analyses the structural underpinning of any civilization to get sharp and historically framed portrait of religion, caste, village, state formation, land relations and so on. The followers of this perspective believe that a social system, a nation, or a civilization has to be understood in a historical-civilizational frame.

Further, in order to understand the civilization, one has to undertake study based on cataloguing (listing of cultural traits); cultural essence (to identify the essential underlying process); and cultural communication (enduring elements that are transmitted among the parts of the society).

N.K. Bose and Surajit Sinha, Bernard S. Cohn and others use civilizational perspective in the understanding of Indian society. They have tried to explore the historicity, continuity and interlinkage of various structures in India. In this context, we would focus our attention on N.K. Bose and Surajit Sinha.

# 17

# N.K. Bose

Nirmal Kumar Bose (1901–1972) was born at Calcutta in Bengal on 22nd January 1901 and passed away on 15th October 1972 after a remarkably fruitful life devoted in equal measure to the pursuit of science and the service of humanity. He has left behind standards of work that will both daunt and inspire succeeding generations of anthropologists and sociologists.

Bose received his school education from different schools of three states in the country, namely, Bihar, Bengal and Orissa. He passed his Matriculation, Intermediate (Science), Bachelor of Science with Honours in Geology and Master of Science (Anthropology) in the year 1917, 1919, 1921 and 1924 respectively. He studied first geology and then anthropology at the University of Calcutta. He did M.Sc. from Calcutta University in 1923–24.

Bose had an unusually varied career. He taught for some time at the Department of Anthropology and was till 1959 Reader in Human Geography in the Department of Geography at the Calcutta University. He was invited as Visiting Professor at the University of California, Berkeley and at the Department of

Anthropology, University of Chicago in 1959. He was also invited to deliver lecture at the University of Wisconsin and Michigan. He was also Director of the Anthropological Survey of India from 1959 to 1964 and in later years, between 1967 and 1970 held the high office of Commissioner for Scheduled Castes and Scheduled Tribes.

Bose was remarkably devoted in equal measures to the pursuit of science and the service of humanity. Although he held various high positions with great distinction, this was a small part of his life. He was drawn into the national movement at a young age and this gave a distinctive stamp to his scientific and literary work. He also went to jail for nationalist activities during the movement for India's independence.

In recognition of his excellent work in anthropology, Bose was awarded Annandale Gold Medal of the Asiatic Society of Bengal in 1948. He was elected as the President of Anthropology and Archaeology Section of Indian Science Congress in 1949. He was elected a fellow of the National Institute of Science of India in 1955. He was a devoted social worker and served in various capacities in many philanthropic organizations. He received Padma Shri in 1966.

## Influence of Gandhi

The greatest single influence on Bose's life was his association with Gandhi. Bose was interested in Gandhi's ideas on the creation of new society in India, and began by making a detailed study of his writings. He was soon drawn closer to Gandhi who said to him that the only way of understanding a living man's ideas was by seeing him put them into action. He was Gandhi's secretary and close companion. His association with Gandhi at Noakhli is too well-known to bear repetition. What impressed Bose most about Gandhi was his search for truth through experience. Gandhi was, in his view, the quintessential fieldworker, always ready to see and listen, and never drawing conclusions about a human situation without first experiencing it. Bose was very much influenced by Gandhi's *The Story of My Experiments with Truth* (1957).

## Writings of Bose

As an anthropologist, Bose was no narrow specialist. He conducted archaeological excavations in Mayurbhanj and wrote with D. Sen a pioneering work on the Palaeolithic culture of the area. He wrote much in both Bengali and English. His best published works are perhaps his three Bengali books, *Maben o Pracheen, Paribrajaker Diary* and *Hindu Samajer Garhan.* The first two are collections of essays and sketches, and the third is a brief but very bold and imaginative account of the basic features of Hindu social structure in which the perspectives of ethnography, Indology and history are combined with singular felicity.

Bose has written authoritatively on temple architecture – a subject that was very dear to his heart. He had an abiding interest in the material culture of the tribal people, and wrote with professional skill technology of shifting cultivation, and on various crafts such as oil-pressing, pottery and weaving. But, as an anthropologist, he wrote mostly on society and culture in India, covering the entire range from the simple Juang tribe of Orissa to the complex metropolitan city of Calcutta. Then, there are his several books on Gandhi, including *Selections from Gandhi's Writings.* Finally, he edited almost single-handedly India's oldest anthropological journal, *Man in India.* His major writings are given below:

(i) *Canous of Orissan Architecture* (1932)
(ii) *Excavations in Mayurbhanj* (1948)
(iii) *Hindu Samajer Garan* (1949, in Bengali) English translation by A. Béteille in 1976
(iv) *Studies in Gandhism* (1959)
(v) *Cultural Anthropology* (1961)
(vi) *Peasant Life in India: A Study in Indian Unity and Diversity* (1961)
(vii) *Culture and Society in India* (1967)
(viii) *Problems of National Integration* (1967)
(ix) *The Structure of Hindu Society* (1975)

## Methodology

Bose had basically interest in Indian civilization and culture. His approach was historical and inductive in nature. He developed a classification based on Indian textual categories to study the distribution of cultural traits. He was also a follower of the functional approach of Malinowski. This is highlighted in his work on *Nature of Culture*, i.e., the adaptive function of culture.

Bose, a great anthropologist, tried to present a single framework involving three approaches of ethnographers, Indologists and social historians. He was of the opinion that in order to understand Hindu civilization, an anthropologist should go beyond the applied aspect.

He emphasized the need to bring ethnology and Indology together in the study of Indian society. It is possible to reconstruct the structure of Indian civilization through the twin approaches of ethnology and Indology. Along these approaches, the study of social history also becomes vital in our own understanding of Indian civilization.

## Contributions of Bose

In his book, *The Structure of Hindu Society*, Bose gives civilizational view of Indian society. He has divided it into three parts. The first part mainly belongs to the domain of ethnography, where he presents material based on his own fieldwork. Fieldwork is mainly done among tribal communities. The second part is predominantly Indological, where he presents an account of the theory and practice of Hindu social life. The third part deals with social history.

### *Ethnography*

Bose uses ethnographic data to show the nature of tribal communities of Orissa and Chhota Nagpur and their relations with wider community. He states that the tribal communities of India are not of the same nature and they do not share the same kind of relation with the wider society. He recognizes that there are certain broad stages through which the simpler communities generally pass. He uses two related criteria for classifying the tribal communities in India: their level of technological development and the degree of their geographical and social isolation.

Bose did his anthropological fieldwork among the Juangs and often used this tribe as an example of communities left relatively untouched by what he calls the Brahminical civilization. Bose raises the question whether Juangs should or should not be regarded as Hindus. They are regarded as non-Aryan community falling broadly within the Hindu fold. Juangs had started worshipping a Hindu Goddess, although it was done in their own way. They bath in the morning, the offerings of sun-dried rice, the terms *satya, devata, dharma* – all prove how strongly Juang religious ceremonies have been influenced by those of the neighbouring Brahminical people. In nearly all respects, the Juangs are a tribe living outside the pale of Hinduism. They have their own language; they perform their marriage and funeral customs all by themselves. They eat beef and are not considered by the Hindus to be one of the Hindu castes. Yet, there is clear indication that Hindu religious ideas have penetrated into their culture. At the same time, one has to make a broad distinction between Hindu society with its elaborate caste-based division of labour and marginally situated communities like the Juangs.

Bose also discusses the two main tribes of Chhota Nagpur, viz., Mundas and Oraons. These tribes were not only larger in size but also represented a higher level of technological development. The nineteenth century witnessed a number of social movements among Mundas and Oraons. The Oraons sought escape from Hindu domination in a return to an idealized past which, however, was constructed substantially from elements taken out of Sanskritic Hinduism. Oraons and Mundas were living the life of a pure Hindu. It is interesting to note that Hindu castes like Ahir, Lohar and Midha also join the tribal people in their celebrations, and unless one is told who is who, no distinction can be drawn between them.

Hindus hardly left any economic freedom to the castes, but they left intact the original social and religious culture of the tribes in so far as that was possible. Their policy was not to eradicate beliefs and practices where they were not consistent with Brahminical moral ideas. But, it was nevertheless necessary to do something in order to bring the tribal cultures in line with Brahminism. The co-existence and inter-penetration of two modes of social organization – 'Brahminical' and 'tribal' – was investigated by Bose in the field which clearly indicates his capacity as a field scientist. As an anthropologist, Bose was interested not merely in revealing a certain pattern of culture but also in discovering the theory behind the pattern. He did not believe that the working of Hindu society in its details could be explained solely by this theory. But, the theory was an indispensable aid in understanding how the society actually worked.

## *Indology*

Bose seeks evidence from the domain of Indology to test his ideas about the design of Hindu society. He has taken material from a variety of sources such as the epics, the *Smritis,* Buddhist texts etc. He quotes a story from *Ramayana* as an example of attempts made by individuals of the lower castes to adopt the practice of the twice-born. Bose tries to identify the design of the 'varna' system from a reading of the epics and the *Smritis*. He finds in them the continual attempt to explain the ranks occupied by particular communities according to their origin and function. He also gives brief ideas of the king's duties as laid down in various texts.

Bose discusses the village life and focuses on the division of labour. The division of labour in the traditional Indian village was fairly elaborate. The villagers produced most of what they consumed and to this extent that village was a self-sufficient unit. But, the self-sufficiency of the village was relative and not absolute. What was not produced within the village could be procured from weekly markets or fairs or pilgrim centres, which were visited by many people from far and wide. Bose also gives some glimpses of city life, drawing mainly from the work of Vatsyayna.

Muslim rule brought some changes in Indian society. Some new crafts were introduced, but these were confined mainly to towns and cities. And, even when they penetrated into the rural areas, they did not alter the basic pattern of economic organization in the village. Bose gives two examples of attempts to challenge the very basis of Hindu social organization, i.e., Buddhism in the ancient period and the Bhakti movement of Chaitanya in the medieval period. These movements rejected the ascription of status by birth and the hierarchical ranking of castes. They brought new life into religion but they failed to make a significant dent on the existing social order. They did not generate any fundamental changes in the organization of production.

### *Social History*

Bose felt that an exploration of the past would be used to the present and the future only if it were conducted in a truly scientific spirit. Using historical examples, Bose discusses some of the ways in which the structure of Hindu society began to loosen and change under the impact of British rule. By examining the family history of the Sinhas of Raipur, Bose shows how the Sinhas took advantage of their connections with the East India Company to become traders, landowners, factory owners and professionals. The manner in which they moved from one occupational sphere to another within two or three generations was contrary to the spirit of the traditional economic organization and was made possible by the release of new economic forces.

The new economic forces introduced during the British rule steadily eroded the traditional division of labour based on caste. Bose shows from an analysis of census data that the association between caste and traditional occupation began to weaken, although not at the same rate for all castes.

*The Structure of Hindu Society* is an exposition of the ideas on which Hindu society was constituted. Bose attached great significance to the economic factor as a source of both stability and change in social life. He was also aware of the importance of agriculture technology. It is a common knowledge imparted by anthropology that the tribals learned the skills of agriculture from the caste Hindus. The tribals had an opportunity to come closer with the caste Hindus because of the Gandhian struggle for freedom. Bose believed that one very prominent contribution of freedom struggle was that that it narrowed down the society's diversity. He also talked about the importance of material or economic factors. He took special interest in the economic organization of the tribal people. He believed that the best way of classifying the numerous tribal groups in India is not by language, religion or race but by mode of livelihood. This type of classification enables one to see more clearly the relationship between the 'tribal' and the 'non-tribal' dimensions of Hindu civilization. Bose believed that the 'tribal' and 'non-tribal' people have been in continual interaction, and the key to understanding of this interaction lies in the different types of productive system under which they lived.

Bose felt that the tribal people were under constant pressure to abandon their isolation in favour of absorption into the wider society. This pressure was generated mainly by economic circumstances. Similarly, Bose refers to the view that Muslim impact on India did not alter substantially the basic features of Hindu society whereas the British impact did. The reason for this, according to him, is that the British bought with them a new technology and new system of production which the Muslim did not.

Besides the above, Bose also wrote on the following issues in *The Structure of Hindu Society:*

1. Study of Architecture
2. Indian Civilization
3. Caste System
4. Tribal Studies

### *Study of Architecture*

During his lifetime at Puri in Orissa, Bose came in contact with a master *shilpi* (temple architect) named Ram Maharana, who initiated Bose to the traditional canons of Orissan architecture (Shilp-Shastri). He edited an Oriya manuscript on *Shilpa-Sastra*, which was later published in 1932. He learnt from the field that a student of civilization will have to integrate information from various levels: the text as well as the product of arts. The elegance of ancient Orissan temples fascinated Bose so much that he started giving lectures on these temples to the visitors of Puri.

### *Indian Civilization*

In his Jagdish Bose Memorial Lecture of 1971, Bose stated that Indian civilization was in contrast to the civilization of Europe.

The civilization of Europe was essentially based on repeated experiences of war leading to the spirit of nationalism. On the other hand, the civilization of India developed a pattern of cultural pluralism under relatively peaceful conditions. Indian civilization encouraged diversity of culture, but in its economic organization, it tried to weave all communities into a network of interdependence, but distinct, entities.

The creative potentialities of the traditional structure of Indian civilization cannot be properly assessed, if the observations are only limited to the post-medieval period and the recent phase of recession of the civilization. Bose stated that the study of civilization should be done in phase of expansion and confidence. In his Bengali article, "The Temples of Konark", Bose refers to the expansion and confidence of phase of Indian civilization in a vivid manner. The temples of Konark were built in a glorious period of Orissan history. The king Narsingdev of Ganga dynasty had just defeated the Sultan of Gaura with his powerful army. The state was prosperous and people were infused with a passionate mood to enjoy life and to assert independence. The architects were brought up in this atmosphere and tried to give shape to this confident and livelihood in their work. The sculptures are full of light. The sculptors' minds were not laden with any false shame. Even today, partly buried under a debris of broken stone pieces, withstanding the ravages of time, the temples of Konarka present a vivid picture of a by-gone confident past.

Bose was the Director of Anthropological Survey of India (ASI) from 1959 to 1964. In organizing the research programme of the ASI, he suggested the following successive phases of research to be done on the all-India level:

Phase I: Survey of selected material traits of India and mapping out the pattern of their distribution vis-à-vis linguistic areas.

Phase II: Study of a few selected important ancient craft techniques such as pottery and metal craft. Study of carrying capacity on land of different productive techniques such as hunting and gathering, shifting cultivation, terrace cultivation etc.

Phase III: Study of social organization of crafts and caste associations and mobility in different regions of India.

Phase IV: Study of higher integrative institutions such as temples, the chain of *mathas* established by *Adi* Sankaracharya and the kinships.

Phase V: Study of the process of modernization in castes, occupation, urbanization, tribal movements and social movements in different regions of India.

Bose has tried to capture the expressive modern thrust of Indian civilization through a number of critical character sketches of a few outstanding personalities. In a Bengali book, *Nabin-O-Prachin*, he writes about Gandhi's *satyagraha* and search of truth, Tagore's creative pursuits and paintings, Jamani Roy's views on art and Ramkinkar Baiji's paintings.

### *Unity and Diversity of Indian Civilization*

In India, there has always been a history of cultural divisions, for example, the Aryan in North vis-à-vis the Dravidian in South. Bose observed that the division of Indian population on the basis of language was obvious on a different set of cultural divide in terms of items of material culture – North-West, continuous with West Central Asia, and East, continuous with Southern Asia. This proposition was later on elaborately worked out on the basis of extensive survey of the distribution of a set of material traits, forms and techniques of potters all over India. Bose tried to bring archaic link to indicate how regions or states of India, which are today separated by difference of language, share many elements of material culture in common. Thus, we find a pattern of unity in India though it has different cultural zones.

In his book *Peasant Life in India: A Study of Indian Unity and Diversity*, Bose proposes a pyramidal imagery of unity of Indian civilization. It is apparent that the degree of differentiation is less in respect of the country's social organization if the regionalization is in evidence to a certain extent in relation to the material arts of life. The structure of Indian unity can be compared to a pyramid. There is more differentiation at the material base of life and progressively less as one mounts higher and higher.

In another article, 'The Geographical Background of Indian Culture (1950)', Bose discusses as to how a kind of uniformity grew up between geographically and even ecologically distinguishable regions of India through the tradition of caste system. He also discusses about the various traditional cultural media, which provided a mechanism through which the unifying thoughts and feelings of thinkers, artists and saints of India were brought to the door of most distant communities and enabled them to share some common intellectual and emotional elements of civilization.

In the particular case of encounter of East and West in Bengal, Bose is of the opinion that the civilization of Bengal cannot be defined in terms of spatial and temporal continuity of tradition. Bengali culture has always been in the process of becoming, instead of merely being in formidable and venture of cultural recognition. This refers to the characteristics of any civilization. Hence, the study of civilization is essentially a study of inner most, i.e., matters of the mind responding to changing life experiences of people.

### *Caste System*

Bose's interest in the study of caste system in India appeared in his mind when he was working among the untouchables in the slums of Bolpur town under the Gandhian Reconstruction Programme. He rejected the myth of divine origin, reincarnation and notion of purity and pollution. In a series of articles 'Hindu method of Tribal Absorption' (1941), 'Caste in India' (1951) and 'Some Aspects of Caste in Bengal' (1958), Bose proposes that the root of persistence of the caste system is to be found in the economic and cultural security provided by the non-competitive, hereditary, vocation-based productive organization, which operated in isolated village communities guided by general norm of inter-ethnic cultural tolerance. Bose viewed that the recent developments indicate deviations from the non-competitive ascribed traditional system towards a competitive one. In other words, the old structure being used in various combinations in new social meaning.

Besides having interest in change-oriented study of Indian caste system, Bose also developed interest in the study of castes as self-regulating corporate groups, guiding the social life of their members. A number of studies on operation of caste associations in different regions of India were initiated by him. In some of these, the roles of kings, temples, *mathas* etc. were also brought into focus in regulation of caste norms.

### *Tribal Studies*

Bose wanted to begin his professional career with an intensive empirical research on the Juangs of Orissa but after a brief field work in 1928, he had to leave the state of Keonjhar. The data gathered during the short period of fieldwork among the Juangs, resulted in publication of three short papers (Bose, 1928, 1929, 1930). The brief field study provided him the basic insight into how tribes following a relatively primitive technology like swidden cultivation were being absorbed into agriculture and craft-based Hindu society. In his various insightful papers on tribals, he attempted to highlight the tribal economy, absorption of tribes into the Hindu caste system and the root of tribal separatist movement. In his book on *Tribal Life in India* (1970), Bose has observed that barring a very small fraction, there is little difference in economic life of tribals and peasant and artisan communities. The difference between our rural folk and urban classes is undoubtedly greater than that between peasants and the tribal communities so for as their occupations are concerned.

### Conclusion

N.K. Bose studied the material traits for analysing their distribution at various places in India. His understanding of tribals' absorption to caste is a significant angle to analyse the unity of Indian culture. He focuses on how similar material culture helps in binding zones of India into one framework. Further, the linkage of India through traits, customs, beliefs etc. placed his analysis at the significant platform. Although Bose was a student of Indian civilization, he has not made any conscious effort to distinguish the civilization from culture. He has used both of them in an overlapping manner.

The contributions of Bose are immensely valuable. But we should always keep in mind that Bose was essentially an anthropologist and an ethnologist. He was also a linguistic anthropologist. Anthropology is a holistic social science. It has great faith in ethnological field work. Bose was skilled in these canons of anthropology but despite his persistent association with Gandhi, he did not take into account the diversity and plurality of Indian society. He very much wanted the integration of tribals into Hindu society. He shows all sympathy and softness towards tribals. He is comfortable to find the absorption of tribals into the Hindu society. This made him a sectarian anthropologist; in other words, he was a champion of Hindutva ideology. The present-day tribals would not digest the prescription of Bose.

The theory of N.K. Bose has always been weak and it has been the weakness of all empirical anthropologists. However, it must be observed that Bose attempted to respond to the challenges of his era.

Bose used traditional textual categories such as *Satva, Raja and Tamas*, and *Dharma, Artha, Kama* and *Moksh* in the classification of cultures but he was very critical about simplistic of textual notion in the study of Indian civilization, without taking full note of historical and social contexts.

## Bose's Framework Summarized

### *Background*

1. Educated and trained in anthropology at Calcutta
2. Academic career at Calcutta
3. Interests in Indian civilization and culture, national movement

### *Aims*

1. Analysis on civilizational perspective

### *Assumption*

1. Pyramidal imagery of the unity of Indian civilization

### *Methodology*

1. Historical
2. Inductive

3. Textual
4. Functional

### *Typology*

1. Distribution of culture traits
2. Textual categories

### *Issues*

Different aspects of Indian society:

1. Indian civilization and culture
2. Architecture
3. Caste system
4. Tribal studies
5. Peasant life

## Select Bibliography

Bose, N.K. (1934, 1952 and 1968), *Selection from Gandhi*, Bombay: Navjiwan Publishing House.

— (1959, 1962), *Studies in Gandhism*, Calcutta: Merit Publishers.

— (1957), *Problems of National Integration*, Shimla: Indian Institute of Advanced Studies.

— (1961), *Cultural Anthropology*, New Delhi: Asia Publishing House.

— (1961), *Peasant Life in India: A Study in Indian Unity and Diversity*, Memoir No.8, Calcutta: Anthropological Survey of India.

— (1967), *Culture and Society in India*, New Delhi: Asia Publishing House.

— (1969), *Problems of Nationalism*, Calcutta: Allied Publishers.

— (1975), *The Structure of Hindu Society*, New Delhi: Orient Longman.

Desai, A.R. (1969), *Rural Sociology in India*, Bombay: Popular Prakashan.

Singh, K.S. (1989), 'Indian Anthropology 2000 A.D.: Problems and Prospects', *Bhartiya Samajik Chintan*, Vol. XII, No. 1–2, March-June, pp. 53–68.

Singh, Yogendra (1986), *Indian Sociology: Social Conditioning and Emerging Concerns*, Delhi: Vistaar Publications.

# 18

# Surajit Sinha

Surajit Chandra Sinha was born on 1 August 1926 in Durgapur Upazila in the Bengal Presidency (now in Bangladesh), British India. He was diagnosed with Alzheimer's disease in 1993 and died after a prolonged illness at Santiniketan, West Bengal on 27 February 2002. He was the eldest son of Maharaja Bhupendra Chandra Sinha of Susang. His mother was a daughter of Jogendranath Moitra, the Zaminda of Sithlai in Pabna District. Her family members traced their origins to the reign of Emperor Jahangir. Sinha's youngest sister is Purba Dam, the eminent exponent of Rabindrasangeet. Sinha was married to Dr. Punima Sinha, a physicist, author and music scholar, who was the daughter of the eminent legal scholar and Bengali novelist, Naresh Chandra Sen Gupta.

After his education in a high school in Mymensingh and at Ballygunj Government High School, Calcutta, he started his college education in physics at Presidency College, Calcutta, but then changed to geology and then finally to anthropology. Nirmal

Kumar Bose, the eminent anthropologist, became his mentor soon after they met in the viva examination for the master's degree, where Bose was one of the examiners. Later, Sinha completed his Ph.D. in anthropology from Northwestern University in Illinois, United States on a Fulbright Scholarship. He was trained in social anthropological fieldwork at Calcutta University by Tarak Chandra Das who first introduced Sinha to take up the Bhumij community of the then Bihar state for his doctoral work.

Surajit Sinha was an anthropologist. He held a number of academic and administrative posts such as Deputy Director and Director of the Anthropological Survey of India in Calcutta. At this time, he was considered to be an advisor of the then Indian Prime Minister, Indira Gandhi. He was the Professor of Anthropology at the Indian Institute of Management, Calcutta. He became the up-acharya of Visva Bharati, Santiniketan. After retirement he became the second Director of the Indian Council of Social Science Research sponsored Centre for Studies in Social Sciences, Calcutta.

A close paternal uncle, Maharajkumar Mani Singh was a well-known Communist Party leader who wrote *Jiban Sangram*. In his youth, he (Sinha) followed in the footsteps of his paternal uncle. Sinha was committed to the ideologies of both Mahatma Gandhi and Rabindranath Tagore, arguably the two most eminent Indians in the nineteenth and the twentieth centuries. The difference between the views of these two men was that whereas Gandhi wanted every Indian to be (in the best sense) a Shudra, Tagore wanted every Indian to be (also in the best sense) a Brahmin, Sinha held a self-critical view on Indian anthropology. According to him, Indian anthropologists save a few exceptions, largely remained 'Western apprentice' and could not develop their own tradition.

Sinha distinguished himself in the field of social and cultural anthropology. Upon returning to India from the United States, he continued to conduct field research. His main areas of interest was Indian tribes, especially the Bhumij tribe in central India. While in USA, Sinha did a unique field study in an American village on religion. His research report entitled 'Religion in an Affluent

Society' was published in *Current Anthropology*. Surajit Sinha's original contribution in Indian anthropology could be found in his articles on 'Tribe-Caste and Tribe-Peasant Continuum in Central India' (1965), 'State Formation and Rajput Myth in Tribal Central India' (1962) and 'Bhumij-Kshatriya Social Movement in South Manbhum' (1959) in which he viewed tribes and castes not as separate and isolated social and cultural categories but as parts of the greater Indian civilization in an evolutionary scheme under which formation of the early states in India took place. Sinha was basically a pioneering historical anthropologist of India who combined field and archival data in a very early period of Indian anthropology.

He has done extensive field work on the Bhumij tribe of Bengal and Bihar. His special interests include tribal transformation in central India and the structure of Indian civilization. His work focuses on following themes:

(1) Tribe-caste and tribe-peasant continuum
(2) Levels of economic initiatives, and ethnic groups
(3) Tribal movements
(4) Sociology of religion
(5) Field studies on the people of India

Sinha demonstrated the possibility of orthogenetic development of civilization in India from a primitive cultural level, roughly comparable to cultures of the less acultured tribes of peninsular India. He also found elements of transaction in the tribal cultures in the direction of peasant cultures, on the line of Redfield's scheme of folk–peasant–urban continuum. Sinha examined the tribal-caste interactions and proposed several useful concepts like 'tribal–peasant continuum', 'Bhumij–Ksatriya continuum' as well as 'tribal–Rajput continuum' which provide the model for understanding the process of transformation in the whole of middle India.

In his study of Bhumij, scheduled tribes of West Bengal and Bihar, Sinha found that how tribals become integrated with the regional Hindu caste system. He tried to define two ideal levels of socio-cultural systems – the 'tribal' and the emergent level of

'Hindu peasantry' in terms of a set of characteristics in habitat, economy, social structure and ideological system. The peasant level included a number of emergent features like a surplus in economy based on settled agriculture, social stratification, ethical religion and puritanical value system as distinguished from the essentially egalitarian and non-puritanical tribal level.

Sinha viewed tribe as a system of social relations as well as a state of mind and cultural traditions; both characterized basically by isolation and lack of stratification. The upper Hindu castes have not only feeble social interaction with the tribes but they also think that tribes have their basic distinctive 'unsophisticated' and 'wild' way of life.

## Major Writings of Sinha

1. *Science, Technology, and Culture: A Study of the Cultural Traditions and Institutions of India and Ceylon in Relation to Science and Technology.*
2. *Tribal Polities and State Systems in Pre-Colonial Eastern and Northeastern India* (ed.), (Calcutta, 1987).
3. *Tribes and Indian Civilization: Structures and Transformation* (Varanasi, 1982).
4. *Ascetics of Kashi: An Anthropological Exploration*, (co-edited with Baidyanath Saraswati) (Varanasi, 1978).
5. *Field Studies on the People of India: Methods and Perspectives, (In Memory of Professor Tarak Chandra Das)* (ed.), (Calcutta, 1978).
6. *Anthropology in India, Tribal Thought and Culture* (ed.), (Calcutta, 1976).
7. *Aspects of Indian Culture and Society: Essays in Felicitation of Professor Nirmal Kumar Bose* (ed.), (Calcutta, 1972).
8. *Cultural Profile of Calcutta* (ed.), (Calcutta, 1972).
9. *Research Programmes on Cultural Anthropology and Allied Disciplines* (ed.), (Calcutta, 1970).
10. *Ethnic Groups, Villages, and Towns of Pargana Barabhum: Report of a Survey* (ed.), (co-edited with Biman Kumar Dasgupta and Hemendranath Banerjee) (Calcutta, 1966).
11. *Levels of a Economic Initiative and Ethnic Groups in Paragana Barabhum* (ed.), (Durham, N.C., 1964).

## Theoretical and Methodological Understanding

Sinha derives the characteristics of tribe-caste and tribe-peasant polarities from Redfield's earlier concepts of 'folk-urban continuum' and 'peasant society and culture'. He redefines only the polarities, which are specially oriented to deal with the nature of the continuum in central India. Therefore, Sinha deals with the concepts mainly tribe, caste and peasant in his analysis.

### *Tribal Society*

According to Sinha, the tribal society is isolated in ecology, demography, economy, politics and other social relations, from other ethnic groups. This isolation generates, and in turn, is bolstered by a strong in-group sentiment. Internally, the group is characterized by homogeneity on account of lack of social stratification and role specialization other than by age, sex and kinship. Such an ideally isolated, homogeneous and unstratified group is also marked by disconnections from the great traditions of Indian civilization in terms of objective reality and objective awareness, a value system of equality, closeness of the human, natural and the supernatural world; lack of systematization of ideas, and a 'sophisticated' stratum of culture, ethical religion and puritanical asceticism.

### *Caste Groups*

In contrast with the isolated, homogeneous and unstratified 'tribe', 'caste' is typically connected, heterogeneous and stratified and is characterized by the following social structural features: multi-ethnic residence in the local community, and inter-ethnic groups and stratified land tenure, and ranked and interdependent interaction with other ethnic groups. Similarly, the following critical features distinguish the caste pole of the level of 'culture': interaction with the sub-cultures of other ethnic groups in the region; interaction with the great traditions; polarization of lay and elite cultures with elaboration and systematization of cultural ideals in the latter; hierarchic view of social relations bolstered by the concept of ritual pollution; and emergence of ethical religion and a puritanical view of life.

### *Peasant Village*

It is a territorial community of the multi-caste groups as most of the characteristics of ideal caste are found there. The peasant village community has extensive territorial affiliations with multiple centres of civilization through a diverse network of relationships. The cultural system of the peasant village is heterogeneous in terms of internal division into caste and class and its complex external relations with a heterogeneous region having specialized centres of cultural nucleation. The tribal villages in contrast are typically uni-ethnic and their external relations are limited to villages lying in a homogeneous culture area lived in by the same ethnic group. The contacts of the tribes with the neighbouring peasantry have given rise to a sort of tribal-peasant continuum (Sinha, 1957).

## II

Sinha's concept of tribe-caste and tribal-peasant continuum is mainly concerned with the processes by which tribes are integrated with the traditional civilization of India. Sinha elaborates his conceptual ideas further by taking the examples of tribal groups. We would like to discuss here specifically two case studies:

1. The Hill Maria Gonds
2. The Bhumij of Barabhum

### The Hill Maria Gonds

The Hill Maria Gonds, a tribal group of Bastar district, is the most isolated segment of the Dravidian Gondi-speaking people of central India. They occupy nearly 15,000 square miles of the area in the northwest part of Bastar district. Their habitat is typically hill and jungle clad. Communication is mainly based on travel by government as even bullock carts cannot penetrate this difficult terrain. Although plough cultivation has penetrated considerably in the Maria community, even yet the Marias are supposed to value the slash-and-burn form of cultivation in a very emotional way. They regard the crops as the combined labours of the village rather than of the labour of the individuals. If one suffers, all suffers and all combine to support the old and the needy, and to help each fellow villager to get through the heaviest part of the yearly round. Village is the main unit of cultivation. People are, by and large, self-sufficient in their subsistence economy; they do obtain from outside sources such important items as cloth, iron implements, earthenware, brass pots, ornaments, salt etc. The most important means of procuring these items is weekly market. Besides attending the weekly market, the people of Maria also procure some of their materials from the annual religious fair held at Narayanpur. Thus, the Maria have come into contact with about four or five artisan groups either at the market, or as itinerant traders or as transient or, rarely as permanent settlers in their own village.

The Maria social structure is essentially segmentary in character. Patrilineal class is the largest effective corporate group, further organized into motives, 'brother clans' and 'wife clans'. The clans are regarded as equal in status. The tribe is the widest extension of kin-like ties. Although, in theory, the tribe includes the entire Gond (Koitor) people, in reality, the line of endogamy does not extend beyond the Hill Maria group. Most of the villages in the interior are uni-class communities.

It appears that the interior villages, where the Maria live, are almost exclusively under swidden cultivation and as uni-ethnic and uni-class communities. There is no stratification in terms of landholding and the religious headman of the village or the secular headman, the *Gaita*, is only primus interpreter among the village leaders. Although so unstratified within themselves, they are aware of other ethnic groups living within the range of social contact and rank them in some kind of consistent order.

Maria use mainly three criteria for caste ranking in occupation, wearing of the scared thread and acceptance of food. The various castes are not conceptualized as 'high' or 'low' but as 'big' or 'small'. They were placed in the following three major blocks:

**Table 1**

| *Big Caste* | *Own Caste* | *Small Caste* |
|---|---|---|
| Brahmin (priest) | Koiter (i.e., Gond) | Pathan (Muslims shopkeeper, cultivation) |
| Dakar (cultivation) | | Mahar (weaver) |
| Hindu (including Chattisgarhis and Halbas) | | Gadi (weaver) |
| Kallar (distiller, cultivation) | | Ghasia (jewellery maker) |
| Kopal (cowherd) | | Wade (blacksmith) |
| | | Chamar (leather worker) |
| | | Isai (Christian) |

Thus, all the Hinduized groups, other than those who practise 'degrading' occupations, are placed in the 'big caste' category. And Hill Maria seem to have adopted the characteristic of Hindu attitude of regarding the Muslims and the Christians as ritually low. The Hill Maria have strong ideas of the Maria. It lacks spiritual specialists of the Hindu great ideas about tradition, and that recognizable Sanskritic elements are understandably rare in their religion. The Hill Maria, in the characteristic way of many such isolated tribal groups, sharply distinguished between themselves and outsiders or strangers. The natural non-ascetic pleasure orientation of the Hill Maria is quite vivid.

## The Bhumij of Barabhum

While the Hill Maria was marked by intense isolation clan and village solidarity, the Bhumij was characterized by degree of social stratification and rank consciousness among these people which makes them distinguishable from Hindu caste. Risley, who studied them in 1880s, mentioned that here a pure Dravidian race have lost their original language and now speak only Bengali; they worship Hindu Gods in addition to their own and the more advanced among them employ Brahmins as family priests. They still retain a set of totemistic exogamous sub-divisions closely resembling those of the Mundas and Santhals. But they are beginning to forget the totems which the names of sub-division denote, and the names themselves probably soon be abandoned ritual pollution with reference to violation of the rule of tribal endogamy and sexual relationship with members of the lower castes and also with regard to acceptance of cooked food and water from members of the 'smaller' caste block. But in spite of their well-developed concept of ritual pollution and having at least a simplified concept of caste hierarchy (without reference to the varna order), the Hill Maria do not have access to ritual service from any such caste of critical importance as the Brahmin, barber or washerman castes. Caste ranking in this area is based on what Marriott has called 'attributional' in contrast to 'interactional' factors.

The Maria interactions are largely restricted to their own ethnic area in terms of kinship, marriage and ritual ties. However, a good deal of similarity between the contents of Maria religion and that of the Hindus in ordinary peasant village has found such as worship of ancestral spirits, mother goddess, powerful male gods; a vague belief in a great god or supreme being, feasting, dancing and noisy processions as prominent features of ceremonial life, animal sacrifice and ritual offering; use of certain ritual objects as red power, grain, iron, peacock feathers and chains; a belief in reincarnation and more vaguely in karma. The tribe will then have become a caste in full sense of the word and will go stripping itself of all customs likely to betray its true descent (Risley, 1889, 1915). During 1950–53 and 1956–59, when Sinha studied the Bhumij, he observed that Bhumij had moved even farther in the direction of Hinduization since Risley's times.

Barabhum is a developed area as compared to Bastar area. It is accessible by road. The northern part of the Pargana main estate of Barabhum is relatively plain and the whole area has been subjected to extensive deforestation. Bhumij are regarded as the earliest inhabitants of Pargana. They live in a demographically denser and ethically heterogeneous region when compared with the Hill Maria.

The Bhumij, like the neighbouring Santhal and Mahato, are settled agriculturists cultivating rice with the plough. Agriculture is mainly subsistence-oriented and is not a major source for earning cash. The important cash crops are oilseeds and tobacco, but the main regular source of cash earning is rearing the lac resin on privately owned trees. Unlike the Maria, the Bhumij have strong concern for individual ownership of land. The class does not have any corporate property other than the class ossuary site, and the lineage only exerts some pressure against sale or transfer of shares of ancestral landed property to people outside the group. The village headman holds the maximum acres of land rent free as service tenure and he also gets rent from his tenants in the village. These various types of people include landowners, landless labourers, poor cultivators, substantial cultivators and the village headmen. Within this village of seven ethnic groups, the Bhumij own more than four-fifths of the land.

Although the Bhumij hold the bulk of the traditional feudal tenures and in a large number of villages dominate land, ownership their dominance is not uniformly distributed over the region. As many as 49 villages were given to Brahmins as rent-free religious tenures by the king of Barabhum. In these villages, the Bhumij are subordinate tenure-holders. They are in subordinate tenure relation to other castes such as Mahato, Kayastha and Baniya in some villages in the Pargana.

Whereas there is not a single weekly market in the 1,500 square mile area on the Abujhmar Hill, the typical habitat of the Maria, the area of 635 square roots of Barabhum contains 12 weekly markets. At a distance of 3 to 5 miles, across to the one corner has a weekly market. The total number of ethnic groups participating in the market might be over 30.

Like the Maria, the Bhumij are divided into a number of patrilineal endogamous clans or gotras, which are affiliated with the respective ancestral villages where the class ossuaries are located. The clans lend to be localized around the ossuary village, but there is no clear-cut territory or corporate organization in terms of clan. The clans are segmented into functional partrilineages with equivalent status for the further segments. This imparts a sense of equality among the Bhumij families tied by kinship who may possess wealth quite differentially.

Apart from differential landholding and position in the land revenue hierarchy, the Bhumij are divided into several socio-ritually defined marriage classes, partly corresponding with the land revenue hierarchy. At the lowest rung are the 'degraded' Nichu and Patit strata, while the bulk belong to the Nagadi class, who have access to the ritual service of 'degraded' Brahmins, but do not abstain from taking non-vegetarian food or liquor. The

Ataishey classes are the one who also employ 'degraded' Brahmins but avoid taking chicken and liquor. The more prosperous ones aspire to be recognized as Rajput Ksatriyas, and it is likely that the royal Ksatriya lineage of Barabhum is also of Bhumij origin (Sinha, 1962).

The very demographic situation places the Bhumij within easy reach of a number of ethnic groups. And often, having a dominant position in the land revenue administration and in landholding, they have certain advantages in participating in inter-ethnic interactions. It is, therefore, not surprising that whereas the Hill Maria participate quite remotely in stratified ranking in terms of caste, the Bhumij are more vividly involved in it. Their participation in the regional caste system is indeed quite interactional. They have access to the ritual services of the Brahmin, Vaishnava, barber and washerman castes and some very low caste groups such as the Sahis, Dom and Ghasi, who serve as their midwives. A wider range of castes are tied to the Bhumij in terms of ceremonial friendship, participation in festivals, sharecropping and market relationship. In their desire to be recognized as Rajput Ksatriyas, the Bhumij have been intensely involved in social mobility movements under the guidance of the Ataishey upper class (Sinha, 1959).

The Bhumij have a strong feeling that they are the true autochthones of Barabhum, as their ancestors had cleared the forests to develop cultivable lands, and, as such, they look upon most of the ethnic groups of the Paragana, except Kharia and Pahira, as relative outsiders. Beginning with their own groups, the Bhumij range the various ethnic groups of the region at different points of socio-cultural distance from them, beginning with the closest, roughly as follows:

1. Kharia, Pahira and Santhal, Hindu artisan castes, barber, washerman.
2. Mahato.
3. Brahmin, Vaishnava.
4. Rajput-Ksatriya.
5. 'Bengali' castes: Baniya, Kayastha, Tamil etc.

6. Bihari castes, with whom the Bhumij do not share a common language (Sinha, 1957).

This evaluation is mainly based on their idea of relative exogenousness of the various groups mentioned above.

The Bhumij continue to worship many of their traditional gods and goddesses such as Marangburu (the Mountain God), various hill gods, gods and goddesses of the sacred grove and so on. But, the worship of these gods does not have the same prestige as worshipping the gods of the Hindu great tradition, such as Shiva, Durga and Kali.

Sinha, in his interaction with residents, found that a few Bhumij in the village of Madhupur became involved in self-conscious reflection on the Hindu ideological concepts under the influence of wandering Vaishnava sadhus. Some of these Bhumij were also literate and were quite capable of expounding the complex themes in such sacred texts such as *Chaitanya Charitamrita Srimadbhagabat* etc., to the non-literate within their limited social range (Sinha, 1953). The religious theme of the celestial love of Radha and Krishna provides a major stimulus to the composition of the songs and the dances of Barabhum.

The Bhumij share a good lot of the Maria's gay sensuality, but, this again is slightly toned down by a concern to appear good in the eyes of the upper caste Hindus. The zest for mixed dancing, drinking and festivity is opposed by reformist mobility movements (Sinha, 1959). Although a good deal of premarital sexual life is tolerated, there is also considerable overt concern about the chastity of the femalefolk.

The co-existence of segmentary and hierarchic principles in the social structure is reflected in the sphere of the value system. The Bhumij of the village of Madhupur, for example, look upon the headman as equal in terms of lineage membership, but also show some deference to him for holding a position of power, wealth and prestige. The headman is more than primus interpreter. The hierarchic principle is also expressed in male-female relationship, restricting the sphere of activity and freedom of movement of the females as one moves up the social hierarchy.

According to Sinha, the position of the Bhumij in the regional caste system comes out in relief if we compare them with the partially hunting and gathering Kharia and Pahria, who live in isolated hamlets in the foothills of Pargana Barabhum. They are not only ecologically isolated but have not access to the services of the ritual specialists castes too. They have unusually simple notions about the regional caste hierarchy, are internally homogeneous and less puritanical than Bhumij in their notion of premarital sex and have very feeble knowledge of the great tradition. They are comparable to the Hill Maria in many ways, other than the fact that their settlements are like scattered islands in an ethnically heterogeneous Pargana dominated by other castes.

### Difference between Hill Maria and Bhumij Tribes

Sinha differentiates between Hill Maria and Bhumij tribes (see Table 2). According to him, it involves a sharp swing from near the ideal 'tribe' pole to near the 'peasant' and 'caste' pole. There is a systematic and yet sharp progression towards lessening of ecological isolation and increase in ethnic heterogeneity in regional demographic pattern and in social interaction, social stratification and emergence of indigenous elite class and enlargement and diversification of the network of spatially defined social relationship with civilization centres. In cultural structure also, the movement is towards the development of regional cultural heterogeneity in terms of ethnic diversity, social stratification and role specialization, greater inclusion of Hindu great tradition and of ethical slant in religion, and greater emphasis on puritanical values.

The final contours of the two polarities are guided by the degree of ethnic heterogeneity and the degree of the complexity and hierarchy in the pattern of interaction between and within the ethnic groups of a religion. In case of Bhumij, according to Sinha, population density, ethnic heterogeneity and social hierarchy in the area are sustained by settled plough cultivation, regional craft and market organization and the supervisory role of the chief in the hierarchic land revenue organization of the Pargana. It cannot, however, be stated that technological evolution, population growth and increase in settlement size could generate a caste system in a tribal area.

**Table 2**

*The Hill Maria Gond and the Bhumij and their Level of Complexity*

| Tribe (Hill Maria Gond, Madhya Pradesh) | Caste Peasant Bhumij (West Bengal and Bihar) |
|---|---|
| *Ecology* | |
| Hill and forest | 2/3 plain; 1/3 forest |
| *Ethnic Complexity* | |
| Uni-ethnic villages | Average village contains six ethnic groups |
| Uni-ethnic tribal tract | The Bhumij form 15% of the population of Pargana Barabhum containing 64 ethnic groups |
| *Technology and Economy* | |
| Swidden | Wet rice cultivation |
| No market with the tribal tract | Market at regular intervals of 3–5 miles |
| Community ownership of swidden land | A hierarchic land revenue organization involving at least four levels of sub-infendation |
| *Stratification* | |
| Internal stratification practically none | Considerable feudalization of the political structure and corresponding recognition of at least three nearly endogamous socio-ritual classes |
| *Caste-like Interaction* | |
| Ranked in three strata | 20 to 28 ranks |
| Non-tribal ritual specialists employed | At least four categories of caste employed |

The kind of regularity in progression revealed by comparing two societies so obviously apart in their possible position in his ideally conceived continuum may mislead to imagine that it may be a simple task to evaluate the relative position of more nearly related societies on the proposed continuum. It is quite likely that within the proximal range, all the criteria used in defining the continuum will not move at the same rate. A group may be ahead of another in market participation but behind in sharing great tradition gods and ethical slant in religion.

## Tribal Movements

There have been a series of ethnic (tribal) rebellions during the early days of the British rules in the 18th and 19th centuries: Sardar

Larai (1885) and Birsa Movement (1895–1900) among the Munda; Ganganarain Hangama (1832) among the Bhumij; Kol Rebellion (1832); Santhal Rebellion (1857–58); Rebellion of the Kacha Nagas (1880s), and so on.

Here, Sinha is not concerned with all categories of social movements among the tribes. On all categories of social movements, one may refer to Mahapatra's paper on "Social Movements among Tribes in Eastern India with special Reference to Orissa" (Mahapatra, 1968). In his paper on "Tribal Solidarity Movements in India", Sinha (1972) deals social movements in context of the self-conscious socio-political movement aimed at asserting political solidarity of a tribe or a group of tribes vis-à-vis the non-tribals. Therefore, his focus, as an anthropologist, is on political solidarity with exploring the social and cultural context of the movements.

Sinha views that one of the major roots of tribal solidarity movements arise out of ecological-cultural isolation, economic backwardness, a feeling of frustration vis-à-vis the advanced sections. Tribes, who are either too isolated or too integrated with the Hindu social system, are not involved in these movements. The policy implications of this analysis are obvious: there should be provisions for larger economic opportunities and greater understanding with the emerging core of the Indian national culture.

Although it is true that these movements are guided by minority of emerging elite, it would be over-simplification to look into the phenomenon exclusively from the perspective of sub-nationalism engineered by a few self-seeking elites. Sinha discovers in these movements both a process of progressive enlargement of socio-political and cultural experience beyond the primitive tribal units and also a process of drawing solidarity boundaries around the expanded horizon vis-à-vis the Indian core. The review also suggests certain policy guidelines regarding the relatively unintegrated tribes. Assuming that the hitherto isolated tribes should be fully integrated with Indian national polity and the mainstream of the emerging national culture. It may be proposed that economic opportunities made available to these areas should be a little ahead of the political opportunities and as far as possible, the economic opportunities should permeate a broad base of the population instead of being limited to an elite group.

Sinha argues that one need not, and should not, encroach upon 'the cultural autonomy' of these groups, arrangements should be made for greater acquaintance with the 'emerging core' of Indian national culture so that the elite as well as the masses are oriented towards the core pattern rather than seek an escape model in their search for new identity.

It appears that instead of taking an alarmist position about tribal solidarity movements, one should welcome the 'genuine' solidarity movements and resist the 'spurious' ones. The extent to which one is able to properly identify the 'genuine' tribal movements and meet them with 'genuine' nationalism, our task of building a new nation by integrating the relatively isolated tribes will be successful.

## Framework for Research

Sinha (1968) suggests a framework for deciding the topics for urgent research in social anthropology in India and a few general topics for investigations. To Sinha, the urgent problems in social anthropology of the Indian population may be approached from at least three distinct vantage points:

(a) Primitive groups may be selected for covering the missing links in our study of world culture.
(b) Selections of groups and problems for a theoretical understanding of the totality of Indian society and culture as structures, patterns and processes.
(c) Anthropological study of problems urgent needed in national reconstruction and development.

### *Limitations of Approach*

Sinha views that exclusive urgent attention on the 'vanishing' primitives has some essential limitations in the total perspective of Indian civilization:

(1) First of all, the primitive tribes cover a very limited (though significant) dimension of the total complexity of Indian society and culture.

(2) Even the primitives, except perhaps for the remote aboriginals of the Andaman and Nicobar Islands, cannot be properly studied except as historically dependent categories of Indian civilization.
(3) It is generally assumed that tribes are changing at a faster rate than the castes. Except for a few extreme cases like the Great Andamanese, the above assumption is not based on systematic examination of facts.
(4) The cry of alarm about vanishing customs need not be stretched in the case of the Indian population. Our general impression is that social structures and cultural patterns of the marginal tribes are not changing as such a fast rate as to induce to take up a large-scale crash programme in salvage anthropology in terms of ad hoc search for vanishing customs at the cost of a systematic study of the total society and culture in India.

## Perspective of Indian Civilization

The above limitations in the ad hoc search for vanishing customs among the so-called 'vanishing' primitive tribes in India lead to emphasize the choice of urgent problems in the perspective of the totality of the Indian civilization. Urgent anthropological research may be directed towards fully documenting the traditional core of the civilization in terms of significant contemporary social and cultural forms. This approach does not ignore the primitive strata, but only views the latter in the context of the dominant core of the civilization.

Here, again, the choice of problems may be guided by emphasis on either of the following concerns:

(a) Study of forms and processes which are rapidly changing.
(b) Phasing of research in such a way that certain programmes are first systematically completed on an urgent basis so that the next stages of research may be taken up on the basis of sound ground work.

Sinha suggests that the primary emphasis should be on the second approach while paying sufficient attention to the rapidly changing groups and traits. He points out the following areas of research:

(a) Studies on social and cultural economy
(b) Studies on ethnic groups
(c) Studies on local communities
(d) Studies on regional and all-India networks and centres
(e) Studies on organization of specialists

### *(a) Studies on Social and Cultural Economy*

Assuming that we know something about the varied social and cultural organizations of agriculture through the village studies since 1950, very little work has been done in the fields of social and cultural economy of the artisans, fisherfolk, nomads and traders.

### *(b) Studies on Ethnic Groups*

The socio-cultural field of India may also be conceived as clusters of several categories of ethnic groups living in villages and towns: tribes, Hindu castes, religious minorities etc. There is a need to conduct studies on a broad regional or all-India perspective. Dumont's study of the *Pramalai Kallar* (1957), Pradhan's work on the *Jat* (1966), and the earlier monographs on *Mahar* (Robertson, 1938), the *Chamar* (Briggs, 1920), and the *Dom* (Briggs, 1953) are exceptions. Therefore, all-India studies may be taken up on a few selected categories of castes: Brahmins, Rajputs, Kayasthas, some untouchable castes, selected artisan castes, traders (spice vendors and bullion merchants) and fisher folk. It would be worthwhile to study the Moslems in different regions of India as a special project. Similarly, a study of the Jains may also be taken up.

### *(c) Studies on Local Communities*

Although we have several anthropological studies on village communities since 1950, there is a need to study urban communities, specially the relatively ancient towns of various functional categories located in different cultural regions of India. This would provide us an understanding of the traditional urban base of the Indian civilization.

### *(d) Studies of Regional and All-India Networks and Centres*

It is known that apart from ethnic groups, villages and towns, social and cultural forms are stabilized in terms of wide regions such as former zamindaries and feudatory states, dialects and language areas and all-India networks of *maths* and sects, etc. Therefore, it is essential to do studies on zamindaries and feudatory states, the regional pattern of inter-group interaction, stratification and the regional synthesis of styles of life (Sinha, S.C., 1962).

### *(e) Studies on Organization of Specialists*

Any civilization has its own mode of organizing specialists who live in urban as well as rural centres. It is known that the ancient pattern of learning Sanskrit as well as many of the higher arts, such as classical music, dance, painting and sculpture, have undergone considerable change due to competition with emergent new forms and cultural demands in the society and also due to the decline of traditional patronage. Therefore, studies may be taken up on a few important centres of traditional Sanskrit learning in different regions of India and also study of the traditional, colleges or associations and their roles in giving judgments on social norms. The mode of transmission of styles among some of the important schools (*gharanas*) of classical music and dance may also be taken up.

## Surajit Sinha's Framework Summarized

### *Background*

1. Studies in social and cultural anthropology
2. Interests in pattern of Indian civilization and changes in tribal India

### *Aim*

To analyse tribal transformation in central India and the structure of Indian civilization.

### *Assumption*

Tribes are integrated with the traditional civilization of India.

### *Concepts*

1. Tribe 2. Caste 3. Peasant

### *Methodology*

Folk-urban continuum

### *Typology*

1. Field work
2. Ecological and socio-cultural isolation

### *Issues*

Different aspects of Indian society, namely,

1. Tribe-caste and tribe peasant continuum.
2. Levels of economic initiatives, and ethnic groups.
3. Tribal movement
4. Sociology of religion.
5. Field studies on the people of India.

## Select Bibliography

Briggs, W. (1920), *The Chamars*, London: Oxford University Press.

— (1953), *The Doms and their Relations*, Mysore.

Cohn, Bernard S. (2000), *India: The Social Anthropology of a Civilization*, New Delhi Oxford University press.

Dumont, L. (1957), *Une Sous-Caste de L'Inde du Sind: Organization sociale et religion des pramalai Kaller*, Paris.

Madhurima (2003), *Surajit Sinha*, Panjab University, Chandigarh.

Mahapatra, L.K. (1968), "Social Movements among Tribes in Eastern India with Special Reference to Orissa", *Socilogus*, New Series, Vol. 18, No. 1, pp. 46–63.

Pradhan, M.C. (1966), *The Political System of the Jats of Northern India*, Calcutta.

Robertson, A. (1938), *The Mahar Folk: A Study of the Untouchables in Maharashtra,* Calcutta.

Roy, S. (1970), *Anthropologist* in India, Calcutta: Indian Anthropological Association.

Singh, K. Suresh (1972), *The Tribal Situation in India*, Shimla: Indian Institute of Advanced Study.

Sinha, Surajit (ed.) (1978), *Field Studies on the People of India: Methods and Perspectives*, Calcutta: Indian Anthropological Society.

Sinha, Surajit, "Levels of Economic Initiative and Ethnic groups in Pargannah Barabhum", *Eastern Anthropologist*, 16 (2):65:74.

— (1957). "Tribal Cultures of Peninsular India as a Dimension of Little Tradition in the Study of Indian Civilization: A Preliminary Statement", *Man in India*, Vol.37, No.2.

— (1959). "Bhumji Kshatriya Social Movement in South Manbhum", *Bulletin, Department of Anthropology*, Government of India, Vol.8, No. 2, pp. 9–32.

— (1962) "State Formation and Rajput Myth in Tribal Central India", *Man in India*, Vol. 42, No. 1.

— (1965), "Tribe-Caste and Tribe-Peasant Continuum in Central India", *Man in India*, Vol. 45, No. 1, pp. 35–80.

— (1968), "Tribal Solidarity Movements: General Cultural Anthropology and Related Discipline", *Anthropological Survey of India*, Calcutta.

— (1968), 'Tribal Solidarity and Messianic Movement Review Article', *Contribution to Indian Sociology, New Series*, (a) II, pp. 112–18.

— (1968), "Urgent Problems for Research in Social and Cultural Anthropology in India: Perspectives and Suggestions", *Sociological Bulletin*, Vol.XVII, September, No. 2.

— (1972), 'Tribal Solidarity Movement in India', in K. Suresh Singh (ed.), *Tribal Situation in India*, Shimla: Indian Institute of Advanced Study.

Sinha, S., Sen, J. and Panchbhai, S. (1969), "The Concept of *Diku* among the Tribes of Chotanagpur", *Man in India*, Vol. 49, No. 2, pp.121–38.

Sinha, S. and Bhattacharya, R. (1969), "*Bhadralok* and *Chhotolok* in Rural area of West Bengal", *Sociological Bulletin*, Vo. 18, No. 1, March.

# VIII

# Subaltern Perspective

The word 'subaltern' as given in the Oxford Dictionary stands for the general attribute of subordination, which is expressed in terms of a caste, class, age, gender, office or any other way. It includes the characteristics of defiance and submission. Thus, in literal sense, it conveys 'view from below', i.e., a view or understanding from the bottom of society or the flow of knowledge from below.

Populist discourse refers primarily to 'people' or masses (Laclau, 1979). The significance of ideology needs not be viewed merely in terms of dialectical tension between the people and the classes where conflicting situations provide meaning. It can also be viewed within the frame of composite and integral world view and life ways. In this frame one can observe the possible clash between self and society, transcendence and secularism, unity and diversity and between holistic understanding and individuality.

Obviously, such a proposition raises several uncomfortable questions for sociology as a discipline at the level of generality. In the history of ideas, academia has evaluated critically the relationship between ideas and social forces in terms of its forms and content. Specific societies are always important in making such evaluation. Ideas and ideologies are developed by people in society which are always associated with the issues of social existence and social forces. Knowledge is also construction of cognitive consciousness, which is creative and also delinks itself from socially-induced consciousness.

It is an important approach to the study of tribal peasant movement. This perspective seeks to restore a balance by highlighting the role of politics of the 'masses' as against the elite politics. The whole thrust of subaltern historiography is on reconstructing the other history, i.e., the history of people's politics and movement and their attempt to make their own history. This perspective emphasizes not to view peasant or tribal insurgents merely as 'object' of history but to treat them as makers of their own history – endowed with a transformative consciousness of their own. The important proponents of this perspective in India are David Hardiman, B.R. Ambedkar, Ranajit Guha, Kapil Kumar and others.

These subalternists claim to have unfolded the incapacity of nationalist and elitist historiography to incorporate the voices of the weak into the project of history re-writing. Subalternists focused their attention on the circle of elite politics and have emphasized the insurrectionary activities and potential of the 'subaltern' classes (artisans, poor peasants, landless labourers, tribals etc.) to make these classes possessed self-conscious and coherent conception of resistance that was directed against rich peasants, urban traders or the colonial revenue administrators.

# 19

# B.R. Ambedkar

Dr Bhimrao Ramji Ambedkar was born on 14th April, 1891 in a small town at Mhow Cantt near Indore in Mahar caste, which is known as untouchable caste in Maharashtra. He died on 6th December, 1956. His name was Bhim Sakpal, during childhood. His father was Ramji Sakpal, who was the follower of Saint Kabir. Therefore, he never believed in caste. He adopted Buddha religion along with 5 lakh people in a historical congregation on 14th October, 1956 at Nagpur.

After doing High School from Satara (Maharashtra) in 1907, Ambedkar got admission in Elphinstone College, Bombay. He was given 'Gayakwad scholarship' by Maharaja Gayakwad of Baroda for his study in college and with this scholarship itself, he got admission in Columbia University, USA and did his M.A. from there in 1915. He was the first Indian among untouchables who went abroad for higher education. He got PhD in 1917 from Columbia. In 1916, after submission of his PhD thesis, he went to London for the study of law and also took admission in London School of Economics and Political Science for the study of economics. In 1921, he got the degree of Master of Science and also PhD on his thesis entitled, "The Problem of the Rupee" from London University. Simultaneously, he did Bar at Law.

In 1923, Ambedkar started his law practice and also devoted himself for the upliftment of Dalits (depressed class) and poor. In 1930, he became the president of the All India Depressed Class Association. In 1936, he formed an Independent Labour Party, which later on turned into All India Scheduled Castes Federation. On 7th August, 1942, Ambedkar became the member of the Council for Governor General. In his chairmanship, the Constitution of India was drafted. On 3rd August, 1949, he took the charge of the Law Minister in the Government of India. In 1955, he formed Bharatiya Buddha Mahasabha. Ambedkar always felt that the depressed class has no honour in the Hindu religion which also reflects in his writings and actions.

## Writings of Ambedkar

1. *The Untouchables, Who are they?*
2. *Who were the Shudra?*
3. *States and Minorities*
4. *Emancipation of the Untouchables*
5. *Annihilation of Caste*

## Concept of Dalit

Generally, the word Dalit includes those who are designated in administrative parlance as Scheduled Castes (SCs), Scheduled Tribes (STs) and Other Backward Classes (OBCs). However, in common political discourse, the term Dalit is so far mainly referred to Scheduled Castes. The term 'Scheduled Caste' was used for the first time by the British in Government of India Act, 1935. Prior to this, the untouchable castes were known as depressed classes in public discourse. Mahatma Gandhi gave them the name *Harijan* – man of God. Gandhi himself did not coin the name. He borrowed the name from a Bhakti saint of the 17th century – Narsimh Mehta.

Traditionally, according to the Hindu code of conduct, the untouchables were placed at the bottom of hierarchy and had different names in different parts of the country. They were called

Shudras, Atishudras, Chandals, Antyajas, Pariahas, Dheds, Panchamas, Avarnas, Namashudras, Asprusthas, etc. The word *dalit* is a common usage in Marathi, Hindi, Gujarati and many other Indian languages, meaning the poor and oppressed persons. Shah (2001) views: "*Dalit* includes all the oppressed and exploited sections of society. It does not confine itself merely to economic exploitation in terms of appropriation of surplus. It also relates to the suppression of culture – way of life and value system – and more importantly the denial of dignity. It has essentially emerged as a political category. For some, it connotes an ideology for fundamental change in the social structure and relationships." The word *dalit* indicates struggle for an egalitarian order (Zelliot, 2001: 232).

Dalit is a by-product of the Ambedkar movement and indicates a political and social awareness. Ambedkar adopted a different approach and philosophy for the emancipation of Scheduled Castes. He wanted to liberate the Dalits by building an egalitarian social order which he believed was not possible within the fold of Hinduism whose very structures were hierarchical which relegated the Dalits to the bottom. He asserted that the Dalits should come forward and assert for their own cause. He gave them a mantra – educate, organize and agitate.

## Dalit Liberation: Subaltern Approach

With the advent of Ambedkar into the Indian political arena during 1920s, the issue of social reforms achieved a new dimension. He was of the opinion that until and unless the downtrodden themselves came forward to fight their battle, no one else could alleviate their grievances. No one else could know better than them about their own state of affairs. Ambedkar impressed upon the people to understand their own affairs themselves. Self-awakening, he believed, could provide them necessary strength to fight against evils in society. "Ambedkar (started) exercising the spirit of despair from the minds of dumb millions who had been forced to live the lives of sub-human beings. Here was a liberator preaching them the grand universal law that liberty is neither received as a gift; it has to be fought for. Self-elevation is not achieved by the blessing of others but only by one's own struggle and deed. Those inert dormant masses lacked courage and needed a vision and a mission. Ambedkar was aspiring them to do battle for their human rights. He was driving them to action by acting himself.... Ambedkar was displaying energy by his own action; arousing their faith by showing faith" (Keer, 1971).

Ambedkar realized that caste and Brahminic Hinduism reinforce each other and discriminate against the downtrodden sections of the society. He traced the genesis of the oppressive nature of the caste-dominated Indian society to the 'sacred' *Shastras* of the Hindus who guarded them so closely that if any one except them read or hear them he would commit any act of sacrilege. *Manusmriti* sanctioned severest punishment for such a sacrilegious act. According to Ambedkar, the *Vedas, Smritis* and *Shastras* were all instruments of torture used by Hinduism against the untouchables (Lobo, 2001). In fact, it was Ambedkar's subaltern perspective, which pierced through the *Shastras* to reveal their true face. He emphasized in his *Annihilation of Caste* that the *Smritis* and *Shastras* were not the embodiment of religion but a system of rules to deprive the untouchables even of their basic needs and deny them equal status in the society. Therefore, he said that there is no hesitation in saying that such a religion must be destroyed and there is nothing irreligious in working for the destruction of such a religion that discriminate against its own people whom it bracketed as untouchables.

An another aspect of Ambedkar's subaltern approach for the emancipation of Dalits and their empowerment was his distinct formulation of Indian nationalism in opposition to the dominant discourse of Hindu nationalism as represented by Raja Rammohan Roy, B.G. Tilak, Mahatma Gandhi and Jawaharlal Nehru. His conception of nationalism articulated and synthesized the national perceptions and aspirations of the downtrodden. Ambedkar's alternative form of nationalism, popularly known as 'Dalit-Bahujan Samaj', also incorporated the subaltern philosophy of Jyotirao Phule and Periyar E.V. Ramaswami Naicker. It constructed an anti-Hindu and anti-Brahminical discourse of Indian nationalism. It aimed at establishing a casteless and classless society where no one would be discriminated on the basis of birth and occupation.

Within the Dalit-Bahujan framework of Indian nationalism, Ambedkar built up a critique of pre-colonial Brahamanism and its inegalitarian social set-up based on low and high dichotomy of graded caste system. This system of inegalitarianism led to the process of exploitation by the unproductive Brahminical castes of the various productive castes. Thus, Ambedkar provided a subaltern perspective to see clearly the chameleon of Indian castes-ridden social set deceptively appearing in crimson colours and the ways to guard the interests of the Dalits.

## Analysis of the Writings of Ambedkar

Rodrigues (2002) made an attempt to highlight the best of Ambedkar's writings, reflecting the depth and range of his life's work, his intellectual incisiveness, and his realistic assessment of the social and political issues. We find that the analysis given by Rodrigues is very useful for the understanding of Ambedkar's writings. Therefore, we are describing here the abridged version of the Rodrigues' analysis on the following issues as reflected in Ambedkar's writings.

### *Exploration of Concepts*

Ambedkar found the need to reflect upon a wide range of concepts either to substantially explore them, decipher their different determinations, or to chisel and fine tune them by removing the dross. He adopted different approaches to present them, sometimes in the light of historical developments and at other times, in view of contentions. There are times when he attempted to extrapolate them from a mass of data. Occasionally, he appropriated a concept from a scholar and suggested certain innovations, or drew on his or her authority to reinforce certain dimensions of a concept at hand. There are certain concepts that he radically overhauls and as, for instance, the concept of 'Kamma'.[1] Sometimes, the determination of a concept is brought out by contrasting it with kindered concepts[2] such as between religion, *dhamma* and *sadhamma*. Dealing with different types of concepts, he is much more at home with concepts that are less abstruse and closer to experience, lending themselves to actual practice and illustration by example.

With his focus on concepts and arguments, Ambedkar contributed to building not merely a framework for social sciences in India but also the basis of healthy public debate.

### *Methodology*

Ambedkar undertook different types of studies, some involving the collection of sizeable data and the other processing such as the election studies of 1937 and 1945, focusing on the constituencies reserved for Scheduled Castes.[3] He undertook several case studies, often to drive home a point better.[4] There are studies where he attempted to locate the major changes in policy or issues over a period by dividing the period into appropriate stages. These projects required resort to documents and archives for necessary data, such as doctoral studies of Ambedkar, which drew not merely from official documents but also from archival data. In them, there are the standard references to the manuscripts and texts. There are studies such as *Who were the Shudras?*[5], exegetical in nature, which delve into texts but propose an alternative thesis because the existing explanations of these texts do not account for certain known details or passages.[6] Studies, such as *The Untouchables*, resort to the method of constructing a distinctive thesis centred on a characteristic feature in a determinate group, existing solely in that group and universally shared by it. Ambedkar also dwelt a great deal on interpretation and on the criteria appropriate for it.[7] He argued that Gandhi's interpretation of Hinduism did not stand up to the criteria of interpretation, Further, he felt that interpretations which do not take popularly held beliefs and strong evaluations into account, do not materially affect the situation studied.

### *Ideological*

The ideas and ideals of John Dewey, Edwin R.A. Seligman, the Fabians and the British Idealists had a deep impact on Ambedkar. He described himself as a 'progressive radical'[8] and occasionally as a 'progressive conservative,'[9] the qualification, 'progressive', being generally present, distinguishing himself from the liberals and the communists depending on the case. He saw the Directive Principles of State Policy of the Indian Constitution as upholding economic democracy. His notion of liberty was avowedly that of the T.H. Green kind.[10] Although he talked of equality before law and considered it as a major contribution of the British rule in India, he was not satisfied with this notion and advanced stronger notions such as equality of consideration, equality of respect, and equality of dignity. He was sensitive to the notion of respect, and the notion of community was central in his consideration. The demand for 'fraternity' in the French Revolution was seen by him as a call for 'community'. The Buddha, he argued, strove for building communities while Brahminism attempted to fragment them.

At the same time, Ambedkar recognized the critical role of the state, the legacies of Columbia University, London School of Economics and the colonial state in India being in consonance with such recognition. He strongly defended a developmental and ameliorative, and consequently an interventionist approach, as against the Gandhians and the Liberals. The state was invested with a pivotal role in the economy. But, whenever such pivotal role for the state is alluded to, it is based on the premise of a regime of rights that suggested the reasons and limits of interventions. He was deeply suspicious of embedded identities asserting themselves in the name of ethnic, linguistic and cultural claims, relating such assertions to the problem of majorities and minorities. When identity assertions took place, he felt, the minorities are likely to be the victims. He qualified majoritarianism with strong grids of the rule of law, special privileges to minorities, and the existence of a civil society which could nurture democracy as a civic virtue. His opinion that politics and institutions deeply affect the question of representation, found expression in his suggestion before the Simon Commission, that if adult franchise was introduced, he would favour a joint electorate with reservation for depressed classes and if limited franchise was continued he would demand a separate electorate.

One of the Ambedkar's most important arguments against Hinduism was that caste and untouchability did not let Hindus act as a community. There is an emphasis on moral order. He rarely gave a deductive picture of religions but went into the sociological moorings that threw up a diversity of beliefs and practices. At the same time, he admitted that a commonly held religious belief has an impact on socially differentiated constituencies. He found a lot of doctrinal cleavages within Hinduism. He had no great fascination for *bhakti* with which he was nourished in his childhood, castigating the *bhakti* saints for failing to attract the *Shastras*, which provided the normative and sacred grids for sustaining and justifying unjust social institutions.

Ambedkar showed an extraordinary interest in Marxism, particularly in the 1950s. All his major writings during this period, viz., *Buddha and the Future of his Religion*, *The Buddha and his Dhamma* and *Buddha and Karl Marx*, refer to Marx as the central figure. He identified certain crucial areas on which he agreed with Karl Marx: the task of philosophy is to transform the world; there is conflict between class and class; private ownership of property begets sorrow and exploitation; and good society requires that private property be collectivized. He found that on all these four issues Buddha is in agreement with Marx. He, however, rejected the inevitability of socialism, the economic interpretation of history, the thesis on the pauperization of the proletariat, dictatorship of the proletariat, withering away of the state and the strategy of violence as a means of seize power. He felt that the Buddhism, which called for self-control and a moral foundation for society, could provide the missing dimensions for a socialist project and for the purpose, called for a dialogue between Marxism and Buddhism. Therefore, while liberal and modernist alliances of Buddhism were taking place elsewhere, Ambedkar wanted to relocate Buddhism in the trajectory of Marxism and vice versa.

### Religion

A large part of Ambedkar's writings had a direct bearing on Hinduism, most of which remained unpublished and in the initial draft form during his lifetime. In these studies, which he undertook mainly from the second half of the 1940s, Ambedkar argued that Buddhism, which attempted to found society on the basis of reason and morality, was a major revolution, both social and ideological, against the degeneration of the Aryan society. It condemned the *varna* system and gave hope to the poor, the exploited and the women. It rallied against sacrifices, priestcraft and superstition. The *Buddhist Sangha* became the platform for the movement towards empowering and ennobling the common man. However, Brahminism struck back against the revolution through the counter-revolution launched by *Pushyamitra.* Here, Ambedkar deployed a specific terminology employed to explain mainstream European transitions of nineteenth and twentieth centuries and he felt that the corresponding explanation was appropriate for India too, although the periods in question were wide apart.

For Ambedkar, literature, which legitimized and instituted the counter-revolution, was *Smriti* literature in general and *Manusmriti* in particular. It gave birth to the principle of assigning human beings to social roles, reduced the Shudra to servitude and condemned women to ignominy. On the contrary, the governing principle during the Vedic period for assigning social roles was *varna*, the principle of worth, which allowed wide mobility although it ordered society hierarchically. The trajectory of social transformation that Ambedkar traced was divided into the following phases: the Vedic society and its degeneration into Aryan society; the rise of Buddhism and the social and moral transformation it set into motion; and finally, the counter-revolution and the rise of Brahminism.

Ambedkar found that the Hindu scriptures do not lend themselves to a unified and coherent understanding. There are strong contentions built into them within and across trends and traditions. There are cleavages within the *Vedas*; the *Upanishadic* thought is in contentions with the *Vedic* thought; *Smriti* literature argues against *Sruti* literature; sometimes the Vedas are considered lower than the *Shastras;* gods are pitted against one another; and *tantra* is tallied against *Smriti* literature. The icons of Hinduism such as Rama and Krishna have little to recommend them, in that there is nothing morally elevating about them. Further, Ambedkar generally tended to suggest a later date to the central texts of Hinduism as compared to other Indian scholars.

He did not comment much on the *Upanishads*, and compared to the rest of the Hindu literature, is relatively favourably disposed towards them. As late as 1936, Ambedkar felt that Hinduism could be redrafted on the basis of *Upanishadic* thought. For Ambedkar, the *Gita* is a post-Buddhist text. It is primarily a defence of *karma-kanda*, i.e., religious acts and observance, by removing the excrescence which was grown over it. The *Gita* advances a set of philosophical arguments to save Brahminism in the context of the rise of Buddhism and the inability of the former to defend itself by a mere appeal to the rituals and practices of the *Vedas*. He finds that the *Gita* defends the position of Jaimini's *Mimamsa* against Badarayan's *Brahmasutras*.

Ambedkar developed a new interpretation of Buddhism which made commentators label it "Ambedkar's Buddhism". His magnum opus, *The Buddha and His Dhamma* highlights the central issues that concerned him throughout his life and demarcates his view sharply from that of his adversaries. The work contains the central teachings of the Buddha along with a commentary built into it. The commentary transposes the Buddha's teachings to the present and suggests its contemporary relevance with respect to the problems that confront humanity. He saw Buddhism as an ideology that engages with the world, privileging the poor and exploited. Ambedkar repeatedly asserted that Buddha has a social message. Further, he constructed Buddhism in opposition to Hinduism arguing that if there are some traces of Hinduism in Buddhism, they could be attributed to Brahminical interpolations. Ambedkar also upheld the superiority of Buddhism over other religions, particularly Islam and Christianity.

## Caste

Ambedkar's understanding of caste and the caste system underwent certain significant changes over the period of his writings. Initially, he had argued that the characteristic of caste was endogamy, superimposed by exogamy in a shared cultural ambience. He suggested that evils such as *sati*, child marriage and prohibition on widow remarriage were the outcome of caste. Further, if a caste closed its boundaries, other castes were also forced to follow the suit. The Brahmins closing themselves socially first gave rise to the system of castes. Ambedkar continued to emphasize the endogamous characteristic of caste but roped in other features such as the division of labour, absence of inter-dinning and the principle of birth, which he had earlier largely absorbed within endogamy. He also found that the caste name is an important feature, which keeps inequality in the normative anchor of the caste system. Graded inequality restricts the reach of equality to members of the caste at the most. Ambedkar thought that caste is an essential feature of the Hindu religion. Although a few reformers may have denounced it, for the vast majority of Hindus breaking the codes of caste in a clear violation of deeply held religious beliefs. He found Gandhi subscribing to caste initially and later opposing it but upholding *varna* instead. Gandhi's conception of *varna* is the same as that of caste, that is, assigning social agents on the basis of birth, rather than worth. It led to upholding graded inequality and the denial of freedom and equality, social relations that cannot beget community bonds. The solution that Ambedkar proposed was the annihilation of caste. He suggested inter-caste marriage and inter-dinning for the purpose although the latter by itself is too weak to forge any enduring bonds. Further, he felt that hereditary priesthood should go and it should remain open to all the co-religionists endowed with appropriate qualifications as certified by the state. Ambedkar, however, felt that these suggestions would not be acceptable to Hindus. After the early 1930s he gave up any hope of reforming Hinduism except for a belief while with the Hindu Code Bill which was, in a way, the continuation of the agenda he had set for himself in the 1920s.

## *Untouchability*

Ambedkar's engagement with untouchability, as a researcher, intellectual and activist, is much more nuanced, hesitant but intimate as compared to his viewpoint on caste, where he is prepared to offer stronger judgements and proffer solutions. However, with untouchability, there is often a failure of words. Grief is merged with anger. He often exclaims how an institution of this kind has been tolerated and even defended. He evinces deep suspicions about the bona fides of others in terms of their engagement with it. He distinguished the institution of untouchability from that of caste, though the former is reinforced by the latter, and Brahminism constituted the enemy of both. He felt that it was difficult for outsiders to understand the phenomena. He thought human sympathy would be forthcoming towards alleviating the plight of the untouchables, but at the same time anticipated hurdles to be crossed – hurdles made of age-old prejudices, interests, religious retribution, the burden of the social pyramid above and the feeble resources that the untouchables could muster. He found that the colonial administration did little to ameliorate the lot of the untouchables. He argued that the track-record of Islam and Christianity, in this regard, is not praiseworthy either, although they may not subscribe to untouchability as integral to their religious beliefs.

Ambedkar felt that untouchables have to fight their own battle and if others are concerned about them, then, such a concern has to be expressed in helping them to fight rather than prescribing solutions to them. He discussed attempts to deny the existence of untouchables and to reduce the proportion of their population in order to deny them adequate political presence. He resorted to comparison with what he called the parallel cases, such as the treatment meted out to slaves and Jews but found the lot of the untouchables worse than their's. He argued that in spite of differences and cleavages, all untouchables share common disadvantages and treatment from caste Hindus: they live in ghettos; they were universally despised and kept outside the fold. He maintained a graphic account of the course of the movement of the untouchables, although this was much more specific about the movement in the Bombay Presidency. He threw scorn at the Gandhian attempt to remove untouchability and termed it as a mere façade aimed at buying over the untouchables with kindness. He presented voluminous empirical data to defend such a thesis, and suggested his own strategies to confront untouchability, warning untouchables not to fall into the trap of Gandhism. He exhorted them to fight for political power. Although he did not find the lot of untouchables better among Christians and Muslims, he felt that they had a better option as they did not subscribe to untouchability as a religious tenet. Ambedkar was also deeply sensitive to insinuations offered by others to co-opt untouchables within their political ambit.

Ambedkar rarely went into the question of the origin of untouchability in history. He rebutted the suggestion that race has anything to do with it, and did not subscribe to the position that caste has its basis in race either. However, in one instance, he proposed a very imaginative thesis that untouchables were broken men living on the outskirts of village communities who, due to their refusal to give up Buddhism and beef-eating, came to be condemned as untouchables. He did not repeat this thesis in any central way later to the fold either. It has to be noted that the thesis was proposed when Ambedkar was fighting for the recognition that untouchables were a separate element in India and, therefore, should be constitutionally evolved with appropriate safeguards, while the colonial administration and Gandhian leadership were prepared to recognize only the Muslims and Sikhs as distinct communities.

### *Identity*

As in the case of the untouchables, Ambedkar attempted to construct a separate identity of *Shudras* as well and this too during the second half of the 1940s. He identified himself with the non-Brahmins and attempted to build a non-Aryan Naga identity ascribing to it the signal achievements of Indian civilization. He also proposed to write on the clash of the Aryans and the Nagas much more elaborately than he was to do. However, his exploration of the Naga identity remained quite thin.

We find in Ambedkar's works a great deal of discussions about primitive tribes and what were called 'criminal' tribes. He saw them basically as outside the pale of civilization and blamed Hinduism for confining them to such sub-human levels. He ridiculed the Hindus for applauding their attitude to such degradation in the name of toleration. Ambedkar, however, did not explore the tribal cultures and also not attempted to build a political bridgehead with them, although in terms of deprivation, he felt, the untouchables and these communities formed a common constituency. Ambedkar did recognize a myriad of other identities in India such as sub-castes, castes, groupings of castes such as touchables and untouchables, twice-born or 'regenerated' castes and the Shudras religious groups, regional identities and sometimes identities resulting from the mutual reinforcement of all these groups. Ambedkar acknowledged the presence of linguistic and cultural identities but he was deeply suspicious of them. It is not so much their productivity to cast themselves as a nationality that makes him apprehensive but their tendency to exclude minorities that do not share the dominant identity. He, however, considered the fact of identity seriously, going to the length of suggesting that he was a conservative but arguing that identity should be within the bounds of rule of law, the demands of development, justice and participation. For the same reasons the ideal solution for the problem of linguistic states is not "one language, one state" but "one state, one language".

Social reforms in India were increasingly fragmented into regional ambits by the first decade of the twentieth century becoming part of the emerging regional identities. Ambedkar refocused the reform question at the all-India level once again and, in a way, made Gandhi to accord priority to it in spite of the discomfiture of Jawaharlal Nehru and others. Ambedkar also took an active interest in the working class movement and sometimes occupied formal positions in the trade unions. He understood their concerns as had lived in a working class locality for over two decades. However, he felt that the Indian working class had not come to address the caste question. On the contrary, the division of labour in industrial establishments was based on caste relations and he pointed out that as long as the working class was fragmented into castes, their common bond would prove too fragile to wage determined struggles.

## *Economy*

Unlike in the domain of politics and religion, Ambedkar's intervention in relation to economic thought and issues was intermittent though persistent over a long period. For his Master's at Columbia University, Ambedkar wrote a lengthy dissertation, which he did not eventually submit. It was entitled as *Ancient Indian Commerce* and included three fascinating chapters, viz., "Commercial Relations of India with the Middle East',

'Commercial Relations of India in the Middle Ages', and 'India on the Eve of the Crown Government'. It projected India as a land, which has deep and varied ties with other countries based on the nature of its economy. He portrayed very vividly the exploitative nature of the Company's rule in India. In *The Administration and Finance of East India Company,* Ambedkar provided a lucid account of the organization of the East India Company, its sources of revenue and items of expenditure upto 1857. *The Evolution of Provincial Finance in British India* builds on Ranade's work on provinces and the centre in British India from 1833 to 1919. The arguments for centralization and decentralization almost echo our arguments in the present: with Ambedkar himself discretely subscribing to financial decentralization on the principle that power and responsibility should belong to that level which can make optimum use of it. Such an allocation, while making the states strong and viable, would contribute towards strong and effective central government as well, by taking away from it power and responsibility which it cannot exercise effectively. In his doctoral thesis at the London School of Economics entitled *The Problem of Rupee: Its Origin and its Solution*, Ambedkar favoured the gold standard rather than the silver standard that was introduced in India in 1835 or the gold exchange standard as proposed by scholars such as Professor Keynes. After these major forays into the domain of the economy, Ambedkar made only certain selective interventions in this area. His policy interventions in agriculture were basically four-fold: he demanded the abolition of intermediaries between the direct producer and the state as was manifest for instance in the 'Khoti' system, prevailing in the Konkan. He demanded an end to traditional obligations imposed on inferior public servants belonging to lowly castes and that they be replaced with contractual obligations. He suggested the nationalization of agriculture and distribution of all surplus land to the Scheduled Castes. In 1917, Ambedkar brought out a long article on 'Small Holdings in India and their Remedies', arguing for consolidation of holdings though he did not extend unqualified support to the then prevailing position for the enlargement of holdings. His position was: "To a farmer a holding is too small or too large for the other factors of production at his disposal necessary for carrying on the cultivation of his holding as an economic enterprise."

### *Colonialism and Nationalism*

Ambedkar's critique of colonialism ranges across a whole spectrum from the economy to the nature of the colonial discourse. In terms of the later, Ambedkar demanded that the terms of the discourse be altered. He had no defence to offer in favour of colonialism but he did not want power to go to those who would not promote partisan ends in the name of the people. Ambedkar's considered judgement was that colonialism benefited the untouchables least, except for the rule of law which it inaugurated, allowing some space for them. He insisted on a responsible and accountable government based upon adult franchise, and was one of the first top rung leaders in India to demand universal adult franchise early on in his submission before the Simon Commission, in the strongest possible terms.

However, Ambedkar remained wary of nationalism, particularly given the experience of the Second World War. He was primarily concerned with a regime of rights, based on justice and upholding democracy. In a way, he was forced to engage with nationalism seriously when the Muslim League made the demand for a separate Pakistan in 1940. With respect to nationalism Ambedkar placed a great deal of emphasis on the volitional factor. He felt that once large masses of people begin to believe that they are a nationality, then, their identity as a separate nation had to be faced. He blamed both the Congress and the Muslim League for precipitating this tendency. He, however, felt that different nationalities had often remained within a single state and have negotiated terms of associated living. National self-determination is not something inevitable, but the pros and cons of whether nationalities decide to live together in a single state or wish to go their own ways, have to be assessed. He felt that under certain conditions it might be better to be separated than to live in a united state.

Ambedkar did not take an active interest in international relations except in its broader ideological implications. But, where there were some issues that he felt were significant for the future of India. He located India's place firmly in Asia and in the cultural traditions infused with Buddhism. He saw a threat to India from the Communist bloc, particularly given the age-old strategic interests. He was deeply concerned with the occupation of Tibet by Communist China and the response of the Nehru government to this issue. His view regarding Jammu and Kashmir was that it comprised three regions: Kashmir, Jammu and Ladakh. He considered it appropriate to hand over Kashmir to Pakistan and to integrate the other two regions with India.

### *Constitutional Democracy*

The major area of Ambedkar's work was on constitutional democracy. He was adept at interpreting different constitutions of the world, particularly those that mattered insofar as they were committed to democracy, along with their constitutional developments. This becomes obvious if we note the references that he adduces to the different constitutions, in the debates of the Constituent Assembly. He was a key player in the constitutional developments of India from the mid-1920s and on certain issues such as Uniform Civil Code he was to anticipate some of the major issues that have been the topics of debate in India. Ambedkar evolved certain basic principles of constitutionalism for a complex polity like India but argued that ultimately their resilience would depend on constitutional ethics.

Ambedkar also dwelt on several substantive issues of law. In fact, we can understand the significance that law had in his scheme of things by recourse to his larger social and ideological understanding. He was deeply sensitive to the interface between the law on one hand, and customs and popular beliefs, on the other. He felt that law was definitely influenced by customs and popular beliefs but stressed that customs may defend parochial interests, but may not uphold fairness, and may be based on their usefulness for the dominant classes. They may not be in tune with the demands of time or in consonance with morality and reason. Ambedkar also admitted the possibility of customs having the upper hand over law when they begin to defend vested interests, but that with its emphasis on freedom and democracy, law could be placed in the service of the common good. On the other hand, customs, while promoting healthy pluralism, may give rise to a highly inegalitarian order. At the same time, he defers to pluralism, if it can uphold rights.

In all these qualifications, Ambedkar's contention is that the legal domain is an autonomous sphere. He also deployed a complex understanding of rights to situate the domain of law. He distinguished the realm of constitutional law from the acts of legislature, but acknowledged that popular aspirations and the democratic mandate was the common ground for both. At the same time, it is law which determines what are popular and democratic aspirations and what constitute the relevant categories, given the existence of domain of rights. The constructionist role of the state, confronted with long-drawn and irreconcilable disputes, is so prominent in Ambedkar's writing that quite often he avoids substantive definitions and resorts to the legal fiction that "so and so is that was specified by law". He did not reconcile the tension between democracy and law and in his exposition, the domain of reason and morals are often in contention with that of law. Ideally, of course, he envisaged a democracy informed by law and a law characterized by sensitivity to democracy. At the same time, he looked to a system of law which upheld reason and morality, though he saw reason and morality as far too feeble to ensure social bonds without the authoritative dictates expressed in law. Religion, according to him, could play a major role in lightening the task of law. Ambedkar's views on constitutional democracy were reflected in his relations with Gandhi and Nehru on the issues of untouchability and the Hindu Code Bill respectively.

### *Governance*

One of the issues that Ambedkar paid close attention to was power and governance. He thought that governance must reflect sociological reality as closely as possible lest those wielding power to their advantage suppress the excluded groups. Ambedkar spent a great deal of his time and energy in advancing proposals for the purpose stressing the need to respect justice and equity. While he was opposed to overrepresentation to Muslims as expressed in the constitutional reforms of 1909, he did not accept that minority representation should be exactly in proportion to its population.

His commitment to democracy as the mode of governance was unwavering but he argued that democracy needed to become a way of life. He developed some interesting arguments on why parliamentary democracy was the most suitable form of government for India and advocated feasible modes of representation and franchise. His writings dwell extensively on such monumental issues as the presidential versus parliamentary form of government, the relationship between the executive and legislature, the role of the judiciary and judicial review, constitutional bodies such as the Election Commission, the federal division of powers, states in a federation, the role of the Governor, the Constitution and the legislature, constitutional amendments, political parties, and public opinion.

One of the domains that Ambedkar was engaged in very closely was civil society in terms of its operative dimension. He basically saw it as the conscience-keeper of the political sphere, determining the course of governance in the long run. Civil society is the domain in which one has to struggle for human values. He viewed religion as an important institution of civil society, which included other institutions such as political parties, the press, educational institutions and unions and associations. It is a contentious terrain of agreement and disputations resulting in relatively stable zones of agreement. Religion can play a major role in deciding the nature and stability of such agreement. Ambedkar's loathing for violence as a mode of constituting governmental authority or to settle issues in civil society was to have far-reaching implications for constitutional democracy in India. However, he emphasized the value of transformative interventions, and it is in his own organization of associations and movements and educational institutions, his writings on the need for social transformations, and eventually his conversion to Buddhism, that Ambedkar's role can be seen.

Ambedkar was deeply alive to the fact that ideologies undergo mutation in their interaction with social cleavages. He felt that

Islam in India had not succeeded in eliminating caste cleavages but argued that since Islam does not subscribe to the caste ideology, the convert has access to larger spaces of the community which he would not otherwise have had. He engaged in more rigorous study of Christianity in India than of Islam. He rejected Gandhi's opposition to conversion but felt that, given its resources, Christianity should have attracted more converts but it had not due to its own inadequacies.

Ambedkar was ambivalent towards conversion as a strategy till he opted for Buddhism. This ambivalence was particularly true with respect to conversion to Islam and Christianity, though he dismissed the argument that most of the conversions were done for material gains. Even if it was so, it did not matter in the longer run and he cited many illustrations for the purpose. He did not agree that all religions are different paths to the divine and they are all equal. There are gradations in religions in terms of the basic values they uphold and conversions were attempts to reach out to these values.

### *Disadvantaged and Supportive Polity*

Ambedkar made two major contributions in terms of evolving a polity, which would extend special considerations to the disadvantaged. He was the first major theoretician in India who argued that consideration for the disadvantaged should be the constitutive basis of the state. He developed a complex set of criteria to determine disadvantaged and attempted to specify its various gradations. Untouchability was only one of the disadvantages, although one of the most degrading and poignant. Further, he concentrated on the socially engendered disadvantaged, but because he felt that most disadvantaged are engendered by dominant social relations that attempted to convert them into natural disadvantaged. He distinguished disadvantaged from difference – cultural, religious, ethnic, or linguistic – and approached these issues separately for the adoption of appropriate policy measures.

His second contribution was to develop a system of safeguards for the disadvantaged in general and the untouchables in particular, which could be enforceable, quantifiable and accountable – a system that he evolved from early on but found its shape at the time of his deputation before the Simon Commission. This system further evolved through the participation of the disadvantaged, particularly the depressed classes themselves. These safeguards were negotiated with the broader polity with the inevitable confrontations, such as Gandhi's fast unto death in 1932. A standardized system of safeguards at the all-India level came to be introduced during Ambedkar's tenure as labour member in the Viceroy's Council. The Indian polity has not contested the necessity or range of these policies, for SCs and STs, and segments of society which consider themselves as disadvantaged have resorted to this model to make their claims negotiable, proving the enduring appeal of the scheme that Ambedkar advanced.

### *Disadvantaged and Preferential Treatment*

There are diverse types of disadvantages that men and women suffer and a common yardstick cannot be applied for their amelioration. However, there are common principles on the basis of which ameliorative measures to handle disadvantages can be pursued. It is not enough that equal resources and opportunities are assigned to people. Therefore, the disadvantaged need to be extended certain preferences that result in giving a fair opportunity to them.

### *Concept of Exploitation*

For Ambedkar, economic exploitation was a major issue to contend against. It explains his life-long critical engagement with Marxism. However, he felt that there are other sources of exploitation and marginalization besides economic exploitation, which deprive people of those basic goods indispensable for the constitution of a confident self, a life of a mutual recognition and participation in collective affairs.

### *Reason, Rights and Identity*

Ambedkar argued that it was in modern era that human reason came into its own and extricated itself from bonding with myths, customs and religious ideologies. There has been a reversal of the relation between myths and traditions on one hand, and reason, on the other. He saw freedom, equality and fraternity as essential conditions for a good life and argued that they should be understood and pursued as one entity. It was only on their foundation that a comprehensive regime of rights could be built.

### *Privileging Buddhism*

While Ambedkar acknowledged the possibility of diverse religious and moral standpoints that were reasonable he did not see them as equally predisposed towards freedom, equality and fraternity. Buddhism alone cherished such goals comprehensively and offered a complementarity to freedom, equality and fraternity.

### *Pluralism and its Limits*

Ambedkar felt that a liberal democracy has a natural tilt towards the culture and way of life of the majority. It posits itself as the normal and the expected. If the political society is relatively homogeneous, such a tendency may not provoke deep resentment, but in societies which are culturally plural, it may spell doom for the identity of minorities. Therefore, it is necessary that proper safeguards be provided for the expression of these identities.

### *Constitutionalism and Rule of Law*

Ambedkar felt that to sustain rights, to let identities thrive as well as make them respect rights, to maintain an order favouring the disadvantaged and to facilitate a vibrant civil society, constitutional order expressed in the rule of law becomes imperative.

To conclude, it can be stated that both in his training and in his vision of life, Ambedkar was deeply aware of the larger dynamics of the world, its complexity and differential bearing on social groups, localities and nations. He was pragmatic in his approach although not in his concerns. The backward classes in India, while avowing the political legacy of Ambedkar, are yet to engage with the understanding that marked his political involvement while their counterparts will probably rest content in retaining him merely as a symbol.

Besides, given the size of dalits, low castes and disadvantaged in general, no political party can afford to ignore the electoral dividends that Ambedkar as an ally can bestow. For the state to sustain a modicum of hegemony Ambedkar has become an indispensable necessity today.

## Ambedkar's Framework Summarized

### *Background*

1. Educated in Satara and Bombay in Maharashtra (India), Columbia (USA) and London (UK), and training in economics and law.
2. Interest in the amelioration depressed classes.

### *Aim*

Dalit liberation

### *Assumption*

Ambedkar always felt that the depressed class has no honour in the Hindu religion which reflects in his writings and actions too.

### *Methodology*

1. Documents and also from archival data
2. Subaltern approach

### *Typology*

1. Hierarchical and inegalitarian structure
2. Dalitization of untouchables.

### *Issues*

Different aspects of Indian society, namely,

1. Untouchables
2. States and minorities
3. Annihilation of caste system

## Notes

1. BAWS, Vol. 11, p. 243 and pp. 329–44. 'Kamma' in Pali stands for 'Karma', meaning action, which is a central concept in Buddhism. Ambedkar argued that the Brahminical doctrine of 'Karma' suggests that birth and rebirth are the consequences of one's action. It upholds the caste system, undermines limits of human freedom and subscribes to permanence and eternity of soul. On the contrary, Buddha's conception of 'Kamma' upholds dissolution of existent beings and their reconstitution into new forms of life. The latter inherits the consequences of actions of previous life (see B.R. Ambedkar, *The Buddha and His Dhamma*, Bombay: Siddharth, 1974, pp. 245–47).
2. See BAWS, Vol. 11, pp. 227–325.
3. See BAWS, Vol. 9: Appendix XIV and XV, 'A critique of the proposals: Analysis of the Cabinet Mission for Indian Constitutional changes in so far as they affect the Scheduled Castes (Untouchables)', pp. 357–75 and 'Results of primary elections held in December', 1945, BAWS, Vol. 10, pp. 523–36.
4. See BAWS, Vol. 12, pp. 665–91.
5. See Preface *to Who were the Shudras*?, BAWS, Vol. 7, pp. 9–19.
6. Ibid.
7. See introduction, *The Buddha and His Dhamma*, BAWS, Vol. 11, pp. 225–26; and Vol. 1, pp. 86–96.
8. 'Constitution First Amendment Bill', BAWS, Vol. 15, p. 356.
9. BAWS, Vol. 14, p. 283.
10. See T.H. Green (1986), *Lecturers on the Principles of Political Obligation and Other Writings*, in P. Harria and J. Morrow (eds), Cambridge, Cambridge University Press.

## Select Bibliography

Ambedkar, B.R. (1916) (reprint in 1977), *Castes in India: Their Mechanism, Genesis and Development*, Jalandhar: Bheem Patrika Publications.

—— (1936) (reprint in 1995), *Annihilation of Caste*, Jalandhar: Bheem Patrika Publications.

—— (1946), *Who were Sudras?* Bombay: Thacker and Co.

—— (1948), *The Untouchables: Who were They and Why They became Untouchables?* New Delhi: Amrit Co.

Baxi, Upendra (1995), "Emancipation as Justice: Babasaheb Ambedkar's Legacy and Vision", in Upendra Baxi and Bhikhu Parikh (eds), *Crisis and Change in Contemporary India*, New Delhi: Sage.

Bharill, C. (1977), *Social and Political Ideology of B.R. Ambedkar*, Jaipur: Aalekh Publishers.

Gore, M.S. (1993), *The Social Context of an Ideology: Ambedkar's Political and Social Thought*, New Delhi: Sage.

Keer, Dhananjay (1971), *Ambedkar: Life and Mission*, Bombay: Popular Prakashan.

Kuber, W.N. (1973), *B.R. Ambedkar: A Critical Study*, New Delhi: People's Publishing House.

Lobo, Lancy (2001), "Visions, Illusions and Dilemmas of Dalits Christians in India", in Ghanshyam Shah (ed.), *Dalit Identity and Politics*, New Delhi: Sage Publications.

Omvedt, Gail (1994), *Dalit and the Democratic Revolution: Dr. Ambedkar and the Dalit Movements in Colonial India*, New Delhi: Sage.

Roderigues, Valerian (2002), *The Essential Writings of B.R. Ambedkar*, New Delhi: Oxford University Press.

Shah, Ghanshyam (ed.)(2001), *Dalit Identity and Politics*, New Delhi: Sage Publications.

Zelliot, Eleanor (2001), *From Untouchables to Dalits: Essays on Ambedkar's Movement*, Delhi: Manohar.

# 20

# Ranajit Guha

Ranajit Guha, perhaps the most influential figure in postcolonial and subaltern studies, is also the founding editor of *Subaltern Studies*. He taught history for many years at the University of Sussex, England and also served as Professor of History, Research School of Pacific Studies, Australian National University, Canberra. Guha's works have deeply influenced not only the writing of subcontinental history but also historical investigations elsewhere, as well as cultural studies, literary theories, and social analyses across the world.

## Methodology

Guha used subaltern historiography as a method for his study of peasant insurgency.

## Writings

Guha's important writings are as follows:

1. *A Rule of Property for Bengal: An Essay on the Idea of the Permanent Settlement* (1963)

2. *Elementary Aspects of Insurgency in Colonial India* (1983)
3. *Subaltern Studies* (edited volumes 1 to 10).

Guha focuses on the following aspects of the subaltern perspective:

1. Defining the subaltern perspective through subaltern studies.
2. How did subaltern studies get to be recognized so?
3. The idea of subaltern perspective.
4. The emerging subaltern perspective.
5. The inchoate quality associated with the subaltern perspective.
6. Peasant insurgency.

Guha tried to write the history of subaltern from the subaltern's perspective. Then and then alone would it be possible to notice the kind of role that the majority of the population, the silent majority if you wish, played in directing the courts of history. Inevitably, the issue is who was dominating whom and who revolted against the domination and in what kind of manner came to be central importance in these studies.

### *Defining the Subaltern Perspective through Subaltern Studies*

The word 'subaltern' usually meant a junior army officer in the vocabulary of Indians till the 1980s. At the best the meaning was extended to connote the alternate or subordinates. Then, Guha and a team of scholars linked with him presented their series of academic essays. These essays came out in book-length volumes, virtually each year between 1982 and 1984 and then with a reduced frequency were eagerly awaited by the younger scholars in the social sciences. The volumes were entitled as *Subaltern Studies*. Reading through the volumes one can make some sense of what the subaltern perspective stands for, what kind of research falls within the ambit of subaltern studies and what is out of it, yet, to provide a hard definition for it is impossible even after two decades of this perspective coming into existence it retains an inchoate quality.

The best can be said, even though such defining is unfair to the fair amount of insightful research that exists under the rubric, is that the subaltern perspective is that which is perceived through the various papers presented in the volumes entitled *Subaltern Studies*. Of these it can be said that there are two versions. The first, which exists from volume 1 to 5, when the focus was on the study of politics and rebellion. The other exists from volume 5 onwards where the interest in politics and rebellion seems to have waned and the focus has been shifted to constructing the articulation of subaltern culture and its varied relationship with colonial power, the hegemonic nature of dominant culture and resistance to it in various forms is the focus in the second version of the subaltern perspective.

Between volume 1 and 10 there were 76 published papers in *Subaltern Studies*. The most prolific contributors included Ranajit Guha, Partha Chatterjee (16 papers each); David Arnold, David Hardiman, Gyanendra Pandey (five papers each); and Dipesh Chakrabarty, Gautam Bhadra, Gayatri Chakravorty Spivak and Sahid Amin (more than one paper each). It was the writings of these people which seemed to set the tone for the subaltern paradigm though the fifth volume onwards there was a distinct shift of focus towards cultural studies and away from the discipline of history.

### How did subaltern studies get to be recognized so?

Subaltern studies got recognition because of two things. Very briefly, first and foremost, because they insisted upon it, and secondly, because others accepted it to be so. The sheer persistence with which the volumes of subaltern studies kept appearing, the impatience with which they dismissed the then ruling perspectives in history and the enthusiasm with which a whole lot of scholars waited for them, talked about them and rubbished them, resulted in the creation of what many believed was an entirely new perspective in the social sciences in India – the *subaltern perspective*. This was much in keeping with the kind of schema that Thomas Kuhn, the celebrated historian of science, in his book *The Structure of Scientific Revolutions*, had suggested in his discussion of how revolutions, major paradigm shifts, happen in science. This implied that there would be times when the normal paradigms for research would be broken, either because they had exhausted their explanatory potential or had simply lost the interest of the majority of researchers in them.

### The idea of subaltern perspective

The statement made by Guha in the first chapter of the *Subaltern Studies* (Volume 1) made some accusations. One, that the existing ways of investigating Indian history had ceased to be insightful, had become meaningless and left out of their ambit such large segments of Indian society that it was better that old way of doing history be given up altogether. At the same time, he suggested an alternative, which repeatedly insisted would keep in focus the role of the subaltern, the underdog, those who were the canon folder in the canons being fired in the history.

Moreover, to follow the schema offered by Robert Merton, those pursuing the new paradigm created for themselves the role of gatekeepers. In most interesting twist of intellectual fates this was done not by ousting the old gatekeepers from the discipline of history but by the device of demarcating new gates for the discipline and insisting that these gates led not merely to the study of history but to the society as a whole. The fact that the volumes of *Subaltern Studies* came out with a certain degree of regularity and constantly published high quality academic essays made for greater intellectual legitimacy of the entire intellectual enterprise.

At least in the early years those professing the subaltern perspective did not control access to academic institutions. But their sheer prolificacy was impressive. Six books and 27 articles were written in two decades, many of which were translated into Indian languages, was a very high rate of intellectual productivity. Till 1989 between them the subaltern collective had published 15 volumes on diverse themes of their interest with only one commonality between them: that all of them were illustrative of the subaltern perspective and were also rated highly as competent works of research. Little wonder that a significant number of unrelated scholars too began to insist that a new 'perspective' of doing research had emerged. If everyone said so that it had, then it had.

In its details, in the case of the subaltern perspective, the sheer popularity of the idea among a large number of scholars, even while the initial volumes of *Subaltern Studies* were published, was enough to allow observers to notice that an entirely new perspective had emerged. The chief indicator of the subaltern perspective having arrived, as it were, insofar as the discipline of history was concerned, was when one of its most virulent critics like Mirdula Mukherjee, in 1988, spent considerable effort in explaining that the subaltern perspective was merely so much old wine in a new bottle. It if were merely so, then there would have been little need for a senior historian to rubbish it thus and claim that she and others of her ilk had been sensitive to it even before the term had come into existence. By this time a large number of scholars, even those who were only marginally allied with the new perspective, began to pay homage to it by claiming some kind of kinship. It also helped that the new perspective, some believed, actually had some fresh explanatory potential.

### Emerging subaltern perspective

The initial statement about this perspective was laid down in the first chapter of *Subaltern Studies* (Volume 1). Authored by Guha, it was in the form of points, all of them addressed to historians, all of which simply said that the existing way of writing history had fully concentrated on the elite while being dismissive of the subalterns, the poor, the downtrodden etc. Guha insisted that mostly the writings of historians had focused on the Indian National Movement, and that too seen only from the perspective of the leaders of the movement. All else, he went on to impute, in the history of our society, was left either untouched or not examined enough or examined only as an adjunct of the mainstream of the national movement. What was needed, Guha argued, was a subaltern perspective wherein society could be studied from the point of view of the downtrodden, those who were the fodder in the cannon of history, as it were.

This is not to deny the analysis of some social scientists who have revealed sensitive concern for specific dimensions of problematic of Indian social reality. Scholarly traditions in history and in the ethnography of India have provided significant insights into the peasant and tribal movements. Subaltern historiography seeks to restore a balance by highlighting the role of the politics of the people as against elite politics played in Indian history (Dhanagare, 1993). The contributions made by masses in making society have gone unrecognized and unwritten due to their social placement and ignorance regarding means and mechanisms of speaking recognition (ibid.). Subaltern historiography treats 'people' (subalternity) as autonomous who are not dependent upon elite. The ideological element in the subaltern domain is not uniform in quality and density and at times sectional and sectorial interests have been pursued (Singhi, 1996). Guha has used ideology in subaltern studies as a schema of interpretation of the past in order to change the present world and that such a change involves a radical transformation of consciousness (Dhanagare, 1993: 132). Tribal or peasants insurgents have not to be seen as a merely 'objects' of inquiry but makers of their own history (Guha, 1983). The influence is obviously Marxist. Acceptance of Marxism, as an ideology, has been much easier for Indian sociologists for several reasons. Marxism provided a profound theoretical as well as ideological framework with its rigorous logical and neat framework for alternative society. It had both cognitive and emotive appeals for concerned intellectuals. The existence of abundant literature in the area helped the critique of western imperialism to find solace and shelter in the paradigm of Marxism.

The subaltern studies have immense possibility of projecting, constructing and analysing the people's lives, institutions, problems, movements, values and the processes of their formation, structuration and restructuration at local and regional levels. The meanings thus need not be viewed from Marxist perspective but from Indian historiographical and culturological perspectives. In fact, at theoretical and ideological levels, it can provide the basis for explanation of social existence of Indian people and the way people managed their lives. The Indian culturological perspective can be constructed at ideological, theoretical and empirical levels in terms of continuity and change through analysis of classical texts and folk-rural commonality of existence. The relationship between the two provides significant framework to understand the Indian social, cultural and personality systems, at local micro level and trans-regional macro level. It further provides a scheme to relate past with present, empirical with ideological, segmental with pluralism and mundane with transcendental.

The focus on peasants and workers movements by the subaltern studies reveals only one-dimensionality of cognitive framework, which could be constructed from sociology of people. Movement is a form of protest and assumes significance in the context of relationship of subordination, exploitation, suppression and organized efforts to protest against such a situation ideologically. However, people's lives are influenced by several ideologies, which operate through religion, social institutions, polity and cultural practices.

The role of ideologues in the form of local heroes, community leaders, revered individuals, and aesthetic and literary figures needs to be understood in the context of role of ideology, not in terms of its contents and ideas but also in terms of their influence on the lives of people in everyday life, in their existence itself.

### *The inchoate quality associated with the subaltern perspective*

The subaltern perspective will remain quite inchoate. Yet it became fashionable to have a 'subaltern perspective', even though it was not very clear as to what this particular perspective is, and how it differed in substance from the already existing practices of research and analysis in the social sciences. Just as earlier scholars who kept up with the times were almost invariably 'Marxist' or 'behaviourists' or what-have-you, so now were many 'subalternists', whatever that might mean. There were also a nagging doubt among some observers that belonging to this perspective, or opposing it, was often a matter of personal perspectives. Sumit Sarkar, for example, once part of this perspective, veered away and became a critic when literature and culture-based studies began to dominate. His discomfort was with the shift away from politics that the later essays in subaltern studies demonstrated. His charge that merely listing the contours of the culture of domination and subordination was not enough of a critique of existing hegemonic politics has never been met adequately by those professing to pursue the subaltern perspective. At the same time, the subalternists have not addressed themselves to the charge that their constant focus on cultural aspects and their effort to legitimize the culture of the subaltern allows a valorization of indigenous cultures under the presumption that whatever is indigenous is the best for the merely represent local forms of domination. But, such dilemmas have ceased to bother those publishing in subaltern studies for a long time now.

This new perspective seemed to get body as more and more research was done under its rubric. At the same time, within the social sciences the 'subaltern perspective' attracted a lot of criticism from the discipline of history, and also a considerable amount of admiration. Even its vocal critics like Mridula Mukherjee, a leading historian writing in the *Economic and Political Weekly*, were pressed to say that they themselves were sensitive to this perspective even though they did not use the word 'subaltern' to describe their concerns. Sociologists and anthropologists, watching from the sidelines the battles fought among historians, seemed to be somewhat bemused. The journal *Contributions to Indian Sociology* did carry reviews and review articles on subaltern studies but these articles did not go beyond identifying the insensitivity of the subaltern perspective to the formal institutional set-up of society. The bemusement of the sociologists and social anthropologists was substantially based in the recognition that many of the concerns being expressed in the subaltern perspective were already a standard part of the field studies done on the caste system and various village studies. By the 1990s, however, even the sociologists in India, usually not very vocal about their kinship with historians, began to incorporate the 'subaltern perspective' in their theoretical understandings. Some of them, like Amitav Ghosh, even published in *Subaltern Studies* thereby adding, some would say, a new kind of glamour. Could this be taken to be the point at which it might be said that the 'subaltern perspective' had 'arrived'?

### *Peasant insurgency*

The historiography of peasant insurgency in India has frequently been a record of the efforts of the colonial administration to deal with mass uprisings in the countryside. The colonialists tended to see insurgency as a crime or pathology, seldom regarding it as a struggle for social justice. In his study of *Elementary Aspects of Peasant Insurgency in Colonial India*, Guha (1983) seeks to correct this failure to understand the aims and motives of the insurgent. He adopts the peasant's viewpoint and examines "the peasant rebel's awareness of his own world and his will to change it". The study covers the period 1783–1900 and identifies some of the elementary aspects that characterized peasant rebel consciousness in this period.

The object of this work is to try and depict the struggle not as a series of specific encounters but in its general form. The elements of this form derive from the very long history of the peasant's subalternity and his striving to end it. If one looks carefully at the popular mobilizations accredited to nationalist and communist leaderships – at Rowlett Satyagraha and Quit India or at Tebhaga and Telengana, to take only a couple of instances respectively of each kind – one cannot help noticing the structural similarities between their articulation.

The book consists of eight chapters including introduction and epilogue. The main chapters are: Negation, Ambiguity, Modality, Solidarity, Transmission and Territoriality.

The study reflects a set of historical relations of power, namely, the relations of dominance and subordination, as these prevailed in village India under the British Raj until 1900. It has been said: "The history of all past society has consisted in the development of class antagonism that assumed different forms of different epochs. But whatever form they may have taken, one fact is common to all past ages, viz., the exploitation of on part of society by the other" (Guha, 1983: 12).

The antagonism is rooted deeply enough in the material and spiritual conditions of their existence to reduce the difference between elite and subaltern perceptions of a radical peasant movement to a difference between the terms of a binary pair. A rural uprising turns into a site for two rival cognitions to meet and define each other negativity.

It is clear in the light of the findings that Indian nationalism of the colonial period was not what elite historiography had made it be. On the contrary, it derived much of its striking power from a subaltern tradition going a long way back before the Mahatma's intervention in Indian politics towards the end of the First World

War or Nehru's discovery of the peasantry of his home province soon afterwards.

### Guha's Framework Summarized

#### *Background*

1. Educated and training in ancient history
2. Interests in subaltern studies

#### *Aim*

To examine the peasant rebel's awareness of his own world.

#### *Assumption*

Subaltern historiography seeks to restore a balance by highlighting the role of the politics of the people as against elite politics.

#### *Methodology*

1. Subaltern historiography
2. Ethnography
3. Common approach of studying history from the top to down

#### *Typology*

1. Customs
2. Records

#### *Issues*

Different aspects of Indian society, namely,

1. Subaltern studies
2. Peasant insurgency in India

## Select Bibliography

Dhanagare, D.N. (1993), *Themes and Perspectives in Indian Sociology*, Jaipur: Rawat Publications.

Guha, Ranajit (1963), *A Rule of Property for Bengal: An Essay on the Idea of the Permanent Settlement*, Paris.

— (1983), *Elementary Aspects of Insurgency in Colonial India*, Delhi: Oxford University Press.

Laclau, Ernesti (1979), *Politics and Ideology in Marxist Theory*, London: Verso Publications.

Singhi, N.K. (ed.) (1996), *Theory and Ideology in Indian Sociology*, Jaipur: Rawat Publications.

# 21

# David Hardiman

David Hardiman was born in Rawalpindi (Pakistan) in October 1947. He has taught at the University of Leicester, the School of Oriental and African Studies in London, the University of Newcastle upon Tyne, and the University of Oxford. Presently he is attached to the University of Warwick, UK. In 1980, he was a fellow of the Centre for Social Studies in Surat. In 1981, he was also visiting fellow of the Centre for Studies in Social Sciences, Calcutta. Hardiman is one of the many prolific writers who participated in the creation of the subaltern perspective. He is a founding member of the Subaltern Studies group. Noteworthy is the fact that since 1982 at least all his articles and books were illustrative of the practice of subaltern studies.

## Writings of Hardiman

1. *The Quit India Movement in Gujarat* (1980)
2. *Peasant Nationalists of Gujarat: Kheda District, 1917–1934* (1981)
3. *The Coming of Devi: Adivasi Assertion in Western India* (1987)
4. *Peasant Resistance in India: 1858–1914* (1992)

5. *Subaltern Studies VIII: Essays in Honour of Ranajit Guha* (1994)
6. *Feeding the Baniya: Peasants and Usurers in Western India* (1996)
7. *Gandhi in his Time and Ours* (2003)
8. *Histories for the Subordinated* ( 2006)
9. *Missionaries and their Medicine: A Christian Modernity for Tribal India* (2008)

Hardiman is a sociologically-sensitive historian, who participated in the creation of the subaltern perspective. As a historian, he specialises in the history of Modern India. Since the late 1960s, he has studied and written on South Asian History and during this period he has spent over a decade in all actually working in India. The main focus of his work has been on the colonial period in South Asian history, concentrating in particular on the effects of colonial rule on rural society, relationships of power at various levels, the Indian independence movement with a specific focus on the popular bases to Indian nationalism, and environmental and medical history.

In the late 1970s he became involved with a group of historians studying the social history of subordinate groups in South Asia. The Gramscian term 'subaltern' – meaning 'subordinate group' – was chosen to emphasise the centrality of relationships of domination and subordination in a society in which class divides had not developed as in the industrialized world.

He has carried out a detailed examination of the Indian nationalist movement at the local level in Gujarat – Gandhi's home region – bringing out the disjuncture between the aims and agendas of the Gandhian leadership and local peasant activists. He has examined the power-structures of rural society, carrying out for example a detailed study of the hegemonic controls exercised by usurers and the limits to that hegemony, as seen in particular in revolts. He has also studied a movement of assertion by adivasis (tribal people) against liquor dealers who had been granted a monopoly right of supply by the British and who had enriched themselves at the expense of the adivasis.

David Hardiman has also written a book on Gandhi and his legacy in India and the world. In this, he brings to the topic a deep knowledge of Gandhi's particular social milieu. His engagement with contemporary social issues while living in India has also been of crucial importance in assessing Gandhi's legacy in India.

From 1983 to 1989 he worked as a Research Fellow at the Centre for Social Studies, Surat in Gujarat, India. There was a strong emphasis there on the evaluation of government and NGO development projects, and, besides carrying on his historical research and writing, he became involved in a wide range of development-linked research projects.

In this chapter, we would discuss his following works:

1. Hardiman's Sociological Perspective of Subaltern
2. The Devi Movement in South Gujarat
3. Feeding the Baniya

## Hardiman's Sociological Perspective of Subaltern

In the course of this essay we shall have a glimpse into the subaltern perspective, varying and inchoate such as it is, with special emphasis on the writings of one of their more sociologically sensitive contributors, a historian called David Hardiman. Hardiman's interest in such a topic was stimulated by his participation in the subaltern studies project, which, under the inspiration of Ranajit Guha, has had as one of its chief objectives the study of relationships of domination and subordination in India. He was inspired also by the work of western Marxist historians, notably E.P Thompson on systems of moral economy, and Eugene Genovese and Elizabeth Fox-Genovese on the blend of ruthless exploitation with paternalism in the slave system of the American south. These influences, coupled with insights gained from the writings of Karl Marx, Antonio Gramsci, Michel Foucault,.Pierre Bourdieu and, in the context of western India D.D. Kosambi, Jairus Banaji and Frank Perlin, have provided some of the main foundations for his work.

### *Framework of the Subaltern Perspective*

The study of Indian society has been done by sociologists through various perspectives. Subaltern perspective is one of these perspectives. One of the exponents of this perspective is David Hardiman who has used it in his study *The Coming of Devi*. This is basically a movement among adivasis of western India to change their established way of life. Such movements, although, have been reported from almost all adivasi tracts of India over the past century, they have until now been relegated to the margin of modern Indian history.

One of the enduring secrets of the subaltern perspective is that it existed only as a broad framework. A detailed enquiry, such as undertaken by some of its critics, usually pointed out serious continuities with other kinds of coeval research and that the discontinuities, such as could be noticed, were rather minor and sometimes merely idiosyncratic as when Ranajit Guha insisted in his seminal book on peasant insurgency that one of the ways into the minds of the subaltern was to read the inverse meaning into the routine reports coming from the elite. Three kinds of problems were pointed out: One is that the term 'subaltern' was not adequately defined/identified. Two, the subaltern perspective had already been in use for a very long time. Three, the idea of subaltern was a relative concept; subaltern was always relative to something, or someone else. It referred to something that was 'below'. "Below what?" "Below that which was above." Such distinctions, even though they were not very strict, acquired meaning through the practice of subaltern studies. In this regard, one could take the studies done by Hardiman to be illustrative.

There was also a problem that the distinction between the subaltern and the elite was considerably a context dependent distinction. A little change, as Hardiman noticed in his study of the Devi movement in Gujarat, could place a tribal leader in the role of an exploiter rather than the one who is being exploited.

## The Devi Movement in South Gujarat

Hardiman tried to look at subaltern perspective from his study of the Devi movement in south Gujarat (Western Maharashtra region). He observes the mass movement in south Gujarat in early 20th century by the native masses and it was termed as 'Devi movement'. It was peaceful, led by tribals themselves, spread over a large region, involved a considerable number of people and focused on bringing social reform among the tribals. He noticed that this movement among the adivasis was virtually ignored by the contemporary government, the newspapers, the nationalists and subsequently the historians. There is no full-length monograph on such movements, he remarked, nor were they documented adequately. Insofar as the activities of the tribals were noticed by the nationalists, it was to remark that they were done under the auspices and influence of outsiders, e.g., Gandhi, in the case of Devi movement, or some social worker of tribal origins who would be presumed to have worked for the so-called uplift of the tribals. Even, the socialists, who claimed to be more at one with the common people completely denied any role for the tribals other than as mere followers who could take any decision by themselves and had to be completely directed by the socialists who had come from outside. Hardiman notices that in this way the existing observers of the tribal life had completely denied the tribals any initiative, any decision-making capacity or any ability to decide what is good for them. Such denial of existence to the tribals (or, as a general case, to other subaltern groups) is what Hardiman and others following the subaltern perspective criticized.

### *Genesis of Resistance*

There were many individual and group efforts to warm the adivasis to take liquor. It included rural elite and *Bhajan-Mandal* groups of the village, but the remarkable change in the consciousness of the adivasis came with Devi movement.

*The Coming of Devi* by Hardiman is a work on the assertion of the adivasis in western India against the Shaukars (moneylenders). The Devi movement started as a small propitiation ceremony among the fisher-folk of Palghar taluk in late 1921. Later, it spread in other parts of Gujarat. In the case of Devi movement, Hardiman noticed that the tribals had involved themselves in a social reform movement not merely as an effort of reforming themselves, by getting rid of the drinking habit, but also as a rebellion against the domination of Parsi liquor vendors who had brought them into debt bondage and also against the domination by large landlords.

This 'Devi' was supposed to have come from the mountains to the east, and she expressed her demands through the mouth of spirit mediums. The medium sat before the crowd, holding red clothes in their hands, they began to shake their heads. Then, they pronounced the commands of Devi:

- Stop drinking liquor and toddy.
- Stop eating meat and fish.
- Live a clean and simple life.
- Man should take bath twice a day.
- Women should take bath thrice a day.
- Have nothing to do with Parsis.

When they finished, the girl who was dressed as Devi was offered coins or gifts. Later, they sat for a common dinner (*Bhandara*).

The collective and 'Devi' words have brought remarkable change in the consciousness among the adivasis. This led to their political mobilization and ultimately to raise their standard of living by going away from the clinches of Shahukars and Parsis.

But, what was the result of this kind of quite rebellion, Hardiman asked. It did not result in the total emancipation of the adivasis, he conceded. For, the domination of the Parsis was replaced by the more hegemonic domination of the elite among the adivasis over all others. But it did result in other kinds of benefits. In the region where the Devi movement spread the far more exploitative capitalist farmer could not find roots. The adivasis managed to retain a modicum of dignity and self-control in the face of ever increasing incursions of capitalist relations protected by the colonial government and even after the movement dissolved it still left a lingering impression on the tribals of this region by making them more assertive and giving them memories, which involves self-help and action for the collective good.

So, if the uniqueness and self-dignity in the current existence of the tribals of the forested regions of south Gujarat had to be understood, it could be done so only by first understanding the special way in which the tribals created and responded to the Devi movement. If the social scientists were to ignore the perspective, they would lose out on the special understanding that David Hardiman and others of his ilk provided.

## Feeding the Baniya

The book entitled, *Feeding the Baniya* represents an attempt to understand something of the quality of power which usurers have exercised over subaltern classes in rural India over several centuries. As well as the obvious economic element, this power had strong political and cultural dimensions to it. It was very tenacious, not only surviving the transition to colonial rule, but thriving in the new environment. Even when resisted in popular revolt, usurers – personified in popular imagination by the figure of the Baniya merchant – seemed to have a remarkable ability to bounce back, redefining the terms of their relationship with the subaltern to their perpetual advantage. Hardiman attempts to see how such a domain of power was forged; how, over the centuries, usurers managed to adapt their practice so effectively within succeeding state formations; and how the classes whom they exploited related to them, and also resisted them.

A peasant proverb in western India gives expression to the hegemony of Baniya usurers over the peasants: "I love the Sheth-Baniya so much that I have given him a fat belly." The indebted peasantry feeds the Baniya merchants' never ending demands for agrarian produce, enriching the usurers while being itself trapped in a cycle of poverty.

Hardiman's second major book, *Feeding the Baniya* reflects the integration of a small-scale agrarian society with a larger capitalist economy. Hardiman investigated the deep meanings involved in the relationship between the villager and the moneylender. Anyone who has had any experience of the borrowing practices in villages knows how usurious the village moneylender is. Yet it has often puzzled observers that the villagers prefer going to him for help in times of need rather than visit the local branch of the State Bank of India or other banks even though they provide loans at much cheaper rates and without much difficulty. A crucial part of the answer to this puzzle was provided by Hardiman's study. Rich in historical and sociological details, the study pointed out that the moneylender was located in a complex web of domination exercised by the local dominant classes. The moneylender himself might not always be the dominating person, but he definitely was the front for the other dominant sections of local society. In so far that here was a society not sufficiently suffused with capitalist relations and institutions, the moneylender provided the small-scale agrarian producer with adequate means to relate to the wider capitalist world.

In this detailed and comprehensive study of the relationship between peasants and Baniya usurers in western India, Hardiman examines how and why usurers have, over the centuries, managed to exert their power over the peasantry. An explanation purely in terms of economics of the relationship is, he argues, not adequate. Crucial also has been the support extended to the Baniyas by successive states from pre-colonial to colonial times. But, over and above, this is the ideological or hegemonic power that Baniyas have been able to exert over their clients.

Applying insights derived from the works of Gramsci, Foucault and Bourdieu, Hardiman explores the nature of this hegemony, seeing how a shared set of beliefs could help the Baniyas consolidate their power. Despite this, the relationship was by no means a harmonious one. There was a whole range of tensions which at times gave rise to protest and resistance.

His book *Feeding the Baniya* was conceived initially as a study of usury in Gujarat, which has been his chief area for historical research. However, in the course of the investigations, the project expanded to include other parts of western India. Rajasthan is also included in part because it was the heartland of the Marwari Baniya – a critical group for any study of usury.

*Feeding the Baniya* spans the pre-colonial, colonial and post-colonial periods of Indian history. The role of merchant and usurer capital in the appropriation of the peasants' surplus is examined, revealing crucial changes over time, and it is argued that the institution of usury has undergone a metamorphosis in the period since Indian independence.

Once again, as in the case of his study of the Devi movement, Hardiman had provided an additional perspective into the changing world of the villagers as they tried to cope with the changes in the wider society around them. And it was creating special knowledge that the subaltern perspective has been used to any student of society.

## Hardiman's Framework Summarized

### *Background*

1. Educated at UK
2. Academic career in UK and India
3. Interests in subaltern studies
4. Active in the welfare for Dalits

### *Aims*

Chief objective is to understand the relationships of domination and subordination in India

### *Assumptions*

1. Hegemony of Baniya usurers over the peasants
2. Hegemony of landlords over the agricultural labourers

### *Methodology*

Subaltern perspective

### *Typology*

Dialectical-model

### *Issues*

Different aspects of Indian society, namely,

1. Subaltern studies
2. Studies of Dalits
3. Tribal studies
4. Agrarian system
5. Agricultural labourers

## Select Bibliography

Dhanagare, D.N. (1998). *Themes and Perspectives in Indian Sociology*, Jaipur: Rawat Publications.

Guha, R. (1982). *Subaltern Studies*, V, New Delhi: Oxford University Press.

Hardiman, David (1980). "The Quit India Movement in Gujarat", in Gyanendra Pandey (ed.), *The Indian Nation in 1942*, Calcutta.

— (1981). *Peasant Nationalists Movement of Gujarat: Kheda District* (1917–1934), New Delhi: Oxford University Press.

— (1987) (paperback edition in 1995). *The Coming of Devi: Adivasi Assertion in Western India*, New Delhi: Oxford University Press. Gujarati version published as *Devi Andolan*, Centre for Social Studies, Surat, 1986.

— (1987). "The Bhils and Shaukars of Eastern Gujarat", in R. Guha (ed.), *Subaltern Studies*, V, op. cit.

— (1994) (paperback editions 1996, 1997, 1999), *Subaltern Studies VIII: Essays in Honour of Ranajit Guha* (edited with David Arnold), New Delhi: Oxford University Press.

— (1996) (paperback edition in 2000). *Feeding the Baniya: Peasants and Usurers in Western India*, New Delhi: Oxford University Press.

— (ed.) (1992) (paperback edition in 1994). 'Introduction', *Peasant Resistance in India: 1858–1914*, New Delhi: Oxford University Press.

# IX

# Contemporary Discourses

Contemporary sociological thought has a kit of concepts, which is used – by modern and postmodern thinkers alike. To understand and analyse our thinkers, it is essential to make a conceptual clarity of these terms. The present section discusses some of these key conceptual terms. These will provide us a meaningful understanding of Indian thought. Our argument is that these contemporary terms are embedded in both the western and Indian sociology.

## Meaning of Discourse

Discourse is written and spoken conversation and the thinking that underlies it. According to Michel Foucault, discourse is sociologically important because how we talk and think about the world shapes how we behave and the kind of world we create consequently. It is through discourse that we construct what we experience as reality, and as soon as we learn to think and talk about reality in a particular way, we cannot help but shut off our ability to think of it in countless other ways.

## Discourse Formation

Foucault was particularly interested in discourse formation – how ways of thinking and conversation come into being in a society and how they affect social life. For him two major areas of interest were madness and sexuality, both of which he regarded as socially constructed. There is, Foucault argued, no such thing as sexuality or madness except as human beings create ideas about them through conversation, and other forms of discourse. Whether we regard madness as divinely inspired, or evil, or a biologically caused pathology, for example, depends on what the discourse on madness looks like in our society. Similarly, if we equate capitalism with democracy or sexuality with male-dominated heterosexuality, we cannot help but shape economic and sexual life in ways that make it difficult to consider the possibility of democratic alternatives to capitalism or sexual lives that are egalitarian, gay or lesbian. To explain such things, there are two bases of discourse formation: (1) knowledge, and (2) culture.

### *Knowledge*

Knowledge is what we perceive to be real and true. It can be as simple and commonplace as how to tie a shoe or as rarified and complex as particle physics. Knowledge is sociologically significant because it is socially created and because we depend on it for our sense of reality.

In everyday life we carry with us knowledge of how the social world works, what sociologist Alfred Schutz called 'stock knowledge' (also known as common sense knowledge). We know what to say when answering a ringing telephone, for example, how to tell time, how to behave in restaurant, how to dress in a way appropriate for various occasions, or how to divert attention from someone who is deeply embarrassed. Social life is based on a shared sense of what is real, and this, in turn, is based on knowledge, especially that contained in cultures. Without the existence of knowledge, we would not know how to participate in the countless situations that make up social life. But, it is equally true that without such knowledge, social life itself would not exist. There would be no such thing as 'conversation', for example, without shared knowledge of what a conversation is and how people must behave in order for one to take place. The most long-standing sociological interest in knowledge has to do with the question of where it comes from in the first place. In general, sociologists regard all forms of knowledge as socially produced and shaped by the culture and structure of social systems. Karl Marx argued that ruling economic classes shape knowledge in ways that promote their interest over those of subordinate classes. From a Marxist perspective, for example, the idea that wealth results from hard work rather than from inheritance, luck, or various forms of market manipulation, serves the interests of dominant classes in capitalist societies. It does so by making the true basis of wealth and by keeping the lower classes hard at work (which will rarely make any of them wealthy) and distracted from paying critical attention to the reality of the class system and how it works.

Following Marx, Karl Mannheim argued that the social basis for knowledge is much broader than the economic forces that form the core of Marx's approach. In more recent times, various approaches to knowledge have developed, including postmodernism.

### *Culture*

Culture is an accumulated store of symbols, ideas and material products associated with a social system, whether it be an entire society or a family. It is important to note that culture does not refer to what people actually do, but to the ideas they share about what they do. What makes an idea cultural rather than personal is not simply that it is shared by two or more people; rather, it must be perceived and experienced as having an authority that transcends the thought of individuals. We do not perceive a symbol or idea as cultural because most people share in it, for in fact we have no way of knowing what most people in a society think. Instead, we assume that most people share in a cultural idea because we identify it as cultural.

Culture is the shared symbols of communication and conceptions of reality that is peculiar to a group or society. Words, phrases and ideas have special meanings within a group that make interaction more efficient and give the members a sense of identity and belonging. Outsiders or new members must learn the language and assumptions of the culture or sub-culture before they can understand the subtleties of communication or feel secure as members. Therefore, language and communication are the two important channels of discourse.

### *Language*

This is universal form of human behaviour involving symbolic communication through a culturally accepted system of sound patterns having standardized meanings. Language is a part of culture and expresses its heritage. In language arbitrary sounds are formed into cultural symbols capable of communicating ideas, desires, meanings, experiences and traditions from one generation to another. Language is a social product. Each individual in the culture develops language through prolonged interaction with members who are already socialized, and language represents the accumulated and current experiences, feelings and meanings that can be communicated and stabilized within the culture. Language is essential to human perception, thinking, awareness of self, awareness of others, and to the existence of the social community itself.

### *Communication*

The transmission of information, ideas, attitudes or emotions from one person or group to another, primarily through symbols, is called communication. In effective communication, the meaning conveyed to the recipient corresponds closely to that intended by the sender. Communication forms the basis for all social interaction; it enables the transmission of cumulative knowledge and makes possible the existence of empathic understanding among individuals.

## Issues of Discourses

Contemporary discourses on sociology for India centre around the following four issues:

1. Contextualization
2. Indigenization
3. Use of native categories in the analysis of Indian society
4. Sociology for India

These will be discussed separately in the chapters in this section.

## Select Bibliography


Foucault, Michel (1971), *Madness and Civilization: A History of Insanity in the Age of Reason*, London: Tavistock.

— [(1976) (1979)]. *The History of Sexuality*, London: Tavistock.

Mannheim, Karl (1936), *Ideology and Utopia*, London: Routledge and Kegan Paul.

— (1952), *Essays on the Sociology of Knowledge*, London: Routledge and Kegan Paul.

Schutz, Alfred (1972), *The Phenomenology of the Social World*, London: Heinemann Educational Books.

# 22

# Contextualization

Within the context of history, colonialism, and its impact on the intellectual and cultural traditions in India, of which sociology and other social sciences are at a certain level of manifestations, provide an important historical backdrop for its theoretic, ideological and professional evaluation. Major theoretic orientations in Indian society have shown varying degrees of ups and downs during the last century. The analysis is not possible without a framework of sociology of knowledge within the context of history.

Radhakamal Mukerjee, B.N. Seal and B.K. Sarkar continuously refuted the efforts of western ideologists. Seal thought that institutions could only be compared when they were historically co-existed and parallel. To Mukherjee, Indian social institutions are unique. Therefore, the study of any society should be done in the particular context of that society. Ideology, theory and method are related to the context. Without the context, there is no relevance of any ideology, theory and method. Keeping this in view, we would discuss in this chapter the work of sociologists in Indian context.

The Indian sociology, as an emergent distinctive discipline during colonial and post-colonial phases, has been significantly influenced and patterned on western paradigm. Almost all sociologists in India have taken up studies on the theoretical paradigm of Durkheim, Weber, Marx and Parsons. Besides the western paradigms, according to Singh (1993), Indian sociologists have adopted four theoretical orientations: (i) philosophical, (ii) culturological, (iii) structural and (iv) dialectical-historical.

Before the discussion of these theoretical orientations, we would like to refer an important essay on ideology, theory and method in Indian sociology by Yogendra Singh (1993) which covers a period of about a quarter century from 1952 to 1977:

(i) 1952 to 1960 – a period of adaptive changes and innovations;
(ii) 1960 to 1965 – a period of significant shifts in theoretic priorities and beginning of some critical tensions in theory and ideology of Indian sociology;
(iii) 1965 to 1970 – a period of marked sociological self-awareness and growth of new directions in theoretical and substantive contributions; and
(iv) 1970 to 1977 – a period of new maturity and new horizons of knowledge.

These four periods correspond with four theoretical developments in Indian sociology as mentioned above.

(i) The *philosophical orientation* in Indian sociology is associated with the contributions of Radhakamal Mukerjee, D.P. Mukerji and A.K. Saran. This orientation has not made a significant impact on the theoretical nature of the Indian sociology. According to Singh (1983) it is interesting to note that despite the profoundness of scholarship of these scholars, the impact is minimal. The impact of western sociology was becoming more and more enveloping and empirical bases of societal understanding looked simpler than the rigour of philosophy and pain of meaningfully digging the past; that to swim with the current stream was easy sociological course, than the cognitive grasp of complex historical past.

(ii) The *culturological orientation* begins with the work of Srinivas, *Religion and Society among the Coorgs of South India*. Brahminization, Sanskritization and Westernization were major concepts derived from this study. Sanskritization characterized a change within the framework of Indian tradition.

(iii) The *structural orientation* focuses on power structure, social stratification, family structure, demography and similar aspects, which reveal patterns, arrangements and repetitiveness. The empirical aspects are converted into abstracted concepts, models and categories. The structural studies have also taken comparative framework.

(iv) The *dialectical-historical orientation* is primarily based on Marxist approach and method for the analysis of social reality (Breekenridge and Veer, 1994). The dialectical method has not been termed as Marxist as adaptations have been made keeping in view the Indian social reality. It is, however, a less developed branch of Indian sociology. D.P. Mukerji and Ramkrishna Mukherjee emphasized the significance of dialectical model (Singh, 1983). A.R. Desai had consistently used dialectical-historical approach with ideological fervour and commitment. He has consistently exposed contradictions in policies and programmes of change. The dialectical-historical orientation grew rapidly in the seventies, when micro-empirical realities were subjected to class observation along with macro-structural social and economic processes in India (Singh, 1983).

Singh's typology of four major theoretic orientations is significant and logically coherent. According to Singhi (1993), these theoretical orientations basically have implicit or explicit ideological connotation. The implications can be discerned at the level of analysis, which as a critique rejects the way social reality is managed or justifies the formation of social reality as it has come to be manipulated and constructed. At other level, they imply need for alternatives, modifications and corrections. Knowledge-neutrality is contradictions in terms. Evaluation and analysis of social reality reveals systematic formulation of scattered, diverse and immediate impressions which are mediated through common man's impressionistic perceptions and views. At the third level, dominance of theoretical orientations generated institutionally tends to lead to negation and blinding of our own intellectual traditions.

In his book on *Sociology of Indian Sociology*, Ramkrishna Mukherjee (1979) describes the trends in Indian sociology. He itemized the narratives, which are presented in Tables 1–4 with particular reference to the Indian sociologists who played the pioneering role. The contributions of some of the pioneers of Indian sociology focus mainly on the 'why' and 'what will it be' questions, these constituted their main interests in the dynamics of Indian society. When considered in greater detail, their value preferences, theoretical formulations and research orientations vary considerably. However, so little attention has been paid to the pioneers and their works that a precise account of these variations would be impossible at present. Also, research into this phase of Indian sociology may elicit more names and enables these variations to be understood more comprehensively. Nevertheless, even the superficial analysis of the similarities and differences among the pioneers brings out certain trends which characterize the first phase of Indian sociology and provides the base from which the next phase can be examined.

The Indian society cannot develop under colonial conditions was implied or stated explicitly by the pioneers. At the same time, they regarded the independence of India as merely a stage in the development of the society: it was not the ultimate goal. This goal was also defined differently by the pioneers, as will be noticed from the rough outline of their value preferences given in the Table 1 below:

**Table 1**

| *References* | *Value Preference* |
|---|---|
| A.K. Coomaraswamy | The cultural conquest of the West over the East must be resisted, and colonialism removed because it promotes western cultural domination. |
| B.N. Seal | "Every national personality (like every individual personality in the nation) has a right to the realization of its own ideal ends, satisfactions and values, within the limits imposed by the similar rights of others (individualistic justice), and also a right to co-partnership and co-operation for the common good and common advantage (socialistic justice), within the limits imposed by the preceding clause." |
| B.K. Sarkar | Society is upheld by the 'Might of Man', the growth of which is hindered by colonialism through economic, political and ideological exploitation of the dependent people. |
| G.S. Ghurye | The needs and aspirations of individuals for a better life are to be fulfilled without establishing (or, if it is established coercively by removing) 'a well-divided chequer-board of humanity'. |
| D.P. Mukerji | Development of man is conditioned by the social milieu and, therefore, national independence, economic development and the resolution of class contradictions in society are necessary conditions for man's development but not the sufficient conditions. |
| Radhakamal Mukerjee | Development of man is possible through commonality and cooperation in a free society, and not through contradictions and conflict. |
| S.V. Ketkar | Socialism is to be established by 'economic evolution' in a free society but in harmony with the historically engineered linguistic, cultural, psychological and political distinctions between mankind. |
| B.N. Dutt and K.P. Chattopadhyay | Socialism is to be established by the resolution of contradictions in society, especially the class contradictions traditions, and in the subjugated countries by the resolution of the colonial contradiction as the initial step. |

*Source:* Mukherjee, Ramkrishna (1979), *Sociology of Indian Sociology*, Bombay: Allied, p. 38.

**Table 2**

| *References* | *Theoretical Formulation* |
|---|---|
| A.K. Coomaraswamy | Development of man is possible in his specific social and cultural context which may be harmfully affected by an aggressively dominating culture. |
| B.N. Seal | Social development is not unilinear: instead, there are multiple paths of development along which "nationalism is only a halting stage in the onward march of humanity". |
| B.K. Sarkar | While the 'might of man' is ultimately dependent on the values projected by a few, it is stabilized, promoted or retarded by the contextual social structure and its function. |
| G.S. Ghurye | Development of man is culture-specific since "cultural development is reflected in the trend of thought about man as a living entity". |
| D.P. Mukerji | Indian social reality can be properly appraised only in terms of "its special traditions, its special symbols and its special patterns of culture and social actions". |
| Radhakamal Mukerjee | Since human institutions form an indivisible unity of the individual, society and values, any consideration of social facts without their value-component is unreal; instead, there should be a fusion of 'empirical' and 'normative' sociology. |
| S.V. Ketkar | Indian society is to be regarded as a part of the world society but also it should be examined internally in terms of 'unity in diversity' due to its linguistic, cultural and psychological distinctions. |
| B.N. Dutt | The Indian social reality can properly be understood by taking note of (a) Marx's formulation of the historical stages by social development, and (b) Weber's formulation regarding the role of Hindu religion on the people. |
| K.P. Chattopadhyay | Indian social reality can be best grasped by an analysis of the class character of society in different phases of history but, specially, in the light of (a) the contact of people with different culture and social patterns, and (b) the diffusion of culture among them. |

*Source:* Mukherjee, Ramkrishna (1979), *Sociology of Indian Sociology*, Bombay: Allied, p. 40.

**Table 3**

| *References* | *Research Orientation* |
|---|---|
| A.K. Coomaraswamy | Cultural approach to understand Indian (and Asian) social reality by specifically in a non-western and the Oriental context. |
| B.N. Seal | Bio-sociological approach toward the conceptualization and empirical verification of different paths of social development, with particular reference to the historical and contemporaraneous development of Indian society. |
| B.K. Sarkar | Structural-functional approach to Indian (an Asian) social organization and culture form a historical, contemporary and futuristic perspective in order to dispel the notion of the 'other worldly' outlook of the Orientals and to examine the process of development of the 'might of man', especially in the Indian context. |
| G.S. Ghurye | Structural-functional approach to India's social organization and culture in a historical context and also through an examination of their varied contemporary aspects. |
| D.P. Mukerji | 'Marxologist's' dialectical approach to understand personality and culture in the Indian social context. |
| Radhakamal Mukerjee | Beginning with the structural-functional approach to ascertain the inter-dependence between the economic sphere and the entire socio-historical-cultural order of Indian society, the 'transdisciplinary' approach was to be used for a comprehensive appraisal of social reality in the Indian and world context. |
| S.V. Ketkar | Historical approach through encyclopaedic bibliographical research to establish the thesis that as in the world context India should be regarded as a 'unit' and also that the Indian social organism should be regarded as an expression of 'unity in diversity' |
| B.N. Dutt | Marxist dialectical approach to explain the evolution of India's social and political structure. |
| K.P. Chattopadhyay | Diffusionist and structural-functional approach to India's social organization and culture in the historical context and in analysing varied contemporary aspects, leading in later years to a Marxist dialectical approach to explain India's social reality. |

*Source:* Mukherjee, Ramkrishna (1979), *Sociology of Indian Sociology*, Bombay: Allied, p. 41.

**Table 4**

| *References* | *Contribution to Sociology* |
|---|---|
| A.K. Coomaraswamy | A historic-contemporary overview of the Occidental domination over the Indian and Oriental culture, with a rationalized analysis of the 'meaning' of the latter. |
| B.N. Seal | Concept-formation in order to study social change and social development with special reference to India, and the corresponding methodology for empirical research on an inductive-inferential basis including employing statistical tools and techniques. |
| B.K. Sarkar | A historico-contemporary-futuristic appraisal of Indian (and Asian) social development, dispelling the notion of the 'other worldly' outlook of the Orientals and nothing to the need for (a) intensive empirical research to verify the theoretical formulations and the preliminary empirical findings, and (b) the creation of an extensive data-base. |
| G.S. Ghurye | Data-base for historical and contemporary empirical research on India's social organization and culture. |
| D.P. Mukerji | Theoretical formulations about the role of 'tradition' in order to analyse social change; and a historico-contemporary- futuristic appraisal of Indian society, her classes and culture, pointing to the need for empirical research in a comprehensive manner and irrespective of disciplinary boundaries in social science. |
| Radhakamal Mukerjee | Theoretical formulation about the role and structure of values in all societal manifestations; a methodology for an integrated social science approach to social reality; and the creation of a data-base concerning historical and contemporary perspectives on Indian society. |
| S.V. Ketkar | Creation of a historical and contemporary data-base, essentially from bibliographical research, denoting psycho-social and cultural distinctions among the linguistic regions of India. |
| B.N. Dutt | Constructed a preliminary historical data-base from which to proceed with empirical research on the evolution of India's social and political structure. |
| K.P. Chattopadhyay | Methodology for large-sale survey research, and the creation of data-base for historical and contemporary empirical research on India's social organization and culture. |

*Source:* Mukherjee, Ramkrishna (1979), *Sociology of Indian Sociology*, Bombay: Allied, p. 42.

Table 1 shows that within the framework of man and society, the goals set by the pioneers ranged from an idealized version of oriental culture to the materialistic view of social development as propounded by Marx. Also, between these two polar-opposite goal sets, there are those emphasizing the culture-specific or value-specific development of man or the establishment of a society free from exploitation but coming about through cooperation and harmony among the social segments of the resolution of contradictions and conflicts among them.

Table 2 shows that the theoretical formulations of the pioneers were not unsystematic and abstract generalization about man and society. Also, they did not merely express those characteristics of a social phenomenon, which were spontaneously observed by them – a point in which, like in their value preference, they differed from the modernizers who supplemented them in the social arena. On the contrary, their multi-dimensional comprehension of social reality from historical, contemporary and futuristic perspective meant that their widely divergent theoretical formulations had considerable inductive power to explain the changing reality by accentuating different aspects of social dynamism. The pioneers considered different aspects of the Indian (or the world) society to reveal its substantive reality.

Empirical research was strongly advocated by the pioneers, except perhaps by Coomaraswamy. Following their various value preferences and theoretical formulations, their research orientations registered different approaches to sociological research, as noted in Table 3. However, irrespective of the above formulation of their approaches, which may have to be revised or elaborated in the light of further research into the work of the pioneers, it is evident that their interest in empirical research was not exclusively with respect to any particular social phenomenon like caste, family, national integration, stratification, or rural or urban society. Also, even while dealing with one phenomenon (such as caste), they did not restrict their attention to only one specific aspect, such as the relative positions of the castes variations in that aspect of the phenomenon.

Thus, we find even from an imprecise account of the works of the pioneers in Indian sociology that from different points of view they had proceeded systematically to analyse the Indian social reality is neither an insular nor an imitative manner. Even Coomaraswamy, who appears to have rejected western culture, had the entire Oriental culture with its various mores and modalities in view (see Table 4). The others too did not indulge in repetition of these theories to suit the native situation. Indian thinkers, with one to two exceptions, have been too much dependent on the West for their theory and have been promptly accepting the changing theoretical framework from the West (Saran, 1958: 1023).

It is true that a lot of empirical work has been done during past few decades but it would be difficult to suggest that sociology has gained theoretical maturity of its own in India. New areas of research have multiplied but the theoretical rigour and depth of interpretation seem to be lacking. The contribution of earlier generations of sociologists continues to be regarded and recognized as rigorous and significant by serious scholars. It reflects the following major approaches to the study of Indian society: Indological: Ghurye and Dumont; Structural-Functional: Srinivas and Dube; Marxian: D.P. Mukerji and A.R. Desai, Ramkrishna Mukherjee; Civilizational: N.K. Bose and Surajit Sinha; Subaltern: Ambedkar, David Hardiman and Ranajit Guha; Cultural Approach: Yogendra Singh etc. Most of these approaches have been discussed in the lessons of different units of the course on the Perspectives on Indian Society.

## Select Bibliography

Atal, Yogesh (2003), *Indian Sociology: From Where to Where*, Jaipur and New Delhi: Rawat Publications.

Mukherjee, Ramkrishna (1979), *Sociology of Indian Sociology*, Bombay: Allied Publishers Pvt. Ltd.

Nagla, Madhu (2003), "Approaches to the Indian Society", unpublished paper.

Saran, A.K. (1958), "India", in Joseph S. Roucek (ed.), *Contemporary Sociology,* New York: Greenwood Press Publishers.

Sharma, Surendra (1985), *Sociology in India: A Perspective from Sociology of Knowledge,* Jaipur: Rawat Publications.

Singh, Yogendra (1967), "Sociology for India: The Emerging Perspective", in T.K. Unnithan et al. (eds), *Sociology for India*, New Delhi: Prentice-Hall of India (Pvt.) Ltd., pp.13–37.

— (1986), *Sociology: Social Conditioning and Emerging Concerns*, Delhi: Sage Publications.

— (1993), 'Ideology, Theory and Method', in B.K. Nagla (ed.), *Development and Social Transformation*, Jaipur: Rawat Publications.

Singhi, N.K. (ed.) (1993), *Theory and Ideology in Indian Sociology*, Jaipur: Rawat Publications.

# 23

# Indigenization

## Need for Indigenization

On the intellectual front, the key crisis in social sciences in Asia is related to indigenization. The native scholarship has begun raising questions regarding the applicability and appropriateness of theories and methodology imported from abroad, and has started almost a campaign for their replacement by 'native categories of thought' and indigenous techniques of research. The call for indigenization, however, takes different forms, and lays emphasis on different aspects in different countries. In countries which have recently introduced social sciences, indigenization is merely a plea for the introduction and recognition of social sciences so that native scholarships grow and finally make a contribution to the nation-building process. There, the substantive issues are not discussed. In some others, indigenization is expressed in terms of switch over to the national language as medium of instruction and report writing. Curriculum development, with a bias towards national needs, is also an indicator of indigenization. While considerable reaction against the 'external' theories and methodology is in evidence, there is, however, very little by way of construction of an indigenous social science. Much of the thinking on this issue is guided by the national perspectives, and one is not sure whether any Asian perspective is likely to emerge. One will have to watch carefully whether indigenization will lead to a retreat to national shells or to an emergence of parochial regional social science in place of a universal-global social science. It must also be stated that in the past few years more channels have been opened for the social scientists to act regionally and even internationally. These apertures should guard against any insular tendencies that might develop as part of the process of indigenization (Atal, 2003: 18–19). Development strategists are sloganizing the need for endogenous development, whereas social scientists are agonizing about indigenization.

In the above context, the question of indigenization has been discussed in several national and international meetings organized under different auspices. The movement began to gain momentum in the early 1970s when indigenous scholars from the Third World raised their voice against the implantation of social sciences perpetuating 'captivity' of mind; they were later joined by a number of social scientists from western countries sharing this concern. In Asia, the concern was most eloquently expressed at the first Asian Conference on Teaching and Research in Social Sciences, organized under the auspices of UNESCO in 1973 at Shimla, India. Again, in meeting on International Cooperation in the Field of Social Sciences, organized by UNESCO in Paris in 1976, the participants underlined the fact that 90 per cent of the social scientists of the world came from the developed countries.

The question of indigenization was also taken up by the Conference of National Social Science Councils (CNSSC) and analogous bodies, at its 1977 meeting. In 1978, the Wenner-Gren Foundation organized a conference on indigenous anthropology. The Korean Social Science Research Council convened a seminar to discuss "Organization of Western Approaches to Social Sciences" in early 1979. In September, 1979, the Association of Asian Social Science Research Councils (AASSREC) organized in collaboration with CNSSC – now renamed International Federation of Social Science Organizations (IFSSO) – a special panel discussion during its Third Conference held in Manila.

There is, thus, a worldwide concern with this problem. This lesson attempts to synthesize the major trends of thinking and articulates key concerns related to the call for indigenization. Here, we are heavily dependent on the writings of Yogesh Atal (2003), Surendra Sharma (1985), and Yogendra Singh (1986).

The call for indigenization of social sciences in Asia has not yet gone beyond the reactive phase. Since these reactions come from different sources, albeit all from the professional social scientists, they emphasize different aspects of indigenization. Even, the definitional crisis has not yet been resolved: indigenization means different things to different people.

The social sciences in Asia and the Pacific are at different stages of development. Their introduction to individual countries was determined by their respective colonial masters. The period of their entry, the relative emphasis given to different disciplines, the 'external' orientation of the first generation of native social scientists, and the literature on the society and culture of these countries are all influenced by the colonial heritage.

At the political level, the decolonization process was spelt out as the process of localization or nativization. It is in this sense that Jawaharlal Nehru, and his compatriots, for example, raised the slogan for Indianization during the freedom struggle.

Proponents of indigenization are aware of the dangers of a mere rhetoric of counter-attack. They do not wish to appear as "courageous natives talking back to the alien masters", or as chauvinists. According to Atal (2003: 103–4), some of the positive aspects of indigenization being emphasized by its exponents are:

1. Indigenization is a plea for self-awareness and rejection of a borrowed consciousness. It emphasizes the need for an inside view. Its proponents wish to stimulate such scholarly endeavour so as to promote thoughtful analysis of their own societies to replace the existing trend of knowing these via the West.

2. Indigenization advocates the desirability for alternative perspectives on human societies with a view to making the social sciences less parochial and enriching them. This would, it is believed, emancipate the mind and improve the quality of professional praxis, so that society can be examined through new lenses.
3. Indigenization draws attention to historical and cultural specificities and argues for the redefinition of focus, with a view to developing dynamic perspectives on national problems.
4. Indigenization should not lead to narrow parochialism or to the fragmentation of a single discipline into several insulated systems of thought based on geographical boundaries. It is opposed not only to false universalism but to false nationalism as well. Reduced to the level of national narcissism, indigenization would be rendered futile.

In his article, "Indigenization and Transnational Co-operation in the Social Sciences", Krishna Kumar (1979: 104–5) differentiates between three types of indigenization: structural, substantive and theoretical. To quote his definitions: (a) "Structural indigenization can be defined with reference to the institutional and organizational capabilities of a nation for the production and diffusion of social science knowledge." (b) "substantive indigenization can be conceptualized within the content focus of the social sciences. The essential premise is that the main thrust of these disciplines in a country should be on its own society, people, and economic and political institutions." (c) "Theoretic indigenization indicates a condition in which the social scientists of a nation are involved in constructing distinctive, conceptual frameworks and meta-theories which reflect their worldviews, social and cultural experiences, and perceived goals."

Krishna Kumar does not regard structural and content indigenization as problematic, and dwells at length on the problem of theoretic indigenization and comes to the right conclusion that it is not indigenization but 'transnational co-operation' that ought to be encouraged. In doing so, he touches only one aspect of dilemma.

Although relayed in high accent, indigenization invites thinking about a strategy to match the twin concerns of diffusion of a universal social science culture and the need for roots in different cultural settings. It is not without significance that in this debate the word 'indigenization' is generally preferred to 'endogenous development'. Taken literally, endogenous development signifies development generated from within and orthogenetically, which would, thus, have no place for any exogenous influence. In fact, it was coined in strong reaction to an externally produced and directed strategy of development; it is a different matter that so much outside interest continues to pervade endogenous development, making the newer slogan somewhat redundant. Indigenization, by contrast, at least honestly alludes to outside contact by emphasizing the need for indigenization the exogenous elements to suit local requirements; whether this is done by the 'indigenous' or by 'outsiders' is a mere detail.

It is clear from current academic trends that the concern for indigenization is spreading globally. It is not only the countries of the Third World that are talking about indigenization; one can even find articles on "Canadization". The concern for indigenization among researchers from the developed world is received with a certain pinch of salt. This is how John Samy of Fiji reporting on the discussion on "Theory and Methods" at the recent Young Nations Conference (Mamak and McCall: 1979: 242–43) describes a familiar situation:

> The Conference received and entertained a barrage of attractive and emotionally persuasive developmentalist jargon. Some of these words were local products while others were carefully indigenized to suit the Pacific taste. But even more importantly, much of the talking at the Conference was at cross-purposes, arising from a very sharp dichotomy between foreigners (that is, Australians, New Zealanders and other metropolitan researchers) and the locals (that is, Pacific Islanders, or the researched). ....
>
> Most of the so-called foreign or expatriate researchers ... wanted to know their research could be of benefit to Pacific people. On the other hand, most Pacific Islanders, once they settled down, seemed

to enjoy the privilege of being brought to Sydney to advise and guide the foreigners on relevant research.

## Attempts for Indigenization

According to Atal (2003), in the Asian context, indigenization has been pursued along with four fronts which we would discuss in this section:

1. Teaching in the national language and use of local materials,
2. Research by insiders,
3. Determination of research priorities, and
4. Theoretical and methodological reorientation.

### *Teaching in the National Language and Use of Local Materials*

Several countries of the region are taking steps to introduce the national language as the medium of instructions at higher levels of learning. In the case of India, the problem is further compounded by the fact that the Constitution of India recognizes fourteen regional languages, and the various states are moving towards the adoption of regional languages for the purpose of instructions. The implication of this policy on the growth of social sciences may be noted.

Acceptance of a national language as the medium of instructions requires the production of literature in that language. Most of the books available in non-Asian languages are beyond the comprehension of the majority of students now entering postgraduate departments. As they received their education in vernacular, they are at disadvantage when asked to consult material or listen to lectures in a foreign language. They, therefore, demand books in the national language. But, the demand for books in the vernacular cannot be fulfilled by the seniors who, though experts in the field, lack communication skills in the vernacular or they fear to loose their scholarship as they have to come down from their standard or they do not have time to write the textbook at the cost of their research work.

The new generation of social scientists, because of their lack of competence in an international language, are likely to remain unexposed to the recent developments in their respective disciplines in other countries. Likewise, their own work will not reach foreign researchers and colleagues. Such insulation will isolate them from the world community. The same thing may happen within the country if regional (provincial) languages are made the medium of instructions. On the contrary, due to the globalization, the interest is now developing to learn not only English but also French, German, Japanese, Russian, Korean, Chinese, Spanish etc.

### *Research by Insiders*

One significant step towards indigenization taken by most countries is the promotion of research by the 'locals', and curbing of 'expatriate' research. Several methodological problems concerning research by insiders versus outsiders have come to the fore. It may, however, be maintained that restricting outsiders' research has not always been guided by academic considerations; political considerations have also prevented insiders from doing research on certain themes. Cases can be cited where governments allowed expatriates to carry out research on the most 'relevant' areas while insiders were not permitted to do so. Curbs on the publication of research findings is yet another problem: while the foreign researchers enjoy relative freedom to collect material and publish the findings, the locals may never be allowed to do so.

### *Determination of Priorities*

Another dimension of indigenization is the promotion of research on themes regarded as nationally important and relevant. In the developing countries of Asia, this revolution of relevance has pervaded all sectors. In planning activities, and in the allocation of resources, relevance is used as the key criterion. Priorities are attempted in terms of relevance. Both the introduction of social science teaching and the promotion of research are determined in accordance with this criterion.

### *Theoretical and Methodological Reorientation*

This is happening at a much slower pace. While there is too much iconoclastic talk about the 'domination' of alien models and theories and their inappropriateness, there is very little to commend by way of an acceptable alternative. Along with criticism of so-called 'capitalist', 'status quoist' or 'western' social science, one may come across those who press the claims of Marxists alternatives. But, such alternatives in the name of indigenization are hardly justifiable. By being a 'more desirable' perspective, Marxism does not shed its 'alien' character and become indigenous. Efforts are still needed to test the alleged universality of established theories and models in a variety of settings. It is not so much an alternative, which is really needed if one is to pursue the goal of a universal science – and not the setting up of "schools of thought", like sects, creating priesthood and a blind following. Genuine efforts, which go beyond reactive rhapsodize, are rare. But some effort is being made. One can cite, as an example, the work of the well-known Pakistani economist, Mahhub Ul Haq, whose collection of essays entitled *Poverty Curtain* gives clear evidence of reconsideration of basic premises of a development paradigm learnt at Harvard and Yale, and an attempt at reformulation of the strategy in the light of new facts. Though written in a somewhat belligerent style to attract attention and overcome resistance, Haq is constructive in his approach. He finds that the academic community in the western world which "reacted in shocked disbelief" because "one of its own products had suddenly gone berserk" has now accepted his formulations and premises. More work of this nature is perhaps needed.

## Indigenization: The Case of Indian Sociology

There was almost a worldwide clamour for the indigenization of social sciences in the 1970s. Of course, the call for indigenization came from the social scientists of the developing countries who raised their voice against "implantation of social sciences". But it is interesting to note that even the Conference of National Social Science Councils (CNSSC) and analogous bodies – which later became International Federation of Social Sciences Organizations (IFSSO) – took up this issue for discussion in 1977. It is important to mention here that while IFSSO is international, it is largely an organization of the developed world. Around the same time, the East-West Centre of the University of Hawaii got interested in this issue. America's Wenner-Gren Foundation also organized, in 1978, a conference on indigenous anthropology. Even Canadian social scientists organized a symposium on the Canadization of Social Sciences, not to talk of Korean initiative on Koreanization of Social Sciences.

American interest in indigenization had, however, a different orientation. Since much of the American social science was 'American', it was already 'indigenous' for them. The crisis for them was not to indigenize social sciences but to ensure their universalization through their spread in other intellectual traditions. The call for indigenization appeared to them as a threat to the western social science – that it will restrict its spread, and that this may mean difficulties for the western social scientists in getting clearance from the host governments to carry out field research. From this angle, the demand for indigenization by the social scientists of the developing countries was seen almost as an affront to the American social science. It is interesting that the advocates of indigenization somehow spared the Marxist approach from their criticisms; the campaign for indigenization appeared as a campaign against capitalistic social sciences.

The etiology of indigenization is quite complicated, so is its definition. Advocates of indigenization had different emphases: localization (replacement of foreign faculty with the local), language shift from the foreign language to the mother-tongue paradigm replacement, return to the native categories of thought, non-applicability of western research techniques and methods, and overall condemnation of the foreign academic colonialism. For some, indigenization meant glorification of tradition, and return to the corridors of the past, reducing the demand to some sort of national narcissism.

Indigenization in the 1980s, it must be said, was still largely in its reactive phase in the sense that much of the debate was couched as a reaction to the introduction, or implantation, of western social sciences. There was very little to demonstrate either an indigenized product theory or methodology, or an indigenous social science. Let it be said that the difference between the two is important. The word 'indigenization' connotes the process of indigenizing something that is exogenous from within. Replacement of exogenous categories of thought by the indigenous ones was also regarded as a part of the process of indigenization.

Once the twin disciplines took roots in India – sociology more rapidly than social anthropology, particularly in terms of the number of departments – the professionals addressed themselves to the identity crisis. At once, the practitioners of the two disciplines had to work on several fronts:

- To evaluate the writings of the foreign scholars on India.
- To distinguish sociology from ideology and from social anthropology.
- To formally define the scope of Indian sociology and to set out the priorities for research.

Questions surrounding these three key concerns have provided the impetus to the call for indigenization. Almost as part of a nationalist agenda, the Indian scholarship of the 1940s and 1950s critically reviewed the alien writings on India to detect 'colonial designs' and 'Western conspiracy' to downgrade Indian culture and civilization as if to prove the superiority of the West. The theories of unilinear evolution, Marxism and structural-functionalism were all seen as part of the western agenda to maintain an unequal, vertical relationship. In methodological terms, questions were raised regarding the applicability of the western techniques of research, and also the limitations of an 'outsider' to understand the internal structures of relationships. The insider-outsider controversy became a real methodological issue. A special twist to this problem came in anthropology, which is defined as the study of 'other cultures'. The entire discipline's strength is its ability to investigate the cultures to which the anthropologists do not belong. And, with the technique of 'participant observation', he is able to provide a dependable and scientific ethnographic account of a primitive tribe. If one accepts the criticism that the outsider cannot understand an alien culture, then, all the anthropological researchers will have to be discarded. Moreover, there is also a counter-view that by simply being an 'insider', one cannot claim to have a fuller, better and accurate understanding of the social phenomena. A further complication is created in the case of Indian anthropologists, who have, unlike their western counterparts, mostly studied Indian society and its sub-cultures: "how are these 'other' societies for them?" is the question asked. Even, when Indians went to study anthropology in England, they were sent back to India for fieldwork. Thus, while the Indian society remained the 'other society' for the foreign mentors of Indian anthropologists, it was not so for the latter. They thus studied them as insiders, violating the defining principle of their discipline. Defending the practice, leading Indian anthropologists regarded the distinction between sociology and social anthropology as rather superfluous. Of course, there were, and perhaps are even now, some in the anthropology profession who advocate a separate calling, and maintain closer links between social anthropology, prehistory and archaeology, and physical anthropology and paleontology, with insistence on the study of tribal cultures only.

Sociologists also engaged in an exercise to dissociate their subject from Indology on the one hand, and social anthropology, on the other. On both fronts, the key distinction was located in the methodology. Indology was regarded as the study of the past and anthropology as the study of the 'primitive' by those sociologists who wanted to emphasize the study of the contemporary society with the use of survey research and quantitative techniques. Indology was held responsible for the 'book view' and the 'upper caste view' of Indian society that was very different from what the present-day Indian society is. And, since anthropology focused on the tribal societies, it was considered ill-equipped to study and analyse contemporary Indian society. But, in the 1950s, with heavy emphasis in Indian planning on agriculture and rural development, and with the inauguration of the Community Development Programme (CDP) on a massive scale, both sociologists and anthropologists began studying rural India. The village in India became the meeting ground for the twin disciplines. But, here again, anthropologists continued the use of the ethnographic method while sociologists followed the survey method to distinguish themselves, giving rise to a continued debate in the 1950s and 1960s regarding the status of these disciplines, and questioning the credentials of scholars in terms of whether they are sociologists or anthropologists (Atal, 2003: 115–135).

The new directions that Indian sociology is talking are beautifully summarized by Yogendra Singh:

> Despite the continuity reflected in the quest for social relevance and an indigenous paradigm for sociology, the 1970s and 1980s in India mark several directions in which new explorations have been made. First, sociological studies show a new sensitivity in the choice of concepts and their uses as they move away from a continuum framework of analysis of social process to that of a notion of levels. The use of conceptual typologies, historical data and linguistic or symbolic structural techniques adds new depth and dimension to the studies of social structure. The Marxist historical method of analysis gains momentum as a series of studies on the peasantry, agrarian structure, and working classes gains ground. Instead of preoccupation with the ritual aspects of caste and its cultural and social functions, or with simplistic dichotomization between caste and class, new series of studies sensitive to theoretical orientations such as structuralism, ethnosociology, systems analysis and historical materialist methods of Marxism and neo-Marxism have been conducted to analyse social structure both in specific regional and macroscopic national settings. Such studies tend to be more analytic and to main at explanation rather than mere description, so common in the sociological tradition of the 1950s (Singh, 1986).

## Indigenization of Sociology in India

Surendra Sharma (1983: 43–45) analysed the objectives and discussions of the seminar held at Mount Abu related to the issue of indigenization of sociology in India. The objectives are mentioned as follows:

1. What is the disciplinary status of sociology in India?
2. How far sociological concepts require further re-adaptation and re-conceptualization for a scientific study of the Indian society?

3. What possibilities of interdisciplinary approach and co-operation are available and can be further envisaged?
4. What are the problems of teaching and research in sociology in India?
5. What further improvements can be brought about?
6. What is the role of sociology and sociologists in a developing society?
7. What theoretical and practical problems must be taken up for research by sociologists in India?

Some of the relevant conclusions are:

1. No prescriptive formulae of sociological enterprise could be laid down and the practice of sociology should be left to the academic sensibility of individual sociologists themselves.
2. There was not antinomy between the use of historical fact and the structural-functional approach.
3. The discussions also revealed the faith of sociologists in the universalitistic character of sociology for India.
4. The possibility of a typical and particularistic sociology was rejected (Singh, 1967).

In Delhi University, the Department of Sociology was established in 1959 with M.N. Srinivas as its senior member of the faculty. Under his stewardship studies on caste, kinship, family and village community were carried out with theoretical and methodological orientations of the British social anthropology, particularly the one represented by Radcliffe-Brown. This group led by Srinivas was not represented in either Agra or Mount Abu seminars on sociology for/in India. The Marxists sociologists also were not represented in the two seminars. Saran, who wrote a paper on Indian sociology around the same time, writes: "Marxists sociology has not developed in India in a systematic manner (Saran, 1958)." He further mentions B.N. Dutta's studies in Indian social polity as a Marxist interpretation of the caste system in which its origin is traced from the formulation of economic classes. S.A. Dange's *India from Primitive Communism to Slavery*, and D.D. Kosambi's *Understanding of the Ancient Indian History* are other examples noted by Saran.

Saran also classified the thinking in Indian sociology into: (1) those who totally reject the modern western civilization and advocate the return to the traditional principles; (2) those who want a synthesis of the two; and (3) those who debate the basis of synthesis: (a) traditional concepts and institutions in terms of modern rationalistic-positivistic ideas, and (b) a value-neutral scientific attitude (Saran, 1958). Saran considers Anand K. Coomaraswamy and Radhakamal Mukerjee as the representatives of two traditions, namely, the traditional theory of man and society, and a multidimensional and holistic analysis and outlook, respectively. Saran clubs D.P. Mukerji with Radhakamal Mukerjee. The former was a critic of latter. The other points discussed by Saran are Indian social thought as sociology, community studies and sociology and social engineering. Saran's essay on Indian sociology is an exercise in 'negation' of the existing theories and approaches. He does not point out his own view in this essay. However, Saran seems to be in somewhat conformity with Coomaraswamy's view of a traditional theory of society and man. Saran, as we know, does not accept western theories to be relevant for studying Indian society. He rejects both American and British sociological theories and Marxism.

It is evident that a great deal of awareness exists among the Indian sociologists about the growth of sociology as a discipline. They have taken up self-introspection by analysing the origin of the discipline and level of its growth. The influences of the western sociology (both American and British) and Marxism have been taken up with a view to understand the constraints and challenges shown by the discipline. It is denied that the founding fathers of sociology, namely, Comte, Marx, Weber and Durkheim, did not influence teaching and research in sociology in India. It has also been conclusively proved that sociology in India, particularly in the nineteenth century and the first half of the twentieth century, was not simply an imitation of the western theories, concepts and methods of research. It was contemporaneous to sociology in the West.

The debate in the fifties and sixties was whether sociology in India should have a universal character or it should be unique in nature due to the uniqueness of Indian society. This question was taken up in two seminars and in several papers appeared in books and journals. We find that India's sociologists were divided on this issue. However, a majority of them felt that it should be a part of general sociological theory, and there should be a synthesis and reinforcement of the 'general' with the 'specific'. However, when this debate was going on, Louis Dumont gave a boosting to the 'culturological' view about study of Indian society.

Theory, method and data are the most important elements of a discipline in addition to epistemology and philosophy. Extreme positions are found in Indian sociology, for example, one taken up by Radhakamal Mukerjee and the other by A.K. Saran. Again, Y.B. Damle find Parsons' structural-functionalism as the most appropriate framework for analysing Indian social system. A.R. Desai advocates the orthodox Marxists approach as most suitable for understanding Indian society and state. G.S. Ghurye, R.N. Saxena and A.K. Saran hold views different from each other, but conforming to what is known as a traditionalist perspective. M.N. Srinivas and his associates have found British functionalism as the most suitable approach. Yogendra Singh, Indra Deva and some others adhere to a sort of positivistic-empirical orientation and suggest for a 'synthesis' of general and specific dimensions in regard to sociology in India (Sharma, 1985).

## Conclusion

The concern shown for indigenization has made it necessary to examine coolly and carefully all its implications. The demand for indigenization is an invitation to re-examine the very structure of social sciences and to evolve suitable strategies for their promotion in the differing and challenging situations of modern times. Although the term 'indigenization' has gained considerable currency, there appears to be a lack of consensus on its meeting and desirability.

As we see the status of the concept of Indigenization, there are only a few takers of this concept. The flames of eighties have been cooled down. India has witnessed globalization. There has been an increase of inter-disciplinary research. In such a situation we have the perspectives of modernization and post-modernization. Post-modernization stands for differentiation. It also calls for decentralization and diversity. Now we tend to think globally. In such a fast track of change, it appears Indigenization has no ground to stand. We tend to disqualify great narratives. We plead for meta or literal narratives. The time has come now to encourage Indianization.

## Select Bibliography

Atal, Yogesh (2003), *Indian Sociology From Where to Where*, Jaipur and New Delhi: Rawat Publications.

— (1985), *Social Science in Asia*, New Delhi: Abhinav Publication.

Desai, I.P. (1981), *The Craft of Sociology and Other Essays*, Delhi: Ajanta Publication.

Kumar, Krishna (1979), "Indigenization and Transnational Cooperation in the Social Sciences", in Krishna Kumar (ed.), *Bonds without Bondage*, Honolulu: East-West Cultural Learning Institute.

Mamak, Alexander and Grant, McCall (1978) (eds), *Paradise Postponed: Essays on Research Development in the South Pacific*, Rushcutters Bay, NSW: Pergamon Press.

Samy, John (1978), "Development and Research for Whom? Towards a Critique of Economism in the Paoific, and Session on Theory and Methods", in Alexander Mamak and Grant McCall (1978) (eds), *Paradise Postponed: Essays on Research Development in the South Pacific*, Rushcutters Bay, NSW: Pergamon Press

Saran, A.K. (1958), "India", in Joseph S. Roucek (ed.), *Contemporary Sociology*, New York: Greenwood Press Publishers.

Saxena, R.N. (ed.) (1961), *Sociology, Social Research and Social Problems in India*, Bombay: Asia Publishing House.

Sharma, Surendra (1985), *Sociology in India: A Perspective from Sociology of Knowledge*, Jaipur: Rawat Publications.

Singh, Yogendra (1967), "Sociology for India: The Emerging Perspective", in T.K. Unnithan et al. (eds). *Sociology for India*, New Delhi: Prentice-Hall of India (Pvt.) Ltd., pp. 13–37.

— (1986), *Sociology: Social Conditioning and Emerging Concerns*, New Delhi: Sage Publications.

# 24

# Use of Native Categories in the Analysis of Indian Society

The categories of knowledge, their meaning, content and the methodology of their construction bear the deep imprint of the social and historical forces of the time. We see its evidence in the writings of the pioneers of sociology like Karl Marx, Max Weber and Emile Durkheim. We find similar social conditioning in the writings of the Indian pioneers of sociology (see Mukherjee, 1979; Singh, 1984). This social conditioning, however, is historically constituted. To the western pioneers of sociology, major challenges came from the merging industrial society and its accompanying cultural and epistemological tensions. In the Indian context, the colonial experience, the memory of the past glory and the project for future political and cultural emancipation constituted the major cognitive and moral concerns. These concerns were, as sociology gained its status in India, reflected in problems of concepts, theory and method. A close relationship can be established between the social and historical forces working in Indian society and the evolution of the concepts and methods of Indian sociology. In this context, Yogendra Singh (1986: 1–31) discusses the social conditioning of Indian sociology. We have adapted Singh's ideas in the following pages.

During the colonial period, many British and European writings on Indian society and culture used conceptual categories, which were Eurocentric in cognitive and value terms; some of these also tended to distort history and imputed meanings to Indian reality in the abstract (a historically) as it to perpetuate colonialism. Concepts such as 'caste' 'tribe', 'village', 'community', 'family' and 'kinship' were defined as segmentary entities, often analogous to their socio-historical equivalents in European society. The emphasis was on showing how each of these social entities affirmed the principles of segmentation and autonomy rather than being parts of an organic whole. The element of discreteness was overemphasized and the linkages, both social and cultural, which bound these entities into an organic system of social structure and civilization, were neglected. This bias, which had its roots probably in the colonial ideology of the British social anthropologists and administrators, is obvious in their treatment of 'caste' and 'tribe' as discrete structural and cultural formations. G.S. Ghurye drew attention to this way back in 1943 in his The *Aborigines-so-called and their Future* in response to Verrier Elvin's *The Aboriginals* (1943). He attempted to demonstrate continuities and linkages between the tribal and caste structure and tradition in Indian society. Apart from such biases, the basic social categories of Indian society appeared to be devoid of a dynamic historical viewpoint. The colonial ethnographers, for instance, "took a placid, even a synchronic view of the tribal society. The conceptual framework developed by the British administrators-turned-ethnographers and by anthropologists was inspired by the then prevailing model in anthropology. Tribal communities were treated as isolates, tribals as Noble Savages, and the primitive condition was described as a state of American simplicity" (Singh, 1985: 104).

Similar ahistoricity and segmental treatment of concepts can be seen in the colonial administrators-turned-sociologists' view of village communities in India. As Louis Dumont (1957) rightly observes, Sir Henry S. Maine "hardly ever looked at the Indian village in itself, but only as a counterpart to Teutonic, Slavonic or other institutions". India was to him little more than "the historical repository of veritable phenomena of ancient usage and ancient judicial thought" (ibid.: 830). They treated the village community as an autonomous sociological isolate. This is particularly reflected in the writings of Charles Metcalffe and other British administrators in India. The concept of 'community' was formulated by them in jural administrative terms patterned after Teutonic-Slavonic experiences where the notion of community was postulated as communal expression of individuals' rights and obligations and not as *sangha* – the Indian notion of community. D.P. Mukerji (1958) interprets *sangha* as being devoid of the notion of individual. The absence of the notion of 'individual' in the Indian tradition was later reiterated by Louis Dumont in his concept of the *Homo hierarchicus*. The collective principle not only operated at the normative level but also at the level of market and economy. It demonstrated the macro-structural linkages between caste, tribe, village community and family systems and the integrative role these institutions played in the unity of the Indian society (see Joshi, 1970). The roots of these integrative principles go far back into the historical past of Indian society. Irfan Habib illustrates it for Mughal India when he says: "the village was deeply affected by the requirements of commodity production (i.e., production for the market) ... the towns had not only to be fed by the countryside but to be supplied also with raw materials for their manufacturers" (1963: 37). During the 1950s and 1960s much literature generated by social anthropologists, economists and historians did away with the myth of the autonomy of the basic components of Indian social structure, i.e., the caste, tribe, village, family and kinship. On family and kinship systems, while Dumont (1957) demonstrated the structural similarity between the inter-regional kinship systems, Gough (1979) demonstrated the linkages between these institutions and the modes of production.

The ideology in the interpretation of Indian society and its institutions by the colonial scholars can be seen in the way they defined these institutions and in the methods they employed to study them. Each institution was treated as an ahistorical isolate devoid of linkages, and methodologically, emphasis was more on synchronic descriptions largely with the help of informants, mostly laymen. The contribution it made was not entirely free from conscious or unconscious partiality in the portrayal of social reality. In this context, several orientations in the interpretation of social reality of India emerged during the eighteenth and nineteenth centuries.

Bernard S. Cohn has analysed three such important orientations: the 'orientalist', 'missionary, and 'administrative'. The *orientalists* took a textual view of India offering a picture of its society as being static, timeless and spaceless. "In this view of the Indian society, there was no regional variation and no questioning of the relationship between prescriptive, normative statements derived from the texts and the actual behaviour of individuals or groups. Indian society was seen as a set of rules which every Hindu followed (Cohn and Singer, 1968: 8). The *missionary* view developed a little later. It saw all the roots of degeneration and evil in Indian society in its religion (Hinduism), and offered avenues for its redemption in conversion to Christianity. Unlike the orientalists, who often took a positive or even laudatory view of the Indian tradition, the *missionaries* treated Indian, particularly Hindu institutions as 'degenerate and base'. According to Cohn, the differences in the perspectives on India between the missionaries and the orientalists rested on differences in their social origin. The *administrative* perspective on the Indian social reality was grounded in the British utilitarian tradition (see Stocks, 1978) which also viewed traditional institutions in Indian as impediments to development of a rational modern society; hence, the need for social and institutional reforms.

These perceptions of Indian social reality were conditioned by the social origin of the scholars and by their specific ideological positions: classicism for orientalists, evangelicism for missionaries and rational utilitarianism for administrators-turned-social scientists. In addition, they all held a static, non-historical and fragmentationist view of Indian institutions. Even their economic anthropology of the village tended to circumscribe all relationships within the confines of a village territory, as we see in William Wiser's *The Hindu Jajmani System* (1936). The general theory of the Indian village organization in the writings of Sir Henry Maine and Charles Metcalffe was a near-transplantation of the European model of village organization on the Indian scene, and of course, these generalizations were without an 'intensive ethnographic base'. Thus, the sociology of India from roughly 1775 to 1940 to which Bernard S. Cohn refers was conditioned by the social background, ideology and preferred methods of collection of data by each category of sociologist or ethnographer concerned.

Yogendra Singh discusses four types of theoretical orientations related to the Indian sociology. They are: (1) philosophic – theoretic orientation; (2) culturological orientation; (3) structural theoretic orientation; and (4) dialectical historical theoretic orientation. On the formalization criteria of theory none of these existed in a systematic form. Most of them have operated at styles of analysis or have been evolved into quasi-formal systems of conceptual schemes. We, however, observe the changes in the theoretic structure of Indian society in terms of innovation, universalization of concepts and categories. The first two decades of the twentieth century mark caste, social customs, folklore, land systems and the village communities; and their comparison with similar institutions in the West. Most important meta-theoretic contribution was engendering and also ethno-sociological awareness about Indian sociology. It needs the quest for the universalization of the use of native categories in the analysis of Indian society.

Singh (ibid.) discusses the following conceptual categories, which have been broadly used by different scholars for the study of Indian society:

1. Sanskritization and westernization – M.N. Srinivas
2. Little and great traditions – McKim Marriott
3. Multi-dimensional tradition – S.C. Dube
4. Theory of structuralism – Richard Lembert, D.P. Mukerji, A.R. Desai
5. Historicity of emotions – Louis Dumont

Besides, we have come across some other major categories also, which have been constructed or used by some other scholars. They are, for example:

1. Modernization – Yogendra Singh
2. Dominant caste and caste hierarchy – M.N. Srinivas
3. Reference group model for the caste – Y.B. Damle
4. Universalization and parochialization – McKim Marriott
5. Concept of rural cosmopolitanism – Oscar Lewis
6. Resource group – K.N. Sharma

All the above conceptual categories are constructed or used by the two types of the scholars: one, the Indian scholars, e.g., Srinivas' concept of sanskritization; and second, western scholars, who did fieldwork in India and constructed them for their analysis. Here, we may say that though scholars are western but constructed native categories while doing studies in India, e.g., Marriott's category of little and great traditions.

Keeping in view all these conceptual and theoretical categories, Yogendra Singh presents an integral approach for doing the study in Indian society.

## Village Studies

Sociologists in India have broadly concentrated their studies on the villages of India. Here, excerpts from Atal's (2003: 174–81) analysis of the village studies have been presented to understand the use of native categories in the analysis of Indian society.

Village studies movement in India has gone through a series of phases. As we have noted, it began in the pre-independence period largely as a concern of the administrator, and was led by the practitioners of the discipline of economics; sociologists and social anthropologists arrived on the rural scene much later, and mostly after independence. They began their work in the style of an ethnographer, concentrating on a single village and following a holistic approach. It may be noted that the so-called microcosmic approach of the anthropologists, developed and practised by them in the tribal settings, treated tribe as a unit of study, which consisted of several villages; the villages were parts of the wider whole of the tribe. Application of the same approach in the rural areas was, however, different; in the latter case, the village was treated as a unit of study, a community social system, and 'whole' of a sort. Thus, in a sense, anthropology in the rural setting adopted a still smaller unit for observation and reporting than in the case of tribal studies.

It is in this context that Robert Redfield's seminal concepts of indigenous civilization, little community, peasant society, and great and little traditions were examined, and their validity tested empirically. Taking clues from Redfield, and also from Srinivas' concepts of spread (local, regional, and all-India) and sanskritization (1952), McKim Marriott (1955) came up with two complementary concepts explicating the twin processes of universalization and parochialization. Oscar Lewis (1958) added to this inventory the concept of rural cosmopolitanism. A critical examination of these concepts led by S.C. Dube (1955) to propose a five-fold classification of Indian tradition; he tentatively listed them as classical, regional, local, western, and emergent national.

While researchers continued their village studies in the model of ethnography, these concepts offered them with useful talking points. In the process, the style of description changed, analytical categories began to be used and methodological innovations were made.

Debate on concepts and methodology led to the diversification of village studies. Questions of representatives promoted interest in comparative studies: more than one village, in the same or in a different culture area, was chosen for purposes of comparison. Rather than studying all aspects of life in a village, attention was focused on specific aspects such as caste, family, group dynamics and factionalism, economic life and *jajmani* system, village pantheon and the like. Efforts have also been made to study the same institutions in a number of villages.

Introduction of the comparative approach necessitated proper and usable definition of the key concepts, viz., village, caste, and joint family. Of these three concepts, very little has been written on the concept of village; the definition given by the census has generally been accepted. There are instances where administrative definition was found unacceptable. Two illustrations will suffice: (1) in Rajasthan, one of the places was, on popular demand, classified as town but later, upon the introduction of Panchayati Raj, political leadership of the community managed to reclaim its village status; and (2) the satellite villages, called Nagla in Uttar Pradesh, are generally included in part of the core village though they possess, in many cases, all the sociological attributes of separate village community. Based on these considerations, the present author ignored the revenue definition and treated a *Nagla* as a village in his study in *Local Communities and National Politics* (1971).

Attempts have also been made to classify the villages. Thus, some have taken the degree of nucleation as the key classificatory variable and talked about nucleated and dispersed villages. The concept of nucleated village includes the core village and the surrounding satellites. Similarly, coastal villages have been identified as a separate type. Studies have also been made of the fringe villages. In terms of social demography, classification based on the size of settlement, and the number of ethnic groups (single caste versus multi-caste villages) is also in vogue. In terms of economic pursuit, while there is recognition of the presence of fishing and pastoral villages, studies have mostly concentrated on agricultural villages. A unique village from the Kullu valley has also been reported, which has managed to keep itself from more or less completely insulated from the rest of the village of the region by physically shutting its doors off to the outside world, but speaking its own language, and by practicing its own culture (Rosser, 1955).

The most talked about concept in Indian rural sociology is that of caste. Whether the title of the study emphasizes village or caste, it is the latter which invariably holds the floor. Village studies came in for heavy criticism because of this 'obsession' with caste. The fact, however, remains that caste is a vital element of Indian society, and its neglect in a study would have made the entire exercise worthless. It is only the students of village who started empirical investigation of this most complex phenomenon of Indian social structure.

The great gap between the ideological percepts and the living reality – between the text and the present-day context – that they discovered was an eye-opener. While the urban-based armchair theoretician was content with what has been written about caste in the old scriptures and transmitted it to others with his seal of approval, the village sociologist found it difficult to digest. Controversy was raised as regards the status of this concept – is it to be treated as a cultural concept associated with pan-Indian civilization or is it to be regarded as a social structural category of universal application? Culturologists, following the line of Indology, opted for the former and sociologists for the latter. A seminal essay by Irawati Karve (1958) raising the question unambiguously, what is caste? deserves special mention. Distinction between *varna, jati, gotra, vansha* and the like assumed significance. The concept of sub-caste came under heavy fire, whereas Karve's concept of caste cluster found many followers. Mayer's (1960) distinction of kindered of cooperation and kindered of recognition as two facets of caste was quite attractive but was challenged by Atal (1968). Atal strongly emphasized the need for distinguishing between caste as a unit *(jati)* and the caste system; using the notion of subset he provided a specific definition on the concept of sub-caste. For the caste as a unit, Atal regards endogamy as the pivotal attribute; by the same token caste system is characterized by a plurality of interacting endogamous groups.

Other related concepts are those of dominant caste and caste hierarchy. The concept of dominant was proposed by M.N. Srinivas (1959) in his essay published in the *American Anthropologist*. Soon it caught the fancy of many and became a catchword in rural sociology, as did his earlier concept of sanskritization. The concept of dominant case was challenged by B.R. Chauhan (1967), Yogesh Atal (1968), S.C. Dube (1968), and T.K. Oommen (1970). In this connection, the concept of faction may be mentioned. In village studies in India, this was introduced by Oscar Lewis (1958) in his studies on group dynamics in a north Indian village. While Lewis talked of permanent factions, which were kin-linked, and were cooperative in orientation. Yogesh Atal (1963, 1968) identified short-lived alliances as aspect of village factionalism, which he designated as ephemeral factions. A number of scholars have written on the concept of faction, important among them being Ralph Nicholas (1963), Paul Brass (1965), Richard Sisson (1972), B.K. Nagla (1984) etc. K.N. Sharma (1963, 1969) introduced the concept of resource group.

A major motivating factor for village studies in the 1960s was the Community Development Programme (CDP). Several scholars went to the village to study the process of externally induced, directed, culture change. As a result, a number of case studies on innovation and innovators, and on the leadership, were prepared. These changed the focus of village studies from the description of social structure to social change. Some re-studies have also been attempted: Wiser's *Behind Mudwalls* (1961) and Ghurye's *After a Century and Quarter – Lonikand: Then and New* (1960) may be mentioned. Srinivas has revisited his legendary village of Rampura several times in past 20 years and has written a book entitled *The Remembered Village*.

## Beyond the Village

In more recent years, attention has shifted to a more general process of modernization. This has taken the scholars beyond the village. Employing more sophisticated tools, either of survey research or of psychological testing, a group of villages have been taken up for investigation. There have been studies of communication links, flows of information, voting behaviour, attitudes and aspirations, health practices and family planning, and of economic transactions in the village communities. Some have attempted to analyse class and power relations in a caste society, following largely the Weberian model (cf. Béteille, 1966).

There is, thus, a much more differentiated pattern of village studies in India. Of late, rural research in India has received a certain setback. The interest seems to be on the wane. Indian social science is increasingly getting oriented towards the urban. This shift in focus is understandable, although the neglect of the village cannot be commended.

It must be admitted that considerable data have been generated regarding the villages. There is a need to look at this data with a view to stocktaking. Most of this material is discrete, descriptive and discipline-specific. Very little has been done to consolidate and codify it. While methodological questions have been raised and debated, and concepts have been evolved and conceptual frameworks have been formulated, no rigorous writing on theory has appeared so far.

## Social Structure: Social Stratification

The Indian social structure, in a broader way, is stratified into two divisions: (1) the folks or the unlettered peasantry, and (2) the elites. The folks and peasantry follow the little tradition, i.e., the village tradition. The second division of elites follows the great tradition. The great tradition consists of the traditions contained in epics, *Puranas*, *Brahmins* and other classical Sanskritic works. The roles and statuses of Sita and Draupadi constitute the parts of great tradition. The little tradition, on the other hand, is local tradition tailored according to the regional and village conditions. The great tradition is found clearly in twice-born castes, specially priests, ritual leaders of one kind or other. Some of these corporate groups follow the traits of civilization and the great tradition. The carriers of little tradition include folk artists, medicine men, tellers of riddles, proverbs and stories, poets and dancers, etc.

Little and great traditions help to analyse social change in rural India. The nature of this change is basically cultural. There is a constant interaction between the two traditions which brings about change in rural society. Yogendra Singh explains this interaction as follows: "Changes in the cultural system follow through the interaction between the two traditions in the orthogenetic or heterogenetic process of individual growth. The pattern of change, however, is generally from orthogenetic to heterogenetic forms of differentiation or change in the cultural structure of traditions."

Both Singer and Marriott (1955) argue on the strength of data generated from the villages of their study that the cultural content of social structure at the level of little tradition in a village witnesses changes. First, there is change in the village culture due to the internal growth of village. In other words, the little tradition witnesses changes due to its own internal growth. Second, the little tradition also undergoes change due to its contact with great tradition and other parts of the wider civilization. "The direction of this change presumably is from folk or peasant to urban cultural structure and social organization." The great tradition, i.e., the epic tradition also witnesses universalized pattern of culture resulting from its interaction with the village or little tradition.

Singer has made certain statements about cultural change in rural India. His observations are as under:

1. The Indian civilization has evolved out of pre-existing folk and regional cultures. This aspect of civilization constructed the great tradition – *Ramayana*, *Mahabharata* and other religious scriptures. This great tradition maintained its continuity in India's diverse regions, village, castes and tribes.
2. The cultural continuity of great tradition is based on the idea that people share common cultural consciousness throughout the country.
3. The common cultural consciousness is formed through the consensus held in common about sacred books and sacred objects.
4. In India, cultural continuity with the past is so great that even the acceptance of modernizing and progress ideologies does not result in linear form of social and cultural change but may result in the traditionalizing of apparently modern innovations.

To conclude, it could be safely said that there is one cultural approach out of several to explain rural social change in India. In simple words, one could say that a villager borrows norms and values from the great tradition of country's civilization. In this borrowing, he makes changes according to his village's local conditions and history. The villages vary from region to region and, therefore, the little tradition also continues to remain diverse. On the other hand, the great tradition, i.e., the sacred books, also receives a uniform pattern. The concepts, therefore, explain the cultural change both at regional and national levels.

## Parochialization and Universalization

Parochialization and universalization are complementary to the concepts of little and great traditions. These are processes of cultural change. When the great tradition, i.e., the tradition of epics and sacred books, undergoes change at the local or village level, it is parochialization or localization of great tradition or civilization. Parochialization, therefore, is the cultural change made at the village level.

Universalization, on the other hand, is a cultural change from little tradition to great tradition. Both these processes are related to the interaction between little tradition and great tradition. Interpreting the process of universalization, Yogendra Singh observes that when the little tradition moves upward to the great tradition, it is the process of universalization. And, when the great tradition moves downward to the local or village level, it is parocialization. His interpretation runs as follows: "Elements of the little tradition, indigenous customs, duties and rites circulate upward to the level of the great tradition and are identified with its legitimate forms. This process, Marriott calls 'universalization'. Likewise, some elements of the great tradition also circulate downward to become organic of the great tradition, and lose much of their original form in the process. He (Marriott) used the term 'parochialization' to denote this kind of transaction between the two traditions."

In the process of parocialization, obviously, there is some loss of the elements of great tradition. Whatever is laid down as elements of great tradition is reduced at village level or interpreted differently by local leaders of priestly castes. This process is called de-sanskritization.

## Select Bibliography

Atal, Yogesh (1963), 'Short Lives Alliances as an Aspect of Factionalism in an Indian Village', *The Journal of Social Sciences*, Vol. 3, pp. 65–75.

— (1968), *The Changing Frontiers of Caste*, Delhi: National Publishing House.

— (1971), *Local Communities and National Politics*, New Delhi: National Publishing House.

— (2003), *Indian Sociology: From where to where*, Jaipur: Rawat Publications.

Béteille, André (1966), *Caste, Class and Power: Changing Patterns of Stratification in a Tanjore Village*, Bombay: Oxford University Press.

Brass, Paul (1965), *Factional Politics in an Indian State*, Berkeley: University of California Press.

Chauhan, B.R. (1967), *A Rajasthan Village*, New Delhi: Associated Publishing House.

Cohn, Bernard S. and Milton Singer (eds) (1968), *Structure and Change in Indian Society*, Chicago: Aldine Publishing Company.

Dube, S.C. (1955), *Indian Village*, London: Routledge and Kegan Paul.

— (1968), 'Caste Dominance and Factionalism', *Contributions to Indian Sociology*, New Series No. II, pp. 58–81.

Dumont, Louis (1957), 'For a Sociology of India: Village Studies, Kinship', *Contributions to Indian Sociology* (Paris) 1:7–64.

Elvin, Verrier (1943), *The Aboriginals*, Oxford: Oxford University Press.

Ghurye, G.S. (1960), *After a Century and Quarter-Lonikand: Then and New*, Bombay: Popular Book Depot.

Gough, K. (1979), 'Dravidian Kinship and modes of Production', *Contributions to Indian Sociology* (N.S.) 13 (12): 265–91.

Habib, Irfan (1963), *The Agrarian System of Mughal India*, Bombay: Asia Publishing House.

Joshi, P.C. (1970), 'Review Article', *Seminar*, May.

Lewis, Oscar (1958), *Village Life in Northern India: Studies in a Delhi Village*, Urbana: University of Illinois.

Marriott, McKim (1955), 'Caste Ranking and Community Structures in Five Regions of India and Pakistan', Doctoral Dissertation; Chicago: Chicago University.

Mayer, A.C. (1960), *Caste and Kinship in Central India*, London: Routledge and Kegan Paul.

Mukerji, D.P. (1958), *Diversities*, Delhi: Peoples Publishing House.

Mukherjee, R.K (1979), *Sociology of Indian Sociology*, Bombay: Allied.

Nagla, B.K. (1984), *Factionalism, Politics and Social structure*, Jaipur: Rawat Publications.

Nicholas, Ralph (1963), 'Factions: A Comparative Analysis', in Michael Benton (ed.), *Political Systems and the Distribution of Power*, London: Tavistock.

Nicholas, Ralph W. (1965), *Political System and Distribution of Power*, ASA Monograph, London: Tavistock Publications.

Oommen, T.K. (1970), 'The Concept of Dominant Caste: Some Queries', *Contributions to Indian Sociology,* New Series No. 4, pp. 73–83.

Rosser, Collin (1955), 'A Hermit Village in Kullu', in M.N. Srinivas (ed.), *India's Village,* Calcutta: West Bengal Government Press.

Sharma, K.N. (1963), 'Panchayat Leadership and Resource Group', *Sociological Bulletin*, Vol. 12, No. 1, pp. 47–52.

— (1969), 'Resource Networks and Resource Groups in Social Structure', *Eastern Anthropologist*, Vol. 22, No. 1, pp. 13–27.

Singh, K.S. (1985), *Tribal Society in India: An Anthropo-historical Perspective*, Delhi: Manohar.

Singh, Yogendra (1986), 'Indian Sociology', *Current Sociology*, Vol. 34, No. 2, Summer.

— (1984), 'Relevant Sociology (I) and (II)', 'Indian Situation', *Relevant Sociology*, 1(2):5–17.

— (1993), 'Ideology, Theory and Method', in B.K. Nagla (ed.), *Development and Social Transformation*, Jaipur: Rawat Publications.

Sisson, Richard (1972), *The Congress party in Rajasthan*, Delhi: Oxford University Press.

Srinivas, M.N. (1959), 'The Dominant Caste in Rampura', *American Anthropologist*, Vol. 61, pp. 1–16.

Wiser, William (1936), *The Hindu Jajmani System*.

# 25

# Sociology for India: An Issue for Indian Sociology

The discussion on sociology *in*, *of*, and *for* India came for debate in the year 1950. We, therefore, discuss the following issues relating to the status of sociology in India.

1. Sociology in India
2. Sociology of India
3. Sociology for India

Sociology *in* India deals with the professional activities of sociologists, which are related to the teaching of sociology in India. The discussion on sociology *of* India concerns itself with approaches to the study of Indian society. This is related to the researches, which are done on Indian society, e.g., caste, kinship, village studies etc. But, the western theories are applied in the researches done in India, e.g., Srinivas and Dube applied structural-functional approach in their studies. In the case of sociology *for* India, the effort seems to be one of postulating a set of concepts and theories suitable to study Indian social reality (Oommen, 1986). Therefore, what should be the sociology for India? Young sociologists want emancipation from colonial sociology. Even Dumont was a French sociologist, who did studies on India but he did not agree to the idea of inequality in caste. He talks of hierarchy in the structure of Indian society. There is a need of decolonization of thoughts or deconstruction of western approaches. In this context, there emerge the following issues for ponder the debate:

(i) Emancipation
(ii) Indological sociology (book view)
(iii) Contextualization: Indigenization (Indianization: field view)

All these issues have been discussed in our discourse analysis. Here, our main focus is on the debate of *sociology for India.*

## Ideology, Theory and Methods in Indian Sociology

India had colonial cognitive traditions in the past and it has become an independent nation since 1947. This provides a new context and milieu. Sociology of knowledge perspective would demand examination of the continuity/discontinuity in the colonial approaches, concepts and methods of study.

Yogendra Singh (1986) observes that even the debate – whether sociology has universal concepts and techniques or it refers to culturally cognitive styles and structures – could be seen in the context of the hangover of colonialism in independent India today. Today, the tension in Indian sociology is between:

1. The 'Master Theory' or 'General Theory' and conceptual schemes.
2. Universalism of concepts and proposition and their 'particularism' or 'contextuality'.
3. The role ideology in theory construction.

Singh has analysed the debate on sociology for India. Here, we are giving excerpts of his analysis. Therefore, the details about the references mentioned in the present text may be seen from the writing of Singh (1986). An issue in Indian sociology, which has been carried over from the 1950s to the 1970s and 1980s is that of the quest for 'Sociology for India'. During the late 1950s and the 1960s a debate began on this theme and grew in two directions: the first was initiated by Dumont and Pocock. It was grounded in a structuralist methodology for the treatment of social reality in general and the Indian social reality in particular in the context of ideology. Ideology, to Dumont, "commonly designates a more or less social set of ideas and values", which in the case of social facts, taking care not to mix up facts of 'representation' with facts of 'behaviour' (Dumont and Pocock, 1957: 11) are constituted in the principle of 'hierarchy'. Indian sociology should, therefore, according to Dumont and Pocock, be a sociology of Indian civilization. Its constituents are Indology on one hand and on the other social 'structures' which as 'representations' articulate the specific principle of 'hierarchy' with its own governing components of ideology, dialectic, transformational relationship and comparison (Singh, 1985; Jain, 1985), i.e., the basic elements of a structuralist perspective. In contrast to Dumont and Pocock, F.G. Bailey (1959) postulated that Indian sociology was the study not of 'representations' but of actual behaviour patterns, social roles, and structures from an empirical perspective. This controversy, which was essentially between two theoretical perspectives on social structure in the traditions of European social anthropology, was mistakenly constructed in India as debate about the choice between a particularistic versus universalistic paradigm for Indian sociology. Although both Dumont and Pocock and Bailey did not visualize a particularistic Indian sociology, in the social context of India, their contributions, especially that of Dumont, did trigger a debate on this issue.

## Debate on Sociology for India

The main function of this debate was to help Indian sociologists to reach a level of self-awareness. This debate was carried on in *Contributions to Indian Sociology* edited by Dumont and Pocock, but with the end of its publication and the appearance of *Contributions to Indian Sociology (New Series)* edited by T.N. Madan, a column was assigned to the theme of a 'Sociology for India'. From 1970 to 1985 papers have been continually published on this theme (e.g.,

Yogendra Singh, 1970; Dhirendra Narain, 1971; Imtiaz Ahmad, 1972; W.H. McLeod, 1978; T.N. Madan, 1981; Satish Saberwal, 1982; Kantowski, 1984). Besides, *Sociological Bulletin*, the journal of the Indian Sociological Society, has carried several articles on the paradigmatic issues of Indian sociology, in addition to the addresses by the Presidents of the Society to which we have already referred (e.g., M.N. Srinivas, 1970; S.L. Sharma, 1977; J. Lele, 1981, etc.). One finds substantial continuity of concerns in these articles, especially on the issue of indigenization of Indian sociology, yet, one also witnesses in these debates the emergence of new perspectives. One finds a fundamental change emerging in the ideological basis on which the issue of a sociology for India could be anchored. The focus shift from a debate on sociological colonialism or dependency to the constructive formulation and investigation of grounds on which the specific cognitive structure of Indian sociology could be constituted. One set of contributions seeks to explore the various contextual and historical variations from those implicit in the Dumont-Pocock presuppositions in the observation of Indian or South Asian structure. A few of them challenge the Dumont-Pocock notion of Indian civilization as an exclusively Hindu civilization (Ahmad, 1970). Moreover, within Hindu civilization itself, the role of Hindu and non-Hindu or non-Brahminical elements is emphasized by some sociologists on the basis of intra-cultural variations (Burghart, 1983). An intensive exploration of selected elements of traditions and social structures in India with a view to analysing their symbolic content as well as their inter-cultural and intra-cultural comparability has been undertaken by others (see McLeod, 1978; Selwyn, 1973; Saberwal, 1982). These viewpoints mark a departure from the early concern with the problem of sociology's indigenization. Not that this problem is not debated during the 1970s and 1980s, but in most cases, indigenization is now identified with an emphasis on historicity, conceptual relevance and sensitivity to the distinction of levels (regional, national and cross-national) in attempts to make generalizations through theoretical abstractions in Indian sociology (see Singh, 1970; Narain, 1971).

In the debate on a sociology for India, we thus notice a distinct shift of emphasis in the 1980s. More attention is now paid to the nature of Indian social reality both in its intrinsic and comparative contexts. Burghart, on the basis of his study of the Nepalese social institutions in the setting of a Hindu kingdom, finds Dumont's single system (Hindu) conception of social order theoretically inadequate. He writes:

> I shall argue on theoretical grounds that recourse to single system models commits the anthropologist to understand order in the context of system and this commitment obliges the anthropologist to situate the system in a changeless period of time. Order, however, is quite a different concept from changelessness and until this difference is sorted out I do not see how social change or changelessness can be adequately understood. I suggest instead that an intra-cultural approach to the study of Hindu society permits valid levels of generalization (1983: 276).

Further, the conception of Hindu society as a system and the representation of that system in terms of a scheme of social relations have had the effect of obscuring other schemes which South Asians use to represent their universe of social relations (ibid.: 282). One such other scheme that Burghart identifies in the Nepalese Kingdom is that of tenurial system, by which the king administers his possessions *(muluk)*, its contractual relationships among members enjoying tenurial status, his control over social hierarchy and a serried of other relations and obligations. Similarly, studies of sects and belief systems within Hinduism and its cognate branches have shown characteristics that deviate from a neat structural fit among the components of social system. A significant feature of the new debate on a sociology for India is its grounding in empirical observations and analysis of social reality and its search for principles of social structural integration in terms of contents, meanings and metaphors. Most such studies are deeply influenced by the Dumont-Pocock tradition of social analysis, which offered advantages in studying structures symbolically or in terms of values and beliefs. Hence, one common feature of the new debates on a sociology for India is its overarching symbolic, subjectivist and culturological tendency. Defining structure as representation, this model is more attuned to studying belief systems, ritual practices, the structure and dialectic of textual material, a myth or legend, than the structures of political economy, power structures and social order.

Yogendra Singh (1983: 101) reviewed the main theoretic orientations in Indian sociology. According to him, it may be useful to assess its impact on the process of universalization or particularization of categories and theory. This issue is both ideological and theoretic. Since Dumont and Pocock initiated the debate on "For a Sociology of India" in 1957, this usage has been debated in response to their and Bailey's writings and also independently. Dumont's emphasis in the study of Indian sociology is on its fundamental ideo-structural categories from an "external point of view". He would formulate his sociology from the language of the sources as it were, from the sentiments and ideas of the people themselves. Bailey finds fault with this model for its indifference towards study of 'relations', which are the main sociological category. With this frame of reference, sociology gets reduced to what Bailey calls 'culturology'. In his statement on "For a Sociology of India" in the final issue of *Contributions*, however, Dumont clarifies that he does not see the possibility of a particularistic sociology even though the substantive reality he would prefer the sociologists to deal with would be ideas and sentiments and not relations. Thus, without taking a structural position as that of Bailey, Dumont sees the possibility of a general sociology as the only way out.

The debate between Dumont and Bailey led Indian sociologists to ponder over this problem from an Indian perspective, where the issue was not of two varieties of general sociology, of which the Indian sociology would be a part, but it was mainly whether Indian sociology could be universal or has to be particularistic. A seminar was organized on this problem in 1966 and its deliberations have been published (Unnithan et al., 1967). The conclusion of this seminar was that Indian sociology would have to operate at two levels – the particularistic and the universal. Some concepts and categories, as Srinivas' Sanskritization-Westernization, would be of primarily particularistic and ethno-sociological relevance, but these could be further abstracted for cross-cultural comparisons (see, Singh in Unnithan et al., 1967).

The debate on this issue has not subsided. It was given a sharper edge by linking the problem both of creativity and categories in Indian sociology to the colonial situation. Jit P. Singh Uberoi, in his *Science and Swaraj*, concludes: "Every *swarajist* should recognize what are the essential pre-conditions, under his system (structural asymmetries like rich; poor; international; national; white-black), for the advancement of universal science in our environment. Until we can concentrate on decolonization, learn to nationalize our problems and take our poverty seriously, we shall continue to be both colonial and unoriginal" (Uberoi, 1968: 123). This observation of Uberoi has echoes in many quarters. As we mentioned, Saran (1958) is its strong exponent, who does not see contradictions in methods and categories of the ethno-sociology and general sociology. The problem is ideological and as such it pervades through all levels of sociological thinking in India where normative questions and not merely technology of research are involved.

Even, the universality of methods and tools of research is questioned. Most of these involve translation of cultural idioms and symbols from one culture into another. What is more seriously questioned, however, is the choice of problems and research priorities that sociologists undertake for investigation. In a recent debate on this problem, which is contained in *Social Sciences and Social Realities: Role of Social Sciences in Contemporary India* (1976), edited by S.C. Dube such issues have reopened for a variety of social sciences. The distortions in sociological thinking and practice are created by alienation of the professional sociologists from the other sections of elites and people of the society. This leads to the distantiation of sociologists from the major issues of national concern or with national identity. His uncritical acceptance of models of theory and research tools imported from abroad have come in for thorough examination (see, Singh, in Dube, 1976).

The question of universalization or particularism of sociological categories in Indian sociology or social sciences as such remains open. A more enduring solution to this issue would probably come from accumulation of empirical knowledge through the findings of Indian sociologists and social scientists from studies conducted with self-awareness and scientific objectivity within their own ideological setting. Surendra Sharma (1985) analysed this question as universal versus specific related to the sociology for India. Here, we give excerpts from his book for understanding the issue for sociology in India.

## Universal vs. Specific Sociology for India

Now, let us take up proceedings of the two seminars on sociology in India held in the 1960s. R.N. Saxena, Y.B. Damle, Yogendra Singh, B.R. Chauhan and Indra Deva are contributors to both the volumes. However, R.N. Saxena has the same view in several addresses and papers which he holds in "Sociology in India" and "Sociology for India". The other well-known names are Victor S. D'Souza, K.M. Kapadia, K.C. Panchanadikar and J.M. Panchanadikar. None of these scholars with the exception of Yogendra Singh have joined the debate on Indian sociology in the pages of *Contributions to Indian Sociology*.

An Indological or culturological approach has been the hallmark of several sociologists. They have hammered against the acceptance of theoretical and methodological orientations of the western countries. These scholars emphasize the role of traditions, group rather than individual as the basis of social relations, and religion, ethics and philosophy as the basis of social organizations. R.N. Saxena (1965), for example, stresses on the role of the concepts of Dharma, Artha, Kaama and Moksha. Dumont and Pocock (1957) emphasize utility of the Indological sources for sociological formulations. Saxena observes that sociology in the Indian universities has been shaped on the western pattern. The western sociology is no doubt 'empirical' and 'positivistic', but it fails to provide a proper examination of spiritual values and other super-non- empirical ideas. After arguing a case for the relevance of the study of categorical values and norms, Saxena (1965) writes: "A correct approach to Indian sociology can only be a synthesis of empiricism and intuition and a proper recognition of the fact that spiritual values have an important role on our social life."

Indra Deva (1965) discerns the following points, which might make a reference to the term 'Indian sociology':

1. a body of concepts and generalizations applicable specifically to Indian society and culture;
2. sociological principles derived from traditional Indian sources;
3. the study of social structure and social processes in India; and
4. sociology as it has developed in India.

However, these points are not exclusive when they are used for denoting 'Indian sociology'. After having discussed these points, Indra Deva formulates a view contrary to that of Saxena. He observes that though Indian society has some features of its own, the distinctiveness about it is not so fundamental as to necessitate the development of an 'Indian sociology' in the sense of special conceptual and theoretical framework. The task is to develop the general sociological theories, concepts and methodology, which can be applicable to a pre-modern, mainly peasant society, like India. Coomaraswamy (1948) talked of the essential unity of all traditional societies. In other words, such societies would represent a social formation different from that of the western industrialized societies. Deva suggests that western ethnocentrism must go from the existing theoretical and conceptual framework of sociology, and a theoretical system be evolved, which can do justice to the structural and functional and the dynamic aspects of society (Deva, 1965).

Damle (1965) is very particular with regard to sociology in India. He writes: "In order to take cognizance of both stability and change I would suggest the use of the Parsonian frame of reference for the study of Indian sociology." Parsons' view that personality, culture and society are 'atomistic' as well as interdependent systems and constitute the social system is explained by Damle as relevant for studying Indian society. Damle observes: "Talking in terms of functional prerequisites one finds in India that greatest amount of premium is put on pattern maintenance rather than on adaptation and goal attainment." Later on, Damle adopted Merton's theory of 'reference group' for analysing social mobility in the caste system in India. Damle gives a paradigm adopted from Parsons for application to the analysis of social system in India. He concludes that no special theory is needed for studying Indian sociology.

## Western Social Science and Sociology in India

Yogendra Singh (1965) counts three points relevant to the disciplinary growth of sociology in India: (1) the changing historico-political status of the country; (2) the changing nature of western intellectual contact and its vicissitudes; and finally, (3) the native intellectual traditions from which the sociologists themselves emerged. In the first phase, Indian social structure and values and institutions were analysed but not as a response to the western social science. The second phase refers to the combination of empirical and historico-philosophical analysis of Radhakamal Mukerjee, and the application of a Marxologist approach to the study of Indian society, its tradition and culture, and class structure by D.P. Mukerji. The macro-static studies by B. Malinowski and A.R. Radcliffe-Brown replaced the macro-dynamic studies in Britain at the time when the two Mukerjees were busy in giving a sound shape to Indian sociology. With the freedom of India started the era of sponsored researches in India. However, the researches funded by the western countries were also carried out in the fifties and sixties in India on a bigger scale.

Thus, the ideology of the government on one hand, and of the western social sciences on the other simultaneously influenced social science research in the first two decades of India's independence. Singh (1965) states that (1) increased quantification and abstracted empiricism, (2) increased experimentalism, and (3) greater arbitrariness in regard to concepts and definitions are the significant trends of sociology as a discipline in India. Sociology in India in the early sixties is characterized by functionalism and neo-functionalism, historical comparative method and logico-philosophical and symbolic methods of analysis. Thus, anti-positivism and functionalism, positivism and logico-philosophical orientations influenced Indian sociologists simultaneously in the fifties and sixties. The western 'scienticism' could not overtake Indian sociology completely; it remained in India also as a philosophy of society and history. Singh prefers to have a synthesis of sociological empiricism and analytical quality of vision.

In two essays: (1) "Scope and Method of Sociology in India", and (2) "Sociology for India: The Emerging Perspective" in *Sociology for India*, Yogendra Singh (1967) exemplifies his own view and the resume of the above seminar, respectively. Some of the points mentioned in the Agra seminar have been repeated by Singh in the first paper of the above seminar. He writes: "Sociology in India or the whole university culture in this country has been an extension of the western, primarily the British tradition. Growing American influence is a post-independence phenomenon" and intellectual parasitism and regression. The pre-independence sociology could be characterized by descriptive, evolutionary, analytical and comparative studies and by particularism of Indian society and culture. However, Singh notes that both the organic positivism and mechanistic positivism of nineteenth century European sociology were absent in Indian sociology, and even some sociologists strongly reacted and refuted them (Sharma, 1985: 40–41).

Thus, in the above pages, an attempt has been made to formulate sociology for India or Indian sociology. The significance of the development in the changing conditions reflects the various new areas of research and studies. It indicates the shift in theoretical and methodological issues that took place after 1970s. 1980s signifies a remarkable shift in terms of emphasis. More attention is now paid to the nature of Indian social reality. An important feature of the new debate on sociology for India emphasizes on empirical observation and application of theory in context.

Despite the continuity reflected in the quest for social relevance on an indigenous paradigm for Indian sociology, 1980s and 1990s in India mark several directions in which new explorations have been made.

Sociological studies show a new sensitivity in the choice of concepts and their uses as they move away from a continuum framework of analysis of social processes to that of a notion of levels. The use of conceptual typologies, historical data and symbolic structural techniques adds new depth and dimensions to the studies of social structure. The Marxist historical method of the analysis gains momentum as a series of studies on the peasantry, agrarian structure, and working classes by younger generation sociologists. New series of study became sensitive to theoretical orientations, such as structuralism and post-structuralism, ethno-sociology, functionalism and neo-functionalism Marxism and neo-Marxism, modernity and post-modernity and so on. These perspectives have been used to analyse social structure.

Specific areas of sociological research, such as sociology of development, specifically sustainable development, sociology of education, sociology of health and medicine, sociology of profession, sociology of organization, sociology of management, sociology of communication, sociology of tourism, sociology of environment, sociology of science and technology, and analysis of problems of weaker sections of society, particularly scheduled castes, scheduled tribes, other backward classes, women etc. are expanded in order to promote social reconstruction and development. The understanding of the nature of these problems further enriched sociological insights into the nature of social structure, culture and its dynamics in Indian society.

## Select Bibliography

Coomaraswamy, Anand K. (1948), *The Dance of Siva,* Bombay: Asia Publishing House.

Damle, Y.B. (1965), "For a Theory of Indian Sociology", in T.K.N. Unnithan et al. (eds), *Sociology in India*, New Delhi: Prentice-Hall of India Pvt. Ltd.

Deva, Indra (1965), "Possibility of an Indian Sociology", in T.K.N. Unnithan et al. (eds), *Sociology in India*, New Delhi: Prentice-Hall of India Pvt. Ltd.

Dumont, Louis and D.F. Pocock (eds) (1957), *Contributions to Indian Sociology,* Vol. I.

Oommen, T.K. and Partha N. Mukherji (1986) *Indian Sociology: Reflections and Interpretation*, Bombay: Popular Prakashan.

Saran, A.K. (1958), "India", in Joseph S. Roucck (ed.), *Contemporary Sociology,* New York: Greenwood Press Publishers.

Saxena, R.N. (1965), "Sociology in India", in T.K.N. Unnithan et al. (eds), *Sociology in India*, New Delhi: Prentice-Hall of India Pvt. Ltd.

Sharma, Surendra (1985), *Sociology in India: A Perspective from Sociology of Knowledge*, Jaipur: Rawat Publications.

Singh, Yogendra (1965), "Sociology for India: The Emerging Perspective", in T.K.N. Unnithan et al. (eds), *Sociology in India*, New Delhi: Prentice-Hall of India Pvt. Ltd.

— (1986), "Indian Sociology", *Current Sociology*, Vol. 34, No. 2, summer.

— (1983), *Image of Man: Ideology and Theory in Indian Sociology*, Delhi: Chanakya Publications.

Unnithan, T.K.N. et al. (eds) (1967), *Sociology in India*, New Delhi: Prentice-Hall of India.

# 26

# Globalization: Indian Perspective

Globalization is as fascinating a term these days as modernization, development and change have been for the 20th century. To think of the world as a global village was once a day dreamer's delight. Not any more; instead the end of the 20th century will be remembered for bringing the dream of globalization to reality. On the one side, several outcomes of this transformation are within the reach of a large number of human beings, availability of mobile phones and internet facility are its examples. Who could have thought of its widespread availability in India three decades ago? Globalization as a trend would create its impact on each area of human activity.

## Globalization: Historical Perspective

There is no consensus about the starting point of globalization, although many agree that the process accelerated with the demise of the tripartite division of the world occasioned by the dismantling of the Second World. However, several authors, Karl Marx, Immanuel Wallerstein, Roland Robertson, just to mention three, locate AD 1500 as the starting point of globalization. There are others who pitch it later. For example, for Anthony Giddens, modernity is the theme song of globalization and the 1800s marked its beginning. According to Tomlinson, globalization began as recently as the 1960s with cultural pluralization. But as Nederveen Pieterse points out, that modernity/globalization view is not only geographically narrow but also historically shallow (1994).

Globalization is an outcome of the universal logic of modernity. Giddens (1990) assumes that globalization is the corollary of modernity. The implication of the modernity/globalization view is that the history of globalization begins with the history of west. But it is not precisely the point of globalization as a perspective that globalization begins with world history.

There is no agreed starting point, but understanding of globalization is helped by considering the following:

- The emergence of capitalism is the beginning of globalization. The first great expansion of European capitalism took place in the 16th century, following the first circumnavigation of the earth in 1519 to 1521.
- There was a big expansion in world trade and investment in the nineteenth century.
- The end of the Second World War brought another great expansion of capitalism with the development of multinational companies interested in producing and selling in the domestic markets of nations around the world.
- The emancipation of colonies created a new world order. Air travel and the development of international communication enhanced the progress of international business.
- The fall of the Berlin Wall and the collapse of the Soviet Union ended the Cold War between the forces of capitalism and socialism with capitalism triumphant.
- The development of the internet made possible the organization of business on a global scale with greater facility than ever before. (Pieterse, 1995)

Thus, globalization is an objective, all embracing historical process which began with the breakthrough of capitalism in some countries of Western Europe, notably England, in the early decades of the 19th century. From almost its inception, it developed along with colonialism and later in the century, blossomed fully as imperialism.

## Globalization: Conceptual Clarification

The origin of the concept of 'globalization' is usually traced to Marshal McLuhan (1960), who first introduced the idea of what is today called 'global village' – a notion that implied a sort of compression of the world and intensification of consciousness of the world as a single entity. Therefore, many individuals, organization and countries consider the world in this new millennium as the 'global village'.

Globalization refers to various multidimensional socio-economic and political processes by which the people of the world are incorporated into a single world society, a global village. It tends to homogenize the cultures as well as popularize even unknown cultures of the world. It acts as heterogenizer with a possibility of pluralism. Globalization strives to make the world as its market where all the people are being brought as buyer and seller on unequal terms.

Globalization refers to the multiplicity of linkages and interconnectedness that transcend the nation-states (and by implications the societies) which make up the modern world system. It reflects a process through which events, decisions and activities in one part of the world would have significant consequences for individuals and communities of quite distant parts of the globe. However, for Giddens, globalization embraces much more than a notion of simple interconnectedness. For him, "globalization concerns the intersection of presence and absence, the interlacing of social events and social relations 'at distance' with local contextualties".

It may be understood as a dialectical phenomenon in which events at one pole having distance relation often produce divergent or even contrary occurrence at another. While communication and information are increasingly diffused on a global scale, the individuals locally appropriate these, inherently in contextual and hermeneutic way. Thus globalization becomes glocalization.

## Globalization: The Indian Perspective

Globalization in India started with the new economic policy in July 1991. From then on, India has made tremendous progress in information technology, media sectors, and banking. In this context, globalization, competitiveness and liberalization came to India as a booster and through the backdoor of 'economic reforms'. The sanctity of economic reforms had been derived from it. It was argued that the progress is taking place through globalization and economic reforms.

When the process of economic and social development has been extended, the importance of local cultures and the particularistic expressions of ideology and sentiments have been taken note of in formulation of the public policies as well as in the analysis of 'nation–state'.

The new institutional innovations that globalization may bring about in society are (Dissanayake, 1988):

1. Science and Technology,
2. Media and Communication,
3. Market, Trade and Finance, and
4. Migration and Inter-cultural Transactions.

There are related issues of tourism, mobility of professionals, and the emergence of diasporic sub-cultures. All these function as driving forces of globalization. Briefly, we are describing the following:

### *Science and Technology*

We are being encircled by some visible and invisible powerful global forces day by day. Its hegemony is empowered with hyper-technology and enormous economic resources. From alpines to computer chips, we are using many global products produced by MNCs. In this context, a pervasive global culture as the ideology of consumerism has been knocking every moment on our door. It has occupied a substantial space in our society. A powerful media has been trying to negate our identity to hallow or alter our daily life pattern.

### *Media and Communication*

The electronic media of communication such as radio, television, computer network via satellites, paging services, telephony, electronic mail and internet web, etc. are modes of communication which are revolutionizing the banking, trade and management practices, uses of culture and leisure, and most other modes of inter-cultural and inter-group communicative actions. Most of these media transcend the territorial national cultural boundaries. They may function beyond the sovereignty of the nation-state, and offer individuals enormous amount of choices and freedom in matters of cultural and ideological performances.

The notions of time, space and symbolism of culture undergo new transformation of meanings under the impact of these new telecommunication technologies. Its impact on cultures – local, regional and national – is multifaceted and can be integrative as well as disruptive.

### *Market, Trade and Finance*

In structural terms, globalization is a historical process of transition from agrarian to industrial, post-industrial and finally the stage of information society (Dissanayake, 1988). Globalization strives to make the world as its market where all the people are being brought as buyers and sellers on unequal terms.

The scope of trade and market which was accelerated by the processes of globalization poses formidable cultural problems in developed and developing societies. In India, which traditionally had quite a developed base of trade and market, the impact of the changing role of these institutions has been gradual. The market and trade relations continue to be located in local cultures even today (Ostor, 1980). The economic policy of India up to 1980s has also been that of import-substitution and protectionism in trade and market.

The full momentum of globalization started in 1990s onwards, but many checks and balances continue to persist. Globalization brought changes which altered the traditional mode of cultural expression, usage of language and communication, media at the local, regional and national levels.

### *Migration and Inter-cultural Transactions*

Globalization also accelerates the process of migration, tourism and travel. Its cultural and social homogenizing effects proceed along with creation of pluralism and cultural diversity. Tourism in India is oriented more to religious pilgrimages combined with sight-seeing and for leisure. Over a period of time, it has strengthened the festive and celebrative activities of various religious groups and communities and its diffusion effect has been strong.

## Globalization in India: Challenges and Response

We would like to mention here a free essay on internet written by Gourav on, 'Globalization and India: Challenges and Response'. He describes as follows:

> In the heyday of the Industrial Revolution slogan raised by the British was 'Industrialise or Perish'. Now, in the era of Globalization the slogan has been changed into 'Globalise and Perish'. There is a TINA (There is no alternative) syndrome. Countries know that by globalising them will suffer, their problems will mount up but they feel that there are no choices or alternatives. Therefore, we can agree upon the fact – "Globalization is not a choice". It is an acceptable reality that globalization has both positive and negative impacts.

In this context, one has to analyse 'Globalization'. The idea became popular when media pundit Marshal MacLuhan spotted the 'global village' in the horizon. It was a destination to be reached. At that time many welcomed and few dreaded the prospect. Since then a phenomenal change has taken place in the world as well as in India.

India is one of the civilizational countries in the world. It has a rich cultural heritage. It has seven cultural zones and fifty-eight sub-cultural zones. Language changes every twenty miles in India. All the major religions of the world peacefully co-exist in India. The socio-cultural backbone of the country was broken due to more than thousand years of foreign rule. Though the British were the last to rule the country, they have made both positive and negative contributions. Political integration was possible because of British and we could also learn about the nuances of modern democratic order. But the British colonial policy also weakened us. The drain of resources kept us impoverished. Its policy of divide and rule spread the culture of violence and made us vulnerable to the never-ending threat to communalism.

The modern state in India was born during British rule. After Independence the modern state was built mostly on the western models. Though the people of India had launched a very well organized nationalist struggle. The ethos of the struggle got earled with the new rulers tasting power and privilege in free India. The challenges of new India could not be perceived by an organized political community but by political opposition only. Civil society is a political community having civic virtues. Civicness makes society civil. A sense of group living, group engagements and interactions among individuals for their common interests constitute the major features of civil society. In fact, civil society is defined as the capacity of a political community to organize itself independent of specific directions of state power. Thus civil society is more dependent upon the political culture and the character of a society. The state is rather a product of it. The relationship between the state and civil society is a mutual one. According to Tocqueville, government bodies with a firm-footings in the local community make an ideal breeding ground for democratic civil endeavours. The state cannot be abstracted from civil society and vice-versa.

The political economy of public policy making in India is a peculiar one. It adopted both community development and planned economic development as methods to achieve the twin objectives of growth and social justice. During Nehruvian era, it pursued a policy of welfare, which was centred on subsidy. When Indira Gandhi came to power, the welfare approach was replaced by development. This created a functioning state everywhere. But due to the absence of proper civil society consciousness, it led to bureaucratization and corruption. Rajiv Gandhi replaced development by empowerment which aimed at giving power to the people. The old Gram Panchayat system was revived in order to provide both planning and implementation to the democratically organized lower echelons of the society.

The power to the people is a welcome approach. It is what civil society was striving for. But the background to this approach was mysterious. The failure of centralized planning and rise of theoretical approach for rural development prompted the think-tank of the policy making apparatus for policy ramification. At this juncture globalization comes both as a threat and benefit. When globalization is viewed from its role it is observed that there is both interpenetration and integration. At the same time ethnic formation are also observed. This syndrome can be talked as a dual transformation, super-national integration and sub-national disintegration. The terminology is better understood as 'globalization'.

Let us examine the impact of globalization on India's society, polity and economy. In early 1990s, India was in deep debt crisis. Its credibility was very low. The political process was in turmoil. The society was divided due to Mandir-Mandal controversies.

The New Economic and Industrial Policies adopted during that crisis period opened the doors for foreign loan and investment. This created stiff opposition and acute competition in India. The success of India's producing class was at stake. The policy was commented as anti-agriculture as it would bring disaster. The Structural Adjustment Programme which is otherwise the name for the new policy gave stronger market orientation to agriculture by reducing export subsidies and converting all non-tariff barriers to tariff. This precluded the farming community of India to compete with foreign producing giants. This caused a failure in the production and supply of food grains, particularly of course cereals consumed by the poor, leading to rise in food grain prices. This caused tension among majority of India's population who are poor.

Globalization should be viewed from another angle. In mid 1970s, there was a need for liberalization. It was on reducing the restrictive and complex feature of the previous policies adopted in India. The failure of Nehruvian model of development through planning and public sector dominance warranted such thinking. Though Nehruvian policy caused creation of good industrial base its continuation was treated as a drag in future growth of economy.

India has twin problems of poverty and unemployment. The market economy is not a panacea for these challenges. India needs both growth and social justice. Without human resource development, India cannot achieve the twin objectives. The poor social and human development in India is because of lack of investment in education. Further, if there is more investment in human resource development, funds may not be available for sectors like defence and development. World is globalized but conflict is localized. Hence, defence cannot be given low priority in India as it is encircled by hostile nuclear neighbours.

India is one of the successful democracies and a prominent industrial power. The policy of globalization with its approach of liberalization and privatization has merits and demerits for our society. India cannot be equated with any developed European society as the population, poverty and philosophy of India are different from that of those countries. India has to think globally but will be required to act locally.

## Darker Side of Globalization

Although India has maintained its pace with the rest of the world in globalizing its culture and technology, but globalization too has ill effects. Government policies are guided by the welfare of the multinational companies (MNCs) rather than welfare of its general masses. As a result, the gap between rich and poor has rapidly widened with the globalization. High competition in the market leads to continuous pressure on raising productivity, enhancing consumer service and improving product quality, in order to survive. Due to fierce competition, the emerging technologies are associated with greater risk. Closure of inefficient unit causes voluntary retirement in public sector units, making a large population redundant. Unplanned growth has led to shortage of power and lack of infrastructure and thus affects the industrial expansion in an adverse way. Traffic congestion, growth in consumerism, instability in profits due to too much choice among customers are also deterrents for globalization.

## Conclusion

India is fast emerging as an attractive global hub for low-cost, frugal innovations. The greatest challenge of globalization is to discover and invent indigenous technologies to meet the need of rural areas in our country. A vast domestic market with positive outlook, strong domestic technological base and a relatively open FDI policy enable participation of foreign owned firms for trading in India while Indian firms are creating presence in other markets and thus creating positive country-of-origin effects. Globalization offers a new opportunity for knowledge dissemination, but this does not mean that all the nations and institutions will equally benefit from it. On the contrary, it seems that the institutions that have managed to benefit most from globalization are those that already are at the core of scientific and technological advance. India can benefit from globalization of technology if they implement active policies designed to increase learning and improve access to knowledge and technology (Archibugi and Pietrobeli, 2003).

## References

Archibugi, D. and C. Pietrobeli (2003), "The Globalization of Technology and its Implications for Developing Countries: Windows of Opportunity or Further Burden?" *Technological Forecasting and Social Change*, 70/9, pp. 861–883.

Dissanayake, Ellen (1988), *What is Art For?* Seattle: U. of Washington Press.

Giddens, A. (1990), *The Consequences of Modernity*, Cambridge: Polity Press.

Gourav (2011), Globalization and India: Challenges and Response, Free essay on internet.

McLuhan, Marshall and Edmund Carpenter (1960), *Explorations in Communication*, Boston: Beacon Press.

McLuhan, Marshall (1960), *Report on Project in Understanding New Media*, National Association of Educational Broadcasters, Office of Education, US Department of Health, Education and Welfare, New York.

Nagla, B.K. (2010). "Globalization and Its Impact on Culture", *Quest:* The Journal of UGC-ASC Nainital, Vol.IV, May, pp.1–12.

Nederveen Pieterse, J.P. (1994). 'Globalization as Hybridization', *International Sociology*, Jan. 9(2): 161–84.

Ostor, Akos (1980). *The Play of the Gods: Locality, Ideology, Structure, and Time in the Festivals of a Bengali Town*, Chicago: University of Chicago.

# 27

# Privatization of Education: Challenges Ahead

Education can develop positive attitudes and reflexes, which are important to confront situations such as war or natural disaster. It is also vital to develop an education system or a curriculum that best caters to the needs of crisis-stricken populations, and to ensure that no social groups are excluded or denied the right to education. Equity and human rights are major issues when planning education in countries experiencing situations of emergency and reconstruction. Several factors can hinder children from attending schools, among which are the language of teaching, concerns over personal safety – notably for girls – the characteristics and capacities of emergency teaching staff, and so on. As in most developing countries, but in a much more vivid and complex way, in crisis and reconstruction settings, the need for funding is pressing. The support of organizations – governmental and non-governmental – and donors is often paramount, albeit more in certain countries than in others. Without their participation, countries or areas hosting displaced crisis-affected children would experience great difficulty in providing what is necessary, and the process – which should often be one of immediate urgency – would be greatly delayed. On the other hand, issues of donors' co-ordination have to be dealt with, which require definite skills.

In view of the importance of the subject, the Editorial Board of the IIEP Fundamentals of Educational Planning series asked a well-qualified and experienced person, Margaret Sinclair, to draft a document, which would serve both as a state-of-the-art examination of the present situation of education in emergencies and reconstruction, and a guideline for planning education in emergency and reconstruction environments. Each context has different requirements. Emergencies call for immediate action, while reconstruction is a long-term process. The time required for readjustment and reconstruction varies from one situation to another. Margaret Sinclair summarizes, in a very clear fashion, current thinking on the planning and management of education in such situations. Building on concrete experience in a number of countries, she addresses, in a very practical manner, the question of how in developed and middle income countries, the privatization movement appears to be the answer to an increasingly diversified demand in terms of content or teaching methods and to the desire of families to choose the school to which they send their children. The issue is not so much financing, but rather freedom of choice, management flexibility, private regulation and accountability.

In both developed and developing countries, privately managed and regulated schools – whether owned or financed by public authorities – are generally supposed to be more effective, more efficient, and produce better results than schools managed by the state. But is this the case in reality?

The booklet, written by Clive Belfield and Henry Levin from Teachers College, Columbia University, describes and analyses privatization reforms which have occurred essentially, but not exclusively, in industrialized Western and Latin American countries. Among such reforms, they analyse voucher programmes, the introduction of freedom of choice in the public system, deregulation and private management of largely publicly funded schools, such as charter schools, funding of privately provided education services, etc. They discuss the impact of such reforms on a number of criteria: freedom of choice, efficiency, equity and social cohesion; and derive some lessons for educational planners. They refrain from generalizing across the board: they argue convincingly that all depends on the national context and the way in which the reform is designed and implemented. Certain voucher schemes which are targeted at disadvantaged groups end up being more equitable than traditional, often socially segregated, public systems. When designing a reform, educational planners have to clearly define the objectives and take into consideration its design and modalities. Clive Belfield and Henry Levin, in this booklet, have summarized their wealth of experience in such a clear manner. This document, bearing on a controversial topic, is well balanced in its treatment of the subject. It will be most useful for educational planners from developing and developed countries alike, which are struggling with the need to find additional resources and to make their education systems more efficient, and, at the same time, equitable.

## Privatization of Education

The privatization of education has occupied a large place in the educational debate over the last years. For many, it simply means increasing the role of parents in the financing of education. This movement has thus rather negative and threatening connotations: it is associated with increased inequalities in access to education and the breaking of social cohesion. For others, privatization is a much more positive move, implying more resources for the education sector, more efficient use of these resources, and more flexibility in education delivery. The debate is loaded with ideological considerations, and little evidence is produced (Belfield and Levin, 2002).

In many developing countries, the privatization of education has indeed brought about an increase in the share of private financing, sometimes at the basic education level, but more commonly at the post basic education level. The number of private schools and private universities has increased, at the same time fees have been introduced in some public schools. This trend has emerged largely as a result of the incapacity of the state to satisfy the increasing educational demand at all levels. If an increase in private funding means freeing public resources to support the development of free, quality basic education for all, then it may very well mean a more equitable use of public funds.

The privatization movement is, however, much more complex than a mere increase in private funding. It can take many forms: an increase in the number of fully privately managed and funded schools; privately managed schools financed by public funds; public schools fully or partially financed by private funds; public schools run as private institutions and which compete for public funds; private courses complementing the education provided in public schools or universities; private contracting of certain services; distance courses, etc. New information technology opens the way to many new forms of privately financed education to satisfy many different needs (IIEP, 10). The important question here is: "What is education privatization?"

### *Defining Privatization*

The term 'privatization' is an umbrella term referring to many different educational programmes and policies. As an overall definition, 'privatization is the transfer of activities, assets and responsibilities from government/public institutions and organizations to private individuals and agencies'. Also, privatization is often thought of as 'liberalization' – where agents are freed from government regulations, or as 'marketization' – where new markets are created as alternatives to government services or state allocation systems (Levin, 2001).

The trend towards privatization is strong: it is taking place in many countries and within many sectors of the economy. The education sector – because it is a large expenditure item in government budgets – often faces pressure to privatize. This pressure comes in many forms. For example, education can be privatized if: (a) students enrol at private schools; or (b) if higher education is privately funded. In the first case, schooling is no longer provided by the government; in the second case, the government is no longer funding education through taxpayers' money or loans. So private school students' parents may press for privatization, as may the taxpayers who fund higher education. In general, it is helpful to think of privatization in *private provision.* Education can be provided by private agencies, such as privately owned and managed schools or universities. It need not be provided through government-run institutions; instead, private schools could be operated by religious groups, for-profit entrepreneurs, charities, or other interested parties. Indeed, many families already prefer the private option and choose to forgo the free, public education systems. Internationally, the proportion of students who are educated by private providers varies substantially (IIEP, 20).

In the United States, approximately 11 per cent of school-age children are in private schools, mostly at the elementary level. In the Netherlands, the proportion of schools administered by private school boards is approximately 70 per cent. However, these schools in the Netherlands are privately operated, although they do receive public funds. Similarly, Denmark has a system of publicly funded private schools that enrol about two-thirds of all students, most of which are religiously affiliated. In Belgium, around 50 per cent of all student enrolments are in private schools. There is an equally broad mix of public-private provision in higher education: in the Philippines, over 75 per cent of students are enrolled in private universities; in the United Kingdom and much of continental Europe, the proportion is almost zero.

### Private Funding

Education can be funded by private individuals rather than through government subsidies. Privatization may therefore mean that parents pay for schooling rather than the government (via tax revenues). Often, private schools are supported directly through tuition fees paid by students' families, but in many cases, both families and governments contribute funds in a cost-sharing approach. Public universities in the United States charge tuition fees, but these only cover approximately half of the total costs, the remainder being covered by government subsidies. In the Republic of Korea, private education spending on schooling and on additional tutoring in subjects not covered in school amounts to approximately the same total as that of government expenditures; families pay directly as much for their children's education as they receive in subsidies. Bray (1999) lists 19 countries where at least a quarter of the total students are enrolled in private tutoring programmes. In many developing countries, families must pay additional 'top-up' fees to the local state funded schools (e.g. for textbooks or classroom materials). So privatization occurs when a portion of the total funding is paid by families instead of by the government (Tsang, 2002; IIEP, 21).

## Privatization of Education in India

While India can boast of having the third largest higher education system in the world, reality is that India is facing a severe shortage of skilled human resources. The reason for such a contrasting situation is the extremely low quality of primary, secondary, and college-level education in India. A possible way out of this situation is privatization of the education system, which is predominantly public at present. Privatization of education has the potential to improve the quality of education as well as to reduce the cost. However, to ensure access to education for all, the government must design an effective transfer-payment system. Although India's national literacy rate currently exceeds 75 per cent, a study by Prathama, a voluntary organization, finds that only 53.4 per cent children in Standard V can read a Standard II level text, and that nationally there has been a decline in the children's ability to do basic math. Another study by NASSCOM finds that 75 per cent of technical graduates and more than 85 per cent of general graduates are unemployable. The problem with the present Indian education system is that it is delivering a huge quantity of output, in the name of educated populace, with poor quality. This alarming situation is due to the unavailability of skilled teachers, the lack of determination among the existing teachers to teach effectively, the poor physical infrastructure, and a low level of parental input toward their wards' education. The deteriorating trend in the educational system continues largely because of the lethargy and mismanagement of the public schooling system which accounts for nearly 80 per cent of all schools. Despite many efforts from the government to revitalize the public education system, the quality of public education is dwindling. Consequently, enrolment in private schools, colleges, and universities, is on the rise. For instance, a recent study finds that in the city of Hyderabad, 73 per cent of families in slum areas send their children to private school.

A general realization is that the return on investment in the private schools/colleges is much higher as compared to the government schools and colleges, with some notable exceptions. The reason this is possible is the difference in approach between the two. The public education system – following a top-down approach – is accountable only to the government machinery. So even if the teachers in public schools do not deliver a good quality education, they do not suffer themselves because their jobs are secure. However, in the case of private schools – run through a bottom-up approach – the management and the teachers are directly accountable to the respective parents. If they fail to deliver an expected quality of education, the parents would react. They might even pull out their wards from the school. This implies that the teachers' performance would affect the schools' income and reputation. Consequently, the teachers would lose their jobs. So a private school has to deliver a good quality education. In fact, they do it better than majority of the public schools. Another issue is the cost of education. Most of the public schools are richer than their private counterparts in terms of total expenditure (on record, at least) and incur a much higher expenditure on the teaching and administrative staffs' salary.

The private schools, on the other hand, are thrifty about infrastructure and, in general, pay much lower salaries to their staffs. Thus, on average, at a fraction of the expenditure of a government school or college, a private institution can provide a better quality of education than the public institutions. Thus, private schools can provide a better education at a lower cost. So privatization of the primary and secondary educational systems can help ameliorate the situation by improving the quality of education while reducing the cost. But given India's poverty status (roughly 80 per cent of the population lives below the national poverty line); only a few parents will be able to afford the cost of private education. Hence, one cannot advocate for a blanket privatization of the entire educational system without taking care of the cost. However, given the present scenario, an alternative system which provides a better education, without over-burdening the poor parents, needs to be put in place. Now the question is: What this system should look like? The best solution, of course, is to fix the public education system. But with the track-record of the bureaucratic administration in India, it does not seem realistic to hope for such a positive change. One realistic way, I think, is to gradually privatize the schools and maybe the colleges, too. The government should take care of the educational expenditure by disbursing to the parents/guardians the cost of their wards' attending schools through transfer payments rather than funding the schools and colleges directly. This way, private agencies will run the institutions, and the parents will be able to afford the cost. Since the parents will have a control over the money, they can decide whether or not to send their wards to a certain school or college. This keeps the benefit of the public education system – affordability – intact while bringing in the efficiency – high quality and low cost – of the private system. The challenges of introducing such a system will be manifold. First, the government needs to make sure that schools exist in every locality. Left to the entrepreneurs themselves, they may fight to open too many schools in high-income localities where the students will be better compared to the low income localities. So the policy makers must ensure that low income localities also get a due share of the schools. The government must direct and incentivise the programme so that marginalized areas are not left out. The second challenge is to ensure quality. Although the private schools, in general, are better than their public counterparts, but relying too much on them can also be costly. The quality of the private schools also varies significantly. While some of them may provide a good quality education at a reasonable cost, others may end up becoming money-making machines without caring for the quality of education. So the government should come up with an effective mechanism to determine, monitor, and control the quality of education in the private system. Another challenge to implement this mechanism is to come up with an effective transfer-payment system. This has to take into account the cost of education in a given locality, the frequency of transfer-payments, and a proper utilization of funds disbursed. The policy-makers should make sure to issue the payment checks on a regular basis to families that have school-going children. If the checks or vouchers are not regular or enough to cover the costs, then again, the poor will suffer more. The government must develop a policy framework so that a higher efficiency can be achieved without losing the poorer section of the population. Thus, privatization of the country's education system, coupled with a well-tailored transfer-payment system, can help improve the quality of education in India and reduce costs for parents.

## The Idea of Privatization of Education

Since the impact of privatization is penetrating all sectors of economy, it is bound to affect education sector as well. As it is very difficult to meet the democratic aspirations of the people for further expansion of educational system due to paucity of resources it is, therefore, being felt that private sector is induced in education so that it can share the burdens of the state in funding education.

In India, the privatization of education has been taking place at the school level without much resistance. But it has not made much dent into other levels. However, privatization, though necessary, has some drawbacks. Private education trusts often become merely profit-making business ventures with no special ideals or objectives. Nowadays education has become an industry for private educational institutions at various levels. Now most schools, colleges and universities lay emphasis on professional courses like engineering, management, law, media and communication, etc.

If privatization of education comes into conflict with the equity objective, state intervention would be desirable. It is necessary that state intervention be increased in private sector institutions to increase the opportunity to the poor and deprived sections those who are meritorious students and help in promoting human resources development to keep pace with the emerging requirements which needs change in the education system.

The wave of privatization is sweeping across the world. The essence of privatization lies in the induction of private ownership in publicly owned enterprises. Consequently, within an economy, it is aimed at breaking the monopoly of the public sector in a number of areas including education system. The process involves the private sector in the ownership or operation of a state-owned enterprise.

## Introduction of Private Management

In his *Essay on Privatization of Education in India,* Vikas (2011) raises the question: Why is privatization being recommended in education?

First, it is alleged that the policies followed in India under the Nehru-Mahalanobis Model placed excessive responsibility for the expansion and development of education on state. Consequently, the expansion and establishment of education institutions and facilities have been shouldered mainly by the state. At the elementary levels of education, the state-sponsored schools have been responsible for the spread of literacy, more especially in rural areas, but even in urban areas, bulk of the schools are state-run or aided by the state. At the level of secondary, higher secondary, college and university as well public sector has played a dominant role in the development of education system. A stage has come when the state is finding it very difficult to meet the democratic aspirations of the people for further expansion of the educational system due to paucity of resources, because the demand for funds for the educational sector has to compete with the demand for resources for the other sectors. It is, therefore, being felt that the private sector be inducted in education so that it can share the burdens of the state in funding education.

Second, the expansion of the horizons of knowledge is taking place at a rapid pace all over the world; the underdeveloped economies must keep pace with this explosion of knowledge.

Emphasizing this point the World Bank has stated: Today knowledge explosion is dividing the world into fast moving, rich economies that use knowledge effectively and slow moving poor economies that do not. Education or knowledge industry is becoming a key factor in the process of development. This being so, education is no longer viewed as a social service, it is considered a necessary economic input and as such investment in education is treated as a factor contributory to human resources development. In this effort towards human resource development, the private sector is also expected to play its part since it is a major beneficiary of the knowledge industry.

Third, according to W.W. Rostow, the world is passing through the fourth industrial revolution (1985). This encompasses genetics, communications, robots, lasers and new industrial material and the various tools and products incorporating the micro-chip. The growth of satellite TV and the developments in computer technology have further escalated the information revolution. These technological developments have increased the requirements of highly educated and well-trained technical manpower. The public sector is hampered by lack of resources and cannot meet the needs of industry and other sectors of the economy. Therefore, the private sector must be initiated in the programmes of training skilled manpower to take advantage of hi-tech opportunities.

Fourth, privatization can respond more promptly and efficiently than the public sector which is hamstrung with structural and operational inflexibilities to market signals or market demand for labour and take effective steps to promote human resource development to keep pace with the emerging requirements.

Fifth, over the years, the public sector has failed to generate resources from the recipients of education. Education has become more or less a free public service. This has devalued education in the eyes of the recipients. Privatization, by charging the full cost or a substantial portion of the cost and at times, by charging cost-plus pricing for the service provided is likely to generate greater responsibility among the recipients of the education i.e., the students. As a consequence, students are likely to insist on greater efficiency in teaching and improvement in its quality.

Lastly, privatization, by generating more resources from student fees, will help to reduce fiscal burden on the government. The major components of privatization of education include the following:

- Establishment, in the private sector of institutions imparting education and skills viz., schools, colleges, polytechnics, research laboratories, professional colleges in agriculture, engineering, medicine, management, etc.
- Withdrawal of subsidies by introducing full costing in the individual and institutional domains. In case this is not possible all at once, introducing a system of gradual withdrawal of subsidies by increasing fees over a time and in the interregnum, continuing a decline scale of state support.
- To introduce the culture of private organization by granting the management the right to hire and fire academic and other supporting staff.
- To grant the right to the management to start or stop courses in response to market signals.
- To persuade the users of the output of educational institutions to contribute towards the funding of educational expenditure.

In India, the privatization of education has been taking place at the school level without much resistance. A dual system has come to be established at various levels of school education. In the public sector, we have primary, secondary and senior secondary schools which impart instruction through the mother tongue at the primary stage and thereafter, English is introduced as a language along with other subjects. Up to the 10th standard, all children have a common syllabus. Thereafter, they go in for specialization in different areas at the higher secondary level. The fee charged in these schools is very nominal. Thus, a very large number of students coming from low income groups can afford instruction in these schools.

As against these schools which are directly under the management and control of the state, we have schools run in the private sector which in popular parlance are called "public schools"

– a misnomer, because most of these schools are established and run by private entrepreneurs in education, on commercial lines. These schools impart instruction through the medium of English language. They charge very high fees which cover not only the current cost of education but also contribute towards the cost of buildings and other equipments. The educational entrepreneurs, taking advantage of the high demand of education in English medium schools, generally get land allotted at the nominal cost in the name of some educational society formed for the purpose. In the initial stages, some temporary structures are put up. Later on, as students are admitted, funds begin to flow in the name of development fee, building fee, tuition fee, games fee, cultural programmes fee, etc. These institutions charge cost plus pricing for services rendered by them. Since they are unaided schools and do not receive any grant from the government they pay very low salaries to their academic and other staff. The prevalence of high degree of unemployment helps them to recruit qualified staff which works under a rigid discipline and is liable to summary removal at the will of the management. The high degree of insecurity of service enables the management to extract the maximum output from the staff. Some of the schools functioning under the auspices of reputed educational denominations do pay better salaries and pay scales, but even these do not compare: favourably with the state-run schools. Over a period of time, these schools are able to construct huge buildings and purchase costly equipments to modernize their establishments. In this way, a large percentage of unaided private schools have converted education into business enterprise.

Earlier these schools were confined to metropolitan areas and big cities, but now they are spreading even to smaller towns. Even the charitable trusts like the DAV managements, Khalsa Dewan, Gurudwara Prabandhak Committees, Sanatan Dharam Foundation, etc. which initially were motivated by the urge to impart instruction in Indian languages and propagate Indian culture have been swept off their ideological postures by the entrepreneurial pragmatism of privatization. However, they continue to use the trademarks of their religious or social organization to get concessions and facilities, especially land at throw away prices from the government. In several cases, a chain of English medium schools is operated under a particular organization. With the passage of time, the philanthropic spirit of the founders of these organizations has been replaced by a commercial approach which legitimizes the selling of education at the price possible. These schools cater to the needs of the rich business class and also to the middle and the upper middle class wanting desperately to transcend their present status. In other words, the privatization of school education is rapidly churning out the children from high income groups into English medium 'public schools' while their counterparts from the poor and lower middle classes continue to go to state-run schools. In these English medium public schools, parents pay the full cost of education (generally leaving a good profit margin for the educational entrepreneurs) while, in the state-run schools, highly subsidized education is imparted in the vernacular. At the higher education level, the scenario is very different.

Malcolm Adiseshaiah (1992) has classified higher education institutions in India into four groups: those founded and run by the state governments; those founded, funded and run by private agencies; those founded, and run by private agencies but funded by the government; and those founded and run by private agencies but funded partly by government and partly by non-governmental sources. Majority of the institutions in higher education belong to category 'd', but under the pressure from teachers association, they are moving into category 'c'.

The Acharya Ramamurti Committee that reviews the National Policy of Education (1986), in its report towards an Enlightened and Human Society (1990) mentions: "Though education has been in the Concurrent List in the Constitution since 1976, it remains primarily a state activity; bulk of the investments is made by the state governments. Free and compulsory education is expected to be provided by the states for all children up to 14 years of age. In most states, education is free in the entire school stage. Up to class XII, education is free for girls in all the states. The fee structure for higher education in the colleges and universities has virtually remained unchanged for many years. The pattern of educational development has, consequently, come to be dependent on the availability of public resources for education".

Since privatization should not be treated as synonymous with commercialization, the right to start or stop a course cannot be given to private entrepreneurs due to the very nature of the business in which they have made an investment. However, the need for rationalization of staff due to the limitedness of resources and failure to generate more resources from the recipients of education has to be accepted. Education is a public and merit good and as such, it is incumbent on the society to provide education to its people. It has been enshrined in our Constitution under Article 41 that "the state shall, within the limits of its economic capacity and development, make effective provision for securing the right to work, to education and to public assistance in cases of unemployment, old age, sickness and disablement, and in other cases of undeserved want".

Obviously, as the development of the society takes on rapid strides and the economic capacity of the state is enlarged, it is obligatory on the part of the state to allocate more resources to education with a view to: (a) provide free and compulsory elementary education to all children up to 14 years of age, (b) to provide secondary and higher education to more and more of its citizens so that they can exercise their right to live with dignity, and (c) that the state shall endeavour to provide equality of opportunity among not only individuals of opportunity but also groups of individuals suffering from various disabilities such as that of caste, sex, economic and social deprivation, etc.

On the question of privatization, it would be relevant to consider the forms of privatization: zero privatization of education with total responsibility to be taken over the state at all levels. Mild privatization of education and by gradually increasing recovery cost of education by way of fees to 50 per cent level. The remaining cost should be subsidized by the state. Intensive privatization by insisting that at least 75 per cent cost be covered by student fees and employers' contribution. Total privatization with total freedom to private sector to establish educational institution and recover full cost from the beneficiaries or even charge cost plus pricing and generate profit from investment in education. Out of these forms, the first and the last option cannot be considered as feasible, since in a mixed economy, it is neither feasible nor desirable to depend exclusively either on the public sector to expand the capacity of public sector institutions to fully meet the needs of the economy, nor is it possible for the private sector to cater to total societal needs. There is no doubt that public sector institutions both at the school and college/university level have much better record of responding to the social needs of SCs and STs and other backward sections of the society than the private sector institutions. It is, therefore, necessary that state intervention be increased in private sector institutions to increase the quota of seats to the poor and deprived sections. This can be made applicable to private sector institutions which receive government assistance to cover their deficits. Even in fully financed private sector institutions, as per the Supreme Court judgement, education is a fundamental right and no institution can be permitted to charge capitation fees which deny admission on the basis of merit and permits higher education/professional education on the strength of money power.

The state must enact suitable legislation to impose reasonable restrictions on such institutions consistent with the goals enunciated in Article 21, Article 41 and Article 45 of our Constitution. While framing, it has to be ensured that privatization does not degenerate into commercialization of education. With this end in view, a system of grant of free sops for the economically weaker sections of society has to be built and reinforced. Private sector institutions should also take affirmative action to help the weaker sections to acquire professional/higher education which is otherwise not within the reach of the society. For nearly four decades, fees in higher education have remained stagnant at 1950–51 levels and thus share of fees has come down to only five per cent of total educational expenditure. In the universities, it is less than one per cent. The state has been caving in due to the pressure of organized student unions dominated by student leaders belonging to affluent parents. This trend needs to be reversed. In the course of the next 10 years, fees as a component of total recurring expenditure should contribute at least 25 per cent of total expenditure.

Such stipulation should be made contingent for the receipt of grants. This requires a phased programme of raising fees.

The Ramamurti Committee (1990) made the following recommendation in this regard: "In the circumstances, a justifiable strategy is bringing about an appropriate increase in the fees payable by students going in for higher education. This increase should be appropriately linked to at least the cost of recurring expenditure and levels of income of the parents of the beneficiaries. The richest quartile of the people can be a 75 per cent of the cost of the education; the next richest quartile 50 per cent of the cost and the next richest quartile 25 per cent. The last quartile of the economically weak (to be appropriately defined) need not bear any part of the cost". Although apparently, the recommendation of the Ramamurti Committee appear to be very rational as it prescribes a differential fee structure on the basis of four broad slabs, in practice it is very difficult to implement. In a country, where a small proportion of the population is engaged in salaried employment and a very small proportion pays income tax, it is quite possible that during the course of implementation, the business classes may not get caught in the net and the entire burden may be put on salary earners. A more pragmatic approach would be to prescribe a uniform system of higher fees and, within the system, permit 25 per cent of the students belonging to weaker sections full exemption from fees. Such a step would increase the recovery rate and thus reduce the state burden on education. Coupled with this, there should be periodic revision of fee structure so that resource generation from fees accounts for at least 25 per cent of total recurring expenditure in state-run or state-aided institutions. "Besides tuition fees, fees charged for specific purposes in the higher education institution like laboratory fees, library fees, building fees, magazine fees, games fees, etc. also have to be increased on a rational basis with reference to meet the cost of providing the relevant facilities/services". "With the ever increasing number of examinees, examination fees can also be an important means of raising internal resources to meet the cost of higher education".

The basic purpose of Ramamurti Committee's suggestion is to increase the recovery rate in higher education costs by reducing the element of subsidy. In that sense, the recommendation appears to be overdue. Education cess or graduate tax has also been suggested by the World Bank to be charged from the users of output of higher educational institutions, more especially the corporate sector. The Ramamurti Committee is very sceptical about the suggestion as it states: "Graduate taxes, if any, are to be imposed upon the beneficiaries, i.e. the users of services of graduates, namely, employers. However, the employers are likely to resist imposition of such taxes on ground of economic viability of their own operations getting affected. This is also likely to result in discouragement of employment of the qualified". In our country, the corporate sector is the biggest user of educated manpower, but is not prepared to contribute anything to the higher education sector. This is in sharp contrast to the situation prevailing in developed countries where the universities receive substantial support from the corporate sector by way of grants. Either the corporate sector itself starts funding higher education as a matter of policy, or alternatively the state should impose education cess on the corporate sector so that a certain portion of its gross profits is utilized to fund higher education. This education cess should be a kind of surcharge so that it cannot be evaded.

Ramamurti Committee is unnecessarily apprehensive of the resistance by the employers not to employ graduates. The kind of manpower needed today due to the electronics revolution needs much highly skilled and educated manpower and persons trained in professional education. Such a fear, therefore, appears to be unfounded. Universities/higher education institutions can undertake research projects on behalf of the corporate sector (both the public and the private corporate sector). A part of the research project fund can be used to supplement the deficit of the institutions or to create suitable infrastructure in the form of research laboratories, computer facilities – libraries to conduct research in a competent manner.

## Discourse

As we know that private sector has always been present in the field of education in India. Its role, however, has changed significantly in present times. Earlier, it played more of a benevolent role. Now it has developed business interests in education with its mushrooming growth. That notwithstanding, the fact remains that the need for the involvement of private sector in higher education was never so great as today. What is, therefore, needed is to explore the ways and means to manage its participation so that it becomes a positive force to promote access, equity and excellence in school and higher education.

In the era of globalization, the idea of privatization of education is a great challenging task. The term "globalization" means integration of economies and societies through cross country flows of information, ideas, technologies, goods, services, capital, finance and people. Cross border integration can have several dimensions – cultural, social, political and economic.

In our country, the important thing is that there are various types of schools who adapt different types of teaching methods and syllabus even government has different types of schools like central schools run by central government, schools run by different states, etc. Similarly, the problem of language is also an issue. In the present context, a student should learn at least three languages, namely, English, Hindi, and local language belonging to the student. Therefore, by learning three languages, a student may connect himself at international, national and regional levels. In this context, the total education system of the world requires to come under one roof. In other words, it requires the unification of teaching curriculum, methodology and upgradation of knowledge and system to remain in the context for efficiency and effectiveness by which transformation of knowledge in justified manner to attain the goals of life.

The qualitative study of Misra and Bajpai (2010) is an attempt to describe the concepts of a globalized teacher education, effect of globalization in teacher education, and problems of teacher education in the context of globalization. Globalization contains both opportunities and threats for national development. It considers the recent reforms of teacher education in India and the extent to which they reflect a response to global economic pressures. This paper challenges the determinants of educational policy and argues that any country will need to develop its own national approach to modernizing teacher education in light of the global context. The paper deals with four themes; teacher education in last decade policy; the shift away from the educational disciplines, the shift towards school-based approaches, and the emergence of more centralized forms of accountability of teacher competence.

There is a need to consider the global transformations which require:

(i) People should develop new skills, new experiences, new knowledge and schools have an important role in this sense.
(ii) The role of the teachers and the way they should teach in this new high-tech global economy, and learn in new ways for new purposes.
(iii) Schools and teachers should adapt themselves for this new reality and rearrange their skills, achievements and previous experiences to adapt themselves to new opportunities.

In brief, it may be viewed that education in India has undergone phenomenal transition in the last three decades. It has acquired unprecedented growth of private institutions, salient proliferation of technical and professional disciplines, increasing use of information and communication technology, and expanding global linkages. As a result, there have appeared critical concerns about its commercialization, unequal access, declining quality and low global ranking. In this chapter, we have analysed such trends of change and emerging issues. In particular, we have focused on the upsurge of private enterprise in education and its repercussions on the access and quality of education. Therefore, there is an urgent need to promote quality of education in India with a competitive edge which is the real challenge of globalization.

Private educational institutions have boomed mainly in the field of 'sunrise' disciplines such as engineering and management. Viewing privatization as not an unmixed blessing in globalization, Sharma, Ghuman and Prakash (2014) underlines its following worrisome consequences: unequal accesses and exclusion, low quality, malpractices and corruption. Most worrisome of all is marginalization of social sciences and humanities in the wake of privatization which is equally important for the social development. Turning to globalization, there is a trend of penetration of foreign educational institutions in India in collaboration with their local affiliates. In this context, state is losing its idea of welfare state and market is dominating which is becoming obstacle for unequal access and exclusion. This requires serious thinking.

## References

Adiseshaiah, Malcolm (1992), See in Singh, Katat and Sreenivasan Subramanian (1992), *Themes in Development Economics: Essays in Honour of Malcolm Adiseshiah*, Oxford: Oxford University Press.

Bray, M. (1999), *The private costs of public schooling: Household and community financing of primary-education in Cambodia*. UNICEF.

Belfield, Clive R. and Henry M. Levin (2002), Education privatization: causes, consequences and planning implications, the United Nations Educational, Scientific and Cultural Organization, 7 place de Fontenoy, F 75352 Paris 07 SP.

International Institute for Educational Planning (IIEP) (2021), www.unesco.org/iiep 10, 11, 20, 21.

Levin, H.M. (2001), Privatizing education. Can the market deliver freedom of choice, productive efficiency, equity and social cohesion? Boulder, CO: Westview Press.

Misra, Srikant and Bajpai, Arti (2010), 'Implications of Globalization of Education in India' revised posted on internet April 2, 2011 and July 12, 2014.

Rostow, W.W. (1985), 'The World Economy Since 1945: A Stylized Historical Analysis', *The Economic History Review*, Volume 38, Issue 2, pages 252–275, May and article first published online: 11 February 1985.

Sharma, S.L., B.S. Ghuman and Shital Prakash (2014). *Higher Education in India: The Changing Scenario*, Jaipur: Rawat Publications.

Tsang, Mun C. (2002), 'Comparing the Costs of Public and Private Schools in Developing Countries', in Levin, H. and McEwan, P. (eds) *Yearbook of the American Education Finance Association.*

Vikas (2011), *Essay on Privatization of Education in India*, Free essays on Internet.

# Index